# Contracting for Services in State and Local Government Agencies

# PUBLIC ADMINISTRATION AND PUBLIC POLICY

## A Comprehensive Publication Program

EDITOR-IN-CHIEF

**EVAN M. BERMAN**

Huey McElveen Distinguished Professor
Louisiana State University
Public Administration Institute
Baton Rouge, Louisiana

*Founding Editor*

**JACK RABIN**

Professor of Public Administration and Public Policy
The Pennsylvania State University—Harrisburg
School of Public Affairs
Middletown, Pennsylvania

*Available Electronically*

*Principles and Practices of Public Administration,* edited by
Jack Rabin, Robert F. Munzenrider, and Sherrie M. Bartell

PublicADMINISTRATION*netBASE*

# Contracting for Services in State and Local Government Agencies

## William Sims Curry

### CRC Press
Taylor & Francis Group
Boca Raton London New York

CRC Press is an imprint of the
Taylor & Francis Group, an **informa** business

CRC Press
Taylor & Francis Group
6000 Broken Sound Parkway NW, Suite 300
Boca Raton, FL 33487-2742

© 2009 by Taylor & Francis Group, LLC
CRC Press is an imprint of Taylor & Francis Group, an Informa business

No claim to original U.S. Government works
Printed in the United States of America on acid-free paper
10 9 8 7 6 5 4 3 2 1

International Standard Book Number-13: 978-1-4200-7832-9 (Hardcover)

### Library of Congress Cataloging-in-Publication Data

Curry, William Sims.
    Contracting for services in state and local government agencies / William Sims Curry.
        p. cm. -- (Public administration and public policy ; 148)
    Includes bibliographical references and index.
    ISBN 978-1-4200-7832-9 (alk. paper)
    1. Contracting out--United States--States. 2. County services--United States--Contracting out. 3. Municipal services--United States--Contracting out. 4. Public contracts--United States--States. I. Title. II. Series.

HD3861.U6C87 2008
352.5'382130973--dc22                                                        2008025453

**Visit the Taylor & Francis Web site at**
**http://www.taylorandfrancis.com**

**and the CRC Press Web site at**
**http://www.crcpress.com**

# Dedication

To my wife, Kirsten, for her patience and support
during the course of this project

—Bill

# Note

The subject matter included in this book should not be considered legal advice for specific cases or for general legal guidance. Readers should seek such advice from their own legal counsel. The material in this text is provided solely for educational and informational purposes. However, all possible circumstances could not be anticipated; therefore, individual situations may require further evaluation prior to application of the solutions or recommendations presented herein.

# Contents

# List of Figures

# Preface

The objective of this book project is to present best practices document templates and contracting methodologies obtained through a survey of present practices and a review of documents presently employed by state and local government agencies. The principal documents developed were a Request for Proposals (RFP) and a Model Services Contract (MSC) based on best practices in state and local government agencies. The templates are available for use by all state and local governments.

While one might presume that this project was intended solely for the benefit of contracting professionals, that notion would be based on the assumption that only contracting professionals are involved in contract management activities. This notion, however, is not necessarily applicable in state and local governments. These government agencies often maintain a relatively small central contracting function staffed by professionals who assist department personnel in contracting matters. Therefore, there are numerous agency employees whose primary function and expertise are in fields other than contracting, but who are called upon to participate in the drafting of solicitations, writing sole-source justifications, writing scopes of work, serving on advance contract planning and source selection committees, recommending award of contracts, and assisting in the management of those contracts.

There are others, in addition to contracting professionals and functional department personnel who participate in contracting activities, who can benefit from the document templates and contracting methodologies developed through this project. Board or council members of governing or legislative bodies and chief elected and appointed officials and their ranking staff members, as well as agency financial and legal counsel staff members, have considerable exposure to and responsibility for agency contracts.

The templates developed during the course of this project, described or contained in this book, are intended for the benefit of state and local government agency contracting professionals, as well as the other agency officials and employees mentioned above, who also participate in the contracting function.

The vast number of existing local government agencies — including counties, cities, school boards, universities, and special districts — made it impossible to request participation from every local government agency. Because it was impossible to invite all local government agencies to participate, and because all states would be invited to participate in this project, it was decided to limit the invitation for local government project participation to the cities and counties where the state capitols are located.

While all the participating government agencies made valuable contributions to this project, none of the state or local agencies provided documents or described practices that included all the features in the resultant RFP, MSC, or contracting methodologies presented in the text. Therefore, it is felt that all state and local government agencies can benefit from templates developed through the document review, as well as from the other templates and tools presented to facilitate contract management activities.

**William Sims Curry**
Chico, California

# Acknowledgments

I wish to acknowledge the support and encouragement that I received from Dr. Evan Berman, Huey McElveen Distinguished Professor at Louisiana State University, Editor-in-Chief, American Society for Public Administration (ASPA) Book Series in Public Administration & Public Policy, Taylor & Francis Group, who tirelessly read and critiqued several versions of the text prior to sanctioning it for publication by Auerbach Publications. I would like to thank Raymond O'Connell, Acquiring Editor, Auerbach Publications, Taylor & Francis Group, and Stephanie Morkert, Project Coordinator, Taylor & Francis Group, who performed the multitude of tasks required to bring the rough manuscript to a state where it was ready for marketing and production. Finally, I'd like to acknowledge the efforts of Andrea Demby, Project Editor, and other members of Production who took the manuscript through the final stages of editing and composition to present the book for publication.

The critique and recommendations provided during the early stages of this book project by my friends Dr. Greg Sanger, Ph.D., Optical Sciences, and Terry Hodges, who was twice chosen Writer of the Year by the Outdoor Writers Association of California and, who, in addition to his four books, has been a regular contributor to Outdoor California, are also gratefully appreciated.

The states and local government agencies, named below, participated in a project to develop a best practices Model Services Contract (MSC) and Request for Proposals (RFP). The documents developed through this project are based on best practices found in the participating state and local government agencies. Both documents are included in the book's appendices, and there is also a compact disk (CD) containing a Microsoft Word version of the documents. This book provides a discussion of the resultant best practices MSC and RFP as well as other recommended agency best practices in services contracting.

This acknowledgment is an expression of sincere gratitude extended to those participating agencies that responded to the questionnaire and provided templates of their RFPs and contracts.

## Participating States and Local Government Agencies

State of California
State of Connecticut
State of Hawaii
State of Iowa
Commonwealth of Kentucky
State of Maryland
Commonwealth of Massachusetts
New York State
State of North Carolina
State of Ohio
Commonwealth of Pennsylvania
State of Rhode Island and Providence Plantations
State of South Dakota
State of Texas
State of Utah
State of Washington
State of West Virginia
City of Des Moines, Iowa
City/Borough of Juneau, Alaska
City of Montgomery, Alabama
Maricopa County, Arizona
Oklahoma County, Oklahoma
City of Richmond, Virginia

# About the Author

**William Sims Curry** received a bachelor of science in business management from Florida State University, Beta Gamma Sigma, and a Master's in business administration from Ohio State University.

His initial exposure to the contracting field came as a U.S. Air Force systems procurement officer who was involved in the procurement of or staff support for electronic systems such as command, control, and communications, and radar projects, as well as space systems and ballistic missile programs. Following his retirement as an officer in the U.S. Air Force, he worked in contracting or purchasing for the Stanford Linear Accelerator Center on the Positron Electron Project and for several private-sector corporations in the aerospace and defense field on the Hubble Space Telescope and various Department of Defense programs. Curry's exposure to state and local government contracting began when he became a county purchasing services manager and continued through his subsequent appointments as a county deputy administrative officer and finally as a county general services director. Following his retirement as general services director, he continues his involvement in state and local government contracting through independent research projects and consulting assignments.

Curry has been a member of the National Contract Management Association (NCMA) for more than 30 years. During those years he wrote numerous articles that were published in NCMA periodicals and periodicals published by other professional organizations, and he conducted seminars and workshops on the topics discussed in his articles. He was designated by the NCMA as a Certified Professional Contracts Manager (CPCM) and received the award of NCMA Fellow. Curry was on the board of directors for the Industry Council for Small Business Development (a not-for-profit corporation established to assist small, disadvantaged, and women-owned businesses) and held various elected offices, including president. He developed the curriculum and taught college courses in the field of materials management. Curry also held or holds membership in the Counties General Services Association (CGSA), National Institute for Governmental Purchasing (NIGP), and the California Association of Public Purchasing Officers (CAPPO), for which he also wrote and presented professional development papers. He is also a member of the American Society for Public Administration (ASPA).

# Chapter 1

## The Contracting Cycle and Advance Contract Planning

### Chapter Objectives

The objectives of this first chapter are to introduce the reader to services contracting for state and local government agencies and explain the characteristics of the contracting cycle and processes involved in advance contract planning. The specific topics presented to the readers include:

- Introduction to services contracting in state and local government agencies:
  - Essential elements of a contract
  - Distinctive attributes of contracts for services
  - Participants in state and local government contracting
  - Best practices research conducted in preparation for writing this book
- The contracting cycle:
  - Pre-solicitation phase
  - Solicitation phase
  - Proposal evaluation
  - Contract award
  - Contract administration
  - Contract closeout

- ◾ Advance contract planning:
  - – Implementation of best practices in the contracting process
  - – Implementation of other prudent practices in the contracting process

## 1.1 Introduction

There are numerous references to terminology used in the field of contract management that begin in Chapter 1 and continue to be introduced throughout the entire book. The terms are defined as they are introduced to the readers. However, in recognition of the need for readers to refresh their understanding of these terms, when they appear in subsequent chapters, the definitions are provided in alphabetical order in Appendix A, "Glossary of Terms."

To demonstrate how state and local government agencies will benefit through the establishment of professional contracting standards and procedures such as those presented in this book, a scenario involving the award of a contract featuring problems that can be encountered in the absence of standards and professionalism will be presented. The following is not an actual case; it is a composite case that includes decadent practices found in several actual cases.

Contractor Alpha approached a departmental employee at a government contracting agency with a proposal to provide certain services to the agency. The state procurement code, which also applied to local government agencies, included an exception to the competitive contracting rules for that particular service. The proposal provided for the compensation of millions of dollars to the contractor over the course of the multi-year contract. However, the government agency would realize an increase in revenues resulting in a payback of its investment within five years. The proposal also promised a positive net revenue stream to the agency over the life of the project.

The departmental employee, however, was reluctant to bring the proposal forward to the agency officials who had authority to award the contract. Contractor Alpha presented numerous arguments to the departmental employee in favor of the project including a five-day all expense paid trip to another government agency that implemented a similar project. The departmental employee was also offered additional benefits if he would support their proposal and present it to the decision makers. The government contractor that implemented the similar project was in a location that was several thousand miles distant from the contracting agency, but adjacent to a popular tourist attraction.

The departmental employee finally agreed to present the proposal to the agency officials with authority to award the contract. A competing contractor hired an employee from Contractor Alpha who then alerted Alpha's competitor to the sole source contract being proposed to the contracting agency officials. Alpha's competitor approached the departmental employee with a competing proposal that, in comparison to the Contractor Alpha proposal, would save the agency more than $1 million annually. The departmental employee, however, had taken the all expense paid trip, as well as the other benefits, and felt committed to pursue the sole source contract with Contractor Alpha. He told Alpha's competitor that it would not be recommended for the immediate project but encouraged the competitor to submit its own sole source proposal during the following fiscal year.

Alpha's competitor provided evidence of the impropriety in the award of the contract to Contractor Alpha to a law enforcement agency. Following the law enforcement agency's investigation, an indictment was obtained of two Contractor Alpha officials and the departmental employee. The departmental employee was immediately placed on administrative leave pending investigation by the contracting agency. The contracting agency, along with elected and appointed officials, was criticized in the local and regional media for derelict contracting procedures and lack of controls that permitted approval of such a contract and for failure to detect the indicted employee's nefarious actions.

The Contractor Alpha employees and the departmental employee were convicted of contract fraud and sentenced to fines and imprisonment. The department employee was fired, divorced by his wife, and lost virtually all his assets. Shortly after his imprisonment, he committed suicide. The local and regional media continued to report follow-up stories on their initial reporting, with emphasis on the derelict behavior of the contracting agency officials. One high-ranking appointed official did not have his employment contract renewed and two long-serving elected officials lost to political challengers during a subsequent election.

While the above scenario is fictitious, the events that transpired and outcomes for the participants are based on actual events that occurred in a number of unrelated cases. Adoption of the standards, procedures, and templates presented in this book will not guarantee that the adopting agency will not experience a similar situation; however, implementing the recommendations presented in this book will unequivocally inform the agency's officials and employees of the agency's commitment to professional contracting standards, demonstrate proactive measures to guard against contract fraud, and establish professionalism in the management of the agency's contracting function.

Prior to delving into a description of the contracting cycle and advance contract planning, readers are introduced to the essential elements of a contract, the distinctive attributes of contracts for services, identification of the participants in state and local government contracting, a summary of the methodology, and results of the research project that was conducted in preparation for writing this book. Appendix B, "Best-Practices Research," provides a detailed account of the methodology and results.

## 1.1.1 Essential Elements of a Contract

A contract is an agreement that is legally enforceable and reflects the relationship between two or more parties for a specific time period. Contracts should be crafted to identify potential risks and describe how these risks will be mitigated. Otherwise, the agency may be exposed to risks for which it is not prepared to address and resolve the consequences therefrom. There must also be a meeting of the minds between the parties to the contract such that there is no ambiguity with respect to the understanding of the parties regarding the nature of the agreement. Additionally, contracts must include an offer, acceptance, consideration, competent parties, and a legal purpose.

An *offer* entails the communication of the offeror's willingness to enter into a contract that shall be binding if accepted by the party to which the offer was made. The term "offeror" refers to the party making the offer. The communication of the final unqualified assent to an offer is the *acceptance*. If the individual responding to the offer indicates acceptance of the offer but with some qualification, then there is no acceptance and the original offer is no longer available to the individual who made the qualified acceptance. The qualification could be a change to any element of the offer, such as the time period, quantity, price, or any other element of the offer. The qualified offer is referred to as a counter-offer, is considered a rejection of the original offer, and is treated as a new offer made to the original offeror.

Should the party making a counter-offer have his or her counter-offer rejected, he or she cannot then merely accept that original offer. The original offer, once it has been rejected by the making of a counter-offer, can no longer be considered a valid offer. Of course, the party that had its counter-offer rejected may then indicate that it now would accept the original offer. Should the party that had made the original offer agree to the acceptance of its original offer without further conditions, then acceptance has been realized.

To establish *consideration*, each party must be bound by its promises that constitute a bargain for exchange. However, being bound to perform some preexisting promise does not constitute consideration.

The parties to the contract must also be *competent*. This condition imposes a requirement for all the parties to the contract to be mentally competent and of legal age.

There is also a condition that the nature of the services being contracted can be performed legally in the jurisdiction where the contracts shall be construed and interpreted. In virtually all jurisdictions, for example, a contract with a consultant to facilitate agency employees' conduct to ensure reelection of the existing members of the governing body would most likely not constitute a *legal purpose*.

All the essential elements of a contract also apply to amendments that modify the terms of the original contract. In the case of multiple amendments, the essential elements of a contract also apply to amendments that modify the terms of the original contract as previously amended. If a contractor cannot meet its obligation to complete the contract tasks according to the contractual completion date, the agency cannot merely grant the contractor an extension to the completion date unless the agency receives something of value to the agency in exchange for extending the completion date. Otherwise, the agency has not received consideration for granting the time extension.

## 1.1.2 Attributes of Contracts for Services

Contracting for services is unique and should not be approached in the same manner as contracting for materials. Treating services contracts as though the agency was contracting for materials would ignore the obvious differences and approaches to crafting the solicitation and contracting documents to account for these differences. The services being contracted include janitorial, pest control, landscape maintenance, trash collection, recycling, security, vehicle maintenance, as well as any other services including professional services. Professional services is a subset of services and includes services provided by engineers, architects, attorneys, accountants, professors, consultants, or professionals in another field that require equivalent education and experience.

Unlike materials procured by state and local government agencies that are frequently for off-the-shelf commodities or otherwise made to manufacturer or industry specifications, services are generally tailored uniquely to the contracting agency's needs. The greatest difference between materials and services is that services are intangible while materials are tangible. Another aspect in which services contracting varies from contracting for materials is with respect to inventories. Materials can generally be stored in inventory for use whenever they are required while services are provided solely when the contractor is in position to perform the service. The solicitation documents generally vary with the procurement of materials being solicited by a Request for Quotations (RFQ) or an Invitation for Bids (IFB), while procurement for services is typically solicited by a Request for Proposals (RFP). The selection of contractors that provide materials is usually based primarily on price while contractors for services are normally selected on the basis of price and other factors. It is not unusual to select a services contractor that did not offer the lowest price or life cycle cost, while this practice is rare when purchasing materials.

Most state and local government agencies, such as counties, cities, and special districts, regularly obtain services required for financial auditing, engineering, architectural, legal, temporary help, travel, freight, psychiatric and psychological counseling, computer software maintenance and support, equipment maintenance, trash collection, recycling, and innumerable other services on a contract basis. The need to obtain such services via contract is generally based on the lack of available government employees, or the lack of a sufficient number of government employees, with the requisite skills to provide these services. This skills shortage by the contracting agency could result from difficulty in hiring qualified employees, increases in workload that demand more working hours than available from present qualified employees, or inadequate workload to justify full-time employees to perform the needed services. The availability of trained professionals who have the requisite skills on a contract basis for an interim period, or for the indefinite future, may better suit the agency's needs.

Contracting agencies are compelled to ensure that contracts are not awarded to individuals who actually have an employer–employee relationship with the state or local government agency. Services contracts routinely include an "independent contractor" clause in their standard terms and conditions. Such clauses include provisions professing that there is no employer–employee relationship established as a result of the contract. Furthermore, such clauses typically state that the contractor or contractor personnel are not afforded contracting agency benefits such as retirement or medical insurance coverage. However, should the contract provisions describe an employer–employee relationship wherein the state or local government agency provides the workplace, supervision, determines working hours, and/or instructs the contractor or contractor employees on how the work is to be completed, it is likely that the contractor or contractor employee may be classified as an employee of the contracting agency. There is also the possibility that although the contract clearly describes an independent contractor relationship, the actual practice may more closely resemble an employer–employee relationship. If it is determined that the contractor or contractor employee is, in fact, a state or local agency employee, then an individual (or individuals) providing services to the agency may be eligible for retirement, medical care, or any other agency employee benefits. It may also be necessary for the contracting agency to contribute to the contractor's Social Security and Medicare benefits. A determination that a contractor is actually an employee, at some period in time after the services have been provided, may result in an attempt to compel the state or local government agency to pay such benefits retroactively.

However, that topic is not pursued further in this book other than a caution to contracting agencies that award contracts for services to ensure that their services contracts do not include either an express or implied employee–employer relationship between the contract employees and the agency. Naturally, when the agency enters into an employment contract with a department head or other contractual employee, such contracts do not include an independent contractor clause.

### 1.1.3 Participants in State and Local Government Contracting Process

The principal participants in public contracting are the public sector, the private sector, and the constituency. Each of these categories is discussed below.

*Public Sector.* Although it is a well-accepted fact that the public sector includes all federal agencies, the federal government is not included in the definition of "public sector" for the purposes of this text on state and local government contracting because federal agency contracting is regulated by the Federal Acquisition Regulations (FAR). However, as discussed in subsequent chapters, there are situations, for contracts that are wholly or partially funded by the federal government, wherein provisions of the FAR and other federal government regulations apply to state and local government contracting.

Additionally, federal laws with respect to fraud and related crimes involving ethics and conflicts of interest apply to state and local government agencies regardless of the funding source. State government includes the principal governing organization that manages the day-to-day operations of the 50 state government offices, as well as decentralized state government agencies such as colleges and universities, highway patrol, air quality, corrections, consumer affairs, employment development, franchise tax, health services, insurance, justice department, medical boards, motor vehicles, public utilities, the state bar, and water resources. Local government agencies include counties, cities, and special districts that operate with a degree of autonomy from the cities and counties. On numerous occasions in this text, state and local government agencies are referred to as "agency," "government agency," or "contracting agency."

The individuals representing the public sector include "members of the governing bodies" such as members of the county board of supervisors, city council, district board, or any other entity that governs a particular local government agency. The "chief elected official" is the ranking elected official for a particular jurisdiction, such as the governor, mayor of a city, chair of a county board of supervisors, or chair of any other special district. These individuals are occasionally referred to collectively as "officials" or "agency officials." Career civil servants, referred to as "employees," are also included among the other groups representing the public sector.

*Private Sector.* The private sector is represented by corporations, partnerships, sole proprietors, joint ventures, or any other designation for companies or individuals providing services to government agencies or other clientele on a contract basis. These individuals and entities are referred to collectively as "contractors." When these individuals are competing for a contract, they are generally referred to as "prospective contractors." Occasionally, agency officials and employees refer to contractors as "suppliers" or "vendors." However, the term "supplier" is not used to describe contractors in this text because it oftentimes refers to companies or individuals who sell commodities. The term "vendor" is not used in this text to describe contractors because of the author's belief that this term should be reserved for the limited number of companies that sell products through vending machines or from vending carts. When services contractors are referred to as vendors rather than contractors, within the body of the contract, an inconsistency is created between the use of "vendor" in the contract body and the contract preamble where the contractor is defined as "contractor."

*Constituency.* Although "constituency" is often reserved for defined voters, this term is used in this book to represent voters and all other residents of applicable jurisdictions. Regardless of which definition is used, this group represents those individuals who are the source of funding to provide needed public services, and some of whom who have the power of the vote to register their approval or disapproval of the actions of elected officials.

## 1.1.4 Best Practices Research

A research project was conducted in preparation for writing this text. All 50 states, the city governments for all 50 state capitals, and all 50 counties where the state capitals are located were invited to participate in this research project. The state and local government agencies that elected to participate in the research project responded to a short questionnaire and submitted or provided access to their templates for RFPs and services contracts. A document review was performed on the documents submitted to identify the best practices as reflected in Figure 1.1 and to prepare templates for an RFP and services contract incorporating the best practices.

| BEST PRACTICES IN CONTRACTING FOR SERVICES | | |
|---|---|---|
| **No.** | **Best Practice** | **Implementation Percentage** |
| 1 | Availability of an Agency Web site | 59% |
| 2 | Web site Provided for Management of Pre-Proposal Communications | 32% |
| 3 | Dollar Threshold where Sole Source Justification is Required | 100% |
| 4 | Preference Not Given to Local Contractors | 82% |
| 5 | "Proposal" and "Bid" Not Used Synonymously | 14% |
| 6 | Reference to Companies Solicited as "Contractor" or "Prospective Contractor" | 18% |
| 7 | Word Used that Best Compels Contractors to Perform Tasks | 100% |
| 8 | Weighted Criteria Established for Evaluation of Proposals | 45% |
| 9 | Price Stated as One Criterion for Evaluation of Proposals | 36% |
| 10 | Format Specified for Proposals | 73% |
| 11 | Page Limit Established for Proposals | 5% |
| 12 | Model Contract Included in RFP | 77% |
| 13 | Late Proposals Acceptable if in the Best Interests of the Agency | 0% |
| 14 | Proposals Opened in Confidence | 32% |
| 15 | One Page Contract Format with Incorporated Attachments | 23% |
| 16 | Cost Plus a Percentage of Cost Prohibited | 5% |
| 17 | Unallowable Costs Specified | 5% |
| 18 | State and Local Government Standard Terms and Conditions | 100% |

**Figure 1.1 Best practices in contracting for services.**

The resultant RFP and services contract templates as well as all 47 contract provisions are included in the Best Practices Model Services Contract provided on the compact disk (CD) accompanying this text, in Appendix E, "Best Practices Request for Proposals (RFP)," and in Appendix F, "Model Services Contract (MSC)." These templates are made available for all state and local government agencies that wish to adapt them for use by their agency. Agencies may wish to add, delete, or modify certain provisions or features of the templates to conform to internal agency codes, ordinances, or practices. The "Acknowledgment" in this book includes the author's appreciation to the states, counties, and cities that participated in this project.

The responses to the questionnaire indicated that 61 percent of the agencies prohibited cost-plus-a-percentage-of-costs (CPPC) contracts; however, all but one of the RFPs and contracts provided for the research project did not make reference to the agency's prohibition against CPPC contracts. This is not necessarily problematical because the agencies could ensure that CPPC provisions were not included in their contracts despite the lack of such a reference in the RFP and contract.

Although all the participating agencies maintain standard terms and conditions and all 47 of the provisions in the best practices contract were in at least one of the terms and conditions provided by the participating agencies, none of the terms and conditions provided for the research project included all 47 of the terms and conditions in the best practices contract.

A complete description of the research project and results are provided in Appendix B, "Best Practices Research Project." In addition to identifying the implementation of best practices that had been determined through the document review of RFPs and services contracts provided by state and local government agencies participating in the research project, other published sources were searched to verify the fact that these practices are indeed best practices. The independent verification is also included in Appendix B. A table showing the titles of the best practices, as well as the percentage of state and local government agencies that implemented the best practices, is provided in Figure 1.1. The agencies that provided copies of or access to their solicitation and RFP templates include sixteen states, two counties, three cities, and one borough/city combination. References are made to the research project in subsequent chapters where there are also more thorough discussions of the best practices.

## 1.2 Phases of the Contracting Cycle

The contracting cycle begins with the pre-solicitation phase and proceeds through development of a solicitation, proposal evaluation, contract award, contract administration, and finally contract closeout.

## 1.2.1  Pre-solicitation

The pre-solicitation phase of the contracting cycle begins immediately following the state or local government agency's decision to send a solicitation to prospective contractors that are qualified, or appear to be qualified, to provide the needed services to the agency on a contract basis. There are numerous decisions that must be made prior to release of a solicitation to the private sector. For high-dollar-value or high-risk projects, an advance contract planning committee is normally formed to establish the methodology and parameters for soliciting and selecting the contractor. For lower-dollar-value or lower-risk contracts, the functions of the contract planning committee may be conducted by one or two individuals. Whenever the term "advance contract planning committee" is used in this text, it implies just one or two individuals whenever the contract price or level of risk does not justify a fully staffed committee.

## 1.2.2  Solicitation

The solicitation phase commences when the RFP is released to the prospective contractors and terminates when the proposals are received by the contracting agency. Although one might intuitively believe that activities conducted during this phase of the contracting cycle would be restricted to prospective contractors, agency personnel do have specific responsibilities during the solicitation phase. This can truly be one of the most precarious times for agency representatives because prospective contractors may elect to engage in intelligence gathering activities to enhance their competitive position during the subsequent proposal evaluation phase. The probability for intensive intelligence gathering is heightened when the sector that provides the services being solicited is highly competitive and the private-sector entities are contentious. The potentially highly sensitive nature of the activities during this phase of the contracting cycle justifies the inclusion of an extensive discussion of the management of pre-proposal communications in Chapter 5, "Management of Pre-Proposal Communications and Evaluation of Proposals." The sensitivity is due to the fact that all prospective contractors must be treated equally, and information relayed to one contractor that is not provided to all other prospective contractors could be considered as favored treatment. Failure to treat contractors equally constitutes serious deviation from agency policy and can result in a protest by a prospective contractor that is not selected or recommended for award of the contract. Protests have the potential for reflecting poorly on the professionalism and ethics of agency officials and, just as with the management of pre-proposal communications, there is extensive coverage in this text dedicated to protests.

### 1.2.3 Proposal Evaluation

The proposal evaluation phase begins upon receipt of proposals from the prospective contractors and ends when the proposal evaluation team selects a contractor or recommends a contractor to the chief elected or chief appointed official, his or her designee, or the governing body. The text provides great detail on the pros and cons of various methods for scoring proposals, comparing the proposals to the proposal evaluation criteria that were included in the RFP, and selecting a contractor or recommending a contractor for award of the contract. One of the more salient considerations when evaluating proposals is the importance of evaluating the proposals exactingly according to the evaluation criteria contained in the RFP. Failure to evaluate the proposals according to the evaluation criteria can result in a protest from an aggrieved contractor.

### 1.2.4 Contract Award

The contract award phase begins when the proposal evaluation team completes the evaluation of proposals and selects a contractor or recommends a contractor for award of a contract. A carefully constructed RFP, such as the Best Practices RFP included in the appendices and on the CD accompanying this book, that includes a Model Services Contract (MSC) and a declaration that the contracting agency intends to award a contract essentially in the form of the MSC, minimizes the time required to award the contract and the significance of this phase of the contracting cycle. However, complications can occur during the contract award phase. For example, protests can be submitted by aggrieved contractors for a relatively brief period of time following contract award. Also, poorly crafted RFPs may result in the presentation of a proposed contract based on a contractor's standard contract template that favors the contractor at the expense of the agency and the constituency or may conflict with the codes, ordinances, or policies of the contracting agency. In either of these events, the time and effort required to complete the contract award phase becomes embarrassingly laborious and time consuming when a protest is filed.

### 1.2.5 Contract Administration

The contract administration phase begins upon award of the contract and continues until the contractor has fulfilled all its contractual responsibilities. This phase of the contracting cycle for services contracts oftentimes extends over a period of time that exceeds all the other contracting cycle phases combined. Although contracts for services may be in effect for a short time period, they are routinely awarded for a period of one year or in certain cases for multiple years. Virtually all the contractor's responsibilities are fulfilled during this phase of the contracting cycle. Agency personnel are generally involved in providing any project activities that remain their responsibility, attending project meetings with the contractor if applicable, monitoring the contractor's performance, evaluating contractor billings and making progress payments, evaluating proposed changes to the contract provisions, negotiating contract changes, and preparing modifications to the contract. Significant involvement on the part of agency personnel is necessitated to deal with problem solving when a contractor's performance degrades to a substandard state.

### 1.2.6 Contract Closeout

The contract closeout phase is normally a routine matter that begins upon completion or termination of the contract and is completed following the period of time that contract records are maintained and the records are destroyed. The activities performed during this phase include the preparation of the contractor's performance report if applicable, relief of financial encumbrances if any, maintenance of the contract records, and eventually destruction of the contract records.

## 1.3 Advance Contract Planning

A novice agency official or employee with contracting responsibilities may be tempted to immediately start drafting a Request for Proposals (RFP) as the first step in contracting for services. However, there are numerous practices that the advance contract planning committee should consider for implementation during the contracting process. Although the committee may not elect to use the entire set of advance contract planning practices, considering implementation of these practices helps ensure that the solicitation, source selection process, and contract instrument best address the project needs. The first 14 of the 18 best practices depicted in Figure 1.1 should all be considered for implementation. The final four best practices are not normally considered for implementation by the advance contract planning committee because these practices are normally implemented agencywide prior to conducting advance planning for individual projects. Because these practices are designated as best practices, their implementation has the greatest influence on enhancing the contracting effort. There are an additional 12 (topics 19 through 30 in Figure 1.2) prudent contracting practices that should be considered for implementation by the committee. Implementation of these practices improves the content of the RFP. The 14 best practices are briefly described below while the 12 prudent practices are described in Appendix C, "Advance Contract Planning Topics Not Included in Best Practices." There are more thorough discussions of these practices in the chapters, indicated in Figure 1.2, that are associated with each practice.

Careful advance contract planning leads to a superior RFP, more insightful source selection practices, a lessened chance of protests, a superior contractual document that includes a meaningful scope of work, selection of the best-qualified

| No. | Topics | Where Discussed |
|-----|--------|-----------------|
| \multicolumn{3}{c}{**TOPICS INCLUDED IN ADVANCE CONTRACT PLANNING**} | | |
| 1 | Availability of an Agency Website | Ch 1 and 5 |
| 2 | Website Provided for Management of Pre-Proposal Communications | Ch 1, 3, 4 and 5 |
| 3 | Dollar Threshold where Sole Source Justification is Required | Ch 1 and 2 |
| 4 | Preference Not Given to Local Contractors | Ch 1 and 2 |
| 5 | "Proposal" and "Bid" Not Used Synonymously | Ch 1 and 3 |
| 6 | Reference to Companies Solicited as "Contractor" or "Prospective Contractor" | Ch 1 and 3 |
| 7 | Word Used that Best Compels Contractors to Perform Tasks | Ch 1 and 8 |
| 8 | Weighted Criteria Established for Evaluation of Proposals | Ch 1, 3, 4, 5, 10 and 11 |
| 9 | Price Stated as One Criterion for Evaluation of Proposals | Ch 1, 4, 5, 10 and 11 |
| 10 | Format Specified for Proposals | Ch 1, 3, 4 and 10 |
| 11 | Page Limit Established for Proposals | Ch 1, 3, 4 and 10 |
| 12 | Model Contract Included in RFP | Ch 1, 3, 4, 8 and 10 |
| 13 | Late Proposals Acceptable if in the Best Interests of the Agency | Ch 1, 3, 5 and 10 |
| 14 | Proposals Opened in Confidence | Ch 1, 3, 7 and 10 |
| 15 | One Page Contract Format with Incorporated Attachments | Ch 8 and 10 |
| 16 | Cost Plus a Percentage of Cost Prohibited | Ch 3, 4 and 8 |
| 17 | Unallowable Costs Specified | Ch 9, 10 and 11 |
| 18 | State and Local Government Standard Terms and Conditions | Ch 3, 4, 8, 9 and 10 |
| 19 | Develop a List of Prospective Contractors | App C Plus Ch 2, 3 and 10 |
| 20 | Establish Required Proposal Content | App C Plus Ch 4 and 10 |
| 21 | Develop the scope of work | App C Plus Ch 3, 4, 8, 10 and 11 |
| 22 | Establish criteria for responsibility and responsiveness | App C Plus Ch 3 and 4 |
| 23 | Establish proposal scoring scheme | App C Plus Ch 3, 5 and 10 |
| 24 | Establish strategy for dealing with possible budget shortfall | App C |
| 25 | Use of proposal evaluation criteria in evaluating proposals | App C Plus Ch 3, 4, 5, 10 and 11 |
| 26 | Use of proposal scoring procedure in evaluating proposals | App C Plus Ch 3, 5 and 11 |
| 27 | Contractor presentations | App C Plus Ch 3 and 4 |
| 28 | Describing the option for debriefings and process for filing protests in the RFP | App C Plus Ch 3 |
| 29 | Procedure for managing protests | App C Plus Ch 3 and 6 |
| 30 | Managing contractor performance | App C Plus Ch 3 and 12 |

**Figure 1.2   Topics included in advance contract planning.**

contractor within the project budget, a work environment that facilitates excellence in contractor performance from project commencement through completion, and effective project management to ensure contractor compliance with its responsibilities as described in the scope of work.

Selection of advance contract planning team members should include consideration of the need for expertise in the project's overall management, technical aspects, contract management, finance, and oversight of the contractor's performance. Failure to select a multidisciplinary team increases the probability of overlooking consideration of certain disciplines that are essential to a successful project. When selecting team members, consideration should also be given to those individuals who can commit to team participation, beginning with advance contract planning and continuing through contract award. Continued participation of advance planning committee members through contract award permits first-hand knowledge of the reasoning behind the decisions made during the advance planning phase. The project manager should also be assigned to the team during the advance contract planning phase. The project manager is the central figure involved in all decision making during the term of the contract, and his or her participation in the advance planning, contractor selection, and contract award activities provides valuable background for decision making during the contract term.

The advance contract planning committee should evaluate the conditions leading to the decision to solicit private-sector companies or individuals to perform the particular services for the agency. Those conditions form the basis for the background statement included in the solicitation that informs the prospective contractors of the project's background. This need not be a lengthy document, but it should be reduced to writing to permit future reference by the committee members. The Best Practices RFP includes a section where the background statement, or a variation thereof, is inserted. The next step is to develop the project objectives. The objectives, understandably, are closely correlated with the project background and agency policy. Development of the project objectives may be accelerated through a brainstorming session and review of the objectives established for similar projects. Once the project objectives are completed, the actions needed to meet those objectives can be established.

At this point in the contract planning process, due to the reasoning discussed above, the committee members should consider implementation of 14 of the 18 best practices in the proposal evaluation guidelines. The best practices are discussed in a summary fashion below in Subsections 1.3.1 through 1.3.14 but are discussed more thoroughly in subsequent chapters.

There are 12 additional practices that are considered good practices that are recommended for implementation consideration by the advance contract planning committee. There is an overview of these practices contained in Appendix C, "Advance Contract Planning Topics Not Included in Best Practices," and more details on these topics are provided in the chapters identified in Figure 1.2.

## 1.3.1 Availability of an Agency Web Site

If the agency maintains a Web site with a link to the contracting function, the committee should ensure that information on its project is included on the Web site. A Web site is an excellent tool to keep contractors and prospective contractors informed of ongoing contracting efforts, provide general information on the agency and the contracting function, manage pre-proposal communications (as discussed in the following best practice), permit companies and individuals to register with the agency as prospective contractors, and to announce the award or recommended award of contracts.

If the agency does not maintain a Web site, or maintains a Web site that does not have a link to the contracting function, the advance planning committee may either establish a Web site for the agency with a link to the contracting function or establish a dedicated Web site for the contracting function.

## 1.3.2 Web Site Provided for Management of Pre-proposal Communications

The contract planning committee should establish a method for managing communications during the pre-proposal phase of the contracting cycle. Failure to manage communications while the contractors are preparing their proposals could easily result in a protest from an aggrieved contractor. This is a sensitive period of time, following release of the solicitation and receipt of the proposals, when allegations regarding inconsistent or unfair treatment of prospective contractors could result in a protest of the contract award or recommendation for contract award. Protests are a serious matter, as discussed in a subsequent chapter that includes a detailed discussion of protests. Obviously, protests should be avoided if possible. The receipt of a protest invariably creates an administrative burden, may delay project commencement, and could result in added agency costs. The provision of a Web site for the management of pre-proposal communications is the superior measure to ensure consistent and fair treatment of prospective contractors.

Advance contract planning can use the Web site provided for management of pre-proposal communications as the primary mechanism for dealing with questions from prospective contractors. Despite efforts to develop the best planned solicitation, which appears to include every conceivable element of information, questions from prospective contractors are virtually inevitable. However, it is possible that the questions in response to thoroughly planned solicitations may actually be well-disguised sales ploys. Questions submitted via telephone, e-mail, traditional mail, facsimile, or requests for personal meetings are inevitable when there is a failure to make provisions for managing pre-proposal communications. Questions posed via telephone or in personal meetings have the potential for creating the greatest problems because of the need to provide all prospective contractors with the same information and the possibility that seemingly insignificant information may be relayed exclusively by telephone or in a personal meeting to just one of the competing contractors. When replies to questions are made by telephone or in person to one prospective contractor, there is a strong probability that other contractors are not treated equally because seemingly insignificant questions and responses are not provided to the other prospective contractors. Another problem associated with responding to questions by telephone or in personal meetings is the administrative burden of preparing a record of the questions and responses that must be transmitted to all prospective contractors. Questions posed via e-mail, traditional mail, and facsimile do not have the same potential for providing incomplete information to the other prospective contractors; however, the administrative burden associated with preparing and transmitting the questions and responses is not avoidable. The ideal method for responding to pre-proposal questions is to establish a Web site where prospective contractors' questions and the contracting agency's responses can be posted for all prospective contractors to read. This method for responding to pre-proposal questions is fast, simple, and ensures that all the contracting agency's responses to questions are available in the same timeframe to all companies competing for the contract. To ensure control over the questions posted on the Web site, the agency should consider having the questions posed via e-mail to the project manager for posting on the Web site. Permitting prospective contractors to enter their own questions directly to the agency's Web site could result in questionable postings on that Web site.

Sections 1.3.1 and 1.3.2 relate to agency Web sites. Agency Web sites typically contain general contracting information such as the organizational structure and personnel assigned to the contracting function, a description of contracting performed directly by agency departments, how to register as a contractor for the agency, descriptions of ongoing contractual efforts, and the announcement of contract awards. The use of a Web site to manage pre-proposal communications is an excellent tool to ensure that all prospective contractors are treated equally because it permits the posting of questions from prospective contractors along with the agency's response on a Web site that provides identical information that is available to all prospective contractors at the same instant.

### 1.3.3 Dollar Threshold Where Sole Source Justification Is Required

Although the dollar threshold where a sole source justification is required is normally the prerogative of the agency or based on law or ordinance, the agency should assess the availability of prospective contractors to determine whether there is competition available for the service to be provided. Virtually every state and local government agency either mandates or encourages competitive contract awards to obtain the numerous advantages stemming from the competitive selection of contractors. This is a subject that is thoroughly discussed in a subsequent chapter. If there is just one company qualified to provide the needed services, the committee needs to determine whether they require approval to pursue the contract on a sole source basis. If it is determined that there is no qualified competition, the sole source justification is prepared at this stage of the process to permit time for approval of the sole source request or for making an attempt to identify additional companies to include in a competitive procurement.

## 1.3.4 Preference Not Given to Local Contractors

If the agency does not have a law, ordinance, or policy that provides a preference for local contractors, there is no need to consider such a preference during the advance contract planning process. However, if preference is regularly given to local contractors, the committee must determine whether any federal funding is provided for this project. If federal funding is provided for the project, then the committee must seek an exception to the practice of providing a preference for local contractors.[1]

Sections 1.3.3 and 1.3.4 relate to considerations regarding competitive contracting. It is important to establish a dollar value threshold above which sole source contracts require written justification. Without such a threshold, effort could be wasted writing justifications for low-dollar-value contracts that can be awarded without seeking competition. The other extreme would be the possibility of awarding high-dollar-value contracts without seeking competition. Naturally, the award of high-dollar-value contracts without seeking competition has the greatest potential for problems. Awarding high-dollar-value contracts without competition increases the probability for selecting a contractor that is not as well qualified as the competing contractors, paying an exorbitant price compared to the services provided, or even the existence of fraudulent acts to obtain the contract. State and local government agencies occasionally establish preferences for contractors within their jurisdiction. Oftentimes, the preferences include award of a contract despite the fact that the local company did not bid or propose the lowest price. Typically, such local preferences establish a limit such as 5 percent or 10 percent by which the local company's bid or proposal can exceed the bid or proposal from the company that is not local. The danger is that if the contract is funded wholly or in part by federal funds, the federal government could conceivably audit the contract and find that the agency must return the federal funding for failure to follow federal grant contracting provisions.

## 1.3.5 The Words "Proposal" and "Bid" Are Not Used Synonymously

When drafting an RFP or adapting an agency RFP template, the committee should ensure that this document does not refer to the expected response from prospective contractors as a "bid" or any term other than "proposal." The term "bid" should be restricted to a response to an Invitation for Bids (IFB) because there are distinct differences between the treatment of bids in response to an IFB and proposals in response to an RFP. If the agency's RFP template refers to "bids" or any term other than "proposals," this anomaly should be corrected in the project RFP, and the department that maintains the template should be advised of the fact that incorrect terminology is present in the template. The department that maintains the template must be aware of template anomalies so that the template can be corrected prior to subsequent use by other advance planning committees. The distinctions between the treatment of bids and proposals are explained in detail in a subsequent chapter on solicitations.

### 1.3.6 Reference to Companies Solicited as Contractors or Prospective Contractors

The use of the term "vendor" or any term other than "contractor" or "prospective contractor" should be treated similar to the incorrect usage of "bid" rather than "proposal." A tremendous majority of contract templates used by state and local government agencies identify the name of the individual or company they are contracting with in the contract preamble and then indicate that subsequently in the contract, the individual or company is referred to as "contractor." This is the primary reason for using the term "contractor" or "prospective contractor" rather than "vendor" or any other term. However, there is added information on this point in a subsequent chapter on the contract document.

### 1.3.7 Word Used That Best Compels Contractors to Perform Tasks

Most state and local government agencies use the word "shall" to best compel a contractor to perform tasks or comply with contract provisions. Although terms such as "may" or "should" can be used to describe truly optional performance or compliance, the word or words that best compel contractors to perform should be used consistently throughout the contract and the attachments to the contract. Otherwise, the contractor is not compelled to perform mandatory tasks.

Sections 1.3.5, 1.3.6, and 1.3.7 all relate to terminology used in government contracting. As in most professions, there is unique terminology and highly specific definitions for certain terms used in the field of contract management. Laypersons often use the terms "bid" and "proposal" synonymously. However, a bid is a contractor's response to an Invitation for Bids (IFB), while a proposal is a contractor's response to a Request for Proposals (RFP). Because different rules are applicable to the government's handling of bids and opposed to handling of proposals, the inappropriate use of terminology could lead to allegations regarding improper government handling of bids or proposals. State and local government agency contracts usually name a contractor in the preamble of their contracts and then indicate that they will subsequently be referred to as "contractor" in the contract text. The resultant ambiguity from referring to a contractor as "vendor" or any term other than contractor can be avoided by referring to contractors solely as "contractor." Most government agencies use the word "shall" to compel performance by a contractor. Some government agencies use "must" or "will" to compel contractors to perform tasks. In either event, it is essential that the word that most compels a contractor be used when describing mandatory contractor tasks. Otherwise, a contract may be interpreted such that the use of a word other than the most compelling word classifies tasks so described as discretionary rather than mandatory. The use of inappropriate terms may have the greatest impact on government agencies in those instances where disputes are settled in a court of law.

## 1.3.8 Weighted Criteria Established for Evaluation of Proposals

Evaluation of proposals and selection of the successful contractor are normally the two final acts of the advance contract planning team. However, in some cases a separate proposal evaluation team may be established to evaluate the proposals and select the contractor. In the event that such a proposal evaluation team is established, one or more members of the advance contract planning committee normally serve on this team as well. The advance contract planning committee should consider the makeup of the proposal evaluation team and ensure that the solicitation requires all prospective contractors to submit relevant information in their proposals. If essential information is not requested in the solicitation, there could be significant delays in the commencement of the project because it may be necessary to extend the proposal due date or cancel and reissue the solicitation to request essential but missing information from the prospective contractors. One critical goal of the advance contract planning committee is the development of a solicitation document that requires competing contractors to provide information required for the proposal evaluation team to select the best contractor on the basis of cost and other relevant factors. It is essential that serious thought is given to the evaluation criteria included in the solicitation and measures established to ensure that the proposals are evaluated solely on the basis of the criteria described in the solicitation. Details on an approach to ensure that proposals are evaluated solely on the basis of the criteria in the RFP are included in Chapter 5, "Management of Pre-Proposal Communications and Evaluation of Proposals." Once the successful contractor is selected, the advance contract planning team, or proposal evaluation team, is normally disbanded and not likely required to meet again as a team unless one of the unsuccessful contractors initiates a protest.

The committee should determine the criteria, based at least partially on the project objectives, that are appropriate for evaluating the proposals and selecting a contractor to provide the needed service delivery. If there is insufficient correlation between the project objective and the proposal evaluation criteria, the agency is likely to select other than the ideal contractor for the project. If the agency has a template for a services contract RFP, that document should be reviewed to determine whether any of the criteria included in the RFP template is appropriate for the project. Evaluation of the criteria in the RFP template can establish the basis for discussing what criteria are relevant for the immediate project. The committee should also consider the relative importance of the criteria and assign weights to each. Following evaluation of the proposals by each committee member, the scoring is weighted according to the relative importance of each criterion to ensure that the most important criteria receive added consideration and the less important criteria receive less consideration.

## 1.3.9 *Price Stated as One Criterion for Evaluation of Proposals*

The committee should ensure that either "price" or "life cycle cost" is included as a criterion, and also determine whether "price" or "life cycle cost" would be more appropriate as a criterion. Failure to include price or life cycle cost as one of the proposal evaluation criteria could easily result in a protest from an aggrieved prospective contractor that discovered that the agency considered price or life cycle cost when it was not identified in the solicitation as a selection criterion. Price refers to the contract price paid to the contractor. This price may be increased or decreased during the contract term through contract amendments based on changes in the scope of work. Price does not normally include agency personnel costs, training or materials not provided by the contractor, contract phase-out, or other miscellaneous project costs not included in the contract. Life cycle cost refers to the price as adjusted during the term of the contract, plus all other agency costs associated with the project not included in the contract.

Merely eight of the RFPs (36 percent) submitted by agencies participating in the best practices research project specified price as a criterion for evaluating proposals. However, it is suspected that all the participating agencies consider pricing in their proposal evaluation process but just failed to include that information in their RFPs. The Best Practices RFP specifies life cycle cost, as an alternative to contract price, as one of the selection criteria. Life cycle cost, which considers all contract costs plus all other agency project costs over a specified number of years, is considered superior to consideration of cost to the agency that is limited to contract pricing. As an example of the superiority of the life cycle cost evaluation, consider one proposal for a three-year contract with annual pricing of $4,000,000 that requires the addition of three agency employees to manage the project at a cost to the agency of $60,000 per employee per year. If a competing proposal includes a three-year contract with annual pricing of $4,050,000 and requires just one additional agency employee to manage the project at $60,000 per year, the company with the higher contract price has a life cycle cost that is lower than the competitor's life cycle cost by $70,000 per year.

Sections 1.3.8 and 1.3.9 both relate to criteria for evaluating proposals. The use of weighted criteria is an ideal tool to use in the evaluation of proposals when an agency wishes to give more weight to one criterion than to another criterion. For example, an agency may use specific experience and development of the project plan as three of the criteria for evaluating proposals. If the agency feels that specific experience carries twice the importance of financial stability and that development of the project plan carries twice the importance of financial stability, then it might assign financial stability a weight of 10, specific experience a weight of 20, and development of the project plan a weight of 40. Price is almost always one of the criteria used to evaluate proposals for services contracts. Agencies frequently mention the proposal evaluation criteria (as they should) in their RFPs; however, they often neglect to name price as one of their criteria.

In the event of the protest of the award of a contract when the agency considered pricing in selecting the contractor but failed to name price as an evaluation criteria in their RFP, officials determining the merits of a protest could be convinced to rule against the government.

## 1.3.10 Format Specified for Proposals

The advance contract planning committee should establish a format for proposals to ensure that all the proposals address the same topics and are organized in the same sequence. If the prospective contractors are permitted to present the topics that emphasize their best attributes and to present them in any sequence, then the proposal evaluation committee is unnecessarily burdened with the task of comparing dissimilar proposals to one another and to the criteria. This problem is avoided by including instructions to prospective contractors, in the RFP, to organize their proposals in a standard sequence and to cover topics that are directly correlated with the proposal evaluation criteria.

## 1.3.11 Page Limit Established for Proposals

The establishment of page limits for each section of the proposal is a logical extension of the practice of establishing a format for proposals. Proposals that cover the same topics in the same sequence and with the same maximum number of pages garner proposals homogenous in all respects except the features that distinguish the prospective contractors from one another. This homogeneity greatly simplifies the efforts of the proposal evaluation committee when comparing the proposals to one another and to the criteria.

Sections 1.3.10 and 1.3.11 both relate to a government agency established format of proposals in response to an RFP. In the absence of an established format, prospective contractors would be free to organize their proposals in any sequence, address the topics of their choosing, and submit as many pages as they wish. Dissimilar proposals are difficult and time consuming for the state and local government agencies to evaluate for selection of the best contractor for the immediate project.

## 1.3.12 Model Contract Included in the RFP

The advance contract planning committee should ensure that there is a copy of its agency's standard services contract template included in the RFP. This practice, especially when there is a statement in the RFP that the agency intends to award a contract essentially in the format of the attached model contract, guards against the possibility of prospective contractors proposing their own standard contract with provisions that are generally unfavorable to the agency. A contractor certification in the RFP that requires prospective contractors to agree to the agency's contract provisions further guards against the possibility that contractors will propose their own contract format.

Section 1.3.12 relates to attaching a copy of the agency's standard contract template to the RFP and including a statement in the RFP to the effect that the agency intends to award a contract essentially in the format of the attached contract. Insistence on the use of the agency's contract format avoids the necessity to negotiate contractor standard terms and conditions that generally favor the contractor over the government with respect to responsibilities and risks. Contract provisions proposed by prospective contractors are certain to vary from one another, thus making it virtually impossible to compare the contract provisions on an equivalency basis. There is also the possibility that the rush to award a contract by some date certain may cause the agency to agree to some provision (or provisions) that, with more time available for analyses, it would have considered such a contract provision (or provisions) to be unfavorable or unacceptable.

## 1.3.13 Acceptance of Late Proposals

Although bids in response to an IFB cannot be accepted if they are delivered late, most states and local government agencies do not have codes or ordinances prohibiting the acceptance of late proposals in response to an RFP. If an agency rejects all proposals that are delivered after the time and date established for receipt of proposals, a proposal or proposals that would have better suited the interests of the agency may be summarily rejected. The rationale for accepting late proposals is that proposals, unlike bids, are treated confidentially; therefore, the prospective contractor submitting a late proposal does not gain a competitive advantage when submitting a late proposal. Should the advance contract planning committee elect to establish an option for accepting late proposals, however, this option should be described in the RFP. Failure to include the agency's option to accept late proposals in the RFP could result in a protest from a contractor that submitted its proposal on time and then the agency accepted a late proposal. The description of the option to accept late proposals should reflect the fact that the agency may accept late proposals if they are in the best interests of the agency, but that prospective contractors should endeavor to deliver their proposals on time because the agency does have the option to reject late proposals. This cautionary advice to prospective contractors is designed not only to provide maximum flexibility for the agency, but also to encourage contractors to submit their proposals on time or risk rejection of their proposal.

## 1.3.14 *Proposals Opened in Confidence*

Because proposals are subject to negotiation, they should be treated as confidential until the contract is awarded or recommended for award. Should proposals be made public prior to selection of the successful contractor, competing contractors would have access to one another's proposals and this access would compromise negotiations. However, because some contractors may be more accustomed to submitting bids in response to an IFB, they may assume that there is a public opening of the proposals. To ensure that there is no misunderstanding regarding the lack of a public opening of the proposals, there should be advice in the RFP that the proposals are treated confidentially until the contractor is selected and there is no public opening of proposals. If such advice is not provided in the RFP, some prospective contractors may expect a public opening of the proposals.

Sections 1.3.13 and 1.3.14 both relate to the receipt and opening of proposals in response to an RFP. Agencies are permitted considerably more informality in the handling of proposals in response to RFPs than in the handling of bids in response to IFBs. Because bids are required to be opened publicly and read aloud, it is not possible to accept late bids because a contractor submitting a late bid could wait until competitors' bid prices were read aloud and then submit a bid scarcely lower than the lowest bid that was read aloud. Proposals in response to an RFP, however, are subject to negotiation and are not opened publicly. Therefore, a prospective contractor submitting a proposal a few minutes, hours, or even a day or two late does not gain an advantage over its competitors. However, the terms of that proposal may be considerably more favorable to the government than the earlier proposals. Therefore, when it is in the best interests of the government, late proposals may be accepted. Because the rules for handling bids and proposals differ so significantly, it is recommended that agencies state in their RFPs that proposals will be treated confidentially until the contract is awarded or recommended for award, that there will be no public opening of the proposals, and that the agency may accept late proposals if they are in the agency's best interests.

All 14 topics listed above are discussed at length in this book. The majority of the material for the proposal evaluation guidelines can be copied and pasted from the Solicitation document and then modified as required for guiding the proposal evaluation team. Details on the content of the guidelines for each of the above topics are not discussed in this chapter because there are thorough discussions on each of these subjects in subsequent chapters.

Four of the best practices, listed below, are not included among the topics to be considered during advance contract planning because they are considered to be in the purview of the agency for implementation on an agencywide basis. If, however, the following topics have not been implemented on an agencywide basis, then the advance contract planning committee should consider these topics as well. Additional information on these topics is available in the chapters associated with each in Figure 1.2:

- One-page contract format with incorporated attachments
- Cost plus a percentage of cost prohibited
- Unallowable costs specified
- State and local government standard terms and conditions

## 1.4 Conclusion

Contracts, to be legally enforceable, must include offer and acceptance, a meeting of the contracting parties' minds, consideration, and reflect the relationship between two or more competent parties for a legal purpose and for a specific time period. These essential elements of a contract also apply to contract amendments. The most likely essential element to be missing from a contract amendment is consideration. Agency officials should ensure that contract amendments include consideration as discussed in this chapter.

Contracts for services have distinct differences from contracts for commodities. Aside from the obvious differences regarding the ability to accumulate commodities in inventory for future use while services are generally provided in real-time, there are also differences in solicitation and contracting documents. While it is true that there are instances when contracts for commodities are solicited through RFPs and contracts for services are solicited through IFBs, this is contrary to the usual solicitation documents used to contract for commodities and services.

The principal participants in state and local government contracting are the public sector including government officials and employees and the private sector including contractors comprising corporations, partnerships, sole proprietors, joint ventures, or any other designation for companies or individuals who provide government services on a contract basis. Of course, constituents, including voters and all other residents of applicable jurisdictions, also have significant roles as financiers for and beneficiaries of the services provided.

A research project was conducted in preparation for writing this book. The research included a short questionnaire sent to all 50 state governments, as well as the city governments in the state capitals and the county governments where the state capitals are located. Additionally, these 150 government agencies were requested to provide copies of the solicitation and contract document templates they use for services contracting. Best practices were identified through the research project, and authoritative publications were researched to verify the fact that such practices were, indeed, considered best practices. The best practices were incorporated in templates for RFPs and services contracts that are thoroughly discussed in subsequent chapters, provided in the appendices to this text, and provided on a CD for agencies that wish to adapt these templates for their own use and for academic exercises for students of state and local government services contracting. A complete description of the research methodology and results is provided in Appendix B, "Best Practices Research Project."

There are distinct facets of the contracting cycle comprised of the pre-solicitation, solicitation, proposal evaluation, contract award, contract administration, and finally the contract closeout phases. The activities conducted during the pre-solicitation phase are accomplished by the advance contract planning committee or, for less-critical or lower-dollar-value projects, by an individual or a few individuals. Advance planning encompasses planning for all subsequent phases of the contracting cycle. The solicitation phase begins with the issuance of the RFP or other type of solicitation document and is completed when the proposals are received by the agency. This is a particularly sensitive time period in the contracting cycle when the prospective contractors are involved in the preparation of their proposals and agency personnel would, intuitively, be relatively idle. However, there are invariably attempts by contractors, during this period, to contact agency personnel to gather information that will assist the contractors in rendering their proposals more competitive. To further the agency's goals for treating prospective contractors on an equal basis, emphasis must be placed on planning and conducting the management of pre-proposal communications. The proposal evaluation phase begins with the receipt of proposals and is completed when the contract is awarded or recommended for award. Two critical considerations during the evaluation phase are (1) to ensure that the proposal methodology process is fair and likely leads to selection of the contractor that best meets the criteria for the project, and (2) that the proposals are evaluated solely based on the criteria stated in the RFP. Careful construction of the RFP, a fair proposal evaluation process, and the inclusion of a statement that the agency intends to award a contract essentially in the form of an attached MSC generally results in a fairly routine contract award phase. However, in the absence of a fair proposal evaluation process, the contract award phase is more likely to be complicated by a protest. In the absence of an MSC attached to the RFP accompanied by a statement that the agency intends to award a contract essentially in the form of the MSC, extended negotiation of contract provisions should be anticipated. The contract administration phase for services contracts generally consumes more time than the combined time for all the other phases of the contracting cycle. This is the phase when the contracted services are actually provided. When the contractor delivers the services in a professional manner, according to the provisions of the contract, this is a relatively routine phase of the contracting cycle. However, contractors that fail to perform according to the contract provisions are likely to create an administrative burden on agency personnel, which could lead to early termination of the contract and the need to select an alternate contractor or to perform the services with agency personnel. Contract closeout generally consists of performance of routine tasks such as preparation of a contractor performance report, relief of financial encumbrances, maintenance of the contract records for the required time period, and the eventual destruction of the contract records.

Advance contract planning is essential to minimize problems during the solicitation, proposal evaluation, and contract administration phases of the contracting cycle. This activity is normally conducted by a committee for high-dollar-value or high-risk projects, or by an individual or a few individuals for low-dollar-value or low-risk projects. The committee or individual (or individuals) performing this function should consider implementation of the best practices as well as other prudent practices described in this text to ensure successful contractor selection and service delivery while avoiding problems associated with poor planning. A comprehensive advance contract plan prepared during this phase contributes to success during all subsequent phases of the contracting cycle. A total of 26 topics, including 14 of the 18 best practices, are recommended for consideration by agency personnel during advance contract planning. The 14 best practices are discussed in this chapter while the remaining 12 prudent practices are discussed in Appendix C, "Advance Contract Planning Topics Not Included in Best Practices." A comprehensive advance contract plan includes the project background and objective statement, list of actions needed to meet the objectives, scope of work to be incorporated in the MSC, specification of content for proposals from prospective contractors, a complete list of firms to be solicited, strategy for managing pre-proposal communications, selection criteria that is consistent with project objectives, guidelines for evaluating proposals, and ground rules for the contract administration phase.

## Note

1. 28 CFR PART 35, STATE AND LOCAL ASSISTANCE, Part 35.936-2, Grantee procurement systems; State or local law, subpart (C) Preference, states, State or local laws, ordinances, regulations or procedures which effectively give local or in-state bidders or proposers preference over other bidders or proposers shall not be employed in evaluating bids or proposals for subagreements under a grant. Similar prohibitions are also included in Subpart 35.938-4, Formal advertising.

# Chapter 2

# Competition and Socioeconomic Contracting

## Chapter Objectives

This chapter provides readers with an introduction to the topic of competition in contracting, disadvantages of sole source contracts, challenges to and benefits from embracing competition, rationale for establishing a dollar threshold where sole source justification is required, as well as situations that do and that do not justify sole source contracts. The readers are also introduced to socioeconomic contracting programs and equal opportunity techniques for developing a successful socioeconomic contracting program. The equal opportunity techniques discussed include:

- Establishment of an incentive awards program
- Motivational training for contracts professionals
- Encouragement by managers to use targeted companies
- Agency participation in a supportive organization
- Establishment of rapport with targeted companies
- Provision of direct assistance to targeted companies
- Promotion of internal networking
- Incorporation of program support as a part of employee job responsibility

## 2.1 Introduction to Competition in Contracting

State and local government agencies have a reputation for purchasing through the use of Invitations for Bids (IFBs) wherein the lowest-priced responsible contractor or supplier providing a responsive bid is selected. Elected and appointed officials, as well as the constituency, normally insist on competitive procurements to ensure that excessive amounts are not paid from tax revenues and that favoritism is not a factor in the selection of contractors. However, the IFB type of solicitation used in full and open competition is normally reserved for the purchase of commodities or for construction contracts. In rare cases, state or federal grants require competition through the use of an IFB for services contracts. Granting agencies, in such cases, normally provide an IFB template and guidelines for use of the IFB by the contracting agency. Solicitations for services contracts, other than in the preceding unusual situations, are normally conducted through use of Requests for Proposals (RFPs) wherein the resultant contract is awarded based on both price (or life cycle cost) and other factors. Occasionally, such service contracts are awarded on a sole source basis or with limited competition. The first portion of this chapter is devoted to the merits of and recommendation for using RFPs in full and open competition for services contracts.

The necessity to provide equal opportunities for all parties to compete for government contracts has its origins in the United States Constitution.[1] Some state constitutions have similar provisions that extend equal contracting opportunities to the state and local government level. However, the absence of such provision in state constitutions does not diminish the applicability to states and local governments of the U.S. Constitution provisions for competitive procurement.

## 2.2 Disadvantages of Sole Source Contracting

Contractors that are well aware of their status as the sole source provider for a particular service have a tendency to propose higher pricing than they would in a competitive environment. Sole source contractors involved in service delivery over the long term also tend to increase their pricing at a rate higher than increases to their costs or the applicable rate of inflation. This tendency for higher initial pricing and excessive price escalation from sole source contractors is intuitive and well understood. Not so intuitive or well understood, however, are additional disadvantages stemming from noncompetitive contracting such as the tendency for some long-term sole source contractors to relax their propensity to complete tasks or deliverables within the expected timeframe and to relax their propensity for meeting expected quality standards. Competition provides a significant incentive for contractors to deliver their services at competitive pricing, produce high-quality services, and adhere to their schedule commitments.

Noncompetitive procurement also encourages a business environment that includes the unwelcome specter of gratuities or other inducements to foster continued limitation or elimination of competition with the objective of corrupting the agency, its officers, and its employees. To counter the propensity for government officials and employees to limit or eliminate competition in return for personal gain, government agencies have established laws requiring competition in numerous situations. Therefore, an additional disadvantage of sole source contracting is the possibility of noncompliance with applicable law.

## 2.3 Challenges to and Benefits of Embracing Competition

The introduction of competition in the selection of contractors presents a significant challenge to the contracting professional when a contractor has traditionally been selected on a sole source basis. As alluded to previously, the introduction of competition in such an environment is expected to result in lower pricing as well as improved quality and improved on-time service delivery. Contracting professionals wishing to capitalize on the benefits of competition, however, may face internal opposition when attempting to introduce competition in a previously noncompetitive environment. State and local government departmental personnel may be satisfied with the service being provided and reluctant to face the uncertainties associated with a new contractor. Sole source contractors occasionally lobby elected and appointed officials to pressure contracting professionals to continue awarding, extending, or renewing the contract on a sole source basis. When these lobbying efforts are successful, the contracting professional feels considerable resistance to her or his efforts to solicit proposals through full and open competition for the follow-on contract.

A state or local code or ordinance and a contracting policy requiring competition for services contracts that exceed a specified dollar value threshold are essential to ensure that the contracting professional has support for her or his decision to proceed on a competitive basis in light of expected pressure to merely renew the contract with the present contractor. A questionnaire was sent to all states, as well as the city and county governments serving the state capitals, to determine the threshold at which service contracts require competition or a sole source justification. Although there was a slightly better response to the request for document templates, the questionnaire received responses from twelve states and merely six local agencies.

## 2.4 Dollar Threshold Where Sole Source Justification Is Required

The questionnaire sent to states and local government agencies asked for the dollar threshold where it was necessary to obtain sole source justification for services

| Response to: At what dollar threshold are sole source justifications required? | | |
| --- | --- | --- |
| States | Local Agencies | Response |
| 0 | 1 | No dollar amount, but sole source must be proven |
| 1 | 1 | $1,000 |
| 2 | 0 | $2,500 |
| 3 | 1 | $3,000 to $3,100 |
| 3 | 2 | $5,000 |
| 0 | 1 | $10,000 |
| 2 | 0 | $50,000 |
| 1 | 0 | $62,600 |

**Figure 2.1  Response to: At what dollar threshold are sole source justifications required?**

contracts. There is an emphasis in this chapter on the importance of obtaining competition when selecting a contractor, and also the introduction of a form that can be used to justify and approve sole source contracts when competition is not available. The responses from the state and local government agencies regarding the threshold where sole source justifications are required are summarized in Figure 2.1.

## 2.5 Justification for Sole Source Contracts

In recognition of the fact that there are cases when there is but one contractor that can provide the required service, the ordinance or contracting policy should provide a basis for contracting on a sole source basis when that is the only alternative. Development of a form similar to the Sole Source Justification/Approval form shown in Appendix D ("Source Justification/Approval Form") can be an effective tool to document the decision to approve a sole source contract. Ideally, a limited number of agency officials are authorized to approve sole source procurements, and such approvals are based on a determination that the recommended sole source contractor is the "only" contractor that can provide the needed service. Two reasons that should not be considered as justification for sole source contracting are (1) determinations that the recommended contractor is the lowest price contractor and (2) that there is insufficient time to award the contract on a competitive basis.

Lowest price should not be justification for a sole source contract. Current pricing can normally be determined only through the competitive process. Therefore, it is necessary to conduct a competitive procurement to determine the current pricing from qualified contractors. When such a competitive process has been recently followed, there is no need to justify a sole source contract. Departments that attempt to justify sole source contracting based on lowest pricing generally base their justification on a previous competitive procurement. However, previously unsuccessful contractors are likely to propose more competitive pricing during subsequent competitive procurements. Contractors presently performing services for the contracting agency may be more inclined to increase pricing for follow-on procurements. This inclination to increase pricing for follow-on contracts is more likely if the present contractor is aware that its previous pricing was significantly lower than the competitors' pricing. Therefore, follow-on competitive procurements are likely to result in a closer alignment of proposed pricing from the competitors.

Insufficient time to conduct a competitive procurement also should not constitute justification to contract on a sole source basis. While it is tempting to criticize departments for failing to plan their work when they base sole source justifications on insufficient time, there are even more constructive arguments against reliance on insufficient time to justify sole source procurements. If there is sufficient time to obtain pricing and a proposal from one company, then there is normally time to obtain pricing and a proposal from numerous contractors on a concurrent basis. The proposals may also reveal that one or more of the competing contractors that may not have been permitted to submit a proposal in a sole source environment could actually ramp up faster and begin service delivery sooner than the company that was being considered for the sole source contract. In the event that the contract in question is a follow-on contract, departments may have a stronger argument for calling out insufficient time as its justification to forego competition. The temptation to criticize departments for failure to plan to obtain competitive proposals for continuation of ongoing contracted services is even greater. However, it is usually preferable to have a policy and mechanism in place to extend current contracts for a limited time period to allow sufficient time to conduct a competitive procurement for the follow-on contract.

State and local government agencies and colleges or universities offering degree programs in public administration or public policy are invited to adapt the Sole Source Justification/Approval form, and any other materials in the appendices, for their own contracting or academic programs. A compact disc (CD) containing the material in the appendices is included with this book to facilitate the adaptation of materials in the appendices. The sole source form is designed for completion on a computer, typewriter, or in handwriting. Detailed sole source justification and approval instructions for completing the Sole Source Justification/Approval form are provided in Appendix D along with a copy of the form.

## 2.6 Introduction to Socioeconomic Contracting Programs

*Socioeconomic programs* are equal opportunity or affirmative action programs that promote social or economic goals based on the award of contracts to targeted companies. "Targeted company" is the generic term used for companies that an agency targets for increased contracting opportunities through the agency's socioeconomic contracting program. Examples of targeted companies include small business, minority-owned small business, women-owned business, veteran-owned business, and disabled-veteran-owned business.

Such programs encourage the award of contracts to contractors that fit certain criteria such as a maximum number of employees or ownership of and management by a person or persons fitting one of the classifications cited in the preceding sentence. *Equal opportunity programs* involve outreach efforts to discover prospective contractors in targeted groups that historically have had less than full access to state or local government contracts. Equal opportunity programs usually provide outreach efforts to identify such companies and offer them the chance to compete with traditional contractors, but do not afford any competitive advantage with respect to price, quality, or schedule adherence. Equal opportunity programs are normally established on the assumption that management of small, minority-owned, woman-owned, or other targeted contractors is not inherently less qualified to compete with more traditional contractors in a capitalistic environment. Therefore, to succeed as state or local government contractors, they only need be given the opportunity to compete. They do not require a competitive advantage that might be considered unfair by traditional contractors and the constituency. Affirmative action programs can be differentiated from equal opportunity programs in that contractors that are targeted for a particular affirmative action program may be awarded a contract despite the fact that competing non-targeted companies may have proposed lower pricing, higher-quality services, or earlier project completion.

Socioeconomic contracting programs are normally enacted by law or administrative procedures to institute the furtherance of goals for expanding contracting opportunities to targeted companies. In addition to the targeted companies identified in the previous paragraph, state or local government agencies occasionally provide similar advantages to companies based within their jurisdiction. State and local government agencies that contract for services when federal funds are involved, however, should consider suspending such local preference programs for contracts that are funded either fully or partially through federal funding because local preference programs are restricted when federal funding is used.[2] In the case of affirmative action programs, targeted companies may be awarded contracts despite the fact that their competitors offered lower pricing (or life cycle costs), superior service, or earlier project completion. Additionally, constituents are likely to consider paying more than the market price, determined through the competitive process, as a wasteful practice.

Four of the twenty-two RFPs (18 percent) submitted by state and local government agencies in support of the research project described earlier revealed a preference given to local contractors in the proposal evaluation process. An earlier paragraph discussed the prohibition against providing local preferences when federal funding is included in the project budget. Other objections to local and other types of socioeconomic preferences in the selection process are also included in the chapter on solicitations. Eight of the RFPs (36 percent) submitted by agencies participating in the research project included socioeconomic preferences for targeted companies other than local contractors. The Best Practices RFP does not include any socioeconomic preferences that are employed in the selection process. However, this chapter does include proven methodology for establishing outreach programs that increase contracting participation from targeted contractors.

Equal opportunity programs do not include the award of contracts to targeted firms based solely on the makeup of their ownership and management, nor do they permit the award of contracts to targeted companies despite higher pricing, lesser quality, or untimely service delivery. However, targeted companies are sought out by agencies through outreach programs and may be offered assistance short of a competitive advantage over non-targeted companies. While this may be considered by some advocates for targeted companies as a minimal effort, a program relying solely on equal opportunity measures that proved highly successful in significantly increasing the participation of targeted companies is outlined later in this chapter.

It could be argued that, through affirmative action programs, targeted companies are justified in receiving contracts despite the fact that they might have proposed higher pricing, have a poor history of service delivery and cannot complete the project within the requested schedule, or that their owners and managers are less capable than their competitors. However, companies should not be judged as being lesser qualified based on ownership or management by women, members of minority groups, veterans, or disabled persons. Certainly, government agencies do not consider their own employees less capable because they may belong to one of these groups. Therefore, there is a strong argument to design socioeconomic contracting programs around equal opportunity measures rather than affirmative action.

## 2.7 Equal Opportunity Techniques for Developing a Successful Socioeconomic Contracting Program

The balance of this chapter, with the exception of the conclusion, is dedicated to the discussion of methods for facilitating success in the implementation of socioeconomic contracting programs by state or local agencies while relying solely on equal opportunity measures.

There are eight measures that, when applied simultaneously, proved to significantly increase the number of contracts and dollar value of contracts awarded to targeted companies. Implementation of six or seven of these measures may prove successful. However, when all eight measures presented in this chapter were employed by a private sector company to increase awards to minority-owned businesses and women-owned businesses, significant and continuous improvement was measured over the program's nine-year duration. The measures are all categorized as equal opportunity tools because they do not provide price, quality, or schedule advantages to targeted companies. The company[3] where this socioeconomic contracting program was implemented had historically awarded 2 percent of contracted dollars to minority-owned companies and 1 percent of contracted dollars to women-owned companies. The dollar value of awards to minority-owned companies increased from 2 percent to more than 15 percent. This represents an increase of more than 600 percent in the dollar value of contracts awarded to minority-owned contractors. The dollar value of awards to women-owned businesses increased from 1 percent to more than 6 percent. This represents an increase of more than 500 percent in the dollar value of contracts awarded to women-owned companies.

While it is unlikely that state and local government agencies have socioeconomic contracting programs that specifically target, as in this example, women-owned and minority-owned companies, all eight of these measures are applicable to any category of targeted companies. In addition to the likelihood that state and local government agencies do not target the exact categories of companies used in this example, there are other differences between this example and socioeconomic contracting programs for state and local government agencies. One obvious difference is that the example was taken from a private-sector company. An additional significant difference is that the contracts in the example were primarily for the procurement of commodities with a significantly lesser percentage for services contracts. However, despite these differences, the measures described in this chapter are readily applicable to state and local government agencies when they contract for services or commodities.

Although the company that developed the program described below had the option of using both affirmative action and equal opportunity tools, they elected to use only the available tools that fit in the definition of equal opportunity measures. Despite the fact that the affirmative action measures including price advantages for targeted companies and set-asides were not employed, impressive results were achieved. "Set-asides" is the term used to describe procurements for which solicitations are sent only to a targeted class of contractors (such as small businesses or disabled-veteran-owned businesses), and responses to the solicitation are not considered unless the responding companies are members of the targeted class of contractors. The targeted companies in this example, in fact, were required to compete with traditional contractors on an equal basis without set-asides or other advantages. In addition to competing equally with respect to competitive pricing, the targeted companies were also required to meet the same high-quality and on-time completion standards as the traditional contractors.

At the onset of the socioeconomic contracting program used as this example, there was considerable concern that higher prices would be paid for inferior products that might also be delivered late. To guard against the possibility of such abhorrent results accompanying increased procurement from targeted companies, all the contractors that were historically solicited remained on the solicitation list, but at least one targeted company was added to each list of contractors solicited. This practice ensured that the targeted company would not be selected unless its pricing was lower than that of the traditional contractor's pricing, the number of traditional companies competing for contracts would not be reduced, and other selection factors for the targeted companies were required to be equal to or better than the selection factors for traditional contractors. Pricing, schedule performance, and quality had been measured for numerous years prior to implementing this socioeconomic contracting program that would remain in place for a period of nine years. The pricing, schedule performance, and quality measurements were continued throughout the duration of the program. Not only did the continued reporting indicate that the worst fears did not occur, but there was actually a slow but continuous improvement in pricing, on-time project completion, and product quality throughout the duration of the program. Such outstanding results should not be surprising because minorities and women who are employed by state and local government agencies require no special compensation to compete in the workplace with non-minority males. Therefore, one would expect that minority-owned and women-owned companies, when provided an equal opportunity, are capable of successfully competing with non-minority, male-owned companies.

The company used in this example is a prime contractor for the Department of Defense (DOD). Based on that classification, that company was authorized to employ affirmative action measures to increase its awards to minority-owned and women-owned companies. Affirmative action programs, such as providing a price advantage to targeted companies or establishing set-asides wherein only targeted companies could compete for contracts, thus limiting the benefits of full and open competition, would certainly increase the cost of materials and possibly result in lesser-quality products and late deliveries, all of which would have an adverse impact on profit for the DOD contractor. The increases in price would occur as the result of lessened reliance on full and open competition. The increased chance of receiving lesser-quality and slower deliveries is based on the tendency for companies operating in less than a fully competitive environment to take their future market share for granted and relax their efforts to meet or exceed quality and delivery standards.

Although state and local government agencies need not be concerned with profit, the same disadvantages to private-sector companies that employ affirmative action measures are likely to also have an adverse impact on contracting agencies. Constituents who contribute the revenue for state and local government operations certainly expect that such tax revenues are expended in a fair and rational manner. It would be difficult to justify higher expenditures to the public for purchase of inferior products or services that are not provided on time. This is especially true when most targeted companies, such as those in this example, can compete with historical contractors on an equal basis. The eight measures employed to obtain the results in the above example are described below.

## 2.7.1 Establish an Incentive Awards Program

Contracting agencies generally recognize the benefit of providing programs for rewarding employees who excel in their work performance. Success in discovering targeted companies and developing them to the point where they can compete with historical contractors is readily measurable. Because it is a noble cause that can be readily measured, an incentive awards program for contracting professionals who excel in their support for the socioeconomic contracting program is recommended for contracting agencies that wish to have a successful socioeconomic contracting program.

The types of activities that can be measured to recognize contracting professionals for their success in support of the socioeconomic contracting program include attendance at trade shows where targeted companies demonstrate their capabilities, providing targeted companies with opportunities to compete for agency contracts, first-time contract awards to targeted companies, the number of or percentage of contracts awarded to targeted companies, and the dollar value or percentage of dollars awarded to targeted companies. Because some contracting professionals may specialize in services for which there are fewer targeted companies, adjustments may be made to the recognition criteria to ensure fairness to the contracting professionals. Another measure for ensuring that more contracting professionals have an opportunity to be recognized for their efforts is to limit the frequency in which employees may be recognized for recognition. In the example from the private sector, the award was presented twice each year and employees could not receive the award more than once in any two-year period.

The types of recognition provided to contracting professionals for outstanding support of the socioeconomic contracting program could include one, or any combination, of cash, government bonds, a plaque, favorable mention in the employee's performance evaluation, a letter or certificate placed in the personnel files, an article in the agency's newsletter, lunch or dinner in a local restaurant, or any other recognition deemed appropriate by the contracting agency.

## 2.7.2 Motivational Training for Contracts Professionals

Certain employees are predisposed to wholeheartedly embracing the implementation of a socioeconomic contracting program while other employees are inclined to remain neutral or even hostile. The contracting professionals who are first to excel in discovering and developing new targeted companies are those who embraced the program from the beginning. Appropriate recognition of those early successes is an excellent tool to encourage continued success by other motivated employees as well as to encourage program support by the more neutral and hostile employees.

Establishing a recognition program with a forum that permits the contracting professional who received the most recent award an opportunity to describe how the targeted contractor or contractors were discovered and developed is encouraged. Public recognition of employees who excel in meeting socioeconomic subcontracting goals and the positive impact on their careers should help convince the more neutral and hostile employees to more actively participate in the socioeconomic contracting program. Sharing successful techniques for achieving socioeconomic contracting goals with their colleagues by employees that exceeded the objectives should also be considered. This sharing approach encourages the adoption of successful techniques by the previously less successful contracting professionals, and thus improves their performance in reaching socioeconomic contracting goals.

## 2.7.3 *Managers Encourage Use of Targeted Companies*

Managers of contracting professionals control the assignment of contracts to the employees who prepare the draft solicitation, create the list of contractors to be solicited, evaluate the proposals, and select or recommend the company or individual as the successful contractor. When assigning a project or contracting effort to a subordinate, the manager has an excellent opportunity to identify targeted firms that appear qualified to perform the contracted services. This identification of targeted companies to contracting professionals at the time a project is assigned is highly recommended.

Managers who elect to follow this recommendation obviously need to be familiar with targeted companies and their capabilities. One advantage managers have in this respect is that, by reviewing the work of all contracting professionals in their organization, they become aware of targeted companies that have been awarded contracts by other contracts professionals. More importantly, managers become aware of targeted companies that have performed well on contracts awarded by other contracting professionals.

## 2.7.4 *Participate in a Supportive Organization*

Development of a socioeconomic contracting program can be an overwhelming task for one government agency that may be using virtually all of its resources just to perform its primary contracting mission. However, if a contracting agency joins with similar organizations to jointly develop an entity that facilitates the tasks required to develop a socioeconomic contracting program, all member agencies significantly relieve the strain on their resources. An excellent organization[4] of this type was formed in the San Francisco Bay Area, and could be used as a model for state and local government agencies that wish to develop a world-class socioeconomic contracting program without overextending their resources.

The founders of this model organization are all private-sector companies with federal government contracts requiring the establishment of socioeconomic subcontracting programs. Targeted companies and government agencies were permitted to join as non-voting associate members. Their membership has since grown to include private-sector companies that are not required to develop socioeconomic subcontracting programs as a condition of federal contracts, but wish to provide the same targeted companies with improved opportunities to compete for their contracts. The model organization holds monthly luncheons that afford a venue for the large corporations, targeted businesses, and government agencies to network. The model organization also holds periodic procurement fairs where organization members, government agencies, and targeted companies have an opportunity to be exhibitors.

Regardless of whether state and local government agencies are required or elect to develop a socioeconomic contracting program, they should consider a cooperative arrangement such as the model organization discussed above. It is likely that following the initial, extensive efforts to form such an organization, the participating contracting agencies are able to develop a superior socioeconomic contracting program while expending fewer resources than would be required to develop a less successful program on their own.

## 2.7.5 Establish Rapport with Targeted Companies

The initial sales contact between a contracting agency and a targeted company may be at a networking event as discussed in the section above, receipt of sales literature through the mail, a telephonic cold sales call, a sales representative who personally arrives in the contracting agency's lobby, or any of innumerable contact methods that the sales or marketing representatives might devise. Contracting professionals who are novices at dealing with targeted companies may find it difficult to initially establish rapport with the representative. If efforts are not taken to establish a meaningful dialogue during the initial sales contact, a valuable resource can be lost forever.

Contracting professionals are accustomed to dealing with sales representatives who are aggressive and persistent. Although there is no shortage of aggressive, persistent sales representatives from targeted companies, contracting professionals should realize that some sales representatives may blame an unproductive sales contact on their perceived impression that the contracting professional is prejudiced, chauvinistic, or even dedicated solely to the existing contractor base because of a less than admirable business relationship. One reason for expressing blame in this manner is that there are contracting professionals who possess these unfortunate characteristics.

While every individual may have his or her own approach to establishing rapport with new business contacts, some suggestions are provided here. First, it is not necessary to establish a friendly, personal relationship. The sales representative is normally more interested in developing a business relationship than a personal relationship. The path to establishing meaningful rapport is by taking a genuine interest in the targeted company's resources and capabilities. If this is not forthcoming from a possibly inexperienced sales representative, leading questions should help reveal a possible match between the targeted company's capabilities and the needs of the contracting agency. The representative should be asked about the targeted company's capabilities, projects performed for other government agencies, what the contractor can do to support the needs of the state and local government agency, and any other questions along these lines to express an interest in the company and to learn about the company's strengths and how they can contribute to the contracting agency's objectives.

Many targeted companies are in great demand by other contracting agencies. Missing an opportunity to discover a match between the needs of the public agency and the capabilities of a targeted company during the initial contact could result in missing the only opportunity to develop that targeted company as a service provider. This is especially true if another contracting agency makes a connection, recognizes the ability of that particular targeted company to contribute to its agency's success, and provides a sufficient quantity of work to cause the targeted company to scale back its sales and marketing program.

## 2.7.6 Provide Direct Assistance to Targeted Companies

As mentioned earlier, direct assistance in the form of providing a price advantage or forgiving poor-quality services or tolerating late performance is not advocated. Likewise, set-asides for targeted companies are not advocated. Assistance, short of these measures that are included in the definition of affirmative action, however, may prove to be acceptable measures that can be provided to targeted companies.

One form of assistance that is normally valuable to a recently established targeted company is a critical review of its sales or marketing literature. When viewed from the perspective of a contracts professional, a critical evaluation of information intended for the targeted company's customers can be highly valuable. In one extreme example, a newly established company prepared, printed, and distributed a flyer that did an excellent job of describing the company's capabilities and potential value to its customers, but failed to include the company name or any contact information. While such obvious shortcomings are extremely rare, simply providing feedback on material content that tends to either encourage or discourage the contracts professional from pursuing a business relationship with the targeted company can be immeasurable.

Suggesting venues, such as trade shows, where targeted companies can reach contracts professionals who are prospective customers is, likewise, valuable information for targeted companies. Supportive organizations, such as the one cited earlier in this chapter, hold periodic trade shows where targeted companies are provided an opportunity to demonstrate their company's capabilities to large businesses and government agencies. Such trade shows typically provide large businesses and government agencies a venue for providing opportunities to targeted companies for directly marketing their services.

Contracting professionals who do not have the need to contract for the products or services provided by a targeted company that approached them may have contacts at large businesses or other government agencies that do have a need for the targeted company's products or services. Making referrals in such a situation is appreciated by large companies and government agencies seeking targeted companies as well as by the targeted company that is attempting to expand its customer base.

### 2.7.7 Promote Internal Networking

The internal networking advocated is networking among the contracts professionals within a particular contracting agency. Targeted companies that have proven valuable contributors to the success of one department of a state and local government agency may have the potential for making a similar positive contribution to other departments within the same state or local government agency.

State and local government agency department heads and managers of contracting offices can generally promote internal networking during periodic interdepartmental meetings. An excellent opportunity to promote such networking is immediately following the award of a significant contract to a targeted company or completion of a successful project by a targeted company. In addition to recognizing the targeted company, this becomes an occasion that also provides an opportunity to recognize contracting or departmental personnel who participated in the successful project.

### 2.7.8 Incorporate Program Support as Part of Job Responsibility

Whenever a state and local government agency or contracting activity adopts a socioeconomic contracting program, the success of that program depends highly on the performance of individual contracting professionals. Therefore, it is essential to garner support for the program from these professionals. While the incentive program discussed earlier in this chapter encourages certain contracting professionals to support these programs, placing support of the socioeconomic contracting program on the same level as other job performance measures ensures that all contracting professionals accept responsibility for supporting the program.

Job performance measures for contracting professionals often include the success, or lack thereof, in developing contractors that deliver high-quality services that are delivered on time and within budget. If development of targeted companies that likewise deliver high-quality services that are delivered on time and within budget is included as a job performance measure equal to the traditional job performance measures, contracting professionals acquire a clear incentive to provide unequivocal support to the public agency's socioeconomic contracting program.

## 2.8 Conclusion

Award of contracts for services contracts through the use of competitive RFPs should be just as prevalent as competition for commodity or construction contracts through the use of IFBs. Requiring contractors to compete for services is likely to result in lower prices. Because certain contractors that operate in a sole source environment tend to increase prices faster than they do in a competitive environment while also failing to maintain the high-quality standards and on-time service delivery standards that they would in a competitive environment, there are advantages to competitive contracting other than merely improved pricing. Contractors vying for contracts on the basis of competitive proposals, therefore, are likely to have an incentive to provide superior services and on-time schedule performance as well a competitive pricing.

If a contracting agency attempts to justify its sole source selection on the fact that a contractor prices its services lower than its competitors, there is little opportunity, in the absence of competition, to verify that fact. Existing contractors that are required to compete for follow-on contracts are likely to propose lower pricing than if their contracts were renewed on a sole source basis.

These advantages to contracting in a competitive environment are not only consistent with the contracting professionals' expected goals for reducing costs while improving the quality and timeliness of service delivery, but are also consistent with the goals expected of all state and local government agencies. Therefore, the arguments in favor of the contracting professionals' use of competitive contracting should be useful in overcoming the objections of departmental personnel who argue against contracting on a competitive basis.

It is recognized, however, that there are situations wherein there is just one contractor qualified for certain contracts for services. When there are no opportunities for obtaining competitive proposals, that fact should be documented. A form to document the justification and approval of sole source contracts is provided in Appendix D, "Sole Source Justification/Approval Form."

Contracting professionals may harbor strong feelings about the benefits of certain socioeconomic contracting programs. A true contracting professional may provide rationale and recommendations against adoption of a proposed socioeconomic program based on the fact that such programs may not comply with expectations for full and open competition, may not be constitutional, may not be in the best interests of the public, may result in higher costs than services available from other companies, or services could be made available later and with lesser quality than what is being offered by non-targeted competitors. However, once a particular socioeconomic contracting program has been adopted as mandatory, the true professional pursues successful program implementation regardless of her or his personal feelings.

In certain cases, a particular program may provide for a number of tools available to the contracting professional to achieve specific goals. If those tools are optional and include a mix of affirmative action and equal opportunity tools, the contracting professional who is adverse to the use of affirmative action tools (because he or she feels that such tools may not be in the best interests of the constituency) may be in a position to meet the agency's goals while implementing only those tools that are considered equal opportunity measures.

Eight equal opportunity contracting measures that were proven successful in increasing contracting results for targeted companies are described in this chapter and recommended to agencies that wish to increase contracting opportunities for targeted companies without increasing costs and without accepting less than optimal quality or timely service delivery.

## Notes

1. United States Constitution, Privileges and Immunities Clause, Commerce Clause and the Equal Protection Clause.
2. 28 CFR PART 35, STATE AND LOCAL ASSISTANCE, Part 35.936-2, Grantee procurement systems; State or local law, subpart (C) Preference, states, State or local laws, ordinances, regulations or procedures which effectively give local or in-State bidders or proposers preference over other bidders or proposers shall not be employed in evaluating bids or proposals for subagreements under a grant. Similar prohibitions are also included in Subpart 35.938-4, Formal advertising.
3. The socioeconomic contracting program in this example was implemented at the Electron Devices Division of Litton Industries in San Carlos, California. The program was implemented in 1986, and the increased percentage of dollars awarded to minority-owned and women-owned companies steadily increased until the referenced increases were achieved in 1995. As a result of the success of this program, Litton Electron Devices Division was awarded the Dwight D. Eisenhower Award for Excellence by the United States Small Business Administration. The Electron Devices Division of Litton Industries has since been acquired by L-3 Communications.
4. The Industry Council for Small Business Development (ICSBD) in Sunnyvale, California, was formed by federal government private-sector contractors that were required to establish socioeconomic subcontracting programs as a condition of one or more of their federal contracts. The ICSBD maintains a Web site at www.icsbd.org.

## Chapter 3

# Solicitation Documents: Information for Prospective Contractors

## Chapter Objectives

This chapter provides readers with a description of the various types of solicitations commonly used in government procurement. The reason for recommending the use of Requests for Proposals (RFPs) as the solicitation document for services contracts is also explained in this chapter.

The Best Practices RFP was developed by incorporating the best features from all the RFPs provided by state and local government agencies participating in the research project undertaken in preparation for writing this book. In certain cases, the solicitation documents provided by state and local government agencies participating in the research project were not entitled "Request for Proposals." However, in virtually all cases, the solicitation documents met the characteristics of RFPs better than any other type of solicitation document. Every section of the Best Practices RFP is displayed later in this chapter in italics and is followed by an explanation of the rationale for including that particular text in this document. The characteristics of the Best Practices RFP that are displayed and explained in this chapter are:

- Cover page
- Table of contents

- ■ Notice to prospective contractors:
  - − Comments and questions
  - − Communications with agency personnel
  - − Accommodations
  - − Confidentiality of proposals
  - − Contact information
  - − Address and due date for proposals
  - − No public opening
  - − Questions regarding this RFP
  - − Contractors without e-mail access
  - − RFP addenda
  - − Questions and responses posted on Internet site
- ■ RFP introduction
- ■ Background
- ■ Scope of work
- ■ Contractor selection process:
  - − RFP release
  - − Due date for receipt of questions
  - − Paper and CD-ROM versions of proposals
  - − Due date for proposals
  - − Opening of proposals
  - − Evaluation of proposals
  - − Presentations, discussions, or negotiations
  - − Right to reject proposals
  - − Weighted evaluation criteria
  - − Debriefing
  - − Protests
  - − Agency rights

## 3.1 Types of Solicitations

"Solicitation" is the generic term used to describe documents sent to prospective contractors to advise them that a state or local government agency is seeking proposals, quotations, or bids for services provided by the private sector. Examples of solicitations traditionally used in state or local government contracting are Requests for Proposals (RFPs), Requests for Contractor Qualifications (RFCQs), Requests for Quotations (RFQs), and Invitations for Bids (IFBs) (Figure 3.1).

"Request for Proposals" (RFP) is the term for the type of solicitation normally used to solicit proposals for services provided by private-sector contractors. RFPs typically include a short introduction of the state or local government agency soliciting proposals; background of the services to be contracted, to include the present manner in which the services are being provided; a description of the services to be

Comparison Between Types of Solicitations

| Type of Solicitation | Acquisition of Services or Property | Contractor Response | Public Opening | Late Responses Acceptable | Basis of Evaluation | Subject to Negotiation |
|---|---|---|---|---|---|---|
| Request for Proposals (RFP) | Normally used for acquisition of services. However, may be used for acquisition of property or a combination of service and property. | Proposal | No | Yes, but only if in the best interests of the contracting agency. | Proposals are evaluated on the basis of criteria identified in the RFP. The criteria normally includes the contract price or lifecycle costs. | Yes |
| Request for Contractor Qualifications (RFCQ) | Normally used for acquisition of services. However, may be used for acquisition of property or a combination of services and property. | Statement of Qualifications (SOQ) | No | Yes, but only if in the best interests of the contracting agency. | SOQs are evaluated on the basis of criteria identified in the RFCQ. The criteria does not include the contract price or lifecycle costs. | Negotiation is not applicable. SOQ should not result in contract award primarily because it does not include pricing. |
| Request for Quotations (RFQ) | Normally used for purchase of relatively low dollar value property. | Quote or Quotation | No | Yes, but only if in the best interests of the contracting agency. | Quotes or Quotations are evaluated primarily on the basis of price. | Yes |
| Invitation for Bids (IFB) | Normally used for purchase of relatively high dollar value capital equipment, construction or commodities. However, an IFB is occasionally used for the acquisition of services when price is the primary factor affecting contractor selection. | Bid | Yes | No | Bids are evaluated solely on the basis of price if the bid is responsive and the contractor is responsible | No |

**Figure 3.1   Comparison of types of solicitations.**

provided; evaluation criteria to be used in selecting the successful contractor; rights reserved by the contracting agency; format for preparing proposals along with page limitations, when appropriate, and a copy of a model services contract that includes the terms and conditions, required insurance coverage, and scope of work. This chapter includes an extensive discussion of the RFP provided in Appendix E, "Best-Practices Request for Proposals (RFP)" and on the CD accompanying this book. Proposals are responses to RFPs from prospective contractors. Proposals describe the approach that contractors intend to employ to meet the services needs of the state or local government agency that released the RFP. The proposals also typically describe the prospective contractor's experience and qualifications to perform such services, as well as their proposed pricing and any other information requested in the RFP. Unlike bids in response to IFBs, proposals are not opened publicly, are treated as confidential until the contract is awarded or recommended for award, and are subject to negotiation and change. While proposals may be rejected for being nonresponsive or delivered after the due date and time, they are not normally rejected summarily for these reasons. Nonresponsive proposals can be modified through negotiations to render them responsive. If the agency states in its RFP that it may elect to consider proposals received after the due date and time, it may consider late proposals if that would be in the best interests of the agency.

"Request for Contractor Qualifications" (RFCQ) is the term for a document that is similar to the RFP except that its use is limited to obtaining information on the qualifications of various private-sector entities that may be qualified to deliver the services. Prospective contractors, in response to the RFCQ, submit a statement of qualifications to the contracting agency. The contracting agency, in turn, evaluates the contractors' qualifications to determine which firms or individuals are qualified. Once a list of qualified contractors is developed, an RFP is normally sent to all the firms that were determined to be qualified through the RFCQ process. The RFCQ is a type of solicitation that is normally not used when the contracting agency is familiar with the prospective contractors for the service to be contracted. RFCQs are also not normally used when time is of the essence for placing the services under contract, because the need to follow-through with an RFP after the list of qualified contractors is developed significantly extends the time required to obtain proposals. Some agencies refer to RFCQs merely as Requests for Qualifications (RFQs) or Requests for Information (RFIs). However, use of the term "Request for Qualifications" (RFQ) can lead to confusion between requests for quotations and requests for qualifications, and Request for Information (RFI) is not sufficiently descriptive of the nature of the solicitation. Statements of qualifications are the responses to RFCQs from prospective contractors. They describe the contractor's qualifications to perform the services to be provided to the state or local government agency that released the RFCQ. A statement of qualifications does not normally include pricing.

A Request for Quotations (RFQ) is an informal solicitation document that is normally used to solicit quotes for low-dollar-value commodities that are easily described. RFQs are normally not used to solicit quotations for services. Quotations, or quotes, are responses received from prospective contractors or suppliers in response to RFQs released by state or local government agencies. Quotations, or quotes, are typically prepared by completing blanks on a quotation form that is prepared by the contracting agency. The information provided by the prospective contractors on the quotation form may be limited to pricing, delivery time promised, payment terms, identifying company information, and the signature of a contractor representative.

An Invitation for Bids (IFB) is a formal solicitation normally used to solicit bids for high-dollar-value commodities, capital equipment, or construction work. IFBs are normally not used to solicit bids for services. However, there are certain grants that require solicitation for services with IFBs. If solicitation by IFB is a condition of a grant, then compliance with grant terms requires adherence with the need to use an IFB to solicit bids for the specified services. IFBs solicit bids that are opened publicly, and result in award of a contract to the responsive, responsible contractor with the lowest price. When grants require solicitation through an IFB, an IFB template is normally provided by the granting agency for use by the state or local government agency. Bids are responses received from prospective contractors or suppliers in response to IFBs released by state or local government agencies. Like quotations or quotes, bids are typically prepared by completing blanks on a bid form that was prepared by the contracting agency. The information provided by the prospective contractors on the bid form is similar to the information provided for quotations or quotes; however, it may include added information that is required based on high-dollar-value projects solicited via IFBs as opposed to low-dollar-value projects solicited via RFQs. Unlike proposals, statements of qualifications and quotations or quotes, bids are opened publicly and the prices are read aloud for all to hear. Bids are normally recorded on a spreadsheet, and copies of the spreadsheets are also considered public information that can be provided to anyone who submits a request or provides a self-addressed stamped envelope.

"Addendum" is the term used to describe the instrument used to make changes to an RFP or any other type of solicitation after the solicitation has been sent to prospective contractors and before contractor responses are due.

Three of the twenty-two RFPs (14 percent) provided by state and local government agencies in support of this book's research project referred to the response requested from the prospective contractors exclusively as "proposal" while all the remaining RFPs (86 percent) used "bid" as a synonym for "proposal." There are distinctly differing terms for the various types of solicitation documents such as Request for Proposals (RFP), Invitation for Bids (IFB), and Request for Quotations (RFQ). These terms cannot be used interchangeably because each type of solicitation is unique and subject to differing rules. Likewise, responses from prospective contractors to each type of solicitation depend on the type of solicitation selected. For example, proposals are the only appropriate response to an RFP, bids are the only appropriate response to an IFB, and quotes or quotations are the only acceptable responses to RFQs. If the text of an RFP states that bids are due at a time and date certain, then prospective contractors may expect that there is a public bid opening or that bid results are available on the due date for bids, as is customary when contractors respond to an IFB. Proposals are not normally opened publicly. Proposals are treated initially as confidential and are subject to negotiation. Therefore, proposals differ distinctly from bids that are opened publicly, immediately become public information, and are not subject to negotiation. When agency officials use terms synonymously for distinctly different responses to the various types of solicitations, considerable confusion is created. Such confusion could easily lead to a protest from a prospective contractor that became convinced the agency mishandled its response to the solicitation and that the agency used the incorrect methodology for selecting the contractor.

As discussed above, "solicitation" is the generic term for specific types of solicitation documents such as Invitation for Bids (IFB), Request for Quotations (RFQ), Request for Contractor Qualifications (RFCQ), or Request for Proposals (RFP). IFBs and RFQs are used almost exclusively for capital equipment, construction, or commodity procurements. Therefore, the discussion in the balance of this chapter is limited to RFCQs and RFPs.

Solicitation by RFCQ is the first step of a two-step solicitation process. The RFCQ typically identifies the contracting agency, provides some background on the need to contract for services, and invites the prospective contractors to submit a statement of qualifications that describes the contractors' capabilities, their experience in providing services similar to those required by the contracting agency, and contact information for references. Upon receipt of the statements of qualifications submitted by the contractors in response to the RFCQ, the contracting agencies evaluate the contractors' qualifications to establish a list of qualified contractors. The second step of this two-step process is initiated by soliciting the qualified contractors with an RFP. However, it is essential at this point to clarify the fact that an alternative, preferred method for soliciting proposals is to forego the RFCQ entirely and use an RFP as the initial solicitation document. Although it is possible to reduce the number of proposals expected in response to a solicitation through the initial evaluation of the statements of qualifications, this two-step process requires additional time to sequentially release two solicitation documents (RFQC and RFP) and to convene the evaluation committee once to evaluate the statements of qualifications and then again to evaluate the proposals. Duplication of information contained in the statement of qualifications and the proposal introduce redundancy to this two-step process. This need to extend more than the normal amount of time required to select the successful contractor and the inherent redundancy consume added time and resources that are rarely available to state and local government agencies. Therefore, contracting agencies are encouraged to use an RFP almost exclusively in a one-step solicitation process.

## 3.2 Best Practices RFP

The balance of this chapter is devoted to the preferred one-step RFP solicitation process. The Best Practices RFP developed through the research project involving states and local government agencies is included as Appendix E, "Best Practices Request for Proposals (RFP)." A compact disc (CD) containing the material in the appendices is included with this book to facilitate agency adaptation of the RFP or for academic exercises. A model services contract and other contracting documents developed for state or local government agencies or for academic endeavors are also included in the appendices and on the accompanying CD. A matrix is included as Figure 3.1 to illustrate the similarities and differences between the four types of solicitations discussed in this chapter.

The RFP and Model Services Contract (MSC) that were developed using the best features of the solicitation and contract documents provided by participating state and local government agencies were developed for high-dollar-value projects. In those cases where this volume of documentation is not justified due to the reduced risk often associated with lower-priced contracts, and the tendency for prospective contractors is to shun voluminous documentation for relatively low-dollar-value contracts, the agency should consider a short-form RFP with scaled-back certifications and MSC terms and conditions that are more in line with the reduced risks associated with lower-dollar-value projects. Failure to use a short-form RFP and MSC for small, low-risk projects requires use of the more complex, longer version, which likely contains provisions and features that are not needed when the dollar value and exposure to risk are lower. Contractors may also be resistant to dealing with the more complex RFP and MSC documentation when the profit potential is less significant. One approach to developing such a short-form RFP is to begin with a full-scale RFP, such as the one described in this chapter, and eliminate or scale back those provisions that would not be significant in a relatively low-dollar-value contract. There is a discussion of a short-form services contract in Chapter 10, "Short Form Contracts, Short Form RFPs, Emergencies, and Letter Contracts," and a short-form RFP and services contract template is provided in Appendix G, "Short Form Model Services Contract."

Similar to the RFCQ, the RFP normally identifies the contracting agency and provides some background on the need to contract for services. However, unlike the RFCQ, the text of the RFP normally invites the prospective contractors to submit priced proposals rather than mere statements of qualifications. Proposals are similar to statements of qualifications in that they usually include the prospective contractor's experience in providing services similar to those required by the contracting agency and customer references that are willing to discuss their experiences with the contractor. Requests for proposals differ even further from requests for supplier qualifications in that they normally request prospective suppliers to submit a workplan that describes their approach to providing the needed services.

The Best Practices RFP contained in Appendix E is provided as a template that can be adopted by state or local government agencies. Each element of the Appendix E, "Best-Practices Request for Proposals (RFP)," is discussed below. An MSC is included as an integral part of the RFP; however, discussion of the MSC in this chapter is limited because detailed features of the contract document are provided in Chapter 8, "Contract Document." "Model Services Contract" is the phrase used to describe a contract that is included in the solicitation and is identified as the contract document essentially in the form that the contracting agency intends to award to the successful contractor. Model contracts ideally include the contracting agency's standard terms and conditions, insurance requirements, and the scope of work. Including a model contract in the solicitation and advising the prospective contractors that the contracting agency intends to award a contract essentially in the form of the model contract helps to discourage attempts by contractors to enter into a contract in their format with their terms and conditions. Contractors' terms and conditions often favor the contractor and may require extensive negotiations to render them acceptable to the contracting agency. The model contract should include all the essential elements of the contract awarded to the successful contractor, such as offer, acceptance, consideration of competent parties, and a legal purpose. Failure to incorporate all the essential elements of a contract into the MSC may render the resultant contract not legally enforceable.

Because it would be awkward for the reader to continually refer to the RFP in Appendix E and then back to this chapter to follow the discussion of the RFP contents, sections of the RFP are provided later in this chapter, in italics, followed by a discussion of that portion of the Best Practices RFP.

## 3.2.1 Cover Page

The RFP cover page would normally include information such as that shown in Figure 3.2. The information included on the cover page is sufficient to preclude the need to send a cover letter to each prospective contractor. The cover page would typically include the name of the state or local government agency, and the phrase "Request for Proposals," which could be followed by an RFP number that is assigned sequentially to help manage the receipt of proposals. Cover pages also normally include the project title; department name; and agency contact information such as mailing address, telephone number, and facsimile number. Some agencies may choose to include their Web site address on the cover page. The date of the solicitation is also shown on the cover page. The due date for receipt of questions regarding this RFP is also included on the cover page to alert the prospective contractors of this key date immediately upon their receipt of the RFP.

There are several choices for locating the project manager's name and contact information in the RFP, as well as for locating the deadline for submitting questions

---

[*AGENCY NAME*]

*REQUEST FOR PROPOSALS (RFP) #:*

*PROJECT TITLE:*

*USING AGENCY:*

*CONTRACTING AGENCY:*

*AGENCY PROJECT MANAGER:*

*PROJECT MANAGER E-MAIL ADDRESS:*

*AGENCY MAILING ADDRESS:*

*AGENCY INTERNET SITE:*

*RFP ISSUE DATE:*

*DUE DATE FOR RECEIPT OF QUESTIONS REGARDING THIS RFP:*

---

**Figure 3.2    RFP cover page.**

regarding the RFP. The RFP template reflects the project manager's contact information and deadline for posing questions on the cover page, and the RFP text refers the
prospective contractors to the cover page to avoid the need to duplicate the contact
information in the text of the RFP.

## 3.2.2  Table of Contents

A table of contents is recommended for documents that are relatively long. Including a table of contents in the RFP template reminds the preparer to insert page
numbers in the document, and to consider including material on the topics
included in the RFP template table of contents. The table of contents and page
numbers are useful when referencing sections of the document after the RFP has
been released. The table of contents shown in Figure 3.3 is provided under the
assumption that federal funding provides at least a portion of the compensation
paid to the contractor. If federal funding is not applicable, agencies should remove
the (1) Certification Regarding Lobbying; (2) Certification of Compliance with
Pro-Children Act of 1994; and (3) Certification Regarding Debarment, Suspension, Ineligibility and Voluntary Exclusion — Lower Tier Covered Transactions
from the RFP and from the table of contents because they are not required unless
federal funding is involved.

**TABLE OF CONTENTS**

| *Topic* | *Page* |
|---|---|
| *Notice to Prospective Contractors* | 3 |
| *Introduction* | 5 |
| *Background* | 5 |
| *Scope of Work* | 5 |
| *Contractor Selection Process* | 5 |
| *Proposal Requirements* | 9 |
| *Prospective Contractor Certification* | 12 |
| *Certification Regarding Lobbying* | 16 |
| *Certification of Compliance with Pro-Children Act of 1994* | 17 |
| *Certification Regarding Debarment, Suspension, Ineligibility, and Voluntary Exclusion – Lower Tier Covered Transactions* | 18 |
| *Certification of Cost or Pricing Data* | 20 |
| *Proposal Preparation and Submittal Instructions* | 21 |
| *Model Services Contract* | 25 |
| *Attachment I – Contract Insurance Requirements* | 26 |
| *Attachment II – Scope of Work* | 28 |
| *Attachment III – Agency Services Contract Terms and Conditions* | 30 |

**Figure 3.3    RFP table of contents.**

## 3.2.3 *Notice to Prospective Contractors*

### 3.2.3.1 *Comments and Questions*

*Prospective contractors should carefully review this solicitation for defects and question-able or objectionable matter. Comments concerning defects and questionable or objectionable matter must be made to the agency project manager at the e-mail address on the cover page, and must be received by the agency prior to the deadline for written questions also shown on the Request for Proposals (RFP) cover page. Questions concerning the specifications must be posed through the same e-mail address provided on the cover*

*page. The date limitation for posing questions will permit this agency to issue any neces-*
*sary corrections and/or addenda to this RFP in time for all prospective contractors to*
*react by adjusting, if needed, their proposals. A summary of all questions from prospec-*
*tive contractors and agency responses to those questions will be posted by RFP number*
*on the agency's Internet site, which is also provided on the cover page.*

The above first paragraph of the Notice to Prospective Contractors cautions the contractors to carefully read the RFP and to submit all comments via e-mail by the established deadline. Agencies are free to select any method for prospective contractors to submit their concerns and questions; however, designating e-mail as the only method for posing questions facilitates the handling of the questions and feedback to all prospective contractors; creates a uniform, rapid method of communications; and provides the capability to prepare a paper or electronic trail of the pre-proposal activities. Prospective contractors are not afforded the opportunity to enter their questions directly onto the Web site, thus permitting the contracting agency to maintain better control over the Web site content. Questions and concerns expressed via telephone or in person are not recommended because they are susceptible to inconsistent responses to prospective contractors and there is no paper or electronic trail. The time limit for posing questions is established to ensure that all questions, concerns, and agency responses are posted on the agency's Web site in sufficient time for evaluation by prospective contractors prior to submitting their proposals. There should be specific instructions to direct prospective contractors to the agency's Web site and the specific location where they can find postings regarding the RFP. Failure to provide this important information results in unmanageable pre-proposal communications and risks the possibility of less than equal treatment of the prospective contractors.

## 3.2.3.2 Communications with Agency

*Prospective contractors are prohibited from communicating directly with any agency*
*employee except as specified in this RFP, and no agency employee or representative other*
*than the agency's project manager is authorized to provide any information or respond*
*to any question or inquiry concerning this RFP. Prospective contractors may contact the*
*agency's project manager solely via e-mail.*

The above second paragraph of the Notice to Prospective Contractors is intended to discourage prospective contractors from contacting members of the selection committee who are not acting as spokespersons, and to clearly instruct prospective contractors where and how to pose their questions.

## 3.2.3.3 Accommodations

*The project manager may provide reasonable accommodations, including the provision*
*of informational material in an alternative format, for qualified prospective contractors*

*with a disability. Prospective contractors requiring accommodation shall submit requests in writing, with supporting documentation justifying the accommodation, to the project manager. The project manager reserves the right to grant or reject any request for accommodation.*

This notice regarding accommodations specifically mentions only informational material in an alternative format. An example of what might be provided is a version of the RFP printed in a larger font size for persons with a sight disability. Other accommodations, although not ruled out, are not mentioned because visits from prospective contractors are not anticipated prior to the receipt of proposals. Pre-proposal visits are not expected because:

■ Prospective contractors that are selected as finalists may be invited to the agency's facility and should, at the time of the invitation, be offered accommodations relevant to a visit from disabled persons. Failure to offer accommodations for persons with disabilities could result in visits by disabled persons who do not have access to essential services, and could result in a lawsuit for noncompliance with the ADA. However, if the agency's facilities are compliant with ADA regulations, there should be no reason to provide accommodations beyond an alternative format for the informational material offered in the RFP.

■ Prospective contractors that do not become finalists would not likely need to visit the agency's facilities because pre-proposal meetings are not encouraged, and only finalists would be invited to the agency's facilities for presentations. Pre-proposal meetings are discouraged because the RFP should include all the information needed to prepare a proposal, and pre-proposal meetings often provide a venue where the prospective contractors have an opportunity to evaluate their competition. If it is determined at the pre-proposal meeting that there is little or no competition, the contractor is likely to submit a proposal that is less favorable to the agency than a similar proposal submitted in a full and open competitive environment.

### 3.2.3.4 Confidentiality of Proposals

*Proposals will be treated confidentially until either the contract is awarded or recommended for award. Late proposals may be considered if that would be in the best interest of the agency. Errors in the proposals or nonresponsive proposals may be corrected during the negotiation process. However, prospective contractors are advised that they should endeavor to submit responsive, error-free proposals on time because failure to do so may result in rejection of their proposal.*

The above notification regarding the confidential treatment of proposals, possibility of accepting late proposals, and potential for correction of erroneous or nonresponsive proposals is included in the RFP to ensure that prospective contractors are aware of this treatment of proposals, which differs significantly from the treatment of bids. Because the agency may reject nonresponsive proposals, late proposals, or proposals replete with errors, the RFP also includes advice for prospective contractors to submit responsive, error-free proposals on time to avoid the possibility of their proposal being rejected.

### 3.2.3.5 Contact Information

*Prospective contractors that receive this RFP from the agency Web site or from any source other than the agency and wish to assure receipt of any addenda or additional materials related to this RFP, should immediately contact the project manager and provide their contact information so that RFP addenda and other communications related to this procurement can be sent to them.*

The fourth paragraph of the Notice to Prospective Contractors advises contractors that are unknown to the contracting agency to contact the agency's Project Manager to advise her or him that they wish to be considered as a prospective contractor. Although all RFP addenda may be posted on the agency's Web site, this contact information is important in the event that all prospective contractors need to be contacted immediately to discuss schedule changes or other urgent matters.

### 3.2.3.6 Address and Due Date for Proposals

*Receipt of sealed proposals for furnishing the services described herein is due no later than [**Insert Time**] p.m. on [**Insert Date**].*
*SEND ALL PROPOSALS DIRECTLY TO THE CONTRACTING AGENCY ADDRESS AS SHOWN IN FIGURE 3.4.*

The above information on the due date and time are essential elements of the RFP. However, it should be noted once more that, unlike bids in response to IFBs, proposals in response to RFPs may be considered even though they are received after the due date and time. Of course, late proposals cannot be considered if they are not received until after the contract is awarded or recommended for award.

The format shown in Figure 3.4 provides for separate addresses for proposals sent via the United States Postal Service (USPS) from proposals sent by any other carrier. Differing addresses are needed because addresses that include a post office box number are suitable only for deliveries by the USPS while other carriers require street addresses.

*IMPORTANT NOTE: Indicate ["Technical Proposal" or "Cost Proposal"] (if applicable), and the RFP number on the front of each sealed proposal envelope or package, along with the date for receipt of proposals in response to this RFP.*

The note regarding "Technical Proposal" and "Cost Proposal" markings on the proposal envelopes or packages is needed only if the contracting agency elects to have the technical proposal and cost proposal sent in separate envelopes or packages. If the

| *DELIVERED BY US POSTAL SERVICE* | *DELIVERED BY ANY OTHER MEANS* |
|---|---|
| *RFP NO.* | *RFP NO.* |

**Figure 3.4  Addresses for proposals.**

entire proposal can be sent in the same envelope or package, the information in parentheses as well as the comma and the word "and" may be omitted from this note.

### 3.2.3.7 No Public Opening

*There will be no public opening of the proposals. Proposals will be treated as confidential until the contract is awarded or recommended for award.*

The above information is provided for prospective contractors to advise them that their proposals in response to the RFP are not opened publicly. This is to ensure that prospective contractors do not assume that there is a public opening as provided when opening bids in response to an IFB.

### 3.2.3.8 Questions Regarding this RFP

*Any question submitted in response to this RFP via telegraph, facsimile (FAX) machine, or telephone is not acceptable. Prospective contractors are required to make all inquiries concerning this RFP via e-mail to:*
**[Insert Address]**

Inquiries restricted to e-mail are encouraged because this is the most efficient communications method that also best ensures that prospective contractors are treated equally. Potential problems with other communications modes were discussed earlier in this chapter.

### 3.2.3.9 Contractors without E-Mail Access

*Prospective contractors that do not have access to e-mail may make written inquiries to the following address:*
**[Insert Address]**

Although submittal of inquiries via e-mail only is recommended, the above section is provided as an option should the agency wish to permit the submittal of written inquiries via mail or courier for prospective contractors that do not have e-mail capability. However, serious consideration should be given to omitting this instruction and requiring contractors to have e-mail capability to participate in agency contracting opportunities. Omitting this instruction avoids the duplication of the agency's processes for managing pre-proposal communications that is established merely to accommodate contractors that are not incorporating current technology in their business processes.

### 3.2.3.10 RFP Addenda

*It is the prospective contractor's responsibility to assure that all addenda have been reviewed and, if need be, signed and returned or noted in the proposal.*

To ensure that all prospective contractors have considered all addenda in their proposals, the RFP provided in Appendix E includes a space for acknowledging receipt of addenda in the Prospective Contractor Certification. Should prospective contractors fail to acknowledge all addenda in their proposals, the contracting agency could ask the contractors to include addenda acknowledgment after proposal opening. However, all contractors should be afforded the same opportunity. If all contractors are not afforded the same opportunity, it could be argued that they are not being provided equal treatment.

### 3.2.3.11 Questions and Responses Posted on Web Site

*A copy of all inquiries along with the agency response will be posted at the agency's Internet site indicated below:*

**[Internet Site]**

Posting all inquiries and responses thereto on an Internet site best affords all prospective contractors an equal opportunity for access to the inquiries and responses. This approach also simplifies the task of the agency when responding to inquiries and provides a process that facilitates a prohibition against making inquiries other than via e-mail.

**Note:** The "Notice to Prospective Contractors" should not be confused with "Advertising," which constitutes a public notice printed in local newspapers to advise potential contractors of the fact that the agency is releasing an RFP, and informs interested parties how they may obtain a copy of the RFP. Advertising may help increase the number of competitors, and is recommended when there is limited competition and the agency has had difficulty locating local qualified contractors. The provisions of certain federal and state grants may require advertising RFPs for grant funded contracts. In this event, or if local rules require advertising contracting opportunities, then advertising is mandatory.

### 3.2.4 Introduction

*[Make an introductory statement, provide guidance regarding the intent to use the agency's standard contract, and refer to the scope of work for a description of the work to be performed.]*

Bolded text in brackets represents advice to agency representatives that are using the RFP template. Bolded text in brackets should not be included in the completed RFP. In this case, the agency representatives are being offered advice on writing the introductory statement. An example of the information that might be provided in an introductory statement is provided below in bold:

> **The agency is seeking a firm to develop a [*Name of Project*] for the [*Agency*], [*Department*]. The agency intends to award a contract to a firm that will meet agency qualification criteria and has successfully performed services on similar projects in the past. The successful firm will be required to enter into a contract with the agency for the services requested in this RFP within a reasonable time after award. A firm submitting a proposal must be prepared to use the agency's standard contract form rather than its own contract form. The contract will include terms appropriate for this project. Generally, the terms of the contract will include, but are not limited to: (1) completion of the project within the timeframe provided; (2) no additional work authorized without prior approval; (3) no payment without prior approval; (4) funding availability; (5) termination of the contract under certain conditions; (6) indemnification of the state or local government agency; (7) approval by the state or local government agency of any subcontractors; and (8) minimum appropriate insurance requirements. A model services contract is attached to this RFP. The state or local government agency intends to award a contract substantially in the form of the attached model services contract to the selected contractor.**
>
> **The scope of work in the model services contract describes the work to be performed by the successful contractor.**

### 3.2.5 Background

*[Describe how the services fit into the using agency's function, legislation, or new initiatives that necessitate these services, other solutions tried in the past, etc. Reference to attachments may be helpful here.]*

The background for the project should be clearly described to permit the prospective contractors to determine whether this is a contract that they wish to pursue.

Background information that should be included here is whether this is a service presently being performed by an agency department. Contractors have an interest in this information as it may influence their decision on whether or not to submit a proposal. If the work is presently being performed by an agency department, the reason for the decision to contract out this service should be provided. Failure to provide this important information to prospective contractors is likely to result in time-consuming questions from all the contractors that may have an interest in submitting a proposal. There should also be a statement with respect to the fact that an agency department was asked to submit a competing proposal. Providing this information is also essential in fairness to prospective contractors that wish to know if they are competing with a government agency. If the service is presently being performed on a contract basis, the reason for seeking competitive proposals at this time should be provided. Alternatively, should this be a new service that has not previously been performed by the agency or a contractor, background information should be provided to explain why the agency has now assumed responsibility for providing this service. This is important background information for prospective contractors that may be able to prepare a more responsive proposal when they are aware of the complete background behind the agency's decision to contract out such services. Anticipated changes in the manner or extent of services provided should also be included in the background information. This information is also essential to contractors to permit them to prepare fully responsive proposals.

## 3.2.6 Scope of Work

*The scope of work for this project is contained in "Attachment II — Scope of Work" in the Model Services Contract included in this RFP.*

The scope of work is an essential part of the RFP and resultant contract. It describes the nature and extent of the contractor's work during the contract period of performance. In virtually all cases, the agency is capable of drafting a complete scope of work to incorporate in the MSC. However, in rare cases the work may be performed for the first time and the agency may not be totally familiar with the details of the services performed by the successful contractor. However, there may be an existing pool of contractors experienced in performing these services. In these rare cases, the RFP may instruct all prospective contractors to submit a draft scope of work with their proposals. When the prospective contractors are required to submit a draft scope of work with their proposals, the scope of work should be included in the evaluation criteria. The reason for including the scope of work in the evaluation criteria is that, in this event, the scope of work is a contractor-prepared document that reflects its understanding of the agency's needs and the contractor's responsibilities. The agency may consider preparing a final scope of work from the best features of the various drafts, and then asking all the prospective contractors to submit a BAFO based on the final scope of work.

As an alternative to requesting a draft scope of work in the proposals, the agency might consider sending a draft RFP to all the prospective contractors to determine whether their comments lead to an improved scope of work, as well as improvements to other features of the RFP.

## 3.2.7 Contractor Selection Process

*The following is a general description of the process by which a contractor will be selected for award of a contract to perform the services described in this RFP.*

### 3.2.7.1 RFP Release

*The Request for Proposals (RFP) is released to prospective contractors.*

This is the first step in the contractor selection process as explained to prospective contractors. It is essential that prospective contractors understand the contractor selection process and the rules that must be followed. The time period beginning with release of the RFP and ending with the award of the contract is an especially sensitive time when agency errors could result in a protest by an unsuccessful contractor and a resultant delay in the award of the contract or a delay in project commencement.

### 3.2.7.2 Due Date for Receipt of Questions

*To help ensure that all prospective contractors are treated consistently during the selection process, all questions regarding this RFP, as well as the agency's responses to the questions, will be posted on the agency's Web site. A deadline for the receipt of written questions has been established. (See the cover sheet of this RFP for deadline date.) After issuance of an RFP by the agency and prior to the date and time for receipt of proposals, persons or entities who intend to respond to such an RFP by submission of a competitive proposal may wish to pose questions, objections, or requests for information, or request clarification or an interpretation regarding terms, provisions, or requirements of the RFP. In this event, prospective contractors shall not attempt to communicate with, in writing, electronically, or orally with any agency official or employee other than the agency's project manager. The project manager may be reached at her or his e-mail address on the RFP cover page. Prospective contractors shall not contact any other agency officials in an attempt to gather information regarding this RFP, or in an attempt to influence the agency's consideration of its proposal. All inappropriate communications with agency officials or employees will be forwarded to the agency's project manager as well as the proposal evaluation committee. Inappropriate communications by a prospective contractor may, at the discretion of the project manager, constitute grounds for disqualification of that prospective contractor's proposal. Alternatively, the evaluation committee may, at its discretion, consider such inappropriate communications when evaluating and scoring proposals.*

This instruction to prospective contractors provides the rules for submitting questions or queries about the solicitation, and the prohibition against contacting agency personnel other than the project manager, and the possibility that a proposal may be disqualified or that the prospective contractor may be penalized during the proposal evaluation process should the rules be violated. Some of the text of this instruction is duplicated in the Notice to Prospective Contractors to ensure that it is clearly communicated.

## 3.2.7.3 Paper and CD-ROM Versions of Proposals

*Proposals in one original and [**at least two**] copies are required in a sealed envelope or package from each prospective contractor. Each original proposal shall be signed and dated by an official authorized to bind the contractor. Unsigned proposals may be rejected. In addition to the paper copies of the proposal, prospective contractors shall submit one **complete and exact** copy of the technical proposal on CD-ROM in Microsoft Office or Microsoft Office-compatible format. Prospective contractors shall make no other distribution of its proposal to other agency officials or consultants. Each proposal page shall be numbered for ease of reference.*

This instruction to prospective contractors prescribes the number of copies of the proposal to submit. It also includes the requirement that the proposal be signed by a company official who is authorized to bind the contractor, and advice that unsigned proposals may be rejected. There is also an optional requirement to include a CD-ROM version of the proposal. Agencies that do not require a CD-ROM version should delete this requirement to prevent unnecessary effort on the part of prospective contractors and prevent receipt of unneeded information by the agency. CD-ROM versions may be helpful in the proposal evaluation process or to copy-and-paste portions of the successful contractor's proposal for incorporation into the resultant contract or scope of work. The requirement for page numbers is to assist the agency in referencing portions of the proposals during the proposal evaluation process.

## 3.2.7.4 Due Date for Proposals

*All proposals must be received by the issuing agency no later than the date and time specified on the cover sheet of this RFP. Late proposals may be considered if that would be in the best interests of the agency. However, the agency may elect to reject any proposal that is received after the due date and time.*

This instruction describes the need to meet the date and time established for receipt of the proposals. However, unlike bids in response to an IFB, the agency is provided with the option to accept or reject late proposals. In the event that a superior proposal is received shortly after the deadline, this provision provides the agency with the flexibility to consider that late proposal should it be in the best interests of the agency. Experience has demonstrated that despite the possibility that the agency may accept late proposals, contractors do not have a greater tendency to submit their proposals after the due date and time because they are well aware that their late proposal may be rejected.

### 3.2.7.5 Opening of Proposals

*Following the date and time when proposals are due, the envelope or package containing the proposals from each responding firm will be opened by agency personnel. **The opening of the proposals is not open to prospective contractors or the public.** Proposals are subject to change, clarification, and negotiation following the receipt date; therefore, the proposals will be treated as confidential until the resultant contract is awarded or when a recommendation is made to award the contract.*

The above instruction is to ensure that the prospective contractors are aware that the proposals are not opened publicly like bids in response to an IFB. Should proposals be opened publicly, competing prospective contractors would be aware of the content of their competitors' proposals and, because the proposals are subject to negotiations, they could submit revisions to their proposal to gain an advantage over the competition. It is recommended that the agency treat not only the content of the proposals as confidential, but to also not release the names of the contractors that submitted proposals. Prospective contractors that realize that they have limited competition or no competition during the selection process may elect to submit changes to their proposals that make them less beneficial to the agency.

### 3.2.7.6 Evaluation of Proposals

*The agency's Proposal Evaluation Committee expects to take the following actions to determine the relative merits of the proposals that are submitted:*

- *Review the proposals to determine whether they are responsive to the RFP and that they were submitted by responsible companies.*

This sixth instruction is divided into numerous steps to explain the actions taken by the proposal evaluation committee upon receipt of the proposals. This first step is to determine responsiveness of each proposal and the responsibility of each prospective contractor. If any proposals are not responsive, the agency may be able to negotiate changes to make proposals responsive. If the contractor is not responsible, it is not eligible for contract award. Agencies need to establish the criteria for responsible contractors, and also ensure that prospective contractors are aware of this definition. Possible reasons for determining that a particular contractor does not meet the responsibility standards are past instances (within specified time periods) of the material breach of an agency contract, a conviction (or convictions) for bribery, fraud, conflict of interest, violation of environmental laws, or any other convictions specified by the agency.

■ *If there are six or more responsive proposals from responsible companies, the agency will review the proposals, according to the criteria included in this RFP, and assign scores to each criterion using a color-coded scheme, with green being assigned to proposals that are among the best of the proposals, yellow for the average proposals, and red for the marginal proposals. This color-coded rating system will be used to narrow the number of proposals to five or fewer.*

This instruction describes the actions to be taken by the Proposal Evaluation Committee if there were too many proposals received to effectively evaluate them via the ranking method.[1] In this event, there is an initial screening to reduce the number of finalists to five or fewer to facilitate evaluation through the ranking method.

Prescribing the selection process to the extent that selection criteria are described is highly recommended to ensure that the selection process is structured and fair to all prospective contractors. In situations where the expected dollar value of the contract is relatively high or the selection environment is contentious, weighted criteria should be considered to further structure the process and to be better prepared in the event of a protest or protests.

■ *The five, or fewer, finalists will be subjected to a more stringent evaluation that will require individual members of the Proposal Evaluation Committee to rank each criterion with the exception of life cycle cost. Life cycle cost will be scored proportionally rather than ranked. In the event that there are four proposals among the finalists for the ranked criteria, each committee member will assign a 4 to the highest ranked proposal, 3 to the next highest ranked proposal, 2 to the penultimate ranked proposal, and 1 to the lowest ranked proposal.*

This instruction to prospective contractors provides details on the ranking process to be used in the evaluation of the proposals and advises them that life cycle cost is scored on a proportional basis.

■ *The committee members will then meet to discuss their rankings and the rationale therefore. Following this meeting, the committee members may elect to modify their rankings based on those discussions. The committee members will then turn in their evaluation sheets.*

Some agencies may wish to have their Proposal Evaluation Committee members complete their evaluations independently without the benefit of discussions with other committee members. In this event, this instruction should not be included in the RFP. Otherwise, the prospective contractors would be misinformed regarding the proposal evaluation process.

■ *The individual committee member rankings will then be averaged to provide a single combined score for each of the finalist prospective contractors.*

This instruction merely states that all the committee members' scores are averaged to obtain a combined score.

■ *The single combined scores will then be adjusted according to the weights assigned to the criterion to obtain combined weighted scores.*

This instruction advises the prospective contractors that the scores are adjusted to incorporate the weighting of the criteria to provide a greater influence on the total score for those criteria considered more significant by the agency.

■ *The life cycle cost figures will be evaluated separately. The lowest net life cycle cost to the agency will receive a score that is equal to the weight assigned to the life cycle cost criterion. To obtain weighted life cycle cost criteria scores for the higher dollar value life cycle cost proposals, each higher dollar value life cycle cost proposal will be assigned a score that is proportionally lower based on the net life cycle cost to the agency.*

Life cycle cost, or pricing when applicable, should be considered a relevant criterion for selecting contractors for virtually all types of service contracts. Failure to include life cycle cost or pricing as one of the evaluation criteria would, technically, prevent the agency from considering the life cycle cost or price when selecting the successful contractor. Should the contracting agency elect to use weighted selection criteria, it is not unusual to see a very high weighting assigned to the life cycle cost or pricing. An exception may be made in those instances where it is essential to select a contractor that employs experts who are considered leading authorities in their field. In this instance, the agency may elect to evaluate the proposals to determine the best-qualified contractor or individual and then open only the best-qualified contractor's or best-qualified individual's life cycle cost proposal. The agency may then elect to award the contract to the best-qualified contractor or individual if the life cycle cost proposal is within the department's budget or if the cost proposal can be negotiated to fit within the department's budget.

This instruction describes the differing treatment given to the life cycle cost criterion in the proposal evaluation process. Because the life cycle cost is a truly objective criterion, the scores should not be ranked. For example, if there were a forced distribution of life cycle cost scores for proposed prices of $4,000,000, $4,500,000, and $8,000,000, they would receive a ranking of 3, 2, and 1, respectively. However, it is obvious that the two lower life cycle costs, which vary by just $500,000, should receive scores that are relatively similar, while the $8,000,000 proposed life cycle cost should receive a score that is considerably less favorable than both of the lower life cycle cost proposals.

This justification for assigning proportional scores for the life cycle cost criterion could raise an argument against the forced distribution of scores for the subjective criteria when, in fact, some proposals appear to have nearly identical benefit to the agency for certain criteria. In the event that an agency would like to include a provision for assigning tied scores for certain criteria, then the agency might consider permitting tied scores when an evaluator determines that the proposed solution by two prospective contractors would provide equal benefit to the agency. One way to achieve this is to average the scores that would have been assigned in the forced distribution scenario and require the evaluator to include a written justification for assigning equal scores to two contractors. If in a forced distribution situation the prospective contractors would have received scores of 2 and 3, then the tied contractors would both receive scores of 2.5. One example of scores that would likely be tied is the case where a particular criterion is contained entirely within a function that two or more contractors have proposed to subcontract to the same subcontractor.

■ *The combined weighted scores for the criteria, other than life cycle cost, will be added to the weighted life cycle cost criterion scores to obtain a final score for each prospective contractor. The contractor with the highest score will then be awarded the contract or recommended to the governing board or chief elected official for award of the contract.*

This instruction merely advises the prospective contractors of the methodology for combining the scores to achieve a combined score for each proposal.

## 3.2.7.7 Presentations, Discussions, or Negotiations

*At the option of the Proposal Evaluation Committee, the evaluators may request oral presentations, discussions, or negotiations with any or all prospective contractors for the purpose of clarification or to amplify the materials presented in any part of the proposal, or make adjustments to the details of the proposals. The evaluators may also request best and final offers (BAFOs) from one or more prospective contractors. However, prospective contractors are cautioned that the evaluators are not required to request clarification or conduct negotiations and may award a contract based on the original proposal. Therefore, all proposals should be complete and reflect the contractor's most favorable terms.*

This instruction describes the fact that the agency may elect to request oral presentations with one or more prospective contractors, or may wish to conduct negotiations. The use of the word "may" is to provide the agency with maximum flexibility with respect to steps that are involved in the selection of the successful contractor. If one contractor can clearly be identified as the leading candidate during the initial review of the proposals, it is likely unnecessary to continue through a lengthy evaluation process. However, if there is considerable doubt or disagreement with respect to identifying the best qualified contractor, the agency may wish to have the flexibility to proceed through a more formal proposal evaluation process. Also, because the proposal evaluation committee may select a contractor on the basis of its original proposal, the solicitation should advise the prospective contractors that their initial proposals should contain their most favorable terms. This advice is recommended to discourage contractors from submitting proposals that include provisions unfavorable to the agency and, therefore, require negotiations to discover the contractors' most favorable terms.

### 3.2.7.8 Right to Reject Proposals

*Prospective contractors are cautioned that this is a request for proposals, not a request to contract, and the agency reserves the unqualified right to reject any and all proposals when such rejection is deemed to be in the best interest of the agency.*

The above instruction merely states that the agency has a right to reject any or all the proposals when such a rejection is in the best interests of the agency. Additional agency rights are provided in Section 3.2.7.12 below.

### 3.2.7.9 Weighted Evaluation Criteria

*Proposals will be evaluated according to the criteria indicated in Figure 3.5, and because the agency has determined that some criteria are more significant than others, Figure 3.5 also reflects weights that have been assigned to the criteria to permit more emphasis being placed on the more significant criteria.*

The above instruction informs the prospective contractors of the evaluation criteria and that weights have been assigned to the criteria as indicated in Figure 3.5. Evaluation Criteria (or Selection Criteria) are the factors considered for evaluation of proposals to select the successful contractor from among the competing contractors. Evaluation criteria should be described in the solicitation to permit the prospective contractors to understand the basis for selecting the successful contractor by the contracting agency. When evaluating proposals, it is essential to base the selection of the successful contractor solely on the evaluation criteria stated in the solicitation. Therefore, great care should be taken to ensure that the evaluation criteria included in the solicitation measure significant and relevant attributes for a contractor with the desired attributes. In the event that an unsuccessful contractor protests the contract award or recommendation for award, selection committee records that indicate strict adherence to evaluation criteria in contractor selection help to defend the contractor selection being challenged by an unsuccessful contractor. Weighted Evaluation Criteria are identical to evaluation criteria, defined

| PROPOSAL EVALUATION CRITERIA AND CRITERIA WEIGHTING | |
|---|---|
| **Criteria** | **Weight** |
| **Past Performance** | 10 |
| ☐ *Corporate experience with similar projects*<br>☐ *Feedback from references regarding qualifications to succeed on this project* | |
| **Financial Stability** | 10 |
| ☐ *Evaluation of contractor's financial stability based on analysis of most recent financial statements or similar evidence* | |
| **Risk Assessment** | 20 |
| ☐ *Identification of risks to the agency associated with this project*<br><br>☐ *Evaluation of the prospective contractor's proposed approach to reducing, mitigating or eliminating these risks* | |
| **Project Plan** | 20 |
| ☐ *Evaluation of the prospective contractor's plan for accomplishing the tasks outlined in the scope of work*<br><br>☐ *Determination of contractor's understanding of the problem based on the contractor's description of each project task, contract deliverables and the project schedule submitted by the prospective contractor*<br><br>☐ *Evaluation of contractor's proposed staffing, deployment and organization of personnel to be assigned to this project as well as minimum qualifications such as education, certification and experience on similar projects for personnel in key positions*<br><br>☐ *Evaluation of contractor's qualifications and experience of all executive, managerial, legal, and professional personnel to be assigned to this project*<br><br>☐ *Evaluation of contractor's proposed project schedule and methodology for monitoring performance according to the schedule milestones* | |
| **Outsourcing** | 10 |
| ☐ *Evaluation of risks associated with reliance on subcontractors located outside the United States*<br><br>☐ *Evaluation of subcontractor qualifications*<br><br>☐ *Evaluation of risks associated with over reliance on subcontracted work* | |
| **Life Cycle Cost** | 30 |
| ☐ *Evaluation of all agency costs associated with acceptance of the contractor's proposal. Life cycle costs include the contract price plus all other project costs borne by the agency including the need for added personnel, equipment, space, training, disposal of equipment or chemicals, eventual contract closeout and any other costs associated with the contract.* | |
| **Proposal Score** | 0–100 |

**Figure 3.5   Proposal evaluation criteria and criteria weighting.**

above, with the exception that weights are assigned to each of the criteria to differentiate between the relative importance of the various criteria. For example, if price has twice the importance of contractor's reputation, price might be assigned a weight of 40 while contractor's reputation is assigned a weight of 20. Although it is not essential, the sum of the weights assigned to the criteria typically equals 100. Weighted criteria should be considered when the contractor selection could potentially be contentious or controversial. The incorporation of weighted criteria introduces a greater level of objectivity into the proposal evaluation process, thus providing the agency with more convincing evidence supporting its selection of the successful contractor to defend against potential protests from aggrieved contractors. Examples of weighted criteria are provided in Chapters 3 and 5.

## 3.2.7.10 Debriefing

*Any company that submitted a proposal and feels that its proposal was not given adequate consideration or not given a fair evaluation may request a debriefing from the agency proposal evaluation committee.*

The Best Practices RFP includes the above offer to provide a debriefing on the source selection process and decision. Providing such a debriefing may satisfy the concerns of a particular unsuccessful contractor and, thereby, avoid a formal protest.

## 3.2.7.11 Protests

*Companies that received a debriefing, but continue to feel that their proposal was not given adequate consideration or a fair evaluation, may wish to protest the procedures for selection or the actual selection of a particular contractor. Contractors wishing to file a protest should abide by the following procedures. Failure to follow these procedures may result in a summary rejection of the protest:*

■ *Any actual or prospective contractor that is aggrieved in connection with the solicitation or award of a contract may protest to the [ ]. The protest shall be submitted in writing to the [ ] within seven (7) working days after such aggrieved person or company knows or should have known of the facts giving rise thereto.*

The above provision advises the prospective contractors of the procedures for lodging a protest against the selection process or the actual selection of a contractor. Inclusion of this feature in solicitations is highly recommended. Advising all prospective contractors of the procedure for filing protests should avoid the possibility that contractors might use some highly unorthodox or untimely venue and date for submitting their protests.

■ *Upon receipt of such a protest, the [**Title of Agency Official**] shall issue a written determination within ten (10) working days following receipt of the protest. The determination shall:*

   (1) *State the reason for the action taken;*

   (2) *Inform the protesting company that a request for further administrative appeal of an adverse decision must be submitted in writing to the [**Organization or Agency Official That Will Consider Any Appeal of the Determination**] within seven (7) working days after receipt of the determination by the [**Title of Agency Official Making Determination**].*

The above provision adds the time limit for filing a protest and making an appeal of the determination.

## 3.2.7.12 Agency Rights

*The agency reserves the right to:*

■ *Reject any or all submittals*
■ *Request clarification of any submitted information*
■ *Waive any informalities or irregularities in any proposal*
■ *Not enter into any contract*
■ *Not select any firm*
■ *Cancel this process at any time*
■ *Amend this process at any time*
■ *Interview firms prior to award*
■ *Enter into negotiations with one or more firms, or request a best and final offer (BAFO) or BAFOs*
■ *Award more than one contract if it is in the best interests of the agency*
■ *Issue similar solicitations in the future*
■ *Request additional information from prospective contractors*

Agency rights are rights of the contracting agency that are enumerated in the solicitation. They typically include the right to cancel the solicitation, modify the provisions of the solicitation, refrain from awarding a contract, engage in negotiations with prospective contractors, or any other rights that the contracting agency wishes to enumerate in the solicitation. Agency rights are called out in numerous sections of the solicitation. This provision (i.e., agency rights) contains an all-inclusive list of rights to provide the agency with maximum flexibility with respect to its actions during the contractor selection process.

## 3.3 Conclusion

There are numerous alternative documents available for solicitations used in state and local government contracting. The characteristics of RFPs, RFCQs, RFQs, and IFBs were described, and the RFP was recommended as the solicitation type for services contracts. The solicitation documents provided by state and local government agencies participating in the research project were, in virtually all instances, consistent with the characteristics of RFPs. The primary reason for recommending RFPs as the solicitation document for services contracts is that the services provided cannot always be described exactly as required when an IFB is used as the solicitation document. Additionally, agencies generally prefer to select the successful contractor based on price *and* other factors rather than on price alone as required when an IFB is selected as the solicitation document. RFCQs were not recommended because the RFCQ is merely the first step in a two-step solicitation process with the second step using an RFP as the solicitation document. Agencies that wish to pre-qualify contractors prior to release of the RFP, and when time is available for such a two-step selection process, may wish to use an RFCQ followed by an RFP that is sent solely to the prequalified contractors.

The discussion of the Best Practices RFP described the fact that this RFP was developed by incorporating the best features from all the RFPs provided by state and local government agencies that participated in the best practices research project. One essential attachment to the RFP is a Model Services Contract (MSC). Failure to include an MSC as an attachment to the RFP is tantamount to requesting the prospective contractors to propose their own services contract template. There are significant problems associated with prospective contractors proposing their own version of a services contract. Differences in the standard contract provisions from each of the contractors submitting proposals are a certainty. The differing contract provisions compromise the agency's need to evaluate the proposals and thereby fail to treat the prospective contractors on an equal basis. Additionally, contractors have a tendency to incorporate contract provisions that favor the contractor at the expense of the agency. Contractor-prepared services contracts are certain to include some objectionable provisions that require extraordinary negotiations, thereby delaying contract award and possibly delaying project commencement.

Each of the provisions in the Best Practices RFP depicted in the chapter was followed by an explanation of the rationale for including that particular provision in the Best Practices RFP.

## Note

1. There is a discussion in Chapter 5 that describes the problems associated with attempting to rank a large number of proposals.

# Chapter 4

# Solicitation Document: Proposal Requirements and Preparation Guidelines

## Chapter Objectives

This chapter presents the text from the Best Practices Request for Proposals (RFP) that imposes requirements on prospective contractors when preparing proposals in response to an RFP. The text with respect to preparation guidelines for prospective contractors is provided in italics. An explanation of the rationale for including each of these sections in the RFP follows the text materials.

The solicitation material on the format for proposals includes the following topics:

- Past performance
- Financial stability
- Risk assessment
- Project Plan
- Outsourcing
- Life cycle cost

- Life cycle cost format
- Certifications:
  - Prospective contractor certifications
  - Certification regarding lobbying
  - Certification of Compliance with Pro-Children Act of 1994
  - Certification regarding debarment, suspension, ineligibility, and voluntary exclusion — lower tier covered transactions
  - Certification of cost or pricing data

The solicitation material on the guidelines for preparing proposals includes the following topics:

- Exceptions to provisions of the RFP
- Oral explanations
- Reference to other data
- Elaborate proposals
- Desired recycling considerations
- Cost of proposal preparation
- Time for acceptance
- Right to submitted material
- Prospective contractor's representative
- Subcontracting
- Proprietary information
- Historically underutilized business
- Accommodations

Readers are advised of the necessity for attaching a Model Services Contract (MSC) to the RFP accompanied by a statement in the RFP regarding the agency's intent to award a contract substantially in the format of the attached MSC. If an agency does not attach an MSC to the RFP and indicate that it plans to award a contract essentially in the format of the MSC, prospective contractors are likely to propose their own contract templates. The numerous complications associated with contractors proposing their own contract templates are addressed in this chapter.

## 4.1 Proposal Format

The text from the proposal format section of the RFP is provided below and followed by the rationale for the inclusion of this text.

*The response to this RFP shall consist of a completed Prospective Contractor Certification (included in this solicitation), a cover letter limited to a maximum of two pages including an executive summary of the proposal. The cover letter shall indicate whether or not the contractor had any contract terminated for default in the past five years. If no such termination for default has been experienced by the prospective contractor in the past five years, this fact shall be stated in the cover letter. Proposals shall be divided into six sections in the same sequence, and with the same titles, shown below. Proposals shall be prepared on 8½ × 11 paper; however, larger foldouts are acceptable for milestone charts and similar documentation. The font size shall be 10 point or larger:*

| Section Title | Page Limitation |
|---|---|
| Past performance | 6 |
| Financial stability | 4 |
| Risk assessment | 8 |
| Project plan | 8 + resumes |
| Outsourcing | 4 |
| Life cycle cost | 8 |

This section of the proposal format sets forth the rules for preparing and assembling proposals in conformance with the agency's requirements. Proposal format is the phrase used to describe the contracting agency's prescribed organization of proposals submitted in response to an RFP. Specification of topics presented in the proposal that have a direct relationship to the evaluation criteria simplify the work of the selection committee and help ensure that the prospective contractors are treated equally. The requirement to prepare the proposal in a certain format, sequence, and maximum length greatly simplifies the agency's task when comparing the proposals to determine which proposal best meets the agency's requirements. Should contractors be permitted to prepare proposals without regard to such rules, the task of comparing proposals is greatly magnified. When all the proposals are prepared in the same format, in the same sequence, and with a maximum number of pages, it is a relatively simple matter to compare each proposal with respect to the evaluation criteria, and the time required to evaluate the proposals is optimized. Most agencies provide a template for use in preparing an RFP that contains sample selection criteria. However, most agencies permit departments to modify the criteria as needed to match the project particulars. Certain agencies also provide templates for evaluating proposals that include the standard criteria included in the RFP template. When an agency provides templates for the RFP and for evaluating proposals, it is essential that any changes made to the RFP criteria be made to the criteria in the proposal evaluation template. To avoid the possibility that the proposal evaluation team evaluates the proposals based on criteria differing from the criteria in the RFP, the changes to the criteria in the RFP need to be duplicated in the proposal evaluation template. Otherwise, the contractor is selected on the basis of criteria that had been determined to be inappropriate for the project. In the event of a protest based on selection of the contractor using inappropriate criteria, the agency is faced with the embarrassing task of explaining why the proposals were evaluated by criteria that differed from what had been selected for the project and communicated to the prospective contractors. Although the protesting contractor is not likely to have the contract award made to their company based on such a protest, the agency's approving official is required to take corrective action in response to the protest. The least burdensome corrective action is to reconvene the proposal evaluation team, or establish a new proposal evaluation team, to evaluate the proposals based on the appropriate criteria. An alternative corrective action is to require requests for best and final offers (BAFOs) from the competing contractors, and to evaluate the BAFOs according to the appropriate criteria.

### 4.1.1 Past Performance

*This section shall be limited to a maximum of six pages, shall include background information on the organization, and provide details on company experience with similar projects. A list of references (including contact persons, organizations, e-mail and regular mail addresses, and telephone numbers) for each of the above similar projects shall be included.*

*If the prospective contractor's past performance with the agency requires response to the bulleted items below, such responses shall be on a separate sheet and shall be excluded from the maximum number of pages indicated above:*

- *If the prospective contractor or any prospective subcontractor contracted with the agency during the past 24 months, indicate the name of the agency, contract price, the contract number and project description, and/or other information available to identify the contract.*
- *If the prospective contractor or prospective subcontractor has a staff member who was an employee of the agency during the past 24 months, or is currently an agency employee, identify the individual by name, the agency previously or currently employed by, job title or position held, and separation date from the agency.*
- *If the prospective contractor has had a contract terminated for default in the past five years, describe each such incident. Termination for default is defined as a notice to stop performance due to the prospective contractor's non-performance or poor performance and the issue of performance was either*
  - *Not litigated due to inaction on the part of the prospective contractor, or*
  - *Litigated and such litigation determined that the prospective contractor was in default.*
- *Submit full details of the terms for default including the other party's name, address, and telephone number. The agency will evaluate the facts and may, at its sole discretion, reject the proposal on the grounds of the prospective contractor's past experience. If no such termination for default has been experienced by the prospective contractor in the past five years, state so in the cover letter.*

This section explains how the prospective contractors are to prepare the section of their proposal as it relates to the first criterion of *past performance*. Some limitation of pages as indicated in this provision is highly recommended as without such a limitation some prospective contractors are prone to submitting lengthy, verbose proposals that provide superfluous information requiring extensive time to read and for isolating the relevant information.

## 4.1.2 Financial Stability

*This section shall be limited to a maximum of four pages, and shall include the prospective contractor's most recent audited financial statement or similar evidence of financial stability.*

This section merely calls for the submittal of the most recent audited financial statement or the equivalent. Financial stability of the contractor is likely to be relevant. This is especially true for long-term, high-dollar-value contracts for services that are not conducive to contractor substitution on short notice. The prospective contractors' financial stability may be evaluated by requesting submittal of recent, audited financial statements or obtaining company profiles from organizations that provide performance reporting on businesses.[1] Because there is limited opportunity to include superfluous information to this section, consideration may be given to elimination of the page limitation for financial stability.

## 4.1.3 Risk Assessment

*This section shall be limited to a maximum of eight pages, and must identify all risks to the agency that must be addressed should the agency enter into a contract in furtherance of this project. The prospective contractors shall also identify measures that will be taken by the contractor or should be taken by the agency to mitigate the risks.*

The section on Risk Assessment requires the prospective contractors to describe risks faced by agencies that enter into a contract for the type of service proposed by the contractor and proposed methods for mitigating those risks.

## 4.1.4 Project Plan

*This section shall be limited to a maximum of eight pages (not including resumes), and shall include a thorough description of the prospective contractor's approach to accomplishing the tasks outlined in the scope of work. This section shall include the proposed staffing, resumes for key staff members, deployment, and organization of personnel to be assigned to this project. A description of each task and contractor deliverables shall be included in this section along with a schedule for accomplishing all contract milestones.*

The Project Plan is typically a key element of prospective contractors' proposals and is generally assigned a relatively high weighting when weighted criteria are applicable. The page limitation would normally be longer for this section of the proposal to provide adequate space to include all the relevant information needed for selecting the successful contractor. The page limitation is recommended; however, in this RFP, the resumes are not counted against the page limitation.

## 4.1.5 Outsourcing

*This section shall be limited to a maximum of four pages, and shall include a description of the work (including the percentage of the total contract effort) performed by company employees, subcontracted resources, as well as any work performed outside the United States by company employees or subcontractors. The proposal shall also include the percentage of work to be performed by specific subcontractors, evaluation of subcontractor qualifications, and identification of the geographical area where all work will be performed.*

This section is where the prospective contractors describe all the work for this project that they expect to subcontract to another firm or individual.

## 4.1.6 Life Cycle Cost

*Contract Price: The life cycle cost proposal shall be limited to a maximum of eight pages, and shall be submitted in a separate, sealed envelope or package and marked accordingly. The agency prefers to contract on a firm-fixed-cost basis whenever permitted by the nature of the work. However, it is understood that in some instances the proposal must be based on incurred expenses. In this latter case, the proposal shall include the following contractor costs:*

- *Personnel costs (including job titles, hourly rates, and total hours)*
- *Travel and subsistence expenses*
- *Subcontractor costs (if any)*
- *Other costs (e.g., office expenses) shall be identified by the nature of the costs*
- *Not-to-exceed price (A total Not-to-Exceed [NTE] price representing the maximum amount for all work to be performed by the contractor and any subcontractors must be clearly indicated under this heading.)*

*Incremental Agency Costs: The contractors' proposals shall include, in addition to contract costs, all incremental agency costs associated with entering into the contract. Agency costs generally include the costs of required additional personnel to support the contracted effort, training, equipment, and facilities, as well as any other incremental costs associated with award and administration of the contract for the term of the contract, or a period of five years, whichever is longer. No contract costs are to be included in incremental agency costs.*

*Life Cycle Costs: The life cycle cost is the total of the contract price plus the incremental agency costs. This information shall be depicted in the proposal on a monthly basis for the first year of the project and on an annual basis for the duration of the project.*

Life cycle cost (or occasionally contract price) is almost always included as one of the criteria for contractor selection and usually is highly weighted when compared to other criteria. Occasionally, the life cycle cost proposal is requested in a separate envelope or package to permit evaluation of life cycle costs at a later time or by evaluators who evaluate only costs. The weighting of life cycle cost is usually highest when the successful contractor is expected to deliver commodities along with the services. The weighting of life cycle cost is usually lowest when highly qualified professionals are expected to provide the services. For projects that include the services of highly qualified professionals such as physicians, psychiatrists, or engineers, the selection of the successful contractor may employ minimal weighting for life cycle cost or discount life cycle cost entirely if the proposed cost is within the agency's budget for the specific project.

## 4.1.7 Life Cycle Cost Format

*A life cycle cost proposal format has been provided as Enclosure [ ]. All prospective contractors shall include all contract life cycle costs, including the NTE cost or incremental agency costs to the agency should a particular proposal be accepted, or risk the possibility of having their proposal declared to be nonresponsive.*

A standard life cycle cost proposal format is often desirable to ensure that life cycle costs are proposed on the same basis by each contractor, and that life cycle costs can, therefore, be compared on an equivalent basis. The life cycle cost proposal format should be designed for individual projects and should include a breakout of contract pricing for individually priced efforts such as engineering, legal, administrative, travel, reports, consultants, incremental agency costs, etc., as well as a space for the total cost or not-to-exceed cost. This design to match the project parameters and the pricing breakout are necessary to provide a basis for tracking the contractor's performance during the term of the contract. The incremental agency costs might consist of costs for added personnel, equipment, facilities, supplies, and other miscellaneous agency costs associated with award of a contract.

## 4.1.8 Certifications

*The certifications identified in the following section are to be submitted along with the proposal and do not count against the page limitations.*

### 4.1.8.1 Prospective Contractor Certification

*By submitting this proposal, the prospective contractor certifies the following:*

■ *The contractor representative who signs below certifies that she/he has carefully read and understands the provisions of the solicitation and associated documents attached thereto, and hereby submits the attached proposal to perform the work specified therein, all in accordance with the true intent and meaning thereof. The contractor representative further understands and agrees that by signing this certification, all of the following information in the certification is true and accurate to the best of her/his knowledge. If this certification cannot be made unequivocally, a written description of all instances wherein the prospective contractor cannot unequivocally make this certification is provided with this proposal:*

This first section of the Prospective Contractor Certification is to ensure that the person signing the certification has read and understands the provisions of the RFP and that the information provided in the certification is true and accurate. There is also a provision that permits the signing of the certification even if the certification cannot be made unequivocally provided that all exceptions are described in the proposal.

- *Prospective Contractor is:*

  ☐ *Sole Proprietor*   ☐ *Partnership*   ☐ *Corporation*\*   ☐ *Joint Venture*
  ☐ *Other*_____
  *\*State of Incorporation*

This space above is provided for prospective contractors to certify as to their business organization classification.

- *Other entities or individuals shall not be allowed to perform work or take data outside the United States without express advance written authorization from the agency's project manager.*

This certification requires the successful contractor to obtain the agency project manager's authorization to allow others to perform work or take data outside the United States.

- *All personnel provided for work under this contract, who are not United States citizens, will have executed a valid I-9 form, Employment Eligibility Form, and presented valid employment authorization documents.*

This certification requires the successful contractor to have work performed by United States citizens or to comply with applicable immigration laws.

- *This proposal is signed by a representative who is authorized to commit the prospective contractor.*

*The company identified below is the prime contractor.*

The certification above is included in the RFP to ensure that the employee or representative of the prospective contractor is authorized to commit the company, and that their company is the prime contractor.

■ *The prospective contractor's insurance carrier(s) can provide insurance certificates as required within ten (10) calendar days following notice of award.*

The above certification is required to commit the prospective contractor to furnishing the insurance certificate within ten calendar days of the notice of award.

■ *The proposed costs have been arrived at independently, without consultation, communication, or agreement for the purpose of restricting competition as to any matter relating to such process with any other organization or with any competitor.*

*Unless otherwise required by law, the costs proposed have not been knowingly disclosed by the prospective contractor on a prior basis directly or indirectly to any other organization or to any competitor.*

*No attempt has been made, or will be made, by the prospective contractor to induce any other person or firm to submit or not to submit a proposal for the purpose of restricting competition.*

The above certifications are made to further ensure that the proposal pricing was developed independently and without collusion.

■ *The cost and availability of all equipment, materials, and supplies associated with performing the services described, including associated indirect costs and profit, herein have been determined and included in the proposed cost. All labor costs, direct and indirect, and profit have been determined and included in the proposed cost. The incremental costs expected to be incurred by the agency, should it enter into this contract, have also been estimated to the best ability of the prospective contractor. It is understood that the life cycle cost includes the total of the contract cost plus the estimated costs to be incurred by the agency should it enter into this contract.*

This certification is to ensure that the prospective contractors have certified that all relevant contract and non-contract agency costs are included in the life cycle cost.

■ *The prospective contractor can and shall provide the specified performance bond or alternate performance guarantee (if applicable).*

The above certification is required in the RFP only if the successful contractor is required to provide a performance bond or equivalent. If a performance bond or equivalent is not required, this certification should be deleted from the RFP.

*In submitting its proposal the prospective contractor agrees not to discuss or otherwise reveal the contents of the proposal to any source outside of the using or contracting agency, government or private, until after the award of the contract. Prospective contractors not in compliance with this provision may be disqualified, at the option of the agency, from contract award. Only discussions authorized in advance and in writing by the contracting agency are exempt from this provision.*

Above is an additional certification to ensure that the prospective contractor is not colluding when proposing a price or life cycle cost.

■ *The prospective contractor hereby certifies that it and all of its affiliates collect appropriate taxes and remits them as provided by law.*

The above certification is to ensure that the prospective contractor and all its affiliates collect and remit applicable taxes.

■ *The prospective contractor certifies that all insurance policies required by this contract shall remain in full force and effect during the entire term of this contract. All insurance policies and any extensions or renewals thereof shall not be canceled or amended except with the advance written approval of the agency. The contractor agrees to submit certificates of insurance, which indicate coverage and notice provisions as required by this contract, to the agency upon execution of this contract. The insurance certificates shall be subject to approval by the agency. The insurance certificates shall include a statement in the certificate that no cancellation of the insurance shall be made without at least thirty calendar days' prior written notice to the agency. Approval of the insurance certificates by the agency shall not relieve the contractor of any obligation under this contract.*

The above certification is included in the solicitation to ensure that the successful contractor maintains all applicable insurance coverage in place during the term of the contract, to submit insurance certificates for approval by the agency, and to provide thirty days (30) advance notice of insurance coverage that is scheduled for cancellation.

■ *The prospective contractor has read and understands the conditions set forth in this RFP and agrees to them with no exceptions. (If exceptions are taken, attach a written description of each exception to this certification.)*

The above certification requires the prospective contractor to comply with all provisions of the solicitation or to attach a description of all the exceptions.

■ *The prospective contractor warrants, represents, and certifies that no elected or appointed official or employee of the agency has, or will, personally or indirectly benefit financially or materially from this contract.*

This certification is to ensure that the contractor has not made any arrangement with any elected or appointed official or agency employee to benefit financially or materially from the award of the contract.

■ *Any contract and/or award arising from this RFP may be terminated by the agency if it is determined that gratuities of any kind were either offered to, or received by, any of the aforementioned officials or employees from the prospective contractor, the prospective contractor's agent(s), representative(s), or employee(s). Any contract and/or award arising from the RFP may also be terminated if it is determined that the contract and/or award was obtained by fraud, collusion, conspiracy, or other unlawful means, or if the contract and/or award conflicts with any statutory or Constitutional provision of the State of [**Insert State**] or of the United States.*

This certification permits the agency to terminate the contract if gratuities were offered or received by any of the officials or employees mentioned in the certification statement immediately above this certification. There is also a provision for terminating the contract if the contract was obtained by fraud, collusion, conspiracy, or other unlawful means, or if the contract award conflicts with any applicable law.

■ *Therefore, in compliance with this Request for Proposals, and subject to all conditions herein, the undersigned offers and agrees, that if this proposal is accepted within [**Insert Number of Days**] from the date of the opening, to furnish the subject services for a Firm Fixed/Not-to-Exceed (delete "Firm Fixed" or "Not-to-Exceed") Contract Price of $_____.*

This certification specifies the period of time when the proposal remains valid. The agency enters the applicable period of time prior to release of the RFP. The certification also indicates the proposed total or not-to-exceed contract price. The contract price differs from the life cycle cost in that the contract price does not include incremental agency costs to be incurred through execution of the resultant contract.

■ *The following addenda have been received, and considered in the preparation of this proposal:*

The space above is for the prospective contractors to indicate the solicitation addenda that they received and considered in the preparation of their proposals. Should a prospective contractor fail to include any or all of the addenda in this section, the company representative should be provided with copies of all addenda not included in this section of the Prospective Contractor Certification, and advised to certify in writing that all relevant addenda were obtained and that they were considered in calculating the contract price and life cycle cost. This action is necessary to ensure that all the addenda were included while calculating the contract price or life cycle cost, and that proposals from all competing contractors were made on identical bases. Based on the nature of the addenda, it may be necessary for the contractors that had not previously received the addenda to adjust their proposals accordingly.

> ■ *I further affirm that: neither I, nor to the best of my knowledge, information, and belief, the business identified below, or any of its officers, directors, partners, or any of its employees directly involved in obtaining or performing contracts with public bodies has been convicted of, or has had probation before judgment imposed pursuant to criminal proceedings, or has pleaded nolo contendere to a charge of bribery, attempted bribery, or conspiracy to bribe in violation of any state or federal law,* **except as indicated on the attachment** *[indicate the reasons why the affirmation cannot be given and list any conviction, plea, or imposition of probation before judgment with the date, court, official or administrative body, the sentence or disposition, the name(s) of person(s) involved, and their current positions and responsibilities with the business]:*

The above certification is provided for prospective contractors to reveal all instances of bribery, attempted bribery, or conspiracy to bribe in violation of any applicable law.

*Attachments to Prospective Contractor Certification*

___ *A description of a potential instance(s) of collusion or violation is attached.*
___ *A list of exceptions to the RFP is attached.*
___ *A description of instances involving bribery, attempted bribery, or conspiracy to bribe in violation of any state or federal law is attached.*

The above certification requires the prospective contractor to indicate whether it has attached a description of potential instances of collusion or other violations, and or has attached a list of exceptions to the RFP.

> ■ *The agency may initiate proceedings to debar a contractor or subcontractor from participation in the proposal process and from contract award if it is determined that the contractor has refused to disclose or has falsified any information provided in its proposal.*

This notification is included in the Prospective Contractor Certification to ensure that the prospective contractors are aware of the consequences for refusing to disclose information or providing falsified information in their proposal.

■ *Due to the existence of federal funding in the revenue that funds this contract, the agency included the following additional certifications, which are attached hereto if applicable, and which shall be completed by all prospective contractors, and returned to the agency with their proposal:*
 – *Certification regarding lobbying*
 – *Certification of Compliance with Pro-Children Act of 1994*
 – *Certification regarding debarment, suspension, ineligibility, and voluntary exclusion — lower tier covered transactions*

The above section of the Prospective Contractor Certification may be deleted if no federal funds are provided for the project. Copies of the referenced certifications are provided below on the page following the contractor representative's signature on the Prospective Contractor Certification:

*PROSPECTIVE CONTRACTOR NAME:* _____

*BUSINESS STREET ADDRESS:* _____

*CITY/STATE/ZIP+4:* _____

*PAYMENT ADDRESS (IF DIFFERENT):* _____

*CITY/STATE/ZIP+4:* _____

*TELEPHONE NUMBER:* _____ *FAX:* _____

*FEDERAL EMPLOYER IDENTIFICATION NUMBER:* _____

*E-MAIL:* _____

*BY:* _____ *TITLE:* _____

_____
*(Signature)*

*DATE:* _____

*(Typed or Printed Name of Contractor Representative)*

**Unsigned certifications may result in a determination that the proposal is non-responsive.**

This section is provided for the prospective contractors to complete their contact information and sign the certification. There is also a caution that unsigned certifications may result in a determination that the proposal is nonresponsive.

The certifications required for contracts that are federally funded or that have partial federal funding, as referenced earlier, are included below and are also provided on the CD that accompanies this book.

Following those three certifications is a Certification of Cost or Pricing Data that is recommended for inclusion in solicitations in all high-dollar-value services contracts. However, the cost or pricing certification is not needed for fixed-price contracts awarded competitively.

## 4.1.8.2 Certification Regarding Lobbying

*The undersigned certifies, to the best of his or her knowledge and belief, that:*

■ *No federal appropriated funds have been paid or will be paid on behalf of the sub-grantee to any person for influencing or attempting to influence an officer or employee of any federal agency, a member of the Congress, an officer or employee of the Congress, or an employee of a member of Congress in connection with the awarding of any federal contract, the making of any federal grant, the making of any federal loan, the entering into of any cooperative agreement, or the extension, continuation, renewal, amendment or modification of any federal contract, grant, loan or cooperative agreement.*

■ *If any funds other than federal appropriated funds have been paid or will be paid to any person for influencing or attempting to influence an officer or employee of any federal agency, a member of the Congress, or an employee of a member of Congress in connection with this contract, grant, loan, or cooperative agreement, the applicant shall complete and submit Standard Form LLL, "Disclosure Form to Report Lobbying," in accordance with its instructions.*

■ *The contractor shall require that the language of this certification be included in the award documents for all sub-awards at all tiers (including subcontracts, sub-grants, and contracts under grants, loans, and cooperative agreements) and that all sub-recipients shall certify and disclose accordingly.*

*This certification is a material representation of fact upon which reliance was placed when this transaction was made or entered into. Submission of this certification is a prerequisite for making or entering into this transaction imposed by Section 1352, Title 31, U.S. W.C.A. Any person who fails to file the required certification shall be subject to a civil penalty of not less than $10,000 and not more than $100,000 for each such failure.*

*Signature:* _____

*Typed or Printed Name:* _____

*Title:* _____

*Organization:* _____

*Date:* _____

## 4.1.8.3 Certification of Compliance with Pro-Children Act of 1994

*Contractors shall comply with Public Law 103-227, Part C Environmental Tobacco Smoke, also known as the Pro-Children Act of 1994 (Act). This Act requires that smoking not be permitted in any portion of any indoor facility owned or leased or contracted by an entity and used routinely or regularly for the provision of health, day care, education, or library services to children under the age of 18, if the services are funded by federal programs either directly or through state or local governments. Federal programs include grants, cooperative agreements, loans or loan guarantees, and contracts. The law also applies to children's services that are provided in indoor facilities that are constructed, operated, or maintained with such federal funds. The law does not apply to children's services provided in private residences; portions of facilities used for inpatient drug or alcohol treatment; service providers whose sole source of applicable federal funds is Medicare or Medicaid; or facilities (other than clinics) where WIC coupons are redeemed.*

*The contractor further agrees that the above language will be included in any sub-awards that contain provisions for children's services and that all sub-grantees shall certify compliance accordingly. Failure to comply with the provisions of this law may result in the imposition of a civil monetary penalty of up to $1000 per day.*

*Signature:* _____

*Typed or Printed Name:* _____

*Title:* _____

*Organization:* _____

*Date:* _____

## 4.1.8.4 Certification Regarding Debarment, Suspension, Ineligibility, and Voluntary Exclusion — Lower Tier Covered Transactions

*By signing and submitting this proposal, the prospective contractor is providing the certification set out below:*

- *The certification in this clause is a material representation of fact upon which reliance was placed when this transaction was entered into. If it is later determined that the prospective contractor knowingly rendered an erroneous certification, in addition to other remedies available to the federal government, the department or agency with which this transaction originated may pursue available remedies, including suspension and/or debarment.*
- *The prospective contractor certifies that it has not and will not provide any gratuities to any agency elected or appointed official, employee, representative, or consultant in connection with the award or administration of the contract that is expected to result from this solicitation.*
- *The prospective contractor shall provide immediate written notice to the person to whom this proposal is submitted if at any time the prospective contractor learns that its certification was erroneous when submitted or had become erroneous by reason of changed circumstances.*

■ *The terms covered transaction, debarred, suspended, ineligible, lower tier covered transaction, participant, person, primary covered transaction, principle, proposal, and voluntarily excluded, as used in this clause, have the meaning set out in the Definitions and Coverage sections of rules implementing Executive Order 12549. You may contact the person to which this proposal is submitted for assistance in obtaining a copy of those regulations.*

■ *The prospective contractor agrees by submitting this proposal that, should the proposed covered transaction be entered into, it shall not knowingly enter into any lower tier covered transaction with a person who is proposed for debarment under 48 CFR Part 9, Subpart 9.4, debarred, suspended, declared ineligible, or voluntarily excluded from participation in this covered transaction, unless authorized by the department or agency with which this transaction originated.*

■ *The prospective contractor further agrees by submitting this proposal that it will include this clause title, "Certification Regarding Debarment, Suspension, Ineligibility, and Voluntary Exclusion — Lower Tier Covered Transaction," without modification, in all lower tier covered transactions and in all solicitations for lower tier covered transactions.*

■ *A participant in a covered transaction may rely upon a certification of a prospective participant in a lower tier covered transaction that it is not proposed for debarment under 48 CFR Part 9, Subpart 9.4, suspended, ineligible, or voluntarily excluded from covered transactions, unless it knows that the certification is erroneous. A participant may decide the method and frequency by which it determines the eligibility of its principals. A participant may, but is not required to, check the List of Parties Excluded from Federal Procurement and Non-procurement Programs.*

■ *Nothing contained in the foregoing shall be construed to require establishment of a system of records in order to render in good faith the certification required by this clause. The knowledge and information of a participant is not required to exceed that which is normally possessed by a prudent person in the ordinary course of business dealings.*

■ *Except for transactions authorized under paragraph 4 of these instructions, if a participant in a covered transaction knowingly enters into a lower tier covered transaction with a person who is proposed for debarment under 48 CFR Part 9, Subpart 9.4, suspended, debarred, ineligible, or voluntarily excluded from participation in this transaction, in addition to other remedies available to the federal government, the department or agency with which this transaction originated may pursue available remedies, including suspension and/or debarment.*

   – *The prospective contractor certifies, by submission of this proposal, that neither it nor its principals, nor its prospective subcontractors are presently debarred, suspended, proposed for debarment, declared ineligible, or voluntarily excluded from participation in this transaction by any federal department or agency.*

– *Where the prospective contractor is unable to certify to any of the statements in this certification, such prospective contractor shall attach an explanation to this proposal.*

*Signature:* _____

*Typed or Printed Name:*_____

*Title:*_____

*Organization:* _____

*Date:* _____

## 4.1.8.5 Certification of Cost or Pricing Data

*The undersigned hereby certifies that the contract price is based upon*

☐ *Established catalog prices (copies of the applicable catalog pages showing the established catalog prices are enclosed).*

☐ *Established market prices (the amounts of contract prices offered to other contractor customers and the name of the contractor customers are enclosed).*

☐ *Statute or regulation (the citation for the statute or regulation and the date and short description of its provisions are enclosed).*

☐ *Other (describe any other basis for pricing on a separate attached sheet signed by the signatory to this Certification of Cost or Pricing Data).*

*Submitted cost or pricing data. To the extent that the contract price is based upon submitted cost or pricing data, I certify, on behalf of the contractor, that to the best of my knowledge and belief, the cost or pricing data submitted is accurate, complete, and current as of the date specified above.*

*I further certify, to the best of my knowledge and belief, that the costs payable by the agency do not include any of the following (unless full disclosure is attached on a separate sheet signed by the signatory to this Certification of Cost or Pricing Data):*

■ *Costs of fines or penalties paid to any government agency*
■ *Contingency fees paid to obtain award of this contract*
■ *Subcontractor profits for goods or services provided by Contractor subsidiaries*
■ *Gifts or gratuities paid to employees of the agency or any other government agency*

*The contractor understands that in addition to any other remedies or criminal penalties, the contract price shall be adjusted to exclude any significant sums by which the agency finds that the price was increased because the cost or pricing data furnished by the contractor was inaccurate, incomplete, or not current as of the date specified above.*

Signature: _____

Typed or Printed Name:_____

Title:_____

Organization: _____

Date: _____

**Note:** The questionnaire, sent to all states and the counties and cities where the state capitals were located, indicates that most states, counties, and cities that responded were not requesting certification of costs or pricing. It is significantly less challenging to complete this suggested certification than the similarly named certification required for federal contracting. The certifications requested of prospective contractors appear to be straightforward and relevant.

## 4.2 Proposal Preparation Instructions

### 4.2.1 Exceptions

*The agency intends to award a contract substantially in the form of and including the provisions of the attached Model Services Contract (MSC). Contractors that take exception to the terms and conditions do so at the risk that their proposal may be declared to be nonresponsive and not considered for contract award. By signing the PROSPECTIVE CONTRACTOR CERTIFICATION included in this RFP, the representative of the prospective contractor certifies that no exceptions are taken to the form of the MSC or to the provisions therein, unless such exceptions are fully disclosed in a document attached to the PROSPECTIVE CONTRACTOR CERTIFICATION.*

The agency's intent to award a contract substantially in the form of the Model Services Contract (MSC) that is attached to the RFP is distinctly stated in this first paragraph of the Proposal Preparation Instructions. Agencies that do not include an MSC in their solicitations are essentially inviting the prospective contractors to submit their own contract format along with their terms and conditions. Contractors' formats for services contracts, as well as their terms and conditions, normally favor the position of the contractor over the agency. Therefore, it is essential to develop an MSC that, while fair to both contracting parties, includes all the provisions that are essential to the agency and do not favor the contractors' position at the expense of the agency. A second benefit to including a model services contract is that the agency's terms and conditions are acceptable to prospective contractors when presented in this manner. When prospective contractors submit their own contract format, delays are incurred to permit negotiation of the contractor's provisions. In the absence of such negotiations, it is necessary for the agency to accept unfavorable contract terms and conditions. Certain disciplines such as Information

Technology (IT) and Equipment Maintenance often have unique considerations that require exceptions to certain provisions of the MSC. Although IT and equipment maintenance contracts may require acceptance of contract provisions that provide less protection to the agency, the competitors providing services in these disciplines are likely to have similar exceptions to the standard contract provisions. When contractors take exceptions to the standard contract provisions, such exceptions are subject to negotiation and subsequent negotiations will likely be required if the exceptions are not acceptable to the agency. In a competitive procurement environment, it is also necessary to ensure that all competing contractors base their proposals on equivalent contract provisions. To reach this objective, it may be necessary for the agency to develop revisions to the contract provisions that are acceptable to all the competing contractors.

## 4.2.2 Oral Explanations

*The agency shall not be bound by oral explanations or instructions given at any time during the competitive process or after award.*

The absence of being bound by oral explanations or instructions protects the agency in the event that one of its representatives, employees, or agents inadvertently responds to questions or provides unsolicited instructions that conflict with the provisions of the solicitation or agency policy.

## 4.2.3 Reference to Other Data

*Only information that is received in response to this RFP will be evaluated; reference to information previously submitted shall not be evaluated.*

This instruction to prospective contractors is merely to advise them that any information submitted prior to submittal of their proposal is not considered unless it is included in their proposal in response to the RFP.

## 4.2.4 Elaborate Proposals

*Elaborate proposals in the form of brochures or other presentations beyond that necessary to present a complete and effective proposal are not desired. Proposals that do not conform to the page limitations or format prescribed in this RFP may be rejected by the agency as nonresponsive.*

Solicitation documents often include a precaution against submitting elaborate proposals. This is more specific than most such notices because it references the page limitations specified in this RFP. Without limitations on the length of proposals, some prospective contractors tend to submit verbose proposals in the belief that lengthy proposals increase their chances for winning the contract. Lengthy proposals, however, create a burden on the contracting agency because the submittal of lengthy proposals results in the need for all the selection committee members to lumber through the reading of extraneous materials.

## 4.2.5 Desired Recycling Considerations

*It is desirable that all responses meet the following requirements:*

- *All copies are printed **double sided**.*
- *All submittals and copies are printed on **recycled paper with a minimum post-consumer content of 30 percent** and an endorsement in the proposal indicating the minimum post-consumer recycled content for the recycled paper.*
- *Unless absolutely necessary, all proposals and copies shall **minimize or eliminate use of nonrecyclable or nonreusable materials** such as plastic report covers, plastic dividers, vinyl sleeves, and GBC binding. Three-ringed binders, glued materials, paper clips, and staples are preferred.*
- *Materials shall be submitted in a format that allows for **easy removal and recycling** of paper materials.*

This **optional** instruction is a variation of an instruction contained in one of the RFP templates submitted to support the preparation of this book. It is provided here as an option for use by agencies wishing to encourage their prospective contractors to prepare green proposals.

## 4.2.6 Cost for Proposal Preparation

*Any costs incurred by prospective contractors in preparing or submitting proposals, as well as costs associated with any resultant presentations or negotiations, are the prospective contractors' sole responsibility; the agency will not reimburse any prospective contractor for any costs incurred prior to contract award.*

This instruction advises prospective contractors that costs associated with the preparation of their proposals, presentations, and negotiations are not reimbursable. Although virtually all companies consider proposal preparation as a usual cost of business, there is always the possibility that in the absence of this text, some contractor may keep records on the cost of preparing the proposal and then attempt to recover those costs from the agency.

## 4.2.7 Time for Acceptance

*Each proposal shall state that it is a firm offer that may be accepted within a period of **[insert at least 30]** days. Although the contract is expected to be awarded prior to that time, the longer validity period is requested to allow for unforeseen delays.*

This instruction is used to establish a time period within which the prospective contractor honors proposals. It is incumbent on the agency to select a number of days that provides ample time to obtain needed contract reviews and approvals to permit award of the contract prior to expiration of the proposal.

## 4.2.8 Right to Submitted Material

*All responses, inquiries, or correspondence relating to or in reference to the RFP, and all other reports, charts, displays, schedules, exhibits, and other documentation submitted by the prospective contractors shall become the property of the agency when received.*

This instruction is provided to ensure that the prospective contractors do not expect to have their proposal or any documentation included in the proposal returned following contractor selection. This is necessary to permit the agency to maintain complete records of the source selection process along with documentation applicable to the resultant contract.

## 4.2.9 Prospective Contractor's Representative

*Each prospective contractor shall submit with its proposal the name, mailing address, e-mail address, and telephone number of the person (or persons) with authority to bind the firm and answer questions or provide clarification concerning the firm's proposal.*

This instruction is recommended to ensure that there is one point of contact at each prospective contractor's facility to answer questions and make arrangements for subsequent presentations or negotiations, and that the named representative has authority to bind the prospective contractor.

## 4.2.10 Subcontracting

*Prospective contractors may propose to subcontract portions, but not all, of the work performed. However, prospective contractors shall clearly indicate in their proposals all the work they plan to subcontract and to whom it will be subcontracted. Prospective contractors shall also provide identifying information for each proposed subcontractor similar to the identifying information provided for the contractor submitting the proposal.*

State and local government agencies require full disclosure with respect to subcontracting portions of the work to other contractors. This information is needed to ensure that there are no unacceptable subcontractors proposed to be responsible for portions of the project. Plans to subcontract a significant portion of the work to one of the unsuccessful competing contractors could question the legitimacy of the competition that was obtained. When federal funding is provided for the project, it is necessary to ensure that neither the prime contractor nor any of the subcontractors have been debarred or determined to be ineligible for federal contracts or subcontracts.

## 4.2.11 Proprietary Information

*Trade secrets or similar proprietary data that the prospective contractor does not wish disclosed to other than personnel involved in the proposal evaluation effort or post-award contract administration will be kept confidential to the extent permitted by the agency as follows: Each page shall be identified by the prospective contractor in boldface text at the top and bottom as "PROPRIETARY." Any section of the proposal that is to remain confidential shall also be so marked in boldface text on the title page of that section. Cost information may not be deemed proprietary. Despite what is labeled as confidential, proprietary, or trade secret, the determination as to whether or not certain material is confidential, proprietary of a trade secret shall be determined by law. If a prospective contractor designates any information in its proposal as proprietary pursuant to this provision, the prospective contractor must also submit one copy of the proposal from which proprietary information has been excised. The proprietary material shall be excised in such a way as to allow the public to determine the general nature of the material removed and to retain as much of the content of the proposal as possible.*

This instruction is included in the RFP to advise the prospective contractors of the agency's policies and procedures with respect to proprietary information that is submitted with the proposal. The state or local government agency's counsel needs to pay particular attention to the provisions of this instruction because policies and procedures with respect to proprietary information may vary greatly between the various government agencies. The word "proprietary" might be preferred to "confidential" because some prospective contractors may also perform under contract with federal agencies that designate National Security information as Top Secret, Secret, and Confidential. The word "proprietary" is more consistent with private-sector terminology for protected information when the exposure of that information would not adversely impact national security.

## 4.2.12 Historically Underutilized Business

*The agency invites and encourages participation in this procurement process by businesses owned by minorities, women, disabled business enterprises, disabled veterans, and non-profit work centers for the blind and severely disabled.*

This is yet another instruction that is considered optional and could vary significantly between the various jurisdictions involved in state and local government agency contracting. The mix of underutilized companies does vary greatly between the agencies that submitted solicitation and contract templates in support of the best-practices research project. Projects funded by federal or state agencies may have specific flow-down provisions for contracting with historically underutilized businesses that are required to be included in solicitations and contracts in support of those particular projects. In such a situation, proposal and contract language provided by the federal or state agencies would normally replace the local government agency's boilerplate language regarding historically underutilized businesses.

### 4.2.13 Accommodations

*Reasonable accommodation will be provided by the agency for prospective contractor personnel who need assistance due to a physical disability. However, the agency must have reasonable advance written notice prior to the pre-proposal conference (if any) or any other visit to the agency's facilities. The prospective contractor must contact [**Insert Agency Official Name**] at [**Insert Contact Information**] no later than the fifth working day prior to the scheduled date and time of the pre-proposal conference to arrange for reasonable accommodations.*

Pre-proposal conferences are discouraged and should not be scheduled if they can be avoided. The reason for avoiding pre-proposal conferences is described in the section of Chapter 5 with respect to management of pre-proposal communications. If it is not possible, however, to avoid a pre-proposal conference, this "Accommodations" provision should be included in the RFP when the agency is not in compliance with the Americans with Disabilities Act (ADA). When a pre-proposal conference is not provided or the contracting agency is fully compliant with the ADA, the above provisions may be deleted.

## 4.3 Model Services Contract

Seventeen of the twenty-two RFPs (77 percent) submitted by the participants in the best practices research project included a copy of the agency's standard contract format in their solicitation. Three of the five RFPs that did not include a copy of the agency's standard services contract, however, did include a copy of their terms and conditions. It was rare to find a statement in the RFP that the agency intended to award a contract that was substantially in the format of the model services contract in the RFP. The Best Practices RFP does include an MSC and a statement to the effect that the agency intends to award a contract substantially in the format of the MSC. The primary problem encountered when an agency does not include a copy of their standard services contract in their solicitations is that this practice encourages prospective contractors to submit their own version of a contract along with their proposals. Contractors are prone to drafting terms and conditions that favor the rights and risks of the contractor over the rights and risks of the agency. Additionally, when contractors submit their own contracts, there is less consistency between risks and rights between the competing contractors. This inconsistency results in one additional element that decreases the probability of evaluating the proposals on an equivalent basis.

The emphasis of this discussion concentrates on the desirability of including an MSC in the solicitation sent to prospective contractors. The MSC should be virtually identical to the contract document that is more fully described in Chapter 8 to obtain the benefits of the contract provisions developed during the best practices research project. As discussed previously, the inclusion of an MSC in the solicitation document alerts the prospective contractors to the fact that the contracting agency intends to award a contract in the local government agency format and with the local government agency's contract provisions. The text of the solicitation should also include a statement to the effect that the contracting agency intends to award the contract essentially in the format of the enclosed MSC. If the solicitation does not include such an MSC and the statement regarding the contracting agency's intent to award a contract in that format, such exclusion is tantamount to inviting the contractors to propose their standard contract with contractor terms and conditions that favor the contractors over the contracting agency. In addition to the agency's inherent benefits from entering into a contract with known palatable provisions, contracts incorporating the local government agency's terms and conditions provide for an accelerated review process, less contentious negotiations, and a lesser risk of awarding a contract with disadvantageous provisions that may not have been detected during the review and approval process. The inclusion of a scope of work and the contracting agency's insurance requirements in the MSC are also highly recommended.

To illustrate the possible detrimental effects that could result from acceptance of a contractor's contract format and associated terms and conditions, a number of examples from terms and conditions actually proposed by contractors to local government agencies are summarized below:

■ Provisions in a multi-year contract for escalating future year billing rates based on actual costs during the present year combined with provisions that permitted the contractor to lease equipment from a wholly owned subsidiary. Basing future billing rates on present costs approximates the provisions of the cost plus percentage of costs (CPPC) contract, which is illegal in federal contracts and some state contracts, and discouraged by the American Bar Association. The only distinction between the proposed provisions and a CPPC contract is that with a CPPC contract, profit for the present year would be based on the present year's actual costs. Although the proposed provisions for basing future billing rates on present costs and leasing equipment from a wholly owned subsidiary, in combination, do not constitute a CPPC contract, they do provide the contractor an incentive to increase costs at a rate far in excess of the inflation rate. Because the contractor is permitted to lease equipment from its wholly owned subsidiary, the contractor could afford to pay such exorbitant lease rates that the parent company actually operates at a loss because the wholly owned subsidiary would earn a windfall profit during the first contract year. Additionally, because the subsequent year's billing rates would be based on the present year's actual costs, the contractor would be able to be compensated at the inflated billing rate for leasing equipment in subsequent years. In fact, the contractor could conceivably increase the first year's inflated leasing rates paid to its wholly owned subsidiary to continually increase the level of windfall profits.

- Provisions in another contractor's terms and conditions regarding reimbursement of expenses provided for payment of all costs charged to a hotel. Considering the ability to charge rented motion pictures of questionable artistic value as well as alcoholic beverages to one's hotel bill, such a provision could certainly lead to charges that would not pass the headline test.[2]
- It is not uncommon to encounter contractor standard provisions that include an indemnification clause that requires the agency to indemnify the contractor, but that include no mutual indemnification of the agency by the contractor.
- Contractor standard terms and conditions that permit contract termination initiated by the contractor without any corresponding rights for the government.
- Contractor provisions that include rates for reimbursable costs but without not-to-exceed provisions.

Local government agency contracts are customarily reviewed and approved by a number of officials in various contracting agency departments. Review and approval of contracts consumes fewer employee hours and is completed in less elapsed time when the officials reviewing the contract observe the contracting agency's standard contract format, insurance requirements, as well as standard terms and conditions comprising the remainder of the contract documents. When the contract format and incorporated exhibits are unfamiliar, by contrast, the review and approval process requires additional time to permit the reviewing/approving official to read and fully understand the unfamiliar text. The unfamiliar contract provisions, including those that may favor the contractor over the agency, or be unacceptable to the local government agency, result in questions or even negotiations that consume significantly ever more employee hours. The added time required for reading, questioning, and negotiating the nonstandard provisions of the contractor's contract format extends the elapsed time required to review and approve the contract and delays the beginning of the contract term and commencement of the project.

The negotiation of unacceptable terms and conditions results in a significant increase in the workload of the local government agency employees who must consult with other departmental employees to establish a negotiating strategy and to conduct the actual negotiations. Proposed revisions to the contract provisions prepared by the contracting agency may not be totally acceptable to the contractor, thus resulting in a counter-offer that requires further consultation with departmental personnel to determine the acceptability of the counter-offer or necessity to develop and communicate yet another position to present to the contractor. Several iterations of this process may continue over an extended time period. Had the MSC been included in the solicitation, the contractor would have had the opportunity to review the terms and conditions concurrent with proposal preparation and prepare a proposal consistent with the requirements of the RFP. Prospective contractors receiving an MSC in the solicitation are also more inclined to be resigned to accept the contracting agency's contract format and provisions, thus simplifying the review and approval process.

Local government agencies that develop their own contract format and provisions generally spend considerable time and effort into development of legally binding provisions that are consistent with applicable laws. When it is necessary to review unfamiliar contract provisions in a contractor's standard contract, there is rarely the luxury of time that had been available during the development of the contracting agency's standard format and contract provisions. The compressed time period allowed for review of the unfamiliar contractor's provisions presents the risk of overlooking an essential contract provision that is not in the best interests of the contracting agency nor consistent with applicable law.

An MSC is listed in the RFP Table of Contents, and is attached to the RFP in Appendix E. Because the MSC is essentially the same document as the contract awarded to the successful contractor, discussion of the MSC text is deferred to Chapter 8, "Contract Document."

## 4.4 Conclusion

Contractors are required to prepare their proposals in a standard format to ensure that the proposal addresses the evaluation criteria and to optimize the time and effort required by the agency's proposal evaluation committee. The requirement for all proposals to conform to the same format, cover the same topics in the same sequence, and be limited to the same number of pages also contributes to the agency's goal for treating prospective contractors equally. Specifying sections for the proposal that directly correspond to the proposal evaluation criteria (e.g., past performance, financial stability, risk assessment, project plan, outsourcing, and life cycle cost) was incorporated in the Best Practices RFP and is recommended for state and local government agencies. It would be appropriate to require the prospective contractor certification with all proposals. The other certifications would be required only if mandated by the nature of the funding or contractor reimbursement methodology. The certifications regarding lobbying, compliance with the Pro-Children Act of 1994, as well as debarment and suspension, etc., are appropriate only when the contract is funded, or partly funded, by the federal government. The certification of cost or pricing data would likely be required when the contract price exceeds some dollar value threshold established by the agency. An exception to the requirement for this certification could be to exempt it for fixed-price contracts that were awarded via adequate competition.

Proposal preparation instructions are specific to ensure compliance with agency policy and to instill consistency among the proposals from the various prospective contractors. The topics included in the instructions include the need for prospective contractors to identify all exceptions that they take to the provisions of the RFP and MSC, not to rely on oral explanations, advise contractors that materials not included in the proposal are not considered when evaluating the proposals, and that material which exceeds the maximum size limitations may result in rejection of the proposal. There is also an optional instruction that describes the agency's desire that contractors prepare their proposals from materials that can easily be recycled. Prospective contractors are advised that the cost of preparing proposals is not reimbursed by the agency, there is an established time period during which the agency can accept the contractors' proposals, all proposal materials become the property of the agency, proposals shall contain the name and contact information for a contractor's representative who can bind the company, full disclosure regarding work to be subcontracted and identification of subcontractors shall be included in the proposals, proprietary information shall be clearly marked to ensure that it is not inappropriately disclosed by the agency, and the agency encourages proposals by historically underutilized businesses and that (in the event of a pre-proposal conference) contractors need to notify the agency of any accommodations required for persons with disabilities.

The need for agencies to attach an MSC was also discussed in the final section of this chapter. Failure to attach an MSC to the RFP is tantamount to inviting prospective contractors to propose their own contract template. Proposals that include award of contracts with the contractor's terms and conditions generally create problems for the agency due to the fact that the contractor's provisions favor the contractor at the expense of the agency. The time delays associated with the need to conduct negotiations delay award of the contract or project commencement date. Inclusion of the contractor's contract template also results in added workload to negotiate contract provisions and introduces the prospect of differing contract provisions for contractors competing for the same contract. Dissimilar contract provisions impede equal treatment of the contractors.

# Notes

1. The Dun & Bradstreet Web site can be located by searching the Internet for "Dun & Bradstreet."
2. The headline test refers to basing one's decision to make some certain decision based on how that person would feel should the result of that decision appear in the local newspaper's headline.

# Chapter 5

**Management of Pre-Proposal Communications and Evaluation of Proposals**

## Chapter Objectives

This chapter introduces readers to alternative methods for managing communications during the time period beginning with the release of the Request for Proposals (RFP) through the date when proposals are received by the contracting agency. This is a critical period of time when uncontrolled communications between the prospective contractors and the agency can result in protests from competing contractors based on the perception of unequal treatment of contractors by agency representatives. The following alternatives for managing pre-proposal communications are discussed, and one is recommended to states and local government agencies:

- Pre-proposal conference
- Questions posed verbally
- Letter, overnight courier, and e-mail
- Providing a Web site for posing questions and providing agency responses
- Submitting questions via e-mail and posing questions and responses to the Web site

There are also alternative methods for evaluating proposals. The readers are, therefore, introduced to the following proposal evaluation methods, and one method is recommended to states and local government agencies. However, a combination of two methods is recommended when a large number of proposals are received in response to an RFP. One method is recommended for an initial screening of the proposals, and another method is recommended for use after the initial screening to narrow the field of contractors competing for a contract:

- Predetermined numerical scales
- Specific adjective scales
- Color code scales
- Narrative description
- Ranking method

The advantages for using weighted proposal evaluation criteria are discussed, and the process for evaluating proposals when weighted criteria are applicable are explained through the presentation of an example of just such a proposal evaluation effort.

## 5.1 Introduction to Management of Pre-Proposal Communications

Certain prospective contractors routinely attempt to initiate communications with contracting agency personnel, other than the project manager, immediately upon release of the solicitation. These attempts are made despite RFP provisions prohibiting the contact of agency personnel other than the project manager. Contracting professionals and other agency officials and employees should perceive such contacts as sales efforts. The extent of contractor efforts to pursue such contacts varies based on the type of service that will be provided and the companies that make up the pool of prospective contractors. The expected dollar value of the resultant contract has a significant impact on the contractor's efforts to establish contact with agency representatives who are responsible for selecting or recommending the selection of contractors.

The importance of identifying the contracting agency's contact point in the RFP was emphasized in the chapters on solicitations (Chapters 3 and 4). Limiting the number of government employees who respond to queries from prospective contractors is essential. Certain prospective contractors contact members of the contracting agency's proposal evaluation committee to pose questions. When they discover a committee member who responds to questions, these prospective contractors take advantage of this breach in communications protocol and continue to query evaluation committee members until they receive the most advantageous response. One measure that helps to avoid this problem is the drafting of an RFP that excludes the names of agency personnel who should not be contacted by prospective contractors during the pre-proposal phase. Limiting the agency's point of contact solely to one person, such as the project manager, is recommended. However, some agencies elect to name a technically oriented employee to respond to technical questions from prospective contractors. When such a second point of contact is named in the RFP, the agency is urged to ensure close coordination between the two agency individuals named in the RFP to ensure proper management of pre-proposal communications and equal treatment of all prospective contractors. If there is a change in the contracting agency's contact points, all companies on the prospective contractors list, as well as all contractors that received the solicitation through alternative dissemination of the solicitation, must be advised in writing of these changes. Prospective contractors must be advised in writing of such changes to avoid adverse impacts on the schedule for awarding the contract and starting the project.

To be absolutely fair to all prospective contractors, they should all be treated identically. In addition to maintaining the element of fairness, treating prospective contractors identically protects the contracting agency by guarding against the possibility of providing grounds for protesting the award or recommended award of the contract. In highly competitive markets for high-dollar-value contracts, the pressure on the prospective contractors' marketing and sales staffs to capture a contract can easily evolve into protests from unsuccessful contractors. The likelihood of a protest multiplies if members of the proposal evaluation committee or the contracts management staff leave their contracting agency exposed to legitimate protests through differing treatment of prospective contractors.

In the case of a contract that was solicited through an Invitation for Bids (IFB), a pre-bid conference is an excellent way for all the prospective contractors to have a venue where all competing contractors have the opportunity to hear all the questions and responses. While the pre-bid conference is an excellent tool when an IFB is the solicitation document and all bidders have an opportunity to witness the opening and public reading of the bids, the use of a pre-proposal conference when an RFP is used as the solicitation document may not be as attractive to a contracting agency, especially when considering the confidentiality afforded proposals. Although there is usually no restriction against holding a pre-proposal conference, the contracting agency should consider the advantages and disadvantages of alternatives to the pre-proposal conference prior to scheduling such an event. The following section on alternative methods for managing pre-proposal communications includes a discussion of the advantages and disadvantages of alternatives to pre-proposal conferences and a recommended alternative for managing pre-proposal communications.

## 5.2 Alternative Methods for Managing Pre-Proposal Communications

There are numerous alternatives for managing pre-proposal communications between the contracting agency and the prospective contractors, including those listed below. However, only one of the following alternatives is recommended.

- Pre-proposal conference:
- Questions posed by contractor representatives by telephone or during visits to the contracting agency that are answered by sending the questions and responses to all prospective contractors by letter, overnight courier, or e-mail.
- Written questions submitted via letter, overnight courier, or e-mail and answered by one of the same methods listed above for responses to telephonic questions.
- Questions posted by prospective contractors to a Web site hosted by the contracting agency, and responses to the questions posted by the agency, thus permitting all prospective contractors an equal opportunity to benefit from feedback available to everyone with Internet access.
- Questions submitted to the contracting agency via e-mail with the questions and responses both posted by the contracting agency to the agency's Web site.

### 5.2.1 Pre-Proposal Conference

A pre-proposal conference would be an excellent tool for ensuring that all prospective contractors hear the same questions and responses from the contracting agency. However, the contracting agency may wish to avoid holding a pre-proposal conference because such a conference affords the prospective contractors the opportunity to assess their competition. Likewise, prospective contractors may not feel free to pose questions regarding the proprietary elements of their proposals in a forum attended by their competitors. Conducting a pre-proposal conference does not guarantee that no questions are posed following the conference. Questions posed subsequent to the pre-proposal conference should be addressed in the same manner as they would have been addressed in the absence of a pre-proposal conference. Therefore, the mere use of a pre-proposal conference does not completely eliminate the need for other means to deal with pre-proposal communications.

The contracting agency may not wish to hold a pre-proposal conference because attendance at such a conference could reveal the companies comprising the field of prospective contractors, and provide insight to the prospective contractors regarding the probable features of their competitors' proposals.

## 5.2.2 Questions Posed Verbally

During a pre-proposal telephone call or contractor visit from a sales representative or technical contact, there is always the probability of a number of questions asked formally that can be readily transmitted to other prospective contractors. However, there is also the risk that the formal questions are followed up by informal questions that could be helpful to the prospective contractor but seemingly unimportant to the contracting agency employee who responded to the questions. In the event that the questions did not seem important to the agency employee, he or she may fail to advise the other contractors of those seemingly insignificant questions and the answers that were provided. Another risk in taking telephonic or other oral questions is that the questions may be inadvertently transcribed incorrectly. If and when the transcription error is detected, it is necessary to advise all the prospective contractors of the question and answer one additional time. Should there be a misunderstanding of the question posed verbally, a delayed response is likely, regardless of the method used for sending questions and responses to all the prospective contractors. Inviting prospective contractors to pose their questions via telephone or in personal visits is, therefore, discouraged.

## 5.2.3 Letter, Overnight Courier, and E-mail

Written questions submitted via letter, overnight courier, or e-mail and answered by one of the same methods would likely be more appealing than the earlier alternatives for a pre-proposal conference or the receipt of questions via telephone or during personal visits. Written questions are superior because they simplify the task of ensuring that prospective contractors are advised of all questions and answers. However, questions submitted via letter result in unacceptable delays while questions submitted via overnight courier are more costly than warranted by the slightly shorter delay. Certainly, questions submitted via e-mail are the preferred choice between these three methods for submitting questions and providing responses. Despite the advantages of speed, lack of expense, and controllability of e-mail pre-proposal questions and answers, this is still not the preferred method for handling pre-proposal communications.

## 5.2.4 Providing a Web Site for Posing Questions and Posting Agency Responses

One additional method is presented prior to describing the recommended method to consider for posing and responding to questions regarding the RFP. This method involves the establishment of a Web site, or use of an existing Web site, where all questions are posted by prospective contractors and answers are posted by the agency. This alternative has numerous advantages over those discussed above.

It is not necessary to expend the time required to send multiple hard copies or e-mails to prospective contractors, and the delays inherent in sending hard copies are avoided. This alternative also avoids an opportunity for prospective contractors to gain insight into the competitive environment. The use of a Web site for handling pre-proposal communications is clearly nondiscriminating and minimizes the probability of protests based on mishandled pre-proposal communications. The clear advantages of using a Web site make its use preferred over the previously discussed methodologies. However, some agencies may not wish to establish Web sites wherein parties other than agency employees are permitted to post text.

### 5.2.5 Submitting Questions via E-mail and Posting Questions and Responses to the Web Site

Based on the above discussion on the advantages and disadvantages of the various alternatives for handling pre-proposal communications, it is highly recommended that agencies forego pre-proposal conferences and require all questions from prospective contractors be submitted via e-mail and that agency personnel post the questions and answers on an agency-sponsored Web site. Establishing a process wherein the prospective contractors submit their questions via e-mail and wherein the agency posts both the questions and responses to the Web site meets most of the advantages of the previous methodology. However, this approach avoids the situation wherein non-agency individuals are permitted to post text to the agency's Web site. Although there is the added effort for agency personnel to enter the question on the Web site, the effort required is not excessive. This added effort by agency personnel is reasonable to achieve the added security afforded by eliminating the ability of prospective contractors, or others, to make undesirable postings to the agency's Web site.

Because there is necessarily a time lag between the submittal of the questions via e-mail and the posting of the questions and responses to the Web site, the solicitation should include a deadline for submitting questions. Such a deadline permits sufficient time for the agency to post the questions and responses to the Web site by a date that allows prospective contractors adequate time to make adjustments to their proposals prior to the due date.

## 5.3 Introduction to Evaluation of Proposals

The discussion in Chapter 3, "Solicitation Documents: Information for Prospective Contractors," stressed the need to include the evaluation criteria in the solicitation. This section of Chapter 5 stresses the importance of establishing ground rules for the evaluation committee, evaluating proposals solely on the basis of the evaluation criteria, and the need to ensure that all the evaluation criteria are considered during the proposal evaluation process. Strict adherence to these principles is essential to ensure that prospective contractors are treated equally and fairly, and to minimize the possibility of providing grounds for protests from unsuccessful contractors.

The evaluation committee requires clear ground rules to ensure that the proposals are evaluated in strict conformance with the agency's policies and the evaluation procedures described in the RFP. Agencies should consider providing written guidance for evaluation committee members, training on that guidance, and training on the agency's policies with respect to the evaluation of proposals. Reducing the guidance to writing combined with training on that guidance and agency proposal evaluation policy minimizes the possibility for misunderstandings by committee members. The development of a confidentiality statement, to be signed by each evaluation committee member, to commit to compliance with the agency's proposal evaluation practices and confidentiality policy should be considered by contracting agencies. Such a confidentiality statement reinforces the committee members' comprehension of the need to maintain confidentiality. The confidentiality statement could also include a certification that the proposal evaluation committee members have no financial relationship that would be affected by the selection of any of the prospective contractors.

Agencies may elect to establish a selection committee, or proposal evaluation committee, to evaluate the proposals and select a contractor, or recommend a contractor, for award of the contract. Selection committee membership is typically comprised of employees from the contracting agency's department that requires the services of the contractor. In some cases, consultants, who themselves are on contract, may also serve on the selection committee. Contracts or Purchasing personnel are also frequently members of selection committees. The departments participating on the selection committee are normally identified in the solicitation. A chairperson is typically designated for each selection committee. The selection committee opens the proposals, evaluates the proposals based on the evaluation criteria, and either selects the successful contractor or recommends a contractor to the governing body or chief elected official for approval and award of the contract. The term "successful contractor" might intuitively be considered a contractor that successfully completes the work described in a contract. However, for the purposes of this discussion, a successful contractor is the contractor selected for award of a particular contract. The term "unsuccessful contractor" is used to describe any contractor that submitted a proposal but was not selected for contract award.

One tool that can help ensure that all members of the selection committee adhere to these principles is a proposal evaluation form that provides for scoring the proposals based solely on the criteria contained in the RFP. An example of just such a form is included as Appendix I, "Evaluation of Proposals in Response to RFP." The form in Appendix I includes a column where the exact criteria contained in the Appendix E, "Best Practices Request for Proposals (RFP)," is repeated on the evaluation form. In the event that the evaluation criteria in the

Best Practices RFP are modified, the criteria on the evaluation form must receive identical modifications.

Agencies that elect to pursue the publication of guidelines for members of the proposal evaluation committee should include a statement of purpose for inclusion in the guidelines. A statement of purpose with emphasis on the need to ensure fairness to the companies that submitted proposals as well as the selection of the contractor (or contractors) whose proposal is in the best interests of the agency helps reinforce these precepts for committee members. Although a generic set of guidelines could be prepared for all proposal evaluation efforts, guidelines tailored to the immediate project are preferred. The task of preparing guidelines tailored to a specific project is highly simplified through the availability of previously prepared project or solicitation documents. These previously prepared documents contain material relevant to the guidelines that can merely be copied and pasted to the proposal evaluation guidelines. One such element that would normally be available from other project documents is the project scope. The project scope would logically follow the statement of purpose mentioned above. Added meaningful features to include in the guidelines are agency policies, committee member responsibilities and tasks, a definition of and procedures for protecting proprietary or trade secret information, the desirability of free and open competition, avoidance of undue influence from certain members of the proposal evaluation committee due to their position in the agency's hierarchy, the application of independent versus consensus evaluations or the combination of independent and consensus evaluations, negotiation rules, the importance of meeting schedules, templates for evaluating the proposals, the need to protect the confidentiality of all proposals until the contract is awarded or recommended to the governing body or chief elected official for award, procedures for responding to requests for debriefings, and the policy and procedure for responding to potential protests and actual protests.

While bids received in response to an Invitation for Bids (IFBs) are opened publicly, cannot be received late, cannot contain significant errors, are not subject to negotiation, and require award of the contract to the lowest priced bidder that is responsive and responsible, these restrictions are not nearly as rigid with respect to the receipt of proposals in response to an RFP. Proposals are not opened publicly. Because proposals are subject to negotiation and change, they are treated as confidential until the contract is either awarded or a contractor is recommended to the chief elected official or governing body for award of the contract. Late proposals can normally be considered if they are received prior to contract award and if awarding a contract to the contractor that submitted the late proposal would be in the best interests of the state or local government agency. Significant errors that would normally result in the rejection of a bid can be resolved through negotiation of a proposal. Likewise, nonresponsive proposals can be made responsive through the negotiation process. Responsive contractors are those contractors that provide a proposal satisfactorily addressing all requirements specified in the RFP. Because proposals, unlike bids, are subject to negotiation, certain omissions or variances may be resolved through negotiations to make the proposal responsive. An example of an omission or variance that could be resolved is a proposed period of performance that would not result in completion of the work within the required timeframe. Should negotiation with the contractor result in an adjustment to the period of performance that results in completion with the required timeframe, the proposal then may be deemed responsive. Responsible contractors are those contractors that meet the contracting agency's standards with respect to a reasonable expectation that the contractor has the management, technical, financial, equipment, and human resources available to ensure adequate performance of the work described in the solicitation. Agencies may have established a policy that specifies certain criteria that contractors must meet to be considered responsible. Those criteria could include companies that have not been debarred or suspended, not convicted of certain offenses, or that have not had a contract terminated for default, all within certain specified time periods. Debarred refers to contractors that have been excluded from government contracting and government-approved subcontracting for a specified time period. Suspended refers to contractors that have been proposed for debarment, debarred, excluded, or otherwise disqualified for government contracting and government-approved subcontracting.

When an agency elects to incorporate the above policies in the evaluation process, it should advise prospective contractors of the agency's practices for treating and evaluating proposals. Failure to include such advice in the RFP may result in a misunderstanding of the practices by prospective contractors, and such misunderstanding could lead to an otherwise avoidable protest. The advice can be communicated to prospective contractors by including statements in the RFP regarding the facts that proposals are treated confidentially until either the contract is awarded or recommended for award, that late proposals may be considered if that would be in the best interest of the agency, and that errors in the proposals or nonresponsive proposals may be corrected during the negotiation process. However, prospective contractors should also be advised that they should endeavor to submit responsive, error-free proposals on time because failure to do so may result in rejection of their proposals. Providing such advice to prospective contractors maximizes the probability of receiving responsive, error-free proposals on time.

Negotiation of proposals may include pricing, delivery, contract provisions, or any element of the proposal. The selection of contractors submitting proposals in response to RFPs is normally based on price or life cycle costs and other factors, as opposed to bids in response to an IFB wherein the lowest price is accepted if it is responsive and received from a responsible contractor.

Appendix I, "Evaluation of Proposals in Response to RFP," does not include space for entering an overall score or spaces for scores assigned to an individual criterion. The lack of a formal scoring technique may be entirely acceptable for evaluating straightforward proposals, especially if the proposals are for a relatively low-dollar-value project. In fact, this informal approach may be acceptable to some state or local government agencies for all projects, including the relatively high-dollar-value projects.

Formal scoring techniques, as differentiated from weighted evaluation criteria, may prove attractive to government agencies that award relatively high-dollar-value contracts in a highly competitive environment wherein a greater level of sophistication is desired in the selection process or wherein there is a greater propensity for protests from aggrieved contractors.

If the advice in Chapter 3, "Solicitation Documents: Information for Prospective Contractors," is followed with respect to a requirement that all proposals be highly structured and similarly organized, then that advice is greatly appreciated once the proposal evaluation task is undertaken. The comparison of one proposal to another, or others, is greatly simplified when all the proposals are approximately the same length, address the same issues, and discuss the various aspects of the proposals in the same sequence. Otherwise, considerably more time and effort are required to compare the proposals to one another, and there is a greater propensity for committing errors by overlooking material that is located in a section of the proposal where it was not expected.

Considerable thought and analyses should be used when considering the advantages and disadvantages of the various scoring techniques that can be used in the evaluation of proposals. Selection of a scoring technique with inherent weaknesses can jeopardize the validity of the agency's proposal evaluation effort. Possible scoring techniques, preferably at the criterion level, could include the assignment of numerical scores based on predetermined scales, assignment of specific adjectives describing acceptability of the contractors' proposals, use of color codes to evaluate the contractors' proposal, or ranking the proposals at the evaluation criterion level. Advantages and disadvantages to each of these scoring techniques are discussed in this chapter. For simplicity, the examples shown in Figures 5.1 through 5.5 reflect ratings at the overall proposal level. An actual proposal evaluation effort would be based on the assignment of ratings at the criterion level. Figure 5.6 is an example of a format for evaluation of proposals rated at the criterion level.

### 5.3.1 Predetermined Numerical Scales

It is not unusual for government agencies to rate individual criteria on a scale of 1 to 10 or 1 to 100. The primary advantage to this technique is that it is easily understood and has likely been used in other applications by selection committee members. The disadvantages are that the end result could very likely be identical or nearly identical final scores for all the proposals or for the highest rated proposals. Tied scores, or nearly tied scores, would negate the results that stemmed from the expenditure of considerable time and effort by selection committee members. An even greater disadvantage to this approach is that one evaluator's score could negate the score of two or more other evaluators if some evaluators spread their scores over the full range of available scores while other evaluators tend to closely cluster their scores, thus resulting in slight differences between the score assigned to the highest

| Assignment of Scores Based on a Scale of 1-to-10 Permits Undue Influence by One Proposal Selection Committee Member | | | |
|---|---|---|---|
| **Evaluator** | **Proposal A** | **Proposal B** | **Proposal C** |
| Alvarez | 1 | 4 | 10 |
| Chung | 9 | 10 | 7 |
| Davis | 7 | 10 | 9 |
| TOTALS | 17 | 24 | 26 |

**Figure 5.1** **Assignment of scores based on a scale of 1 to 10 permits undue influence by one proposal selection committee member.**

rated proposal and the score assigned to the lowest rated proposal. Spreading scores differently may result from one person's tendency to compress the scores closely while other evaluators tend to disperse the scores over a wide range. Naturally, there is also the possibility for an individual evaluator to spread his or her scores over the entire range of available scores to achieve maximum influence over the final overall rating. An example of the possible resultant disparity when evaluators differ in their approach to assigning scores for individual criteria is illustrated in Figure 5.1.

In the example in Figure 5.1, Evaluator Alvarez used the entire range of numbers from 1 through 10 while Evaluators Chung and Davis restricted their ratings to 7 through 10. The resulting total scores provided Proposal C with the highest total score despite the fact that both Evaluators Chung and Davis selected Proposal B as the superior proposal. This undue influence exercised by Evaluator Alvarez could have resulted from his or her natural tendency to spread scores throughout the entire available range, or through an intentional effort to favor the contractor that submitted Proposal C.

## 5.3.2 Specific Adjective Scales

Some government agencies have used adjective rankings such as "good," "average," and "poor." An advantage to this type of rating system is that it is simple to use. However, one problem with this rating system is that there is a high probability of tied scores. When highly qualified contractors are solicited for proposals, one would expect that they would receive the highest rating of "good." While the use of adjectives is not the most attractive scoring technique for selecting the successful contractor, the use of adjectives is practical for the initial scoring of a large number of proposals to select the finalist for further evaluation through a more discriminating scoring technique. The example in Figure 5.2 reflects the problem that could result from the use of adjectives to rate three well-qualified companies that submitted good proposals. Certain evaluators are prone to restricting their ratings to average and good, while others use the entire range of ratings from poor through

| Assignment of Scores Based on Adjectives to Evaluate the Proposals Fails to Identify the Successful Contractor | | | |
|---|---|---|---|
| Evaluator | Proposal A | Proposal B | Proposal C |
| Alvarez | Average | Good | Good |
| Chung | Good | Good | Good |
| Davis | Average | Good | Good |
| COMBINED | Average+ | Good | Good |

**Figure 5.2  Assignment of scores based on adjectives to evaluate the proposals fails to identify the successful contractor.**

good. In this event, the evaluators using the entire range of available ratings exert a greater influence on the final overall evaluation.

### 5.3.3  Color Code Scales

The use of color codes to evaluate proposals has also been employed by some government agencies to evaluate proposals. The color code might use blue for good proposals, yellow for average proposals, and red for poor proposals. Color codes have the same advantages and disadvantages as the use of adjectives. If all the proposals were prepared professionally by well-qualified contractors, there is a high probability of ties. However, just as with the adjective rating system, color codes can be used to narrow a large number of proposals to the finalists that are subsequently evaluated by a more discriminating scoring technique. An example of the evaluation of three well-qualified companies that submitted professionally prepared proposals is illustrated in Figure 5.3. Just as with the use of numerical scales over a specified range and with adjective schemes, color codes also lend themselves to the problem of undue influence by evaluators who use the entire range of available color codes over those evaluators who restrict their ratings to the upper end of the color scale.

### 5.3.4  Narrative Description

The assignment of scores based on predetermined scales, adjective schemes, and color schemes are all subject to distortion when one or more evaluation committee members use the entire range of available rankings and one or more other evaluators restrict their scoring to the upper range of available rankings. When this occurs, the evaluators using the entire range of available rankings have a greater impact on the combined scoring. Agencies may consider the use of a ranking system, as described below, to avoid the inordinate influence on the

| Assignment of Scores Based on Color Codes to Evaluate the Proposals Fails to Identify the Successful Contractor | | | |
|---|---|---|---|
| **Evaluator** | **Proposal A** | **Proposal B** | **Proposal C** |
| Alvarez | Yellow | Green | Green |
| Chung | Green | Green | Green |
| Davis | Yellow | Green | Green |
| **TOTALS** | **Yellow+** | **Green** | **Green** |

**Figure 5.3   Assignment of scores based on color codes to evaluate the proposals fails to identify the successful contractor.**

| Example of narrative description | | | |
|---|---|---|---|
| Narrative Description | Numerical | Adjective | Color |
| Far Exceeds All Minimum Requirements | 10 | Excellent | Green |
| Meets Minimum Requirements & Exceeds Some | 8 | Very Good | Blue |
| Meets Minimum Requirements | 5 | Good | Yellow |
| Meets Most Requirements but Fails to Meet Some | 3 | Poor | Amber |
| Fails to Meet All or Most Requirements | 1 | Inferior | Red |

**Figure 5.4   Example of narrative description.**

combined scores. However, in the event that they wish to continue using one of the schemes discussed above rather than a ranking system, there are several measures that can be taken to lessen the possibility that such an inordinate influence on the combined scoring is realized. Assigning a narrative description of the various rating representations helps avoid the unintentional inordinate influence on the combined scoring. An example of such a narrative description is provided in Figure 5.4.

Other measures that can be taken to guard against inordinate influence on the score by one or more evaluators is extensive training in the assignment of ratings or a consensus meeting following the individual rating sessions to ensure that the evaluators are consistent in the assignment of their ratings. However, these measures may not prevent inordinate influence over the combined ratings by an evaluation committee member who wishes to intentionally exert more influence than other proposal evaluation committee members.

## 5.3.5 Ranking Method

There are several advantages to using ranking methods over the other scoring techniques. By using such a forced distribution of rankings with no possibility of tied scores, there is a tendency to spread the scores to avoid ties and to prevent one evaluator from exerting undue influence over the final result. The primary disadvantage to a ranking scheme is that it does not work well for a large number of proposals. It works best for two, three, or four proposals. Ranking may be practical for up to five proposals; however, it is not practical for the evaluation of more than five proposals. The problems with ranking more than five proposals are that the difficulty of ranking proposals increases proportionally with the number of proposals; and when there are a large number of proposals, there is a greater probability of tied scores. However, there is a practical way to achieve the advantages of ranking even when there are a large number of proposals to evaluate. Evaluation of the large number of proposals through the adjective or color code techniques can narrow the field down to two, three, four, or five finalists that can be further evaluated through the ranking technique. In the example in Figure 5.5, Evaluators Chung and Davis again rated Proposal B the highest while Evaluator Alvarez continued to evaluate Proposal C the highest. However, in this example, because of the forced distribution feature of the ranking technique, Proposal B received the highest overall ranking.

Provisions of the Best Practices RFP advise the prospective contractors that a color scheme be used to reduce a large number of proposals down to five or fewer finalists. The RFP also contains advice to the prospective contractors that finalists are evaluated through a ranking process.

| Assignment of Scores Based on Ranked Proposals is more Likely to Identify the Successful Contractor and Prevents Undue Influence by One Proposal Selection Committee Member. In this Example, High Numbers are Assigned as Scores for the Highest Ranked Proposals | | | |
|---|---|---|---|
| **Evaluator** | **Proposal A** | **Proposal B** | **Proposal C** |
| Alvarez | 1 | 2 | 3 |
| Chung | 2 | 3 | 1 |
| Davis | 1 | 3 | 2 |
| TOTALS | 4 | 8 | 6 |

**Figure 5.5 Assignment of scores based on ranked proposals is more likely to identify the successful contractor and prevents undue influence by one proposal selection committee member.**

## 5.4 Evaluating Proposals with Weighted Criteria

The evaluation criteria included in the Best Practices RFP in Appendix E, although subject to change based on the judgment of the contracting activity, is relevant for many government agencies. However, some criteria may be more critical than others. Varying levels of importance assigned to one criterion over another, or over others, is commonplace. Should the contracting activity elect to assign a higher level of importance to one or more of the criteria, that information should be included in the RFP. Including such information in the RFP is in furtherance of the need to fully inform prospective contractors of the agency's methodology for evaluating proposals. Suggested terminology for inclusion of this information in the RFP, in addition to the present text in the MSC, is provided in Figure 5.6.

As mentioned earlier, the system of ranking proposals is highly recommended for the final selection of the successful contractor. The ranking technique, therefore, is incorporated in an example of a proposal evaluation effort to illustrate the effects of ranking and weighted scoring. Due to the inherent difficulties associated with ranking a large number of proposals, however, an adjective scheme or color scheme can be used to narrow a large number of proposals to a workable number of finalists. As mentioned earlier, Figures 5.2 through 5.5 are simplified examples that reflect a single score for each proposal. In actuality, there would be a number of

| | |
|---|---|
| Addition to the RFP Advising Prospective Contractors of the Use of Weighted Criteria in the Proposal Evaluation Process | |
| **Weighted Criteria:** The state or local government agency has elected to assign weights to the above evaluation criteria. The weights assigned to each of the criteria are indicated in the example below: | |

| Criterion | Weight |
|---|---|
| Past Performance | 10 |
| Financial Stability | 20 |
| Risk Assessment | 20 |
| Project Plan | 5 |
| Outsourcing | 5 |
| Life Cycle Cost | 40 |
| **TOTAL WEIGHT** | **100** |

**Figure 5.6** Addition to the RFP advising prospective contractors of the use of weighted criteria in the proposal evaluation process.

| Format for Combined Weighted Scores by All Three Evaluators for All Three Proposals | | | |
|---|---|---|---|
| **COMBINED WEIGHTED SCORES** | | | |
| **CRITERIA** | **PROPOSAL A** | **PROPOSAL B** | **PROPOSAL C** |
| Past Performance | | | |
| Financial Stability | | | |
| Risk Assessment | | | |
| Project Plan | | | |
| Outsourcing | | | |
| Weighted Life Cycle Cost | | | |
| **WEIGHTED SCORES** | | | |

**Figure 5.7   Format for combined weighted scores by all three evaluators for all three proposals.**

criteria that would be ranked for each proposal. The end result of an evaluation of the proposals by an evaluation committee, based on ranking and weighted criteria, would be a final scoring tally such as in the format presented in Figure 5.7.

To develop combined weighted scores, such as the ones that would be inserted in Figure 5.7, it is necessary to start with proposal scoring sheets prepared by each of the individual evaluators to record their ranking of each proposal at the evaluation criterion level. In this example, there are three proposals and three members of the evaluation committee. Therefore, there are three such rating sheets — one for each evaluation committee member. Examples of such individual scoring sheets are provided in Figures 5.8, 5.9, and 5.10.

The rankings in Figures 5.8 through 5.10 are carried through Figure 5.16 where the combined weighted scores for all three members of the proposal evaluation committee are recorded in a single table. Figure 5.16 reflects the final results of the proposal evaluation committee wherein the successful contractor has the highest score. The ranking scheme may use either low scores or high scores to represent the highest ranked proposals. The one caveat is that if low numbers are assigned to the best proposals, then low scores should also be assigned to the lowest life cycle cost (or lowest price). Likewise, if high numbers are assigned to the best proposals, then high numbers should also be assigned to the lowest life cycle cost. Assigning high scores to the best proposals with respect to some criteria, while assigning low scores to the best proposals with respect to other criteria, would obviously negate the entire scoring process. Because it is relatively simple to assign low scores to the best proposals and life cycle cost, the example illustrates the slightly more difficult

| Total Scores by Evaluator Alvarez for All Three Proposals | | | |
|---|---|---|---|
| **Evaluator Alvarez** | | | |
| | PROPOSAL | PROPOSAL | PROPOSAL |
| **CRITERIA** | A | B | C |
| Past Performance | 3 | 2 | 1 |
| Financial Stability | 2 | 3 | 1 |
| Risk Assessment | 3 | 2 | 1 |
| Project Plan | 2 | 3 | 1 |
| Outsourcing | 1 | 3 | 2 |
| **TOTAL SCORES** | **11** | **13** | **6** |

**Figure 5.8   Total scores by Evaluator Alvarez for all three proposals.**

| Total Scores by Evaluator Chung for All Three Proposals | | | |
|---|---|---|---|
| **Evaluator Chung** | | | |
| | PROPOSAL | PROPOSAL | PROPOSAL |
| **CRITERIA** | A | B | C |
| Past Performance | 2 | 1 | 3 |
| Financial Stability | 3 | 1 | 2 |
| Risk Assessment | 3 | 2 | 1 |
| Project Plan | 2 | 3 | 1 |
| Outsourcing | 1 | 3 | 2 |
| **TOTAL SCORES** | **11** | **10** | **9** |

**Figure 5.9   Total scores by Evaluator Chung for all three proposals.**

scheme that involves the assignment of high numbers to the best proposals and high numbers to the lowest life cycle cost. In the example shown in Figure 5.8, Evaluator Alvarez judged Proposal A to have the highest score and Proposal C to have the lowest score with respect to Past Performance as well as Risk Assessment. Although the criteria are weighted, it is not necessary to consider the weighting at this beginning stage of proposal evaluation.

In the above examples, all the criteria except the weighted life cycle cost are based on a ranking scheme wherein the best proposal for a particular criterion is

Total Scores by Evaluator Davis for All Three Proposals

**Evaluator Davis**

| CRITERIA | PROPOSAL A | PROPOSAL B | PROPOSAL C |
|---|---|---|---|
| Past Performance | 3 | 1 | 2 |
| Financial Stability | 2 | 1 | 3 |
| Risk Assessment | 1 | 2 | 3 |
| Project Plan | 2 | 3 | 1 |
| Outsourcing | 1 | 3 | 2 |
| **TOTAL SCORES** | **9** | **10** | **11** |

**Figure 5.10   Total scores by Evaluator Davis for all three proposals.**

Calculation of Weighted Life Cycle Cost

**WEIGHTED LIFE CYCLE COST SCORE TABLE**

| Proposal | Proposed Life Cycle Cost | Percentage of Total | Inverse | Weighted Life Cycle Cost |
|---|---|---|---|---|
| A | 5,000,000 | 37.0 | 63.0 | 35.8 |
| B | 4,000,000 | 29.6 | 70.4 | 40.0 |
| C | 4,500,000 | 33.3 | 66.7 | 37.9 |

**Figure 5.11   Calculation of weighted life cycle cost.**

assigned a 3, the second-best proposal for that criterion is assigned a 2, and the lowest ranked proposal for that criterion is assigned a 1. The practice of assigning high numbers for the best proposal as shown in Figure 5.1 continues to be used throughout this example. The life cycle cost should not be assigned a score of 1, 2, or 3 because it is an objective number that can be evaluated on a proportional basis as described below.

In addition to the use of proportional numbers for the weighted life cycle cost, all the evaluators use the same score because all of the evaluation committee members have access to the proposed life cycle cost from each of the finalists. Certain agencies may elect to have the life cycle cost (or price) evaluated separately by a different team or person. The life cycle cost proposed by each of the three finalists is illustrated in Figure 5.11.

Calculation of the weighted life cycle cost is accomplished as follows:

- Determine the total of all three life cycle costs: $13,500,000.
- Calculate the percentage of the total life cycle cost for each proposal. For example, Proposal A is calculated by dividing 5,000,000 by 13,500,000 and then multiplying the result by 100 for a percentage of 37.0.
- The inverse is calculated by subtracting the percentage from 100. This is a necessary step to adjust the weighted life cycle cost to obtain a weight wherein the high score is advantageous to the contracting agency.
- The weighted life cycle cost is equal to 40 (the weighted criteria value reflected in Figure 5.6) for the lowest life cycle cost proposal. To calculate the weighted score for the higher life cycle cost proposals, it is necessary to divide the weighted criteria value by the inverse for the lowest priced proposal ($40 \div 70.4 = 0.5681818$) and then multiply the inverse for the higher life cycle cost proposals by the product. For example, the weighted life cycle cost score for Proposal A is calculated by multiplying 63.0 by 0.5681818 for a weighted life cycle cost score that rounds to 35.8.

There is also the necessity to calculate weighted scores for all possible rankings and weights for factors other than life cycle cost. This calculation is more straightforward than the similar calculation for life cycle cost. In the following example there are three possible rankings of 3, 2, and 1 representing the score assigned to the proposals by each of the evaluators. The highest ranked proposal for each factor is assigned a score of 3 while the lowest ranked proposal is assigned a score of 1. There are also three possible weights (the life cycle cost is excluded from this calculation) that apply to each factor. Therefore, it is possible to develop a matrix to reflect the weighted score determined by each evaluator for each factor and each proposal. The matrix developed for this example is provided in Figure 5.12.

Calculation of weighted scores for factors other than life cycle cost is accomplished as follows:

- Enter the possible weights (other than for life cycle cost) in the weight column while ensuring that the number of rows for each weight equals the number of proposals. In this example there are a total of nine rows. There are three rows (representing the three proposals) for the weight of 5, three rows for the weight of 10, and three rows for the weight of 20.
- The rankings are merely the possible rankings of 3, 2, and 1 resulting from the evaluation of three proposals. These rankings are repeated for each weight.
- The multiplier is calculated by dividing the weight by the highest possible ranking. In this example, the weight of 5 is divided by the ranking of 3 to calculate the multiplier of 1.67. The multiplier of 1.67 is used for all rankings with the corresponding weight of 5. The remaining multipliers are calculated

| WEIGHTED FACTOR SCORING TABLE | | | |
|---|---|---|---|
| Weight | Ranking | Multiplier | Weighted Score |
| 5 | 3 | 1.67 | 5.0 |
| 5 | 2 | 1.67 | 3.3 |
| 5 | 1 | 1.67 | 1.7 |
| 10 | 3 | 3.33 | 10.0 |
| 10 | 2 | 3.33 | 6.7 |
| 10 | 1 | 3.33 | 3.3 |
| 20 | 3 | 6.67 | 20.0 |
| 20 | 2 | 6.67 | 13.3 |
| 20 | 1 | 6.67 | 6.7 |

Calculation of Weighted Scores for Factors Other than Life Cycle Cost

**Figure 5.12** Calculation of weighted scores for factors other than life cycle cost.

in the same manner, resulting in a multiplier of 3.33 calculated by dividing 10 by 3, and a multiplier of 6.67 calculated by dividing 20 by 3.

■ The weighted score is calculated by multiplying the ranking by the multiplier.

Once all members of the proposal evaluation committee have ranked all the proposals as shown in Figures 5.8, 5.9, and 5.10, weighted scores for the life cycle cost have been calculated as shown in Figure 5.11, and weighted scores for the other factors have been calculated as shown in Figure 5.12, it is then possible to calculate weighted scores for all the proposal evaluation committee members. The weighted score results, based on the example shown in Figures 5.8 through 5.10, are shown in Figures 5.13 through 5.15.

The final step is to summarize all the weighted scores in one table such as the blank table in Figure 5.7 and the completed table shown in Figure 5.16.

The combined weighted scores are calculated by determining the mean average of all the evaluators' weighted scores for each criterion and for each proposal. For example, the Past Performance for Proposal A is calculated by adding the weighted score for Past Performance for Proposal A assigned by each evaluator (10.0 + 6.7 + 10.0 = 26.7) and then dividing the sum by the number of evaluators (26.7 ÷ 3 = 8.9). The combined weighted score for Past Performance for Proposal A is then entered in the cell immediately to the right of "Past Performance" and immediately below "PROPOSAL A" in Figure 5.16.

| Weighted Scores for Evaluator Alvarez | | | |
|---|---|---|---|
| Evaluator Alvarez | | | |
| **CRITERIA** | **PROPOSAL A** | **WEIGHT** | **WEIGHTED SCORE** |
| Past Performance | 3 | 10 | 10.0 |
| Financial Stability | 2 | 20 | 13.3 |
| Risk Assessment | 3 | 20 | 20.0 |
| Project Plan | 2 | 5 | 3.3 |
| Outsourcing | 1 | 5 | 1.7 |
| Life Cycle Cost | $5,000,000 | 40 | 35.8 |
| **WEIGHTED SCORE** | | | **84.1** |
| **CRITERIA** | **PROPOSAL B** | **WEIGHT** | **WEIGHTED SCORE** |
| Past Performance | 2 | 10 | 6.7 |
| Financial Stability | 3 | 20 | 20.0 |
| Risk Assessment | 2 | 20 | 13.3 |
| Project Plan | 3 | 5 | 5.0 |
| Outsourcing | 3 | 5 | 5.0 |
| Life Cycle Cost | $4,000,000 | 40 | 40.0 |
| **WEIGHTED SCORE** | | | **90.0** |
| **CRITERIA** | **PROPOSAL C** | **WEIGHT** | **WEIGHTED SCORE** |
| Past Performance | 1 | 10 | 3.3 |
| Financial Stability | 1 | 20 | 6.7 |
| Risk Assessment | 1 | 20 | 6.7 |
| Project Plan | 1 | 5 | 1.7 |
| Outsourcing | 2 | 5 | 3.3 |
| Life Cycle Cost | $4,500,000 | 40 | 37.9 |
| **WEIGHTED SCORE** | | | **59.6** |

**Figure 5.13   Weighted scores for Evaluator Alvarez.**

| Weighted Scores for Evaluator Chung | | | |
| :--- | :--- | :--- | :--- |
| Evaluator Chung | | | |
| CRITERIA | PROPOSAL A | WEIGHT | WEIGHTED SCORE |
| Past Performance | 2 | 10 | 6.7 |
| Financial Stability | 3 | 20 | 20.0 |
| Risk Assessment | 3 | 20 | 20.0 |
| Project Plan | 2 | 5 | 3.3 |
| Outsourcing | 1 | 5 | 1.7 |
| Life Cycle Cost | $5,000,000 | 40 | 35.8 |
| WEIGHTED SCORE | | | 87.5 |
| CRITERIA | PROPOSAL B | WEIGHT | WEIGHTED SCORE |
| Past Performance | 1 | 10 | 3.3 |
| Financial Stability | 1 | 20 | 6.7 |
| Risk Assessment | 2 | 20 | 13.3 |
| Project Plan | 3 | 5 | 5.0 |
| Outsourcing | 3 | 5 | 5.0 |
| Life Cycle Cost | $4,000,000 | 40 | 40.0 |
| WEIGHTED SCORE | | | 73.3 |
| CRITERIA | PROPOSAL C | WEIGHT | WEIGHTED SCORE |
| Past Performance | 3 | 10 | 10.0 |
| Financial Stability | 2 | 20 | 13.3 |
| Risk Assessment | 1 | 20 | 6.7 |
| Project Plan | 1 | 5 | 1.7 |
| Outsourcing | 2 | 5 | 3.3 |
| Life Cycle Cost | $4,500,000 | 40 | 37.9 |
| WEIGHTED SCORE | | | 72.9 |

Figure 5.14  Weighted scores for Evaluator Chung.

| Weighted Scores for Evaluator Davis | | | |
| --- | --- | --- | --- |
| **Evaluator Davis** | | | |
| **CRITERIA** | **PROPOSAL A** | **WEIGHT** | **WEIGHTED SCORE** |
| Past Performance | 3 | 10 | 10.0 |
| Financial Stability | 2 | 20 | 13.3 |
| Risk Assessment | 1 | 20 | 6.7 |
| Project Plan | 2 | 5 | 3.3 |
| Outsourcing | 1 | 5 | 1.7 |
| Life Cycle Cost | $5,000,000 | 40 | 35.8 |
| **WEIGHTED SCORE** | | | **70.8** |
| **CRITERIA** | **PROPOSAL B** | **WEIGHT** | **WEIGHTED SCORE** |
| Past Performance | 1 | 10 | 3.3 |
| Financial Stability | 1 | 20 | 6.7 |
| Risk Assessment | 2 | 20 | 13.3 |
| Project Plan | 3 | 5 | 5.0 |
| Outsourcing | 3 | 5 | 5.0 |
| Life Cycle Cost | $4,000,000 | 40 | 40.0 |
| **WEIGHTED SCORE** | | | **73.3** |
| **CRITERIA** | **PROPOSAL C** | **WEIGHT** | **WEIGHTED SCORE** |
| Past Performance | 2 | 10 | 6.7 |
| Financial Stability | 3 | 20 | 20.0 |
| Risk Assessment | 3 | 20 | 20.0 |
| Project Plan | 1 | 5 | 1.7 |
| Outsourcing | 2 | 5 | 3.3 |
| Life Cycle Cost | $4,500,000 | 40 | 37.9 |
| **WEIGHTED SCORE** | | | **89.6** |

**Figure 5.15   Weighted scores for Evaluator Davis.**

| | PROPOSAL | PROPOSAL | PROPOSAL |
|---|---|---|---|
| **Combined Weighted Scores by All Three Evaluators for All Three Proposals** | | | |
| **COMBINED WEIGHTED SCORES** | | | |
| **CRITERIA** | **A** | **B** | **C** |
| Past Performance | 8.9 | 6.7 | 6.7 |
| Financial Stability | 15.3 | 11.1 | 6.7 |
| Risk Assessment | 15.6 | 13.3 | 6.7 |
| Project Plan | 3.3 | 5.0 | 1.7 |
| Outsourcing | 1.7 | 5.0 | 3.3 |
| Weighted Life Cycle Cost | 35.8 | 40.0 | 37.9 |
| **WEIGHTED SCORES** | **80.6** | **81.1** | **62.9** |

**Figure 5.16  Combined weighted scores by all three evaluators for all three proposals.**

The remaining combined weighted scores are calculated in the same manner and entered into the appropriate cell in the table for the combined weighted scores (Figure 5.16). The calculation of one additional example is provided to illustrate this process. The combined weighted score for Financial Stability for Proposal B is calculated by adding the weighed score for Financial Stability for Proposal B assigned by each evaluator (20.0 + 6.7 + 6.7 = 33.4) and then dividing the sum by the number of evaluators (33.4 ÷ 3 = 11.1).

The Weighted Scores in the bottom row of the Combined Weighted Scores (Figure 5.16) are calculated by adding the weighted scores in the cells in the column immediately above the bottom row. For example, the weighted score of 80.6 for Proposal A is determined by adding 8.9 + 15.3 + 15.6 + 3.3 + 1.7 + 35.8.

The process for selecting proposals considered as the finalists should include a determination that the finalists are all responsible contractors that submitted responsive proposals. To do otherwise would be tantamount to a wasted exercise. However, once such a reasonable and responsible determination has been made, the contractor that submitted the proposal with the highest combined weighted score should be the contractor awarded the contract or recommended for award of the contract. Selection of the contractor with the highest combined weighted score is consistent with the agency's intent to select the successful contractor based on submittal of a responsive proposal from a responsible contractor that best meets the agency's needs with respect to the evaluation criteria stated in the solicitation.

Copies of all the tables used in the evaluation process described in this chapter are included in Appendix J and on the CD accompanying this book.

## 5.5 Conclusion

Pre-proposal conferences are not recommended for managing pre-proposal communications because this alternative does not address communications that may occur following the pre-proposal conference and prior to the receipt of proposals by the contracting agency. Additionally, pre-proposal conferences provide prospective contractors with considerable insight into the level of competition to be expected as well as the identity of their potential competitors. This information can be detrimental to the agency in the event that there is little or no competition.

Questions posed verbally, also, are not recommended because questions posed verbally have a greater propensity for misinterpretation than written questions. Additionally, there is a greater chance that when multiple questions are posed verbally, certain seemingly insignificant — to the contracting agency representative — questions may not be communicated along with agency responses to all prospective contractors.

Written questions transmitted via letter, overnight courier, and e-mail are superior to verbal questions because these written questions are less prone to misinterpretation. However, there are even greater advantages to the following alternative methodology.

Providing a Web site where prospective contractors can post questions and where the agency can add its responses to the questions is an excellent approach to providing equal treatment to competing contractors while providing timely responses to contractor questions. The one reservation to this methodology is the possibility that the agency may lose some control over the content of its Web site.

The recommended alternative for managing pre-proposal communications is to require prospective contractors to pose all questions regarding the solicitation to the agency's project manager via e-mail, and then having the agency's project manager post both the questions and agency responses to the agency's Web site. This variation from the alternative wherein the contractors post their questions to the agency's Web site permits the agency to have greater control over its Web site content.

Predetermined numerical scales, such as a scale of 1 to 10, are familiar to most agency personnel who are likely to be assigned to a proposal evaluation team. However, such scales are subject to anomalous results due to the tendency of some individuals to use the entire scale while other individuals have a tendency to use only the upper portion of the scale. Individuals with less than admirable motives may intentionally use the entire scale to gain more influence over the contractor scores than other members of the proposal evaluation team.

Specific adjective scales and color code scales have similar characteristics in that both of these methods have a tendency to result in tied scores rather than achieve the desired discrimination between the qualities of the proposals. There is also the propensity, as with predetermined numerical scores, for proposal evaluation team members to exert greater influence over the other team members by using the entire range of available adjectives or colors while other team members restrict their scores to the higher-level adjective and color scores.

Adding narrative descriptions to the above three proposal evaluation methods alleviates the problem associated with the tendency for some individuals to restrict their ratings to the higher end of the scale while other individuals tend to use the entire scale. However, the addition of narrative descriptions does not guard against individuals who intentionally use the entire scale to achieve greater influence over the combined scores.

The forced distribution feature associated with the ranking of proposals eliminates both the problem associated with the innocent tendency to restrict scores to the upper end of the scale and the intentional spreading of scores over the entire range of the scale to achieve greater influence over the combined scores. The greatest disadvantage of the ranking method is that it does not work well when there are more than five responsive proposals from responsible contractors. However, this disadvantage can be minimized using either the adjective or color scheme to designate a limited number of proposals as finalists, and then using the ranking method to select the best proposal from the finalists.

The use of weighted proposal evaluation criteria introduces a greater amount of objectivity into a process that could otherwise tend to be overly subjective. The use of weighted proposal evaluation criteria is recommended for high-dollar-value projects and/or for projects wherein the industry is highly competitive or comprised of contentious contractors that are prone to filing a protest when they are not selected for contract award.

There are numerous steps involved in the evaluation of proposals when a contracting agency elects to use weighted proposal evaluation criteria. A scenario involving the evaluation of proposals with weighted proposal evaluation criteria was provided to illustrate this process for the readers. In addition to this case, there are several templates used to facilitate the evaluation of proposals when weighted criteria were selected. The templates used in this example are provided in Appendix J, "Tables Used in Proposal Evaluation Process," and on the CD accompanying this book.

# Chapter 6

# Protests

## Chapter Objectives

This chapter introduces readers to the subject of protests. As might be discerned by the term, protests are a phenomenon not welcomed by state and local government agencies. Therefore, legitimate measures for preventing protests are explored. However, despite the implementation of well-conceived measures to prevent protests, state and local agencies almost invariably receive at least an occasional protest from contractors that believe the contractor selection process is flawed or that one of their competitors was otherwise improperly selected for award of a contract that should have been awarded to their company.

This chapter addresses the need to develop policies and procedures, recommendations for features to incorporate in the protest policies and procedures, the role of the agency's legal counsel, the impact from requests for public records in conjunction with a protest, and a discussion regarding how the protest policies are communicated to prospective contractors.

Variations in the nature of alternative approaches to filing protests are addressed. Conventional protests are those protests filed according to the agency's protest policies and procedures. However, there is also the potential for protests being filed contrary to established procedures. Measures to discourage such unconventional protests are explored in this chapter.

Because all state and local government agencies are subject to receipt of a protest from an aggrieved contractor, measures for conducting an investigation and making a determination on the merits of protests are recommended to the readers. The approach to investigating the proceedings of the proposal evaluation committee and making a determination regarding the merits of the protest includes the following activities:

- Read the protest and begin drafting questions for the proposal evaluation committee members
- Read the solicitation
- Read the proposal evaluation team instructions
- Review the policy and procedures
- Review the proposal evaluation record
- Finalize the questions for proposal evaluation committee members
- Interview proposal evaluation committee members
- Synthesize the information to form a determination

The readers are also introduced to the actions to take upon completion of the determination. Those actions include the necessity for advising the interested parties of the determination and to document the activities leading to the determination.

## 6.1 Introduction to Protests

Contractors that believe one of their competitors was improperly selected for award of a contract or that believe the proposal evaluation process was flawed are considered aggrieved. Aggrieved contractors have the right to protest the award of a contract following contract award or the recommendation for award of a contract to one or more of their competitors. The term "protest" is used to describe a challenge to the solicitation, procedure for selecting a contractor, recommendation to award a contract, or actual contract award. Protests are generally initiated by an unsuccessful contractor (or contractors). In the event that the contract was awarded, the intent of the protest is normally to have the contracting agency determine that the contract should have been awarded to the protesting company, terminate the contract, and award the contract to the aggrieved company. In the event that the contract has yet to be awarded, the intent of the protest is to stay the contract award, have the contracting agency determine that the aggrieved company should be awarded the contract, and award the contract to the company that initiated the protest. Contracting agencies normally have one designated official who receives protests, investigates the contractor selection process, and makes a determination regarding the merits of the protest. The official who receives and acts on protests is normally designated for that responsibility on the basis of her or his position within the agency. The majority of the determinations made on the merits of a protest find that the proposal evaluation team followed established procedures and selected the correct contractor. This is not unusual because the vast majority of proposal review committee members are dedicated employees who strive to select the best contractor for the project. If the aggrieved contractor is not satisfied with the determination, there is normally an appeal procedure wherein the contractor can appeal the determination to a higher authority such as the chief elected official or the governing body. If the appeal is denied by the higher authority, the aggrieved contractor can elect to pursue its complaint through litigation.

## 6.2 Preventing Protests

The receipt of a protest creates a major concern for state and local government agencies. The very nature of a protest challenges the competence or ethical practices of the public agency as well as its officials and employees. Receipt of a protest normally delays award of the contract and therefore delays the commencement of service delivery. On certain occasions, a delay in project commencement may lead to cancellation of the project. Every contracting agency is subject to receipt of a protest. The receipt of a protest normally requires significant time and effort on the part of the highest elected or appointed official, governing body, management personnel, contracting staff, legal counsel, and department personnel. Therefore, it is in the agency's best interests to take legitimate steps to prevent protests. Agency officials are encouraged to establish procedures to prevent protests, ensure that protests that could not be prevented are lodged according to agency procedures, and ensure that the agency procedures describe how protests received from aggrieved contractors are processed. This chapter provides insight into measures that can be taken to prevent protests and to ensure that protests are lodged according to agency procedures; however, there are no measures that absolutely prevent protests or ensure that protests are made according to the contracting agency's policies and procedures. Measures to take in reaction to receipt of protests by agency officials and employees are recommended in this chapter.

As mentioned in an earlier chapter on solicitations, it is essential that the selection criteria used in evaluating proposals be described in the Request for Proposals (RFP). This presentation of the evaluation criteria during the initial contact with the prospective contractors demonstrates that the contracting agency's relationship with the contractors is designed to ensure equal treatment of all prospective contractors. It is critical, however, that great care be taken when crafting the criteria to ensure that all essential features of the resultant proposals are considered. For example, if the life cycle cost is paramount to contractor selection but was not included in the evaluation criteria in the RFP, contractors that were not selected for contract award due to a high proposed life cycle cost have grounds to protest the award of the contract.

Another essential measure for the contracting agency to protect against the possibility of receiving a protest, or protests, is to ensure that the evaluation of proposals is based solely on the criteria contained in the RFP. One tool to help ensure that the selection committee restricts its evaluation to the criteria included in the RFP is to prepare a proposal evaluation template similar to the one included in Appendix I. Contracting agencies that provide such an evaluation template for their proposal evaluation committee members should ensure that the criteria included on the evaluation form exactly match the criteria in the RFP template. When the evaluation criteria in the RFP template are modified to better match the features of a particular project, this introduces the possibility that the same changes to the evaluation criteria are not made to the proposal evaluation template. When this occurs, there is a mismatch between the RFP criteria and the criteria used by the proposal evaluation team. Therefore, one additional step to help guard against the possibility of a protest is to provide evaluation committee members with a proposal evaluation form containing the evaluation criteria with safeguards to ensure that there is an exact match between the criteria on the form and the criteria in the solicitation. This could be accomplished by including a cautionary note on the proposal evaluation template regarding the need to determine whether there is consistency between the two sets of criteria.

Another measure to help insulate the contracting agency against protests is to strive for structure and objectivity in the evaluation process while avoiding unstructured and subjective techniques. Use of weighted evaluation criteria, as described in the earlier chapter on solicitations, is an excellent strategy for building structure and objectivity into the evaluation process. This is especially beneficial when the prospective contractors operate in a business climate that is known or believed to be highly competitive or contentious. The ability to demonstrate a superior quantitative rating for the selected or recommended contractor can greatly assist the contracting agency to discourage protests, or at least to defend against actual protests.

If it is discovered that an unsuccessful contractor is aggrieved before it files a formal protest, the agency should consider offering the aggrieved unsuccessful contractor a debriefing on the selection process. Should the contractor's concerns regarding the selection process be allayed on the basis of the debriefing, a formal protest may be avoided.

Agencies should consider inclusion of a debriefing procedure and a description of the debriefing process in their policies and procedures as well as in their solicitations. The existence of a debriefing procedure in an agency's policies and procedures and in their solicitations provides an opportunity for the agency to require contractors to obtain a debriefing prior to lodging a formal protest. The Best Practices RFP does include language that requires aggrieved contractors to obtain a debriefing prior to filing a formal protest.

## 6.3 Policies and Procedures for Dealing with Protests

Defining the method for handling protests in the contracting agency's published policies and procedures as well as in the solicitation may help to keep protests manageable; however, contracts that are approved by the contracting agency's governing body or chief elected official may be protested at a public meeting of the governing body. Most reasonable contractors honor written policies and procedures that require the filing of protests according to established procedures. Contractors that are considering the filing of a protest often contact the public agency to request information on the protest procedures. Policies and procedures should specify the need to file written protests within a specific period of time, say ten calendar days, following the notification that they were not selected or recommended for award of the contract. Without such a specified time period, there would be no established limit to the date when an aggrieved contractor would be required to file a protest. The policies and procedures should also specify the official within the state or local government agency who receives and investigates proposal evaluation activities and makes a determination with respect to the merits of the protest. In the absence of designating an official to receive and investigate protests, the contractor might send its protest to an individual who is not familiar with the process for reacting to protests. The public agency may wish to consider assigning this responsibility to the incumbent of the position who, based on the dollar value or other criteria, normally executes the contract for the contracting agency. Alternatively, the government agency may wish to identify the individual one level higher in the organization as the person who makes a determination based on the merits of the protest. It should be noted, however, that if the protesting contractor is not satisfied with the decision of the official who made the determination, the protesting contractor whose protest was denied has the right to appeal the determination to a higher authority. If the contractor is not satisfied with the result of the appeal, the contractor may bring the matter to litigation. Despite the fact that policies and procedures for handling protests cannot fully insulate the contracting agency against protests, the existence of fair and meaningful policies and procedures for handling protests provides needed protection for unsuccessful contractors to pursue their dissatisfaction with the selection process, and provide the contracting agency with a rational methodology for reacting to the receipt of protests.

The reaction to a protest varies based on whether the protest was received prior to award of the contract or following contract award. The policies and procedures should, therefore, separately address the reaction to protests received prior to award and protests that are received following contract award.

When the protest is made prior to award of the contract, two essential policy considerations to address in the policies and procedures are (1) whether or not to delay award of a contract in the event of a protested source selection, and (2) the time frames established for resolving the protest. The timeframe for resolving the protest could have a significant impact on the functioning of the state or local government agency if a delay in contract award could have an impact on the agency's ability to provide essential services. If a delay in the award of a contract for essential services is unavoidable, and the services have been provided through an earlier contract that is due to expire, consideration should be given to extending the existing contract for a period of time sufficient to resolve the protest. This action permits continuation of service delivery while the agency reacts to the protest. When a protest is received prior to awarding a contract for a service that is not presently being provided on a contracted basis, award of the contract should be delayed, if possible, until the contracting agency can either sustain or deny the protest. Delaying award of the contract in this instance demonstrates good faith on the agency's part and avoids the necessity to terminate the contract in the event the protest is sustained. In either event, it is obvious that the policies and procedures for dealing with protests require expeditious treatment without subjecting the contracting agency to the possibility that it is not able to provide essential services. The provision for sufficient time to investigate the source selection activities and make a rational determination based on the careful evaluation of the facts is essential to maintaining sound contracting practices.

When the protest is not received until after the contract has been awarded, there is less pressure on the contracting agency because the question of whether or not to award the contract is moot. However, the timeframe for making a determination on the merits of the protest rightfully demands expeditious action to obtain resolution of the matter. Should the source selection decision be reversed following contract award, the contracting agency may face excess costs through the necessity for some level of compensation to two contractors during the period of time from the original contract award date until that original contract is terminated and the replacement contract is in place.

Should all protests be referred to the governing body or chief elected official, there would be a needless referral of less significant, small-dollar-value protests to the agency's highest organizational level. The delays associated with the need to wait until all protests can be considered by the chief elected official or agendized for and considered by the governing body would be unfair to all interested parties. One approach to minimizing the number of protests referred to the governing body is to construct the policies and procedures such that the protests are directed to the position where authority to execute the contract rests and provide for appeal to the position one level above the position with authority to execute the contract. This approach minimizes the number of protests referred to the chief elected official or the governing body as well as shortens the time required to resolve the protests in response to the award of relatively low-dollar-value contracts. However, the contracting agency should not entirely rely on the existence of documented procedures for filing protests to completely eliminate protests made directly to the governing body. Whenever agencies conduct public meetings, aggrieved contractors have a venue for lodging a protest contrary to agency policies and procedures.

In addition to identifying the organizational level where protests are to be lodged and appealed, the policies and procedures should include the maximum time periods permitted for filing protests, denying or upholding protests, making appeals in response to denied protests, and for denying or upholding appeals. The failure to include maximum time periods for these actions leaves agencies open to receipt of protests and appeals for an indefinite period of time and can result in a delayed reaction by agency officials.

## 6.4 The Inclusion of Protest Procedures in Solicitations

State and local agencies may elect to remain silent in their solicitations with respect to procedures for filing a protest out of concern that including the procedures for protesting awards, or recommended awards, in solicitations may result in more protests. However, this is unlikely because aggrieved companies are generally aware that there are provisions for lodging formal protests. One advantage to including protest procedures in the solicitation is that providing this information in the RFP discourages unconventional protests or the agency being blindsided by contractors that prefer to present their concerns directly to the chief elected official or publicly to the governing body. When the procedures are included in the solicitation, it is also more likely that protests are made according to the established procedure and can be dealt with more conventionally. Yet another advantage to including the protest procedure in the solicitation is that this also presents an opportunity to include a debriefing option and to require aggrieved contractors to obtain a debriefing before they can lodge a formal protest.

## 6.5 Coordination with Legal Counsel

Upon receipt of a protest, or even the threat of a protest, the individual receiving the protest should contact his or her agency's legal counsel. In addition to providing advice for dealing with aggrieved contractors, legal counsel should be advised of all protests due to the possibility that protests may eventually be resolved through litigation. The need to initiate coordination efforts with legal counsel upon receipt of a protest should be included in written policies and procedures. Including this requirement in written policies and procedures helps to ensure continuation of this important practice in perpetuity. Should the unsuccessful contractor's protest be denied, their company maintains the right to appeal the determination, bring their protest forward during a public meeting of the governing body, and initiate litigation. The fact that unsuccessful protests can be elevated to litigation is one key reason why it is essential to involve the contracting agency's legal counsel at the first hint that a protest may be filed by an aggrieved contractor. However, absent the potential for eventual litigation, legal counsel's insight into the protest or potential protest from an attorney's perspective can provide valuable insight for dealing with the aggrieved, unsuccessful contractor.

## 6.6 Requests for Public Records in Conjunction with Protest

Aggrieved prospective contractors are permitted to seek documentation developed by the proposal evaluation committee through a public records act request. Should the public records be obtained after the protest has been filed, the original protest may be withdrawn or amended, predicated on information discovered in the public record. In the event that there is a modification to the protest, predicated on additional information contained in the public record, the timeline for responding to the protest is normally extended to permit the agency time to react to the amended protest.

## 6.7 Unconventional Protests

### 6.7.1 Blindsiding

Most aggrieved, unsuccessful contractors pursue their protests according to established policies and procedures. However, when the governing body is the final approval authority for the award of the contract, the unsuccessful contractor could conceivably take their protest directly to the governing body during an open public session when the contract in question is being considered for award. There has been at least one case wherein an unsuccessful contractor called on the agency official who was bringing a recommendation to the governing body for contract approval to state that their company had erred in the preparation of the proposal and could not argue against the recommendation for award of the contract to their competitor. However, representatives of that same contractor appeared a few days later at the public session of the governing body to publicly protest the recommendation. The aggrieved contractor appeared with a group of black-shirted employees and potential subcontractors who protested the award, along with corporate executives who based their protest on emotional considerations and unfounded claims that the evaluation criteria were ignored during the evaluation of proposals. Needless to say, any agency official in this situation would feel blindsided and not as well prepared as desired to defend against such an unorthodox protest. Although the protest resulted in a delay in the award of the contract to offer both competing contractors and the opportunity to submit a best and final offer, readers should be pleased to learn that in this case the governing body eventually voted to award the contract to the contractor originally recommended by the proposal evaluation committee.

If the contracting agency's RFP included information on requesting a debriefing and standard protest procedures, the governing body would be justified in rejecting the protest that was contrary to agency procedure. The Best Practices RFP does include suggested language to advise prospective contractors of the proper procedure for requesting a debriefing and filing a protest.

### 6.7.2 Firm Not Solicited

Another type of protest that might be anticipated at a public meeting of the governing body would be from a firm that was not solicited and is protesting the fact that it was not given an opportunity to compete for the contract. Absent the contracting agency's deliberate action to exclude a known company that should have been included in the list of firms solicited, a company that does not lodge a protest until this late date is virtually admitting the failure of its sales or marketing team. Prudent members of the governing body are likely to reject such untimely protests unless it is apparent that the contracting agency knew, or should have known, that the protesting company was unfairly absent from the list of firms solicited. Should it be determined that the protesting firm be given an opportunity to submit a proposal, cancellation of the original solicitation and release of a new solicitation, with the protesting company added to the list of solicited firms, is the most likely course of action.

## 6.8 Conventional Protests

Unlike the extreme examples above with the black-shirted protestors and the protest by the firm that was not solicited, most protests are made in a conventional manner according to the agency's contracting manual. Although conventional protests normally need to be made in writing, the initial contact from the unsuccessful contractor expressing its dissatisfaction with the selection process is almost exclusively made by telephone or in person. In most instances, a spoken explanation of the rationale for recommending award to a competitor is reluctantly accepted. When the spoken explanation is not considered acceptable to the unsuccessful contractor, the next logical step is for the contractor to ask for a copy of the procedure for initiating a protest. Although contracting manuals are public documents and oftentimes posted on the state or local government agency's Web site, contractors almost invariably request a copy of the policy and procedure from an agency official. One notable exception is the contractor that consistently submits a protest on virtually every occasion when the contract is awarded or recommended for award to a competitor. Such habitual protestors are fully aware of the agency's protest procedures and need not request of copy.

Agencies should consider instituting the requirement for a debriefing prior to submittal of a protest. Some debriefings would likely convince certain contractors that the proposal evaluation process was not flawed, and thereby avoid a number of protests. Contractors would not normally be aware of this requirement in the agency's policies and procedures; therefore, this requirement should be included in the agency's RFP template. When contractors ask about the procedures for filing a protest, they should be provided with the procedures and also be advised that a request for a debriefing is required prior to filing a protest. Advising a contractor asking about procedures for filing a protest that they must request a debriefing prior to filing a protest may prevent receipt of a protest from that particular contractor.

Objection to the award of a contract or recommendation for award of a contract that is made over the telephone or during a face-to-face meeting is not normally considered a protest and does not warrant a written determination. In the event that an agency representative receives an unwritten protest, professional courtesy dictates that the contractor be advised that protests must be in writing. In the earlier case, however, when a protest is made directly to the governing body during a public meeting, that verbal protest is normally considered a formal protest. When the agency's RFP template includes advice to prospective contractors regarding the procedures for lodging a protest, however, the governing body would be justified in rejecting the unconventional protest because the contractor, having been duly advised of the need for a written protest, elected to ignore that advice.

## 6.9 Making a Determination on the Merits of the Protest

The individual responsible for evaluating the events leading up to contract award or a recommendation for contract award and then making a determination on the merits of a protest usually finds it necessary to spend considerable time making that determination. The steps normally followed to prepare for making such a determination are provided below.

### 6.9.1 Read the Protest

The written protest should be carefully read and all objections to the selection procedure and decision should be carefully noted. Because there is normally a time limit for investigating the facts regarding the protest and rendering the decision, it is essential that the person investigating the protest fully understand the nature and extent of the protest. The aggrieved contractor should be contacted for clarification if the contractor's claim is not entirely clear. Otherwise, the agency's official investigator may make a faulty assumption regarding the nature of the protest. Communications with protesting companies are preferably done in writing. When written communications are not possible, however, the verbal communications should be meticulously documented. This is necessary because in the event of an unfavorable determination regarding the protest and an unsuccessful appeal by the aggrieved contractor, the matter could be litigated in the courts. The official who makes the determination on the merits of the protest should begin by drafting questions that need to be answered during the following activities. Questions posed to members of the proposal evaluation team and their responses are usually central to the investigation of the facts surrounding the agency's proposal evaluation process, and a timely beginning to the drafting of appropriate questions to be posed to members of the proposal evaluation committee assists the responsible official in the conduct of meaningful interviews of proposal evaluation committee members.

## 6.9.2 Read the Solicitation

It is good practice, at this point in the process, to begin noting any inconsistencies between the description of the source selection process described in the solicitation and the concerns of the aggrieved contractor. The questions for proposal evaluation committee members drafted during the previous step should be expanded during this process. Refining the questions as more facts are discovered assists the responsible official in conducting more meaningful interviews. However, it is also possible that some of the earlier questions can be answered during the reading of the solicitation and, therefore, eliminated.

## 6.9.3 Read the Proposal Evaluation Team Instructions

Any inconsistencies between the instructions provided to the committee members and the solicitation should be noted at this point in the process. Such inconsistencies could have resulted in an anomalous proposal evaluation that would support the aggrieved contractor's contention. The official evaluating the facts, at this point, is able to further refine the questions for committee members to determine whether they performed according to or contrary to the instructions they received.

## 6.9.4 Review the Policy and Procedures

This step is necessary to determine whether the source selection process described in the solicitation and the instructions provided to the committee members were consistent with the agency's policies and procedures.

## 6.9.5 Review the Proposal Evaluation Record

This review is undertaken to determine whether the committee members complied with the source selection process described in the solicitation, ensure that the committee evaluated the proposals according to the criteria in the solicitation, determine whether weighted criteria were properly applied (if applicable), determine whether the committee members used proportional scores for the life cycle cost or proposed price (as applicable), search for inconsistencies between the instructions given to committee members and the record of the proposal evaluation process, note inconsistencies between agency policy and procedures and the record of the source selection process, and draft additional questions to ask committee members during the subsequent interviews.

## 6.9.6 Finalize the Questions for Proposal Evaluation Committee Members

At this point, the questions that were drafted during the earlier activities should be edited and organized to place them in a logical sequence in preparation for interviews of the proposal evaluation committee members. These activities prepare the agency official responsible for evaluating the merits of the protest to conduct meaningful interviews of the proposal evaluation committee members.

## 6.9.7 Interview Proposal Evaluation Committee Members

Completion of the preceding tasks provides the agency official evaluating the merits of the proposal with thorough insight into the solicitation and source selection activities that occurred, as well as the documentation of the proposal evaluation committee's actions. However, it is essential to interview the proposal evaluation committee members to obtain the in-depth knowledge of those activities that is essential for making a determination on the validity of the committee's decision. Failure to reach a fair and logical determination could unnecessarily lead to an appeal to a higher authority within the agency or litigation to resolve the matter through the court system. The objective of the interviews is to evaluate the activities of the committee members during the proposal evaluation process and evaluate their compliance with the ground rules established in the solicitation, instructions given to committee members, and agency policy and procedures. While a review of the source selection documentation provided meaningful insight into the propriety of the committee's activities, the interview process provides considerable insight into the mindset of the committee members and the level of their objectivity and sincerity in selecting the contractor that is best qualified to perform the services contracted out by the agency.

## 6.9.8 Synthesize the Information to Make a Determination

At this point in this process, the agency official synthesizes the information acquired through reading the protest, solicitation, and instructions provided to proposal evaluation committee members; reviewing the agency's policies and procedures governing protests, as well as the records developed by the proposal evaluation committee members during the source selection process; and reviewing the results of the interviews of proposal evaluation committee members. Synthesizing this information prepares the official evaluating the protest to form an opinion with respect to the merits of the protest and to make a determination on the propriety of the proposal evaluation committee's decision. The process should include consideration of the possibility that favoritism was afforded the apparent successful contractor. Although it is unlikely that favoritism was involved in the proposal evaluation process, the mere chance that favoritism could have been a factor requires consideration of this possibility.

This process could reveal that the proposal evaluation team could have committed errors such as using proposal evaluation criteria taken from a standard template when, in fact, the criteria in the standard RFP template had been modified to suit the project. However, that would not automatically result in a reversal of the contractor selection decision or need to cancel the award of the contract and solicit proposals anew. If it could be determined and documented that the proposal evaluation committee would have reached the same conclusion if the error had not been committed, there is a possibility that a determination could be made that the award was proper and the contract should be awarded despite certain inconsequential errors.

If it is determined that the proposal evaluation committee erred and that the contract award decision was flawed, but that there were insufficient grounds to award the contract to the protesting company, there is a compromise solution that would fall short of canceling the solicitation and calling for a new RFP to be sent to all contractors on the original list of solicited contractors. That compromise solution is to request both the contractor that was originally selected and the aggrieved contractor to submit a best and final offer (BAFO). If there were responsive proposals from other responsible contractors that could conceivably be competitive with respect to the contract, they should also be requested to submit a BAFO. This is necessary to comply with full and open competition requirements and to ensure that all prospective contractors are treated equally. The file should be documented with the rationale for not requesting BAFOs from any company that submitted a proposal. This documentation is necessary in the event the company that was not offered an opportunity to submit a BAFO elects to protest that decision. If the original solicitation did not specify a structured evaluation procedure or weighted criteria, local procedures may permit refinement to the selection process for the BAFOs to introduce a more structured evaluation process and possibly the use of weighted criteria. If it is decided to modify the evaluation process, it is necessary to advise all contractors being requested to submit BAFOs of the need to consider the revised evaluation procedures and revised ground rules.

## 6.10 Document the Determination

Once an opinion has been formed with respect to the merits of the source selection decision, the official evaluating the merits of the protest needs to memorialize his or her decision and prepare a response to the aggrieved contractor. A more formal approach may involve a memorandum to the record to memorialize the merits of the source selection decision plus a letter to the aggrieved contractor. However, in most cases, the file copy of the letter to the aggrieved contractor should suffice.

In practice, the evaluation of the merits of the source selection committee results lead to a determination that the committee did follow agency procedures and did make the proper source selection decision. In this event, the company that expended the time, effort, and expense to prepare a proposal and to follow through with considerable added effort to protest the contractor selection is certainly deserving of a comprehensive written response to their protest. The public agency official making the decision to deny the protest signs the letter advising the protesting company of the details of her or his determination. The letter advising the protesting company of such an adverse determination should include instructions for filing an appeal. Without instructions for filing an appeal, the aggrieved contractor may send the appeal to the incorrect official or proceed directly to litigation. The appeal instructions should include the name and address of the official who should receive the appeal, as well as the deadline for filing the appeal and the timeline for the agency's response. Failure to provide this information would likely damage the agency's right to follow through on the determination if the aggrieved contractor sends its appeal to the wrong address or files the appeal after the due date.

If investigation of the activities of the source selection committee led to a determination that the contract should have been awarded to the aggrieved contractor or some other contractor, then an entirely different course of action is required. When it is determined that the contractor was improperly selected, the alternative actions for the agency to consider are:

- Terminate the contract and award it to the appropriate company.
- Request a BAFO from all the responsible contractors that submitted responsive proposals or proposals that could likely be made responsive. In this event, consideration may be given to providing more structure and objectivity to the source selection process for evaluation of the BAFOs.
- Cancel the solicitation and release a revised solicitation. Just as with the request for BAFOs, consideration may be given to incorporating greater structure and objectivity into the source selection process for evaluating the new proposals.

When evaluation of the protest, solicitation, and instructions provided to members of the proposal evaluation committee, agency policies and procedures, record of the source selection process, and interview of proposal evaluation committee members clearly lead to the determination that the contract should have been awarded to the aggrieved contractor, however, the source selection decision must be reversed. If the contract had been awarded erroneously, the termination clause for the improperly awarded contract requires review to determine the process and timeline for terminating that contract and awarding a replacement contract to the aggrieved contractor.

When reversing a source selection decision, notification of the contractor originally selected for contract award is required. In the event that the contract had not been awarded, a letter to the originally selected contractor is recommended. However, because either one of these alternatives is considered a major setback for the contractor that was originally selected for award of the contract, a telephone call alerting the previously selected contractor of this decision prior to receiving the letter is advised. Full disclosure of the facts leading to the reversal of the selection decision should be provided in the letter. This is essential because complete disclosure of the facts leading to the agency's reversal of the selection decision is the best approach to discouraging yet another protest.

When it is necessary to reverse the source selection decision following contract award, termination of the contract that was erroneously awarded is also required. Full disclosure of the reasons for reversing the contractor selection decision and terminating the contract should be included in the first communication to the contractor facing contract termination. Complete disclosure of the facts leading to the agency's reversal of the selection decision is the best approach to discouraging a protest from the contractor that was originally selected for award of the contract. Just as in the case where the contract had not been awarded, the contractor should be advised of this decision by telephone prior to receipt of the letter. The receipt of a personal telephone call to deliver the announcement of such an adverse decision helps avoid the impersonality associated with a letter containing this unwelcome news.

The added workload and general negativity accompanying the receipt and processing of protests should cause public agencies to periodically review the content of the solicitation and source selection practices with the objective of implementing the measures for preventing protests that were discussed in the beginning of this chapter.

## 6.11  Conclusion

Protests are lodged by contractors that are aggrieved because they feel that the contractor selection process was flawed, or that one of their competitors was otherwise improperly selected for award of a contract that should have been awarded to their company. Receipt of a protest is always unwelcome because it is an indication that a contractor perceives that the agency's contractor selection process is deficient or that the integrity of the agency's officials or employees is questioned. Reaction to receipt of a protest normally creates a significant strain on the agency's resources because considerable time is required by the official designated to investigate the circumstances surrounding the contractor selection process. However, this is a necessary process that is needed to make a determination based on the merits of the protest. The investigation normally consumes additional time from the participants in the proposal evaluation process who need to be interviewed by the agency official who investigates the contractor selection process. A protest made prior to the award of a contract most likely delays award of the contract and delays the commencement of the project and could conceivably result in cancellation of the project.

The significance of the impact on agency operations as a result of the receipt of a protest makes implementation of measures to avoid receipt of protests a high priority for state and local government agencies. Legitimate measures to help prevent the filing of protests by aggrieved contractors include a logical process for evaluating proposals that includes equal treatment of all prospective contractors, disclosure of the proposal evaluation process and evaluation criteria in the solicitation, strict adherence to the process and evaluation of the proposals solely on the criteria stated in the solicitation, a description in the solicitation of the agency's procedure for filing protests, and the requirement for prospective contractors to obtain a debriefing prior to filing a protest.

Due to the criticality and sensitivity of protests and because of the complexity of the process for investigating the proposal evaluation process to develop a determination on the merits of the protest, agencies are urged to develop policies and procedures for dealing with protests. Complete and comprehensive policies and procedures require sufficient detail to include implementation of all the measures discussed in the proceeding paragraph that are recommended for avoiding protests. Policies and procedures also require coverage of the need to coordinate with in-house legal counsel upon the initial indication that a protest may be filed or has been filed. Inclusion of the procedure for investigating the proposal evaluation process to develop a determination on the merits of the protest is also recommended.

A thorough and complete investigation of the circumstances surrounding the proposal evaluation process involves a critical reading of the protest filed by the aggrieved contractor as well as reading the solicitation, reading the agency's protest policy and procedures and the proposal evaluation team's instructions, and noting any inconsistencies between these documents. Once this background information has been gathered, the official investigating the proposal evaluation process is ready to review the evaluation team's record of their activities leading to the selection of the successful contractor. During the entire process described above, the agency official needs to begin the drafting of questions to pose to members of the proposal evaluation team. Once the questions are finalized, the official can schedule and conduct proposal evaluation team member interviews.

Following the interviews, the official who must make a determination on the merits of the protest has assimilated a large amount of data to synthesize in order to form a determination. The determination needs to be communicated to all interested parties. The information is normally communicated in writing to document the proceedings; however, a telephone call or personal meeting in advance of the written decision is the professional method for advising parties that are due to receive an adverse determination. If the protesting contractor is to be advised that the protest is denied, it is advisable that the letter to the contractor include the procedures for appealing the determination. Providing information on the option to appeal the decision may avert the initiation of litigation by the contractor.

## Chapter 7

# Contract Negotiations, Ethics, and Conflicts of Interest

## Chapter Objectives

This chapter provides readers with considerable guidance in conducting contract negotiations and on organizational and personal standards for ethics and conflicts of interest. Following a brief introduction to the subject of negotiations, there is an explanation of ethical considerations for government negotiators.

One simplified approach to conducting negotiations is for the government negotiator to request a best and final offer (BAFO). When requesting a BAFO, an agency representative asks one or more prospective contractors to submit a revision to their proposal that is not subject to further negotiations. In some cases, the agency may provide a revised scope of work or other contract changes that must be considered when the contractors prepare their BAFOs. There is also a discussion on how government negotiators can use requests for BAFOs to ensure equal treatment of prospective contractors. Guidance for requesting BAFOs is thoroughly explored in this chapter.

When more formal negotiations are required, the government establishes a negotiating team and assigns roles to team members. Readers are also provided with guidelines to follow when preparing for negotiations. Advice is provided on the agency's reaction to certain objectionable or unacceptable contract provisions that may be proposed by contractors. The contract clauses discussed in this chapter that may include objectionable or unacceptable provisions are:

- Applicable law and forum
- Exorbitant late fees
- Onerous indemnity provisions
- Termination
- Insurance
- Reimbursement
- Cost plus a percentage of cost
- Contract changes
- Nondiscrimination
- Inspection
- Conflict of interest
- Data rights
- Automatic renewal

Additional contract negotiation topics discussed in this chapter include developing the negotiation plan, conducting negotiations, dealing with difficult situations during negotiations, concluding negotiations, and documenting the negotiation proceedings.

Following a brief introduction to the subject of ethics and conflicts of interest, readers are provided with information on organizational ethical standards, to include a threshold for unacceptable gratuities and a zero tolerance policy.

To provide readers with more insight into what they may personally experience during their involvement with state and local agency contracting, they are presented with a scenario involving a newly hired employee and yet another ploy to commit government employees to a particular contractor. These situations are followed by a discussion of government employees who initiate discussions regarding gratuities. The chapter concludes with a recommendation for government officials and employees to develop their own personal ethical standards.

## 7.1 Introduction to Negotiations

Conducting negotiations is considered by many government officials or employees to be more challenging and rewarding than any other aspect of their professional responsibilities. Despite the exhilaration experienced by numerous government negotiators, the thought of negotiating contracts seems foreign to many other state and local government officials and employees. The prohibition against negotiating with contractors that submit bids in response to an Invitation for Bids (IFB) is apparently so ingrained in some government representatives that they are reluctant to negotiate with contractors despite the fact that the terms and conditions, schedules, pricing, and all other aspects of proposals submitted in response to a Request for Proposals (RFP) are subject to negotiation. The right to negotiate should be included in the list of agency rights enumerated in the RFP, just as it is in the Best Practices RFP. The failure to include negotiations in the list of agency rights in the RFP may cause certain prospective contractors to object to the agency's attempt to initiate negotiations. Certain state and local government representatives occasionally resist negotiation. The reluctance by government officials or employees to initiate negotiations could be the result of a lack of training in negotiation techniques or a lack of experience in conducting negotiations. Regardless of the reason that certain state and local government officials avoid conducting negotiations, they are actually retreating from participating in one of the most challenging and rewarding activities they are likely to encounter in their government careers.

Negotiations are considered "undertaken" when the contracting agency enters into discussions with a prospective contractor or present contractor in an attempt to modify the price, schedule, terms and conditions, or any other element of the contractor's proposal or resultant contract. Solicitations often include a statement by the contracting agency to advise prospective contractors that the contracting agency may enter into negotiations or to award a contract based on the initial proposal without conducting negotiations. When such a statement is included in the solicitation, the prospective contractors are normally advised that they should include their best pricing and other terms and conditions in their initial proposal. Government organizations frequently establish objectives to establish pricing for government contracts that is both fair and reasonable. *Fair pricing* refers to pricing that enables contractors to recover their allowable and allocable direct and indirect costs and earn a reasonable profit. The rationale for negotiating pricing that permits contractors to recover their full costs plus a reasonable profit is that the government benefits from a long-term relationship with an ongoing successful company, and companies are not likely to be there for the long term if they are not profitable. *Reasonable pricing* refers to pricing that provides the contracting agency with the receipt of services at a price that does not exceed the reasonable value of the services received.

## 7.2 Ethics for Government Negotiators

Negotiations conducted by government officials or employees differ greatly from mere dickering over prices for commodities purchased for personal use, and also differ from negotiations conducted in the private sector. Government negotiators are generally held to higher ethical standards in that they are required to treat all prospective contractors equally, are prohibited from revealing any features of one contractor's proposal to potential competitors, should avoid requesting multiple best and final offers (BAFOs), and should seriously consider the avoidance of engaging in auctioneering techniques. The word "final" in the term "best and final offer" implies that the government does not ask for multiple BAFOs. Auctioneering techniques place great pressure on prospective contractors to offer prices lower than any of their competitors. The danger in this approach is that contractors may decide to offer pricing that covers their variable cost plus a small contribution to their fixed cost, but actually represents a loss when compared to total costs. Although a contractor may be able to use such pricing occasionally, repeated pricing in this manner may result in company failure and the loss of one of the agency's contractors.

Individuals oftentimes tend to identify a favorite team or participant when observing a competitive event. Developing a favorite contractor during a competitive procurement is, however, a dangerous practice that should be avoided. The danger is that the favored contractor status may cause a government representative to give favored treatment to such favored contractors. During some competitive procurements, the representatives from one contractor may appear to be so obnoxious that the government official or employee may abhor the thought of rewarding their negotiation team through award of a contract to their company. Whenever the government official or employee suspects that she or he has developed a favorite contractor, in such a competitive situation, consideration should be given to recusing oneself from participating in the decision-making process. Failure to recuse oneself in this situation could constitute a conflict of interest. If such recusal is considered too severe a reaction, the government official or employee might consider advising the government negotiation team leader of the potential conflict of interest, or at least make a conscious effort to ensure that all competing contractors are treated equally during all phases of the contractor selection, negotiation, and award process. However, in this situation, recusal would likely be the preferred alternative.

The agency's team responsible for negotiating a new contract is oftentimes a holdover from the proposal evaluation team. However, there could be some adjustment to the team membership prior to commencement of negotiations. Efforts to ensure that information in one prospective contractor's proposal is not revealed to a competitor during the proposal evaluation phase must continue through the negotiation phase of the contractor selection process. Government officials or employees who are experienced in contract negotiations are generally conditioned against violating the precept of proposal confidentiality. However, lesser-experienced government officials and employees may be called on to participate in or even lead the government's negotiation team. Although ethical negotiation policies are likely included in the continuing training for contracting professionals and other government officials who regularly participate in contract negotiations, this should not excuse them from receiving negotiation ethics training along with other negotiation team members whenever an ad hoc negotiation team is formed. The receipt of negotiation ethics training in a group setting increases the consciousness with respect to ethical issues that arise during team activities. If such training is not provided by the agency, then the negotiation team leader may develop instructions, based on the agency's policies, for negotiation team members to conduct ethical negotiations. The instructions would naturally be consistent with agency policy with respect to maintaining the confidentiality of proposals, equal treatment of all prospective contractors, and disclosure of any actual or apparent conflicts of interest, yet reinforce the objective for striving to meet the agency's negotiation objectives.

## 7.3 Requesting a Best and Final Offer (BAFO)

When negotiations are conducted with multiple prospective contractors, consideration must be given to ensure that all contractors are treated equally. Requesting a BAFO from all prospective contractors that have been selected as finalists is an excellent tool to ensure such equal treatment. A BAFO is often requested following negotiations restricted to the contractor that was selected for contract award. However, it is also possible to negotiate the features desired for inclusion in the resultant contract with all the finalist contractors and to ensure that all the finalists have an identical understanding of the contracting agency's objectives and needs. Once the negotiator, or negotiating team, is confident that all the contractor finalists have the same understanding of the contracting agency's objectives and needs with respect to the contract, all finalists can be asked to submit a BAFO. If the agency finds that it is necessary to revise the scope of work or the terms and conditions to resolve any issues that arose during discussions with the contractors, then the request for BAFOs should be conditioned on the revised scope of work or terms and conditions. Conditioning the request for BAFOs on the revised scope of work ensures that the BAFOs are based on the same scope of work and can, therefore, be assumed to be made on an equal basis. To further ensure that the BAFOs are considered on an equal basis, the request for a BAFO should provide a format for BAFO submittals. Providing a format for BAFO submittals is similar to specifying the format for proposal submittals; however, at this point in the selection process, it is likely that the contracting agency has learned enough about the pricing structure to be even more specific when designing the format for contractors to follow. For example, if the contractors are to be reimbursed on the basis of hours charged to the contract by employees from various professional fields, the BAFO format may identify the relevant professional fields and require the contractors to indicate the estimated number of hours and billing rates for each relevant profession. The pricing format may also provide for pricing of several tasks or categories of expenses that were not apparent prior to review of the original proposals. Whenever contractors are to be reimbursed on an hourly basis or for the actual cost of expenses, the BAFO format should provide a space for a not-to-exceed (NTE) price. The NTE price can then be used to compare the price criteria on an equal basis for all the prospective contractors. When overhead is applied to expenses, it is essential that the resultant reimbursement methodology does not constitute a cost-plus-a-percentage-of-cost (CPPC) arrangement that provides an incentive for contractors to spend lavishly. If a contractor insists on charging overhead as a percentage of an actual cost or hourly rate, the CPPC feature can be nullified by including an NTE to the overhead charge, the expenses subject to overhead charges, or to the entire contract.

In the interest of fairness, the government official or employee should not request BAFOs until there has been a meeting of the minds with respect to the contracting agency's expectations for the content and format of the resultant contract. Otherwise, the document might not meet all the essential elements of a contract. Once there is a mutual understanding with respect to the content of the resultant contract, the opportune time for requesting a BAFO has been reached. The government official or employee must be prepared to accept the conditions of the BAFO. Because BAFOs represent the "best" and "final" "offers" from the finalists, the contracting agency must be prepared to accept these submittals as the best offers that the competing finalists are prepared to make, and that they are "final" in that the contracting agency cannot request submittal of additional BAFOs just because they are not satisfied with the initial results. Prospective contractors have the right, although rarely exercised, to increase their pricing when submitting a BAFO. Dissatisfaction with the BAFOs does not mean that the contracting agency is required to accept the BAFO with the most favorable rating. The RFP should have listed all the contracting agencies rights, just as in the sample RFP, to include rejection of all proposals or to cancel the immediate solicitation and prepare a revised solicitation that addresses the problems that resulted in an unsuccessful attempt to enter into a contract for a particular service. Failure to list all the agency's rights could result in a challenge from prospective contractors should the agency wish to exercise any of those rights, such as the right to withdraw the RFP and cancel the procurement.

# 7.4 Assigning Roles to Negotiation Team Members in Interactive Negotiations

A more formal alternative to requesting BAFOs is to conduct negotiations with a prospective contractor on a fully interactive basis. Such fully interactive negotiations are frequently conducted in a face-to-face meeting where pricing and other individual aspects of the contract provisions are addressed. However, the fully interactive approach to negotiations can be conducted by telephone or e-mail in much the same manner. The government negotiator does not necessarily need to be the sole negotiator. A pre-negotiation strategy meeting should be held prior to any significant fully interactive negotiations. This timing is necessary to avoid the possibility that one or more of the agency representatives are installed in a negotiation without adequate preparation. During this meeting, the negotiation team leader should determine what elements of the contractor's proposal or the contract provisions need to be negotiated and identify the desired negotiation outcome or goals. This course is necessary to plan for offers and counter-offers to be proffered by the government negotiating team. The negotiation strategy should be tailored to reach the agency's goals, and a team member or team members should be assigned to conduct the negotiations if the agency is to have an opportunity to reach the desired outcome. During the pre-negotiation strategy meeting, there could likely be a consensus developed that the contract manager negotiates terms and conditions, that the finance (or auditor) representative negotiates the reimbursement provisions, and that the project manager negotiates technical issues and contract price. However, the breakout of negotiation responsibilities should always consider the strengths and weaknesses of the negotiation team members. A team member who is an accomplished analyst but is hesitant to engage actively in negotiations would likely make his or her best team contribution by performing analyses and leaving the negotiations to other team members. Whenever negotiation responsibilities are assigned to more than one negotiator, a lead negotiator needs to be designated to ensure that the negotiation team does not attempt to negotiate a contract without having proper guidance. The selection of an inexperienced lead negotiator or the failure to designate a lead negotiator is likely to impair the possibility of reaching negotiation objectives.

## 7.5  Preparing for Negotiations

Careful preparations are needed to ensure that negotiations are successful and avoid the embarrassment associated with a lack of preparedness when negotiations commence. One straightforward approach to preparing for negotiations is to evaluate the contractor's proposal and identify any features that are entirely unacceptable, objectionable, or merely undesirable. This evaluation should be multidisciplinary and include the project manager, legal counsel, and contracting professional. The multidisciplinary approach helps to ensure that all aspects of the contract that should be addressed are included in the negotiation plan.

When negotiations are scheduled with just one contractor, the need to treat all prospective contractors equally is no longer a burden. However, when a contractor realizes that there are no competitors, the negotiations can be expected to be decidedly more difficult. When negotiating with a sole contractor, the leverage associated with a competitive environment is not available.

Although the contracting agency has less leverage when negotiating with a single contractor, the need to identify entirely unacceptable, objectionable, or merely undesirable features of the contractor's position still exists. The mere fact that a contractor is the only company being considered for a contract may fortify its insistence on maintaining its proposed contract provisions. For example, when negotiating with out-of-state contractors, they may insist that the contract be construed and interpreted according to the laws of the state where the out-of-state contractor is based. However, such terms and conditions would be unacceptable for virtually every state and local government agency because the contracting agency is normally prohibited from subjecting its agency to the jurisdiction of another state. One other category of an unacceptable feature in a contractor's proposal would be an exception taken to a mandatory flow-down provision. When granting agencies require that certain provisions be absent from contracts funded by grants such as the prohibition against giving preference to local contractors during proposal evaluation and contract award decisions, or that certain provisions be included in contracts such as a nondiscrimination clause, it is essential that the contracting agency fully comply with the grant provisions. Subsequent audits of noncompliant contracts could result in the need to repay grant funds to the granting agency.

# 7.6 Objectionable or Unacceptable Contract Provisions

Contracting agencies include a model services contract with the agency's standard terms and conditions, accompanied by a statement that the agency intends to award a contract essentially in the form of the model contract, to encourage prospective contractors to accept the agency's standard contract provisions. If the contracting agency's standard terms and conditions are well balanced with respect to the rights and obligations afforded both the contracting agency and the contractor, there is a considerably higher probability that the standard terms and conditions are acceptable to prospective contractors. However, there is always the possibility that the proposing contractors may wish to substitute their own terms and conditions, supplement the standard terms with their own provisions, or that they may wish to make changes to the contracting agency's standard provisions.

In any event, exceptions to the contracting agency's standard terms and conditions are likely to introduce provisions that are considered objectionable to the government agency. Examples of contractor introduced objectionable provisions are discussed below.

## 7.6.1 Applicable Law and Forum

Contract provisions that would require the state or local government agency to be subject to the laws of a state other than its own, as mentioned earlier, are not only objectionable, but must be considered unacceptable. Contractors are generally willing to concede in negotiations to accept the applicability and forum of the contracting agency's state. Occasionally, a contractor located within the contracting agency's state may propose terms and conditions that require suits to be heard in the contractor's home county. When faced with such a proposal, the government negotiator should consider negotiating a change to a mutually acceptable neutral county. This arrangement eliminates the possibility of home county advantage to both negotiating parties.

## 7.6.2 Exorbitant Late Fee

Exorbitant late fees are often found in contractors' payment provisions. It is not uncommon to discover fees charged for late receipt of payments at the rate of

5 percent per month. A late fee in the amount of 5 percent per month may be overlooked during the reading of verbose contract provisions, or the abject failure to read the contract terms and conditions. However, such an exorbitant rate is equal to approximately 60 percent per year if the payment is made 30 days late. Should the payment be made 15 days late, the percentage rate for the late fee would be approximately 120 percent annually. When faced with the need to review such verbose contract provisions, the reader is advised to call into practice the adage, "Read the contract."

### 7.6.3 Onerous Indemnity Provisions

Contract provisions that require the contracting agency to indemnify the contractor for all acts of the agency's employees while failing to require the contractor to indemnify the contracting agency for even the negligent acts or omissions or willful misconduct of the contractor's employees are clearly unacceptable.

### 7.6.4 Termination

Contract provisions that provide termination rights solely to the contractor and lack any termination provisions for the contracting agency are not entirely uncommon in standard terms and conditions proposed by prospective contractors. However, government agencies should always attempt to negotiate termination rights for their agency that are no less than equal to the contractor's termination rights. There is no known rational reason for a contractor to have contract termination rights that are superior to the government's termination rights.

### 7.6.5 Insurance

Contract provisions that fail to guard against inherent risks associated with the work to be performed also require thoughtful negotiation. Contractors have been known to propose insurance coverage that provides less protection than their standard insurance coverage. There is also the possibility that a particularly high-dollar-value contract or high-risk contract may present a risk to the agency that is greater than the amount of insurance coverage included in the contracting agency's standard terms and conditions. Simply asking the contractor for the level of insurance coverage maintained by the firm may reveal a willingness to increase the coverage to a level commensurate with the risk.

## 7.6.6 Reimbursement

Contract provisions that require payment of invoices within a time period unreasonable to the needs of the contracting agency's ability to process payments, or that specify reimbursable expenses that are not acceptable to the contracting agency, are good candidates for negotiations to reach mutually acceptable alternatives.

## 7.6.7 Cost Plus a Percentage of Cost

Cost plus a percentage of cost (CPPC) reimbursement provisions could constitute the entire reimbursement scheme or just a portion of the reimbursement scheme proposed by prospective contractors. Just as the name suggests, this cost reimbursement scheme involves payment of the contractor for the actual costs incurred plus a fee calculated as a percentage of those costs. The danger with this type of a reimbursement scheme is that the fee, which may constitute the contractor's profit or a portion thereof, results in profits that are proportional to the contractor's expenses. This arrangement has motivated some contractors to spend lavishly to maximize their profits. In some reimbursement provisions, there may be no CPPC arrangement with respect to payment of hourly labor costs, but materials or expenses may be reimbursable on a CPPC basis. If the negotiator is unsuccessful in completely removing the CPPC element from the reimbursement provisions, an alternative strategy is to propose a not-to-exceed (NTE) limit on the fee. Such an NTE limitation effectively nullifies the CPPC element from the reimbursement provisions.

## 7.6.8 Contract Changes

Provisions for changing contracts that do not require all changes to be mutual and written could leave the contracting agency open to contested changes to the contract that are difficult to successfully challenge. The mere suggestion by the contracting agency's negotiator to modify a proposed changes clause to require that changes be in writing and agreed to in advance by both parties to the contract is usually sufficient to effect such a change.

## 7.6.9 Nondiscrimination

Provisions for nondiscrimination that do not include all protected classes or that include unacceptable terminology describing the protected classes definitely require negotiation to reach agreement on acceptable contract provisions. Earlier versions of nondiscrimination provisions contained the currently unacceptable terms "handicap" or "handicapped" in lieu of the now-acceptable "disabled" or "persons with disabilities." Whenever such earlier versions of nondiscrimination provisions are discovered in proposed contract terms and conditions, they should be the subject of negotiations to ensure that current, acceptable terminology is used in the contract. When the use of outdated, inappropriate terminology is discovered in contract provisions, it is recommended that the entire provision be compared to existing mandatory nondiscrimination clauses. Another nondiscrimination clause deficiency that is likely to be discovered in such clauses with outdated terminology is the prohibition for discriminating against persons with physical disabilities. This provision was subsequently changed to prohibit discrimination against persons with physical or mental disabilities.

## 7.6.10 Inspection

Provisions for inspection that fail to provide the contracting agency with reasonable access to the contractor's facilities where the work is to be performed are generally unreasonable. When the representatives of the contracting agency feel that they have a real need for access to the contractor's facilities where the work is to be performed, the negotiator would likely be able to negotiate the granting of access during normal business hours with sufficient advance notice of the visit.

## 7.6.11 Conflict of Interest

Provisions regarding conflicts of interest that are inconsistent and inadequate when compared with the contracting agency's stated conflict-of-interest policies should be cause for concern. Government officials or employees should delve into the reasons that a prospective contractor insists on diluted conflict-of-interest provisions. Insistence on the absence of or diluted conflict-of-interest provisions may be an indicator of a contractor that has integrity issues.

## 7.6.12 Data Rights

Contract provisions for data rights that fail to give the contracting agency ownership of data that is developed during the course of the contract work rewards the contractor with ownership of the work product that was developed through agency funding. Software developers that have developed complex computer systems, and merely develop added coding to permit the contracting agency to use the previously developed software, should not be expected to relinquish their rights to the previously developed software. However, negotiators should seek contracting agency ownership of software or other work products that are developed entirely during the course of the contracting effort. It is reasonable for the agency to seek ownership rights when it paid for the software development.

### 7.6.13 Automatic Renewal

Evergreen clauses are those contract provisions that provide for automatic renewal of contracts in the absence of a termination letter sent a stated number of days in advance of the contract completion date. Such "evergreen clauses" generally require receipt of the termination letter 30, 60, 90, or even 120 days in advance of the contract completion date. Evergreen clauses are often proposed by contractors in industries that typically write multiyear contracts. There is a good chance that between contract execution and the final three or four months of a three- or five-year contract, the agency assigns a new contracts manager or project manager. Even when there is no such change in personnel, there is a fairly high probability that the contract end date is extended automatically due to the failure to send a termination letter on time to the contractor. Evergreen clauses rarely benefit the contracting agency. Therefore, contract professionals or other negotiators that detect an evergreen clause should seriously consider challenging the clause during negotiations. Agency employees occasionally fail to send a termination notice in time to negate the automatic renewal clause and are, therefore, surprised by the unexpected commitment to renew the contract. Evergreen provisions that extend the contract for multiple additional years are very rare; however, provisions for one-year extensions are commonplace. If the negotiator is not successful in negotiating away an evergreen clause, it may be possible to have the contract renew on a month-to-month basis following the initial contract period. If the contractor is entirely unwilling to eliminate or dilute the evergreen clause, the agency negotiator can execute the contract or have the contract executed by the agency's authorized individual, and then immediately following full execution of the contract, send the termination letter to the supplier. Sending the termination letter immediately following full contract execution effectively nullifies the evergreen clause. Termination letters, and other letters that have a significant impact on the contract, should be sent to the contractor via certified mail with a return receipt requested. The return receipt provides proof that the contractor received the letter. A copy of the letter and the signed return receipt should also be filed with the contract documents. Complete contract files are essential for protecting the agency's rights in the event that a contract dispute develops between the agency and the contractor.

## 7.7 Develop the Negotiation Plan

Once all elements of the proposal have been evaluated and the entirely unacceptable, objectionable, and undesirable features have been identified, the negotiation strategy or plan can be drafted. Members of the negotiating team should discuss all the features where changes to contract provisions are desired. Failure to include all required changes is likely to necessitate a subsequent negotiating session that could have been combined with the initial negotiating session. Particular attention should be given to the outcome desired through negotiations and how best to achieve that outcome. Concentration on the desired outcome orients the negotiating team toward negotiation objectives. A typical strategy is to develop an initial negotiation position that leaves room for compromise, the desired outcome, and a fallback position that represents the worst case, yet acceptable, position. For complex negotiations, the negotiation plan should be committed to writing. The initial negotiation position is normally presented verbally; however, it is generally beneficial to provide a written summary of the position to all members of both negotiating teams to avoid any misunderstanding of the offer or counter-offer.

While the contracting professional or any other member of the agency's negotiating team could present the entire position verbally, it is not unusual to divide the presentation such that the team members present aspects of the agency's offer within their particular area of expertise.

## 7.8 Conducting Negotiations

The written summary is necessarily more essential when the initial position is lengthy or complex. Following the verbal presentation of the negotiation position and delivery of the written summary, the opposing negotiating team is likely to pose questions in an effort to clarify the opposing team's understanding of the initial offer. Once the contractor's negotiating team understands the initial offer, their alternatives are to accept the offer or to make a counteroffer. However, in some instances, the contractor's team may reject the agency's offer or counteroffer or they may insist that the agency accept the contractor's previous offer or initial proposal. While acceptance of an initial offer or even a counteroffer could be made at this point, it is more likely that the contractor's team requires a private meeting to evaluate the agency's offer to determine what elements of the initial position are and are not acceptable. Depending on the complexity of the initial offer, the contractor may be able to discuss the offer during a caucus while the agency's negotiating team stands by or returns to their respective offices, or the contractor's negotiating team may prefer to return to their facility to perform a more detailed analysis of the agency's offer. Should the contractor elect to submit a counteroffer, the presentation of the counteroffer generally reflects those elements of the initial offer that are acceptable and those that are not acceptable. The counteroffer would not normally require a written summary unless the complexity of the counteroffer justified yet another summarizing document.

Should the contractor's team present a counteroffer, which is more likely than outright acceptance of the initial offer, the need for clarifying questions from the government team is expected. Once the counteroffer is fully understood, the contracting agency's lead negotiator may request a caucus to discuss the merits of the counteroffer. However, should the counteroffer be straightforward and include demands anticipated by the contracting agency's negotiating team, the negotiations may continue through a verbal exchange until agreement is reached, or until it is deemed necessary by either negotiating team to hold a caucus to decide privately upon the succeeding approach to continued negotiations. These steps can be repeated for numerous iterations until full agreement is reached. However, should it be determined that the discussions are not going to lead to imminent agreement, the agency's negotiating team might consider taking one or more actions discussed in the following section on dealing with difficult situations.

## 7.9 Dealing with Difficult Situations during Negotiations

Although some successful negotiators intentionally establish an adversarial relationship with the opposing negotiation team, establishing rapport and trust is generally a better approach for conducting successful negotiations. Despite the best efforts to establish rapport and trust, and for the negotiation teams to strive for common objectives, difficult situations can develop while participating in negotiations. Oftentimes, negotiators attempt to reach agreement on less significant points in order to begin with some level of agreement between the negotiating teams on the first or several of the first issues being negotiated. Eventually, however, there are likely to be more contentious issues to address. Should the negotiations reach an impasse, the agency's negotiating team may wish to agree to address the more contentious issue that caused the impasse later, make a change in the team member who is conducting the negotiations, take a break from negotiations, or agree to negotiate some less contentious issues. Although the agency may elect to make a change in the team member who is conducting the negotiations, there should be no change in the lead negotiator or dismissal of negotiating team members unless absolutely necessary. Continuity of the lead negotiator and team membership benefits the agency's team focus during the negotiation session. Regardless of the decision made to end the impasse, it would be hoped that the break, change in negotiators, or agreement on lesser issues helps facilitate the negotiation of the more contentious issues. When it becomes apparent that a change such as one of the above is needed, the lead negotiator may call for a break in negotiations or for a caucus. A break usually involves use of restrooms or partaking of snacks, while a caucus involves a separation of the negotiation teams for discussions that need to be kept secret from the opposing team. During the initial strategy meeting, the agency's negotiation team leader should determine who can call for a break and who can call for a caucus. Negotiating teams that permit any team member to call for a break or a caucus can be highly successful; however, such ground rules need to be established prior to the initiation of negotiations to avoid surprises or disagreements between team members.

## 7.10 Concluding and Documenting the Negotiations

At the conclusion of negotiations, when there has been mutual agreement on all aspects of the contract, there is normally a delay before the contract document containing the negotiated changes is ready for review and execution. Acknowledgment of reaching a negotiated position is generally made by an exchange of handshakes between lead negotiators or between the negotiating teams. At the conclusion of negotiations it is possible to generate the negotiated contract, initiate agency staff review, and plan for contract execution by the contractor and the agency.

When the contract itself, or negotiation thereof, is extensive and complex, documentation of the negotiation process provides useful background for future contractual actions. Written policies and procedures for the contracting function should specify negotiations that require documentation to provide the background that should be useful for future contractual actions. This documentation would typically be accomplished concurrently with preparation of the negotiated contract document. Once the contract document and negotiation memorandum are complete, the contract is normally signed by the contractor and then sent through the agency's review process prior to contract execution.

## 7.11 Introduction to Ethics and Conflicts of Interest

The framers of the U.S. Constitution recognized the propensity for conflicts of interest and other ethical lapses on the part of public servants. To discourage such transgressions, the framers included prohibitions against profiting from such lapses in Article I, Sections 6 and 9. Subsequent provisions in federal statutes, state constitutions, laws and codes, as well as local ordinances further prohibit such personal profiting by elected and appointed government officials and other government employees. In addition to these statutory prohibitions against conflicts of interest, moral values instilled through families, religious institutions, friends, and educators also caution against enriching oneself at the expense of others. Despite these constitutional, statutory, and moral prohibitions against profiting through ethical lapses, continuing media coverage of arrests, trials, convictions, incarcerations, and even occasional suicides by government officials and employees bespeaks persistent unethical practices to influence the award of contracts in return for personal gain. Although the number of people who commit such transgressions represents a minuscule percentage of public servants, the constant barrage of media coverage attests to the fact that this is a continuing significant problem facing all those involved in state and local government contracting.

There is no attempt in this chapter to discuss the individual statutes covering ethics and conflicts of interest for all 50 states or the regulations governing ethics issues promulgated by the multitude of local government agencies within the United States. However, there is a discussion of the development of organizational ethical standards by states and local government agencies, the actual experience of one contracting professional who was offered personal rewards from a contractor, agency representative initiated discussions for their own personal gain, and an approach to developing one's own ethical standards.

## 7.12 Organizational Ethical Standards

State and local government agencies, just as with federal agencies and private-sector companies, generally have published standards outlining their organization's policies with respect to ethical behavior and the avoidance of conflicts of interest. These standards typically include restrictions against both actual and perceived conflicts of interest.

The development of organizational standards for ethical behavior and the avoidance of conflicts of interest obviously constitute a challenging task for state and local government agencies. Developing the initial organizational policy, ongoing policy revisions to conform to changes in the organizational philosophy, and to accommodate previously unforeseen circumstances are needed to provide guidance to agency officials and employees, and to assure the constituency that such abuses of public office are not tolerated.

Officials who draft organizational ethical standards need to conduct research and include statutory and other conflict-of-interest restrictions that flow down from higher government levels to the ethical standards established for agency officials and employees.

Ideally, all government officials and employees would develop their personal ethical standards. However, there is always a group of employees that would, without organizational ethical standards, accept gratuities in exchange for favorable treatment of a contractor or prospective contractor. Based on the abundance of instances reported in the media, the existence of statutory prohibitions and organizational policies and regulations restricting the acceptance of gratuities, organizational standards have not entirely prevented the acceptance of gratuities. However, in the hopes that organizational ethical standards discourage certain employees from accepting gratuities and for establishing a framework for dealing with officials and employees who do accept unauthorized enrichment from contractors, it is necessary to develop organizational standards for ethical behavior.

The inclusion of whistleblower protection, compliance monitoring, and reporting requirements helps make agency ethical standards more effective. Whistleblower protection requires sound protection and generous rewards for honest employees who wish to report observed deficiencies in the ethical behavior of agency officials or employees. Monitoring compliance with and equal enforcement of violations of the organization's ethical standards are essential for a successful program to guard against activities that inappropriately enrich public officials and employees for selfish actions they take in their official capacity. The report element pertains to the reporting of income or other revenue received from sources other than the employee or official's agency compensation.

Some difficulties faced when drafting ethical behavior standards, in the absence of a zero-tolerance policy, include the fact that the agency tolerates illicit personal gain when it is below some predetermined dollar threshold, a conflict of interest involving a relative not included in the agency's definition of immediate family, and ethical behavior restrictions usually expire following some stated time period after the official or employee leaves office. Certain agencies may feel that restricting their officials and employees from accepting gifts as seemingly innocent as a cup of coffee and a pastry is acceptable. Other agencies may struggle with a contractor's enrichment of a relative not included in the agency's narrow definition of relatives considered as immediate family. When developing organizational policy, there is the concern regarding the propriety of restricting the enrichment of an official or employee one year or more after he or she left office. Some agencies have also struggled with the establishment of a zero-tolerance policy.

## 7.12.1 *Threshold for Unacceptable Gratuities*

Organizations faced with the task of developing thresholds for differentiating between acceptable and unacceptable ethical behavior, or updating existing ethical standards or thresholds, must face the difficult decisions regarding where to establish the difference between what behavior is acceptable and what behavior is not acceptable. In addition to the difficulty in establishing such a threshold, there is also the probability that establishing the value for some personal rewards involves some level of subjectivity. There is a certain level of subjectivity involved in establishing the difference between an acceptable gift and one that acceptance of which would constitute a breach of policy. In light of this subjectivity, some employees or officials may be tempted to err in favor of accepting the favor. However, more conscientious employees may decline the same or similar contractor offered rewards. The acceptance of low-value favors may lead to less reluctance to subsequent acceptance of more valuable favors and rationalization over the apparent value of gifts offered by contractors or prospective contractors.

When the agency's policy permits receipt of a certain dollar value gift or gratuity, it is necessary to establish the acceptable dollar value of gratuities and address the frequency with which such gifts may be accepted. There is also a need to determine if it is appropriate to establish differing gift and gratuity thresholds based on an official or employee's status or position title. Organizational ethical standards that establish the threshold at which gifts may or may not be acceptable may include differing thresholds for gratuities that must be periodically accepted, and the frequency for reporting gifts and gratuities. A listing of the nature of gifts and gratuities that may or may not be accepted and those that may or may not require reporting for public disclosure should be included in the organization's ethical standards. The organization's ethical standards must be unambiguous to guard against claims that officials or employees failed to understand that a particular situation was reportable. A partial list of gifts or gratuities that might be listed is provided below:

- Admission to conferences
- Entertainment
- Financial remuneration
- Gifts
- Honoraria
- Meals
- Outside employment
- Contributions to employee-supported organizations
- Post-employment offers
- Transportation
- Royalties
- Campaign contributions
- Any reward to relatives

## 7.12.2 Zero-Tolerance Policy

While the zero-tolerance approach would seem to eliminate the problem of establishing the distinction between the extents of personal enrichment that would constitute acceptable or unacceptable behavior, there could be a problem enforcing restrictions as severe as zero tolerance. One problem associated with enforcing a zero-tolerance policy would involve an agency official or employee who held a friendship with a prospective contractor that predated her or his agency employment, or who had a relative who works for a prospective contractor. Such relationships would likely include frequent social interaction and an historical exchange of gifts. One solution for dealing with such relationships would be to require the agency official or employee to recuse himself or herself whenever the prospective contractor in question is being considered for award of a contract or when decisions are made that affect current contractors that employ friends or relatives of agency officials or employees. If the official or employee has been recused in these cases, however, there could be the appearance of a conflict of interest should a subordinate assume the decision-making role. If the recused official is the chief elected or chief appointed official, then there could be little choice but to have a subordinate assume the decision-making role. If the contractor in question competes for a large number of agency contracts, the effectiveness of the official or employee who was frequently recused could also be questioned. Should an agency official or employee accept a cup of coffee from a contractor or prospective contractor, despite a zero-tolerance policy, the agency officials responsible for enforcement of the policy may feel that they would be viewed as petty for disciplining an offender for merely accepting a cup of coffee.

# 7.13 Scenario Involving a Newly Hired Employee

To help put the matter of conflicts of interest and acceptance of gratuities in perspective, it might be helpful to describe the actual experience of a novice contracting professional.

The incident involving the contracting professional occurred shortly after accepting his first contract management position. In this scenario, he was exposed to an outrageous offer from a prospective contractor on his first business trip. Despite the lack of any organizational training in ethics or the avoidance of conflicts of interest, he fortunately recognized the inappropriateness of the proffered rewards and made a determination at that early stage in his career to refuse all gratuities that exceeded the value of a cup of coffee. This decision was made and adhered to despite the fact that more senior members from his agency accepted considerably more generous gifts during that same business trip.

In this scenario, the prospective contractor telephoned the employee's office after the contracting professional boarded an aircraft for an official visit to the contractor's facility. During the conversation between the government agency and the contractor, the contractor's representative asked about the flight information and hotel accommodations for the organization's contracting team that would be visiting the contractor's facility. Upon learning when the team was arriving and where they were staying, contractor personnel made arrangements to arrive at the hotel in advance of the government visitors to prepare for their arrival. Contractor employees made arrangements with the personnel at the hotel registration desk to have the visitors meet them in the hotel bar. Following a round or two of drinks, where there was no visible bill to pay, it was learned that the contractor had made arrangements to travel to a more trendy local establishment. On the way to the second establishment, a contractor's representative asked the novice contracting professional what he liked to do for entertainment. When he responded that the establishment they selected seemed fine to him, the contractor's representative told him to name whatever entertainment he desired. Fortunately, despite the fact that the contracting professional was at such an early stage of his employment that he had yet to attend any agency ethics training, the representative's offer signaled an alarm rather than the promise of a reward. After the briefest of pauses, the professional's response to the offer for whatever entertainment he desired was to merely repeat his initial response. To ensure that he did not feel obligated to the contractor's representative, who was apparently attempting to make him feel indebted by providing drinks, transportation, and the promise of additional entertainment, the contracting professional made arrangements with the waiter at the local establishment to pay for a round of drinks. The contracting professional thereafter refrained from accepting anything further of value from the contractor. The novice contracting professional in a guarded manner handled all future relationships with representatives from this company. Despite the fact that more senior members of his organization appeared to be accepting favors beyond what he considered reasonable, he refused to accept any further corporate favors.

Having received what he considered an outlandishly blatant attempt to gain his loyalty through an initial offering of significant gratuities may have been his good fortune. Initially accepting small-dollar-value favors could slowly, or not so slowly, escalate to more valuable favors that may be more difficult to resist once the habit of accepting favors was established. Although his agency had published guidelines for gifts that could be accepted, he made several more business trips to contractor facilities and had numerous other contacts with corporate representatives prior to attending his first annual training in ethics and conflicts of interest. Fortunately, this early experience led to his development of personal ethical standards that exceeded the standards established by his first employer or any subsequent employers.

Numerous lessons can be learned from the initial business trip taken by this novice contracting professional. Organizations should ensure that training in ethics and conflicts of interest are included in their new-hire training program. Reliance on annual or other periodic training may result in the placement of new employees in situations where they must make decisions regarding ethics or conflicts or interest prior to being trained on these subjects. Agencies should also reconsider their policies to determine whether their policies regarding the acceptance of gifts are overly generous. Some organizations establish a relatively high gift threshold, such as $250, which does not require refusal or reporting of the gift. Some organizations with such relatively high gift thresholds further compromise the integrity of their employees' ethical behavior by permitting multiple gifts that do not exceed this threshold during any given year. Individuals who are interested in establishing their own personal ethical standards can gain insight into this process by reflecting on the above scenario and considering how they would have reacted in a similar situation, or how they will react if placed in a similar position in the future.

## 7.14 Yet Another Ploy to Make Government Employees or Officials Feel Committed to a Particular Contractor

A case of several corporations with significant sales of products to local government agencies is relevant despite the fact that a services contract was not involved in these cases. The corporations in question routinely invite department personnel who operate equipment manufactured by their company or a competitor to three-day to one-week visits at their facility. The trips are ostensibly to evaluate the company's manufacturing processes and determine whether the company is qualified to manufacture the needed equipment. These companies are also eager to assist the department personnel in justifying a sole source contract naming their corporation as the only contractor qualified to manufacture that particular equipment. Sole source justifications are often written shortly following the completion of the visits to the contractor's facilities. The contractor may provide the all-expense-paid trip prior to contract award or may promise the trip during the manufacture of the equipment for the agency. When it is discovered that such trips have been offered and accepted, department personnel have expressed a feeling of incredulity when they are advised that acceptance of such trips constitute a conflict of interest and are contrary to agency policy. To prevent the continuance of such inappropriate practices, contracting professionals and other agency officials need to promote periodic educational programs that inform all agency personnel that the acceptance of contractor or prospective contractor paid trips are contrary to agency policy and that employees who accept such trips are subject to disciplinary action. If department management officials feel that such trips to contractor facilities are needed, they should budget for agency payment for visits to the facilities of all competing contractors. The savings to the department through competitive procurements should more than offset the cost of the visits to the contractors' facilities. Although this example of another contractor ploy was drawn from equipment manufacturers, the lessons learned also apply to services contracting.

## 7.15 Government Employees or Officials Who Initiate Consideration of Gratuities

It is not always the corporation that initiates the discussion of gratuities in exchange for favorable consideration of contractual matters. Some government officials are also capable of initiating such discussions. In one actual instance that did not involve unethical behavior on the part of the contractor, a group of government project and contracting officials managed to undeservedly enrich themselves, although in a small way, without discussing the matter with contractor representatives. At that point in time, their agency's conflict-of-interest rules permitted government personnel to have a working lunch provided by a contractor if the government employees reimbursed the contractor for the fair value of the lunch. The same conflict-of-interest rules required contractors to provide a receptacle for depositing reimbursement by government personnel for the working lunch. The contractors were also required to post a statement indicating the fair value of the lunch. The contractor did provide such a receptacle and a clearly visible statement that the fair value of the lunch was $8.00 per person. Seven government employees participated in the working lunch with the contractor personnel. Several of the government employees were seen placing money in the receptacle that had been provided by the contractor. The receptacle was emptied for deposit of the funds in the appropriate account following the luncheon, and a total of $3.00 had been deposited for all seven government employees. Although the government had the right to audit the applicable account and to match the date that the funds were received with the names of the government officials who participated in the working lunch, that particular account had never been audited. It was possible that the minuscule amount of funds deposited in that account during the contractor's fiscal year precluded it from being flagged for audit. An interesting exercise would have been the examination of the travel claims for the government officials who participated in the working lunch to compare the amount they claimed for reimbursement for lunch with the amount deposited in the receptacle provided by the contractor. Regardless of whether or not the government employees claimed reimbursement for the cost of the working lunch, it was clearly an infraction of their conflict-of-interest rules to deposit nothing or just a token amount for a lunch that had a clearly identified value exceeding their actual contribution.

## 7.16 Personal Ethical Standards

Agency representatives with responsibility for drafting solicitations; writing sole source justifications; evaluating proposals; selecting contractors or recommending contractors for agency contracts; or negotiating, reviewing, or executing contracts and amendments undoubtedly have occasion to make choices regarding their responses to opportunities presented to accept or decline gifts or gratuities or to otherwise deal with actual or apparent conflicts of interest. Some agencies include training on agency policies and regulations regarding these issues for newly hired employees, periodically for those employees who are apt to be exposed to ethical issues, or both the initial and follow-on ethics training. In contrast to agencies with formal ethics training, there are also agencies that merely rely on their employees and officials to read the policies and regulations of their own volition. It is, naturally, preferable for agencies to conduct both initial and periodic follow-on training.

Regardless of the nature of the agency's ethics training, or even the existence of such a training program, the content of the policies and regulations often describe merely the maximum value of gifts or gratuities that can be accepted by agency officials and employees. The policies and regulations applicable to the agency also normally specify the dollar threshold level that requires the reporting of gifts and gratuities. Another view of the ethics policies and procedures is that they describe the maximum value of gifts and gratuities that can be accepted from contractors attempting to influence decisions regarding the contractor's business dealings with the agency. Yet another way to view the agency's ethics policies and regulations is that they describe the level of remuneration that public servants can accept with impunity.

Except for rare instances, the value of any contractor gift or gratuity is not usually great enough to have a significant impact on the official or employee's well-being. The constituency providing financial support and being served by the agency expects the agency representatives to pay for their livelihood through their compensation from the agency without reliance on added compensation from contractors. Based on these facts, public servants should seriously consider the merits of accepting anything of any value from contractors or prospective contractors. In the absence of an agency zero-tolerance gift and gratuity policy, public servants are encouraged to establish their own personal zero-tolerance policy and not accept anything of value from any contractor or prospective contractor. If such a personal zero-tolerance policy appears incompatible with traditional business lunches, contracting professionals should first question whether business lunches are more productive than office meetings. If the agency official or employee fully believes that business lunches are truly more productive than office meetings, then the cost of the business lunches can be evenly divided between the agency and the contractor.

The establishment of such a personal zero-tolerance policy with respect to acceptance of gifts and gratuities is consistent with ethical codes established by professional organizations for contracting professionals. Contracting professionals and other agency officials and employees who establish such a personal zero-tolerance policy certainly have earned the respect of their contemporaries for making such a commitment.

# 7.17 Conclusion

Conducting negotiations is often one of the most challenging, exhilarating, and rewarding activities experienced in the work environment by state and local government officials and employees. Although participating in negotiations may appear threatening to those who have yet to participate in this activity, most individuals who participate in negotiations find the challenges and interaction highly rewarding.

One fundamental approach to conducting negotiations is for the government negotiator to request a best and final offer (BAFO) from one or more prospective contractors. When the government negotiator is merely attempting to obtain a price concession without reducing the level of effort provided by the contractor, one approach would be to merely advise the contractor (or contractors) that their pricing is excessive and that they are requested to submit a BAFO. In certain situations, the negotiator may realize the need to reduce the level of the contractor's effort to achieve the government's pricing objective. In this event, it may be necessary to develop a scaled-back contract scope of work and request a BAFO based on the revised scope of work.

In more complex situations, the government may determine that more formal negotiations are required. In this case, the government normally establishes a negotiation team, assigns roles to negotiation team members, and the team prepares a detailed negotiation plan. Complex offers or counteroffers may be prepared in writing to ensure that there are no misunderstandings generated through the inherent limitations of verbal communications. When written offers are prepared, the contractor is more receptive if the offer is initially presented verbally in a personal meeting and a written copy of the offer is presented concurrently or immediately after the verbal presentation.

When contractors propose contract terms and conditions, they frequently include provisions that favor the contractor at the expense of the government or are otherwise unacceptable to the agency. Such objectionable or even unacceptable proposals relate to contract provisions regarding applicable law and forum, exorbitant late fees, onerous indemnity provisions, termination, insurance, reimbursement, cost-plus-a-percent-of-cost, contract changes, nondiscrimination, inspection, conflict of interest, data rights, and automatic renewal of contracts.

Like most significant activities, preparing for negotiations with a written negotiation plan enhances the preparation of negotiation team members. The development of such a plan that anticipates events that may occur during negotiations helps avoid surprises and provides for more professional conduct during negotiations. Rather than pressing forward with difficult situations during negotiations, it is occasionally better to avoid immediate adversarial relationships and to first establish rapport with the contractor's negotiating team before addressing the difficult issues. When it appears that an impasse is imminent or has occurred, the negotiators might try to reach agreement on less controversial contract provisions. Reaching agreement on simpler issues occasionally results in a more cooperative environment for reaching agreement when subsequently dealing with the more difficult issues. Making a change in negotiators, calling for a break, or calling for a caucus may also help in working through difficult negotiation issues.

Although issues involving ethics and conflicts of interest may seem a recent phenomenon, this problem was recognized and addressed by the framers of the U.S. Constitution. In addition to federal regulations, virtually all states and local governments have programs in place to limit abuses that improperly enrich government officials and employees through contract fraud. State and local government restrictions typically establish a dollar threshold that represents both acceptable values for gratuities that can be accepted and for gratuities that must be reported. Problems associated with these restrictions are that they concurrently establish a limit under which gratuities are acceptable and avoid reporting requirements. The frequency at which gratuities may be accepted are not consistently established, and the thresholds may be established at too high a level. However, establishing very low thresholds or zero-tolerance policies are also challenging. For example, if a zero-tolerance policy for gratuities is established and a government official or representative accepts a cup of coffee, it is unlikely that a government agency would endure the time and expense to discipline an offender for such an insignificant infraction.

It is necessary to establish reasonable thresholds to limit the actions of certain employees who are willing to accept gifts that would not have been proffered if not for their government position. However, the establishment of such thresholds does not prevent those employees who feel that the acceptance of gifts from private-sector companies at any dollar value is inappropriate from establishing their own personal zero-tolerance policy. Current government officials and employees, as well as public administration students who are in training for future careers in state or local government, are urged to establish their own personal zero-tolerance policy with respect to the acceptance of gratuities.

# Chapter 8

---

# Contract Document

---

## Chapter Objectives

Prior to the discussion of the best practices services contract recommended for all state and local government agencies, there are discussions of the essential elements of contracts and the various types of contracts. The best practices contract is based on the best features of the various services contracts provided by state and local government agencies participating in the research project conducted in preparation for writing this book.

Approximately one-quarter of the services contracts provided by the participating state and local government agencies incorporated the recommended one-page contract structure. The reasons for recommending this one-page format are explored in this chapter, along with a discussion of the attachments. The characteristics of the one-page contract format discussed are:

- One-page format
- Preamble
- Recitals
- Incorporation of documents
- Execution
- Contract attachments

Although the recommended contract terms and conditions are one of the three standard attachments, a thorough discussion of the terms and discussions is deferred until Chapter 9, "Contract Terms and Conditions." The attachments are referred to as the "standard attachments" because these three attachments are recommended for all services contracts; however, there are instances when it may be appropriate to incorporate additional attachments. The standard attachments recommended for incorporation in the one-page contract format are:

- Insurance provisions
- Scope of work
- Terms and conditions

## 8.1 Essential Elements of Contracts and Types of Contracts

The contract document awarded to the successful contractor must include all the essential elements of a contract, including offer, acceptance, consideration, competent parties, and must be awarded for a legal purpose. Otherwise, the contract may not be legally enforceable. Additionally, a contract is an agreement that is legally enforceable and reflects the relationship between two or more parties for a specific purpose. Contracts should be crafted to identify potential risks and describe how these risks are mitigated. Failure to identify the risks and means for mitigating the risks may lead to unanticipated problems during the contract performance period. There must be a meeting of the minds between the contracting parties.

As defined in Appendix A, "Glossary of Terms," the term "types of contracts" refers to the basis for compensating the contractor by the contracting agency. The preferred contract type is the firm fixed-price contract wherein the contractor is obligated to provide the services described in the scope of work by a date certain for a predetermined price. This contract type provides the least risk to the agency because unforeseen costs incurred by the contractor cannot be passed on to the agency. The price of fixed-price contracts is not increased unless there is a change in scope. To the contractor, a firm fixed-price contract provides the greatest financial risk but also encompasses the greatest potential for financial reward. The contractor is obligated to perform the services and complete all deliverables. If the predetermined fixed price was insufficient, the contractor is obligated to complete the work even though it would realize a financial loss. Alternatively, if the contractor is able to complete the work well below the estimated costs, it could realize a profit without limitation with respect to the percentage of its costs. While this lack of a limit on profit as a percentage of cost may appear alarming to constituents, government officials, and employees, it should not be of concern if the agency determined the pricing to be fair and reasonable prior to contract award. The preferred method for determining that the price is fair and reasonable is to select the contractor through free and open competition on the basis, for services contracts, of price and other factors.

In the absence of competition, it is more difficult to determine the fairness and reasonableness of the pricing. The amount budgeted for the project could be used for comparison to the contractor's price if the budget was based on an independent price estimate performed by an agency employee or consultant. If the budgeted amount was obtained by merely asking the contractor for an estimate, that amount could not be used to compare against the proposed amount later submitted by the same contractor that provided the budget estimate.

Cost reimbursement contracts, which are often used in federal contracting agencies for research and development programs, are not recommended for state and local government agencies unless they are involved in research and development projects that, due to the difficulty of accurately estimating the price, cannot be awarded on the basis of a fixed price. The Model Services Contract (MSC) is in the format of a fixed-price contract. There are provisions in the MSC to base contractor compensation on billing rates such as hourly rates for certain position classifications that are relevant to the services provided by the contractor. However, the establishment of a not-to-exceed (NTE) price, combined with the requirement for the contractor to provide the services described in the scope of work within the NTE pricing, results in a contract type that functions essentially as a fixed-price contract. State and local government agencies that determine it necessary to award cost reimbursement contracts might consider accessing the Federal Acquisition Regulations (FAR) to evaluate the provisions included in federal cost reimbursement contracts. The following definitions for contract types include both fixed-price and cost reimbursement contracts.

Fixed-price (FP) contracts are those contracts wherein payment to the contractor is based on a fixed price to be paid to the contractor for completion of specific elements of the scope of work or for completion of contract requirements in their entirety.

Firm-fixed-price (FFP) contracts are contracts wherein payment is based on completion of milestones or all the tasks in the scope of work without providing performance or other types of incentives developed to encourage the contractor to provide a product or service that exceeds the minimal specifications or for delivery in advance of the contractual delivery date.

Fixed-price contracts with escalation provisions are fixed-price contracts that provide for price adjustments based on inflation. When contracts contain provisions for inflation, they generally provide for both upward and downward price adjustments based on inflationary, or deflationary, changes during future time periods. The changes also normally are based on inflationary indices that are determined by the U.S. Department of Labor, Bureau of Labor Statistics, or other agency that is independent of either of the parties to the contract.

Fixed-price-incentive (FPI) contracts are similar to firm fixed-price contracts with the exception that the contract terms include a formula for monetary incentives should the contractor exceed the specifications or complete the project prior to the contractual completion date.

Cost-reimbursement type contracts, according to the FAR, permit payment of allowable and allocable costs to the contractor. The costs are prescribed in the contract and there is an estimate of total cost that establishes a ceiling cost. However, unlike the NTE contract described above that requires completion of the work described in the scope of work at a price not exceeding the NTE pricing, the contractor with a cost-reimbursement contract is not committed to completion of the work described in the contract for the estimated total costs. The contractor may not exceed the incurrence of costs above the ceiling without the approval of the contracting officer or acceptance of the risk that those costs will not be reimbursed by the government.[1] Cost-reimbursement contracts are not considered applicable unless the uncertainties associated with performance under the contract prohibit the level of accuracy in the cost estimate that is necessary for use of a fixed-price contract.[2] The definitions below for cost-reimbursement contracts are generally based on the definitions for contract types contained in the FAR. Cost-reimbursement contracts should not be used by state and local government contracting agencies unless they are prepared to employ considerably more resources during contract negotiations and contract administration than they normally employ for awarding and managing fixed-price contracts. The government also assumes a greater share of the risks of contracting when they award cost-reimbursement contracts. The reduced risks shared by the contractor when performing under cost-reimbursement contracts prompted the federal government to place limits on the percentage of fees applicable to cost-reimbursement contracts. Tracking costs is essential with cost-reimbursement contracts, and it is imperative that contractors awarded such contracts have an accounting system capable of such cost tracking. When cost-reimbursement contracts are used, as mentioned above, such costs must be allowable and allocable. Allowable costs are those costs allocable to the contract that are not included in the costs that have been defined by the contracting agency and identified in the contract as unallowable. If costs such as those listed above in the discussion of cost-reimbursement contracts are not designated as unallowable, then the contracting agency could be obligated to reimburse the contractor for inappropriate costs. To ensure that unallowable costs are not reimbursed by the contracting agency, a contract clause permitting audit of the contractor's financial records should also be included in the contract terms and conditions. In the absence of such auditing provisions, the agency is not able to verify that unallowable costs are not being claimed for reimbursement. Allocable costs are those costs that pertain to the contracting agency's contract or project. Costs that are expended to support one contract would not be allocable to more than one contract.

The FAR includes an extensive list of unallowable costs. Some examples of costs that are unallowable according to the FAR include entertainment, advertising, taxes, interest, labor relations, and losses on other contracts.[3] Including provisions for unallowable costs in contracts necessitates more than a mere listing of costs that are unallowable. For example, advertising costs that would be considered unallowable would likely be limited to product advertising, while advertising to recruit employees or to announce upcoming procurement opportunities would normally be allowable. While government agencies may not wish to reimburse contractors for advertising their products, advertising to recruit employees or to announce procurement opportunities are expenses that would be appropriate for reimbursement by government agencies. State and local government agencies that permit cost-reimbursement contracts should seriously consider establishing categories of costs that are and are not allowable. If unallowable costs are not defined in cost-reimbursement contracts, agencies may be embarrassed by some categories of costs that they may reimburse. Based on the numerous negative aspects of cost-reimbursement contracts, as discussed above, they are not recommended for use by state and local government agencies. The various types of cost-reimbursement contracts prescribed in the FAR are briefly discussed below.

Cost-plus-fixed-fee (CPFF) contracts provide for reimbursement of the contractor for allowable and allocable costs plus a fixed fee that is determined at the inception of the contract. Should the contractor overrun the target cost, the fixed fee is not decreased. Likewise, should the contractor underrun the target cost, the fixed fee is not increased. However, if the contract is amended due to a change in scope, the fixed fee is normally increased or decreased in proportion to the increase or decrease in the target cost. The fee normally established for federal contracts cannot exceed 10 percent of the estimated cost for CPFF contracts; however, the maximum is 15 percent for experimental, developmental, or research and 6 percent of estimated construction costs for architect-engineering CPFF contracts.[4]

Cost-plus-incentive-fee (CPIF) contracts provide for reimbursement of the contractor for allowable and allocable costs plus an incentive fee that is based on a formula determined at the inception of the contract. The incentive can apply to cost containment and may include other factors such as technical characteristics or schedule performance.

Cost-plus-award-fee (CPAF) contracts are similar to CPIF contracts except that they do not use an exact formula for determining the amount of the fee. CPAF contracts typically include goals or criteria on which the award fee is based. The award fee factors may be established at the inception of the contract for the first phase of the period of performance, which could be, for instance, the first six months of the contract term. Long-term CPAF contracts typically provide for adjustments to the factors on which the award fee is based. At the end of each award period, the contractor submits a document that supports the award fee at the level at which the contractor feels that it deserves. The contracting agency reviews the contractor's submittal, evaluates the contractor's performance with respect to the award fee factors, and then unilaterally determines the amount of the award fee.

The most extreme departure from the characteristics of a firm fixed-price contract is the cost-plus-a-percentage-of-cost (CPPC) contract. CPPC contracts are unlawful in federal contracting[5] and in some states as well. The American Bar Association (ABA) also recommends the prohibition of CPPC contracts.[6] CPPC contracts provide for reimbursement to the contractor for allowable and allocable costs plus a predetermined percentage of those costs. A cursory analysis of CPPC contracts might conclude that they are not significantly different than CPFF contracts. However, there is a significant difference between CPPC and CPFF contracts. When CPFF contractors overrun their contracts, the fee remains fixed. Therefore, the CPFF contractor's fee as a percentage of the costs is reduced when they experience a cost overrun, and this reduction in the fee as a percentage of actual costs acts as an incentive to control costs. Contrast this to a CPPC contract wherein greater contractor expenditures result in higher fees, and thus higher profits. The method for determining the amount of earned fees clearly provides an incentive for the contractor to engage in uncontrolled spending.

The CPPC contract places virtually all the risks on the contracting agency because the contractor is reimbursed for all its allowable incurred costs plus a percentage of those incurred costs. This arrangement rewards the contractor for excessive spending. If the contractor were, for example, reimbursed for costs plus 5 percent, it would be paid $50,000 over its costs if those costs were $1,000,000. However, if through inefficiency or by design, the contractor's costs for the same task were $2,000,000, it would be paid $100,000 over its costs. This reward for inefficiency, or excess spending by design, is the reason that CPPC contracts are prohibited by the federal government as well as some state and local government agencies. This is undoubtedly the reason that the American Bar Association (ABA) discourages CPPC contracts in its publication, "The 2000 Model Procurement Code for State and Local Governments."

Cost reimbursement contracts, other than CPPC, are generally legal in most jurisdictions. However, contracting agencies should use cost-reimbursement contracts only when they cannot negotiate a fixed-price contract. The administration of cost-reimbursement contracts requires considerably more government resources than the administration of fixed-price contracts. Additionally, cost-reimbursement contracts result in considerably more risk assumption by the government than fixed-price contracts.

When state and local government contractors are reimbursed based on effort expended, such as on the basis of differing hourly rates for senior consultants, consultants, and administrative support plus expenses at cost, it is not necessary to use a cost-reimbursement contract such as CPAF, CPFF, or CPIF. As an alternative to these FAR-type cost-reimbursement contracts, state and local government agencies can usually structure a contract such that costs are reimbursed based on hours worked plus expenses, but contain a not-to-exceed (NTE) price for the entire contract. Not-to-exceed (NTE) refers to a ceiling price that cannot be exceeded except when the contract has been amended to increase the NTE price due to a change in scope.

This compensation structure results in a contract much like a fixed-price contract except that the contract can be completed by a price lower than, but not exceeding, the contract NTE price. One significant differentiation between the NTE contract and cost-reimbursement contracts is that although the price on a cost-reimbursement contract cannot be increased, except at the contractor's risk, those cost are estimates for completion of the work described in the contract. The federal contracting officer can increase the price of a cost-reimbursement contract without changing the scope of work. The NTE contract, however, specifies the maximum that the contractor can charge unless there is bilateral agreement on a change in scope that justifies added compensation paid to the contractor for performance beyond that described in the original contract.

Contractors occasionally propose the reimbursement of labor costs at some certain hourly rate, but reimbursement of expenses at actual cost plus a percentage of that cost. A proposal for paying expenses at costs plus a percentage, however, could result in a hybrid contract with the labor being paid based on a fixed or NTE price and the expenses being paid on a CPPC basis. The fact that there is an NTE price for the entire contract provides some protection from the risks associated with a CPPC contract; however, it would be preferable to negotiate reimbursement of expenses at the actual cost. If that provision cannot be negotiated, the agency might agree to a percentage over the estimated cost of expenses, and then establish the dollar value of that percentage as a separate NTE markup over estimated expenses. Expenses would then be reimbursed at actual costs plus the NTE mark-up over "estimated" expenses. The NTE markup would not be exceeded even if the contractor does exceed the estimated cost of expenses. Because the markup would not increase based on costs that exceed the estimate, there would be no incentive for the contractor to spend excessively.

The best practices services contract is designed for either a firm-fixed-price contract or a contract, as discussed above, with reimbursement based on hours worked plus expenses (or any other defined compensation formula) with an NTE price for the entire contract. The contracting agency could also include a separate NTE fee for reimbursement of expenses. However, the best practices services contract would require significant modification to accommodate the FAR-type cost-reimbursement contracts. Should an agency find it necessary to award a CPFF, CPIF, or CPAF contract, it is recommended that agency representatives consider the FAR clauses as guidance for drafting their cost-reimbursement provisions. Because Web sites are subject to change, a Web site address is not provided here to access the FAR. The phrase "federal acquisition regulation" has proven an effective search term to reach an online version of the FAR.

## 8.2  Best Practices Services Contract

Traditional contracts do not normally include a table containing all the variable information as illustrated in the model services contract (based on the best practices contract) in Appendix F, "Model Services Contract (MSC)." Traditional contracts also are typically multi-page documents that provide space for contract execution on the final page of the document. The page where the traditional contract is executed oftentimes has minimal information regarding the contracting parties, pricing, term, or other essential elements of the contract. In some cases, there is little information on the execution page other than the signatures and identification of the parties execut-ing the contract. This arrangement can cause the individuals executing the contract to feel that they are signing the equivalent of a blank check. In fact, having the execu-tion of the contract on a page that does not include the essential contract elements could facilitate intentional or unintentional substitution of unsigned contract pages that modify the essential contract elements. The possibility of page substitution is guarded against at some contracting agencies by identifying the contract on every page or requiring the individuals executing the contract to initial each page.

## 8.2.1 One-Page Contract Format

Five of the twenty-two contracts (23 percent) provided by agencies participating in the best-practices research project included a one-page contract format with most of the essential contract information on the same page as the executing signatures. The best-practices contract contains the preamble, variable information, recitals, incorporation of attached documents, and execution all on one page. This is an ideal organization for a contract because all the essential elements of the con-tract are on the page where the contract is executed. While government officials may have limited confidence in the contract document when executing traditional contracts with minimal information on the page they sign, those same officials are more confident in signing a contract when the contracting parties are identi-fied; pricing is specified; the terms and conditions, scope of work, and insurance requirements are identified and incorporated in the contract all on the page where the contract is executed. The model services contract in Appendix F has several advantages over the traditional contract format. The variable information table provides convenient spaces for inserting the information that typically varies from the contract boilerplate. Contract boilerplate (or boilerplate) refers to standard terminology that does not normally vary, regardless of the nature of the services for which proposals are being solicited. Standard agency terms and conditions are an example of boilerplate.

A copy of the one-page contract with a variable information table is provided in Figure 8.1. The use of a variable information table facilitates data collection for those contracting agencies that wish to collect information on contracts during preparation of the contract document to populate a computer software database for subsequent automated contract management.

Agencies that wish to collect data in addition to that contained in the variable information table in the model services contract can incorporate additional fields such as account numbers, project name, and project number. A similar table could also be included in the scope of work wherein the deliverables are identified by line item numbers, a description, and the due date. Capturing this level of information on deliverables would be useful for agencies having an interest in tracking deliver-ables with the assistance of computer software.

## *Model Services Contract with Variable Information Table*
## MODEL SERVICES CONTRACT

This contract, dated as of the last date executed by the [***Insert Agency Name***] is between the [***Insert Agency Name***], hereinafter referred to as "Agency," and the Contractor indicated in the variable information table below, hereinafter referred to as "Contractor."

| VARIABLE INFORMATION TABLE | | | | | |
|---|---|---|---|---|---|
| | | Contract Number | | | |
| Term of This Contract (Complete Dates in Just One of the Following Three Shaded Rows) | | | | | |
| √Below | Term Begins | | Term Completion Date | | |
| | On Following Date | | On Following Date | | |
| | Upon Receipt of Notice to Proceed | | Calendar Days Following Notice to Proceed | | |
| | Upon Execution by Agency | | Calendar Days Following Agency Contract Execution | | |
| Agency Department | | | FOB Point | | |
| Terms | | Basis of Price (Do Not√ More Than One of the Following Four Blocks) | | | |
| Price | | Fixed Price | Annual Price | Monthly Price | Hourly Rate |
| Not-to-Exceed Price | | √ If Reasonable Expenses Authorized in Addition to Hourly Rate | | | |

| Contractor Contact Information | | Agency Contact Information | |
|---|---|---|---|
| Contractor | | Project Manager | |
| Address | | Address | |
| City, State & ZIP | | City, State & ZIP | |
| Telephone | | Telephone | |
| Facsimile | | Facsimile | |

**Figure 8.1   Model Services Contract variable information table.**

WHEREAS, Agency, through the Agency Department identified above, desires to have work described in the Attachment II — Scope of Work performed; and

WHEREAS, Contractor possesses the necessary qualifications to perform the work described herein.

NOW THEREFORE BE IT AGREED between the parties to this contract that this contract is subject to the provisions contained in the attachments that are incorporated in this contract, and the provisions that are incorporated in this contract by reference. Should there be a conflict between the provisions of this contract and any of the attachments, precedence shall be given first to the contract and then to the attachments in descending order by the numbers assigned to each attachment.

| *Attachments Incorporated in Contract* | *Provisions Incorporated by Reference as if Attached Hereto* |
|---|---|
| 1. Attachment III — Agency General Contract Terms and Conditions | 2. Agency Special Terms and Conditions available at the following Web site: |
| 5. Attachment I — Contract Insurance Requirements | 3. Compliance with Federal Law available at the following Web site: |
| 6. Attachment II – Scope of Work | 4. Following Contractor Certifications: |

| *Agency* | *Contractor* |
|---|---|
| By _____ | By _____ |
| Name _____ | Name _____ |
| Title _____ | Title _____ |

The preamble, variable information, recitals, incorporation of attached documents, and contract execution are all provided on the one-page model services contract in Appendix F and Figure 8.1. This format is considered superior to the traditional contract format for the reasons indicated in the above discussion.

## 8.2.2 Preamble

The preamble to a contract normally identifies the parties to the contract along with their addresses and a single word or phrase to be used throughout the remainder of the contract to identify each of the parties. The example in Figure 8.1 indicates that the contractor will be referred to as "Contractor" and the contracting agency will be referred to as "Agency" in the balance of the contract and the contract attachments. While it is recommended that agencies that use this template continue to use "Contractor," the template can be modified to indicate use of an alternative to "Agency." The preamble in a traditional contract also frequently contains the effective date of the contract. The preamble to the model services contract consists of the text at the top of the page immediately above the variable information table.

The variable information table provides spaces for all the contract information that regularly varies from contract to contract. It might be said that all the information not contained in the variable information table, other than the scope of work, consists of boilerplate. The variable information in the model contract includes the contract term; applicable department name of the contracting agency; free on board point; payment terms; price; indication of whether the price is fixed, annual, monthly, an hourly rate, not-to-exceed, and whether or not expenses are reimbursable. The parties to the contract and their contact information are also identified in the variable information table.

Contract term (period of performance) is the phrase used to indicate the beginning and ending dates of the work to be performed by the contractor. Free on board identifies the geographic location where title to deliverables changes from the contractor to the agency. In the absence of any other provisions for transportation costs, the contractor would be responsible for transportation to the free on board (FOB) point, and the agency would be responsible for transportation from the FOB point to the agency. The FOB point is not nearly as important with services contracts as it is with contracts for commodities; however, it is recommended that the agency specify "delivered" as the FOB point to ensure that the contractor is responsible for the risks and costs associated with the transportation of any contract deliverables. Payment terms in contracts typically describe the time permitted for the contracting agency to pay invoices following completion of the work and receipt of the invoice. In certain cases, the payment terms indicate cash discounts that may be taken if payments are made expeditiously. When no cash discount is offered by the contractor, payment terms are typically expressed as "Net 30," which indicates that the full amount of the invoice is due 30 days after the invoice and products or services are received by the contracting agency. Cash discounts are occasionally offered by contractors to ensure that invoices are paid in a timely manner. An example of payment terms when a cash discount is offered is "2% 15, Net 45." This indicates that the contracting agency may deduct 2 percent from the invoiced price if payment is made within 15 days of receipt of the invoice and products and services; and that if the payment is not made within 15 days, the full amount of the invoice is due within 45 days of receipt of the invoice and products or services. Cost elements in not-to-exceed price contracts typically include hourly rates that may be charged for various employee classifications such as senior analyst or administrative support personnel, mileage rates for vehicles, per-diem rates for meals, and hotel expenses. However, there is no space in the variable information table for cost elements. Agencies normally include cost elements in the scope of work; however, a separate attachment could be developed for cost elements. Cost elements in firm-fixed-price contracts could be fixed payments paid for milestone completion or a fixed periodic payment that is invoiced monthly during the term of the contract. Billing rates in not-to-exceed price contracts are typically hourly rates for each applicable employee classification, an amount certain for each mile driven such as $0.50 per mile or reimbursement at the then-current rate allowed by the Internal Revenue Service, and meals and hotel expenses could be reimbursed at a per-diem rate such as $50.00 per day for meals and $150 per day for hotels or at actual cost. When certain rates are based on actual costs, it is possible to include a ceiling cost to ensure that contractor employees do not select luxury accommodations and expensive restaurants.

## 8.2.3 Recitals

The term "recitals" refers to the section of a contract that normally follows the preamble and describes the rationale for the parties entering into a contract. The recitals typically indicate that the contracting agency has a specific defined need for entering into the contract and that the contractor has the qualifications to meet the needs of the contracting agency.

## 8.2.4 Incorporation of Documents

Incorporation of documents in addition to the contract itself is essential to ensure that documents accompanying or attached to the contract are enforceable. Mere physical attachment of additional documents to a contract does not make the provisions of those attachments enforceable upon the contractor. To ensure that the provisions of the attachments are enforceable, the attachments should be incorporated in the contract by identifying the attachment by attachment number, title, date, and other identifying information, and then following that description with phraseology similar to "which is attached to and incorporated in this contract." A contractor's proposal is sometimes incorporated in a contract. This can be beneficial because it renders all the contractor's promises in the proposal to be a part of the contract. However, there can also be detrimental effects to incorporating a contractor's proposal because undesirable provisions of the proposal also become part of the contract. Hopefully, the detrimental effects are minimized by placing the proposal lowest in precedence in the event of conflicts between contract provisions. However, an undesirable provision that does not conflict with other contract provisions becomes part of the contract regardless of the precedence assigned to the contractor's proposal if the proposal is incorporated in the contract. An alternative approach to attaching the contractor's proposal is to excise the beneficial portions of the contract and physically add them to the contract or another attachment such as the scope of work.

Incorporation by reference is similar to the incorporation by attachment defined above with the exception that the actual document is not attached to the contract.

Documents cannot be incorporated by reference unless they are readily available to all parties to the contract. The phraseology for incorporating documents by reference should be similar to "which is incorporated in this contract by reference." This is similar to the traditional language that has been determined to be adequate for incorporating documents by reference. In the example in Figure 8.1, a Web site is identified for accessing the documents incorporated by reference. The version of the attached document that was current when the document was executed remains the version applicable to the contract unless the contract is modified to substitute an updated version of the document. Because there is the possibility that a document (or documents) incorporated by reference may be revised following contract execution, the agency should consider revision numbers and dates for incorporated documents, and the need to keep them posted to the Web site while contracts incorporating those versions are active or subject to document retention. These measures ensure that documents incorporated in contracts by reference are available during the contract period of performance and during the subsequent period of time when the contract records are maintained.

The paragraph in the Model Services Contract immediately above the block containing the attached documents specifies the order of precedence for the attached documents in the event that there is a conflict between the contract and the attachments or a conflict between two or more of the attachments. The scope of work is listed as the lowest order of precedence because this document oftentimes includes information provided by the contractor while the terms and conditions and insurance requirements are generally developed by the contracting agency. In some cases, it may be useful to incorporate additional documents such as drawings or specifications provided by the contracting agency or added contract provisions provided by the contractor. Such documents may be incorporated by modifying this section of the model contract to list the additional documents. It is recommended that, as a general rule, contracting agency prepared documents should be higher in precedence than contractor prepared documents. This helps insulate the agency from having contractor prepared documents take precedence over agency prepared documents.

## 8.2.5 Execution

The block of information at the bottom of the first page of the Model Services Contract (MSC) includes signature elements for the state or local government agency and the contractor. The signature by an authorized representative of the contracting agency and the contractor constitutes execution of the contract by both parties to the contract. Execution of the contract by representatives from all parties to the contract constitutes full execution.

## 8.2.6 Contract Attachments

The balance of this chapter is devoted to describing the terms and conditions, insurance requirements, and the scope of work incorporated in the contract.

### 8.2.6.1 Insurance Provisions

The insurance provisions in the RFP's model contract are so extensive that, rather than include them in the standard terms and conditions, a separate attachment is often incorporated in the contract to describe the contractor's responsibilities with respect to maintaining insurance coverage during the term of the contract. Insurance provisions typically describe the types of insurance coverage and limits of liability for insurance policies that must be maintained by the contractor during the entire term of the contract. Typical types of insurance coverage required are general liability, automobile coverage, workers' compensation, and professional liability. Professional liability coverage, however, is normally required only if the contractor is expected to provide professional services such as legal, engineering, architectural, accounting, or other services from other professions requiring similar requisite education and expertise. Added responsibilities that may be placed on all contractors are the requirement to have the insurance carrier name the agency as an additional insured or to provide a specified number of days notice to be provided to the agency by the contractor should the insurance policy approach termination.

Agencies are generally able to establish standard insurance limits that are appropriate for most contracts. However, high-risk contracts may necessitate higher coverage levels. In many cases, contractors engaged in such high-risk activities maintain coverage at rates higher than other contractors. When higher than normal risk contracts are to be awarded, the agency should consider modifying the standard insurance requirements to reflect a higher level of coverage commensurate with the risk. This modification to the standard insurance requirements insulates the agency against the greater risks associated with such contracts. In the event of a low-risk contract that could normally be performed by small companies that may experience difficulty obtaining coverage at the agency's standard coverage levels, consideration should be given to lowering the required insurance coverage to permit a larger field of contractors to vie for the contract.

### 8.2.6.2 Scope of Work

The scope of work also is generally contained in a separate attachment that is attached to and incorporated in the contract. The primary purpose of the scope of work is to describe the work to be performed by the contractor. The scope of work may also include additional information such as certain aspects of the work that will be performed by the contracting agency. Some contracting agencies also include payment rates in the scope of work for not-to-exceed (NTE) price contracts that compensate the contractor on the basis of billing rates. To ensure that the contractor is accountable for performance of the tasks listed in the scope of work, the scope of work should have a preamble that includes a statement to the effect that the contractor shall (or term other than "shall" that best compels a contractor to perform) provide all labor, materials, equipment, supplies, transportation, and pay all required taxes and fees to complete the tasks included in the scope of work. The scope of work is an ideal place for including milestones, reports, and deliverables, along with the scheduled dates for these events.

One common error to avoid when drafting a scope of work, or to search for when reviewing a scope of work prepared by another, is the introduction of uncertainty as to which party is required to perform specific tasks included in the scope of work. This is especially possible when the scope of work does not contain a preamble as described in the previous paragraph. Although the preamble does guard somewhat against uncertainty, it remains possible to include uncertainty despite a scope of work that includes a well-constructed preamble. Innumerable scopes of works have been prepared that state a number of tasks that the contractor shall perform, then a number of tasks that the agency shall perform, and finally a list of tasks that are not assigned to either of the contracting parties. Another example of a poorly constructed scope of work is the use of a word that is not the most compelling but is intended to mandate the contractor's performance. In the majority of states, the most compelling word is "shall," which is considered the most compelling word in this text. An example of a scope of work with errors such as those described in this paragraph is provided in Figure 8.2. A corrected version of this scope of work is provided in Figure 8.3.

---

Attachment II

**Scope of Work**

The Contractor will provide all labor, materials, equipment, supplies, transportation and pay all required taxes and fees to complete the tasks included in the scope of work unless indicated otherwise below:

1. The Contractor will be responsible for furnishing all the labor, supervision and materials to develop a Phase I Plan as described further in paragraph 5. of this scope of work.

2. The Agency will be responsible for providing a suitable work space (including chairs and work surfaces) for up to six contractor employees.

3. Fifty copies of the Phase I Plan will be reproduced and distributed to the organizations listed in Exhibit A to this scope of work.

---

**Figure 8.2   Example of a poorly crafted scope of work.**

---

Attachment II

**Scope of Work**

The Contractor ~~will~~ **shall** provide all labor, materials, equipment, supplies, transportation and pay all required taxes and fees to complete the tasks included in the scope of work unless indicated otherwise below:

The Contractor ~~will~~ **shall** be responsible for furnishing all the labor, supervision and materials to develop a Phase I Plan as described further in paragraph 5. of this scope of work.

The Awarding Agency will be responsible for providing a suitable work space (including chairs and work surfaces) for up to six Contractor employees.

**The Contractor shall reproduce and distribute fifty copies of the Phase I Plan** ~~Fifty copies of the Phase I Plan will be reproduced and distributed~~ to the organizations listed in Exhibit A to this scope of work.

---

**Figure 8.3    Corrected version of same scope of work as in Figure 8.2.**

Despite the preamble in Figure 8.2 that requires the contractor to provide everything necessary to perform under this contract unless indicated otherwise in the scope of work, there remains some ambiguity as to which party to the contract is required to reproduce and distribute the Phase I Plan. Certainly it can be argued that because there is no indication as to which party is responsible to reproduce and distribute the plan, the provisions of the preamble should govern and the contractor should be required to perform these tasks. Despite the provisions in the preamble, the fact that reproducing and distributing the plan is listed immediately after a stated agency responsibility, then it could be argued that the agency is responsible for reproducing and distributing the plan. Whenever there is doubt regarding the interpretation of the provisions of a contract, the courts normally rule against the party that prepared the contract.

The scope of work is a critical element of the contract. Although the boilerplate contract terms and conditions often contain more text, the scope of work generally contains the greatest amount of text that is specific to the contract or project. Because the text of the scope of work is critical to the success of the project, department personnel who prepare the draft scope of work should be trained in the preparation of this document.

Appendix F, "Model Services Contract (MSC)," includes a scope of work template with instructions for completing this document. The template also includes spaces for entering information on milestones and deliverables in a format permitting the capture of this information during document preparation to populate a database for use in automated tracking of the milestone and deliverable dates during the contract administration phase of the contracting cycle.

### 8.2.6.3 Terms and Conditions

A collection of terms and conditions were developed during the document review conducted on the contract templates provided by state and local government agencies that participated in the best-practices research project. A complete set of terms and conditions is provided in Chapter 9, "Contract Terms and Conditions," and in Appendix F, "Model Services Contract (MSC)." Terms and conditions are contract provisions that describe the rights and responsibilities of all parties to the contract. Typical examples of terms and conditions include payment, term of the contract, indemnification, termination, insurance, contract modifications, and independent contractor. Ideally, terms and conditions are balanced to provide equivalent rights to all parties to the contract. An example of a termination clause that is imbalanced is one wherein one party has the right to terminate the contract for either convenience or for cause, while the other party merely has the right to terminate for cause. Contractors that propose their own version of terms and conditions often include provisions that favor their company over the rights and responsibilities afforded the agency. Flow-down terms and conditions may be required if the contracting agency is awarding a contract in support of a grant or contract awarded by a state to a county, city, or district, or awarded by a federal agency to a state, county, city, or district. Oftentimes, grants, state contracts, and federal contracts include terms and conditions that are required to flow down to all state or local government agency contracts awarded in support of that grant or contract. A complete discussion of the MSC terms and conditions is contained in Chapter 9, "Contract Terms and Conditions."

# 8.3 Conclusion

The primary factor used to distinguish between the various types of contracts is the provision for reimbursing contractors. Fixed-price contracts clearly dominate the contract type used for services contracts by state and local government agencies. Contracts that base the reimbursement of contractors according to established billing rates for the resources applied to complete the tasks in the scope of work are frequently used and may resemble some aspects of cost-reimbursement contracts; however, the use of not-to-exceed (NTE) limits for the total contract price combined with the necessity to complete the contract tasks within the NTE limits cause these contracts to be treated as fixed-price contracts rather than as true cost-reimbursement contracts. True cost-reimbursement contracts, such as those frequently used in federal contracting, are not recommended for use by state and local government agencies except in those exceptional circumstances when fixed-price contracts are not appropriate.

The one-page contract format is highly recommended for use by state and local government agencies. This format provides numerous benefits, including provisions for a variable information table and the inclusion of all contract-unique information, except the scope of work, on one page. Consolidating all the variable information, except the scope of work, on the page where the contract is executed by both agency and contractor representatives provides the representatives executing the contract with greater assurance that their signatures represent approval of the essential contract information. The existence of the variable information table facilitates the capture of essential contract information concurrently with preparation of the contract document for population of computer databases used by the agency for managing contracts. Having the essential contract information on the page where the contract is executed also guards against the possibility of accidental or intentional page substitutions that modify essential contract information.

The one-page contract format also includes provisions for incorporating additional documents by attachment or by reference. The three standard contract attachments are the insurance provisions, scope of work, and terms and conditions.

## Notes

1. Federal Acquisition Regulation (FAR), § 16.301-1, Description (Cost Reimbursement Contracts).
2. Federal Acquisition Regulation (FAR), § 16.301-2, Application (Cost Reimbursement Contracts).
3. Federal Acquisition Regulation (FAR), § 31.205, Selected Cost.
4. Acquisition Regulation (FAR), § 15.404-4, Profit, subparagraph (c), Contracting Officer Responsibilities.
5. Federal Acquisition Regulation (FAR), § 16.1, Selecting Contract Types, states the following in subparagraph (c), "The cost-plus-a-percentage-of-cost system of contracting shall not be used (see 10 U.S.C. 2306(a) and 41 U.S.C. 254(b)). Prime contracts (including letter contracts) other than firm-fixed-price contracts shall, by an appropriate clause, prohibit cost-plus-a-percentage-of-cost subcontracts (see clauses prescribed in § 44.2 for cost-reimbursement contracts and § 16.2 and 16.4 for fixed-price contracts)."
6. The 2000 Model Procurement Code, Article 3 — Source Selection and Contract Formation, Part E — Types of Contracts, § 3-501.

# Chapter 9

# Contract Terms and Conditions

## Chapter Objectives

Readers are presented with an accumulation of contract terms and conditions created during the best practices research project by selecting the best terms and conditions from those that were submitted by state and local government agencies participating in the research project. The contract terms and conditions presented here contain more individual terms and conditions than any single set of terms and conditions submitted by the agencies participating in the research project. Although agencies may wish to modify the terms and conditions provided in this chapter, a review of this consolidated group of contract terms and conditions by state and local government agencies is likely to identify new provisions to add to their existing terms and conditions or improvements to existing terms and conditions.

The forty-seven individual terms and conditions presented below in italics (starting with Section 9.1.1) are followed by a commentary on the rationale for including them in the set of terms and conditions presented for adoption or modification, and adoption by all state and local government agencies. The Model Services Contract (MSC) in Appendix F contains an attachment containing all forty-seven terms and conditions, minus the commentary, in a single document.

Figure 9.1 provides a listing of the titles for the individual terms and conditions.

Incidence of Inclusion or Provisions in State and Local Government Terms & Conditions

| No. | Title of Provision | Incidence | |
|---|---|---|---|
| | | Number | Percent |
| 1 | Term | 21 | 100% |
| 2 | Termination for Default | 19 | 90% |
| 3 | Force Majeure | 9 | 43% |
| 4 | Liquidated Damages | 2 | 10% |
| 5 | Termination for Convenience | 17 | 81% |
| 6 | Termination Transition | 2 | 10% |
| 7 | Contractor Reimbursement | 21 | 100% |
| 8 | Payment Terms | 21 | 100% |
| 9 | Set-Off | 5 | 24% |
| 10 | Agency Project Manager | 7 | 33% |
| 11 | Key Personnel | 3 | 14% |
| 12 | Independent Contractor | 13 | 62% |
| 13a | Confidentiality | 10 | 48% |
| 13b | Ownership | 10 | 48% |
| 14 | Indemnification | 18 | 86% |
| 15 | Insurance | 13 | 62% |
| 16 | Amendments | 18 | 86% |
| 17 | Waiver of Rights | 7 | 33% |
| 18 | Compliance with Laws | 14 | 67% |
| 19 | Americans with Disabilities Act | 3 | 14% |
| 20 | Health Insurance Portability and Accountability Act | 1 | 5% |
| 21 | Nondiscrimination | 17 | 81% |
| 22 | Drug Free Workplace | 5 | 24% |
| 23 | Workers' Compensation | 13 | 62% |
| 24 | Contractor's Standard of Care | 10 | 48% |
| 25 | Care of Property | 3 | 14% |
| 26 | Advertising | 4 | 19% |
| 27 | Performance Evaluation | 1 | 5% |

**Figure 9.1  Incidence of inclusion of provisions in state and local government terms and conditions.**

| | | | |
|---|---|---|---|
| 28 | Inspection of Work and Project Site | 2 | 10% |
| 29 | Applicable Law and Forum | 18 | 86% |
| 30 | Successors and Assigns | 16 | 76% |
| 31 | Subcontracting | 17 | 81% |
| 32 | Unallowable Costs | 1 | 5% |
| 33a | Audit & Employee Interviews | 15 | 71% |
| 33b | Document Retention | 16 | 76% |
| 34 | Remedies Not Exclusive | 3 | 14% |
| 35 | Conflict of Interest | 13 | 62% |
| 36 | Contractor Integrity | 7 | 33% |
| 37 | Political Contribution Disclosure | 5 | 24% |
| 38 | Assignment of Antitrust Claims | 3 | 14% |
| 39 | Payment of Taxes | 9 | 43% |
| 40 | Officials Not to Prosper | 6 | 29% |
| 41 | Copyrights | 7 | 33% |
| 42 | Budget Contingency | 12 | 57% |
| 43 | Counterparts | 3 | 14% |
| 44 | Severability | 11 | 52% |
| 45 | Notices | 7 | 33% |
| 46 | Titles, Headings or Captions | 4 | 19% |
| 47a | Entire Agreement | 9 | 43% |
| 47b | Survival of Provisions beyond the Contract Term | 7 | 33% |

**Figure 9.1 (continued)   Incidence of inclusion of provisions in state and local government terms and conditions.**

## 9.1  Contract Terms and Conditions

The terms and conditions that were included in the services contract templates provided by state and local government agencies participating in the research project were subjected to a document review to discover best practices in services contracting. One element of the document review was to transcribe representative provisions included in each agency's standard terms and conditions, and tabulate the incidence at which each of the individual provisions were included. A complete set of 47 provisions discovered in the state and local government agency provisions comprises the terms and conditions for incorporation in the Best Practices

Model Services Contract (MSC). Figure 9.1 provides a summary of the incidence for which each of the MSC terms and conditions appears in the contracts provided by the participating state and local government agencies.

Terms and conditions are provisions that describe the rights and responsibilities of all parties to the contract. Typical examples of terms and conditions include contractor reimbursement, term, indemnification, termination clauses, insurance, independent contractor, amendments, and many of the numerous additional provisions contained in the MSC. Ideally, terms and conditions are balanced to provide equivalent rights for all parties to the contract. An example of a termination clause that is imbalanced is a provision wherein one party has the right to terminate the contract for either convenience or for cause, while the other party merely has the right to terminate for cause. Contractors that prepare their own versions of the terms and conditions often include provisions that favor their companies over the rights and responsibilities afforded the government.

Terms and conditions are essential to the contract document to protect the interests of the agency. There is a vast range of subjects that might be included in any accumulation of terms and conditions. A copy of the terms and conditions discussed below is included in the MSC provided as an attachment to Appendix F. Agencies may determine that all the terms and conditions included in the MSC are essential and acceptable as presented. Some agencies may prefer, however, to modify the provisions presented here, delete selected provisions, or supplement these terms and conditions with additional provisions that are applicable to individual state or local government agencies.

The terms and conditions in the MSC are presented below in italics, and are followed by a commentary in standard font.

## 9.1.1 Term

*The term of this contract is reflected in the Variable Information Table. Should the Agency elect to continue to contract with the Contractor for a continuing period of time beyond the completion of the contract term reflected in the Variable Information Table, the Contractor shall agree to accept an extension of up to six weeks under the provisions of this contract to provide the Agency an opportunity to prepare and execute a formal amendment that includes any changed provisions or compensation rates. No later than ninety (90) days prior to the expiration of a one-year contract, the Contractor may request, in writing, a cost adjustment for the second year of the contract. Any proposed increase in price shall not exceed the rate of inflation as determined by the Consumer Price Index for all urban consumers (CPI-U) U. S. City average all items 1982–84 + 100 published by the Bureau of Labor Statistics as the percent of change at the time of the request, from one year prior (the baseline index). The Agency reserves the right to accept the cost adjustment and extend the contract for one additional year; to negotiate the cost adjustment, scope of work, length of the contract extension, or any other provisions of the contract; or to allow the contract to end at the completion of the period of performance.*

Because the above provisions refer to the variable information table, an example of a variable information table is provided as Figure 9.2. The term of the contract begins with the date when the contractor begins work and ends when the contractor

| VARIABLE INFORMATION TABLE | | | | | | |
|---|---|---|---|---|---|---|
| | | Contract Number | | | | |
| Term of This Contract (Complete Dates in Just One of the Following Three Shaded Rows) | | | | | | |
| √ Below | **Term Begins** | | **Term Completion Date** | | | |
| | On Following Date | | On Following Date | | | |
| | Upon Receipt of Notice to Proceed | | Calendar Days Following Notice to Proceed | | | |
| | Upon Execution by Agency | | Calendar Days Following Agency Contract Execution | | | |
| | Agency Department | | FOB Point | | | |
| Terms | | **Basis of Price (Do Not √ More Than One of the Following Four Blocks)** | | | | |
| Price | | Fixed Price | Annual Price | Monthly Price | Hourly Rate | |
| Not-to-Exceed Price | | √ if Reasonable Expenses authorized in addition to Hourly Rate | | | | |
| **Contractor Contact Information** | | **Agency Contact Information** | | | | |
| Contractor | | Poject Manager | | | | |
| Address | | Address | | | | |
| City, State & ZIP | | City, State & ZIP | | | | |
| Telephone | | Telephone | | | | |
| Facsimile | | Facsimile | | | | |

**Figure 9.2  Variable information table.**

has completed all the work required to be performed under the contract. The dates for both the beginning and ending of the contract term may be expressed as dates certain. However, in some cases, the beginning may be expressed as the date for some future event such as complete execution of the contract, execution of the contract by the agency, receipt by the contractor of a notice-to-proceed from the agency, or any other stated event. The ending date of the contract may also be expressed as other than a date certain. For example, the ending date may be expressed as some time period following execution of the contract or a certain number of days, months, or years following receipt of a notice-to-proceed from the agency. Additional conditions may be included in the "Term" provisions, such as price escalation in the event of a multiple-year contract or whenever price escalation is expected during the term of the contract. In some cases, the term and termination provisions are included in one provision. However, in the terms and conditions for this MSC, there are separate provisions for term and several other provisions covering termination.

### 9.1.2 Termination for Default

*If, through any cause, the Contractor shall fail to fulfill in a timely and proper manner the obligations under this contract, other than for the instances listed below due to "Force Majeure," the Agency shall thereupon have the right to terminate this contract by providing a written notice (show cause notice) to the Contractor requiring a written response due within ten (10) days from receipt of the written notice as to why the contract should not be terminated for default. The Agency's show cause notice shall include a contract termination date at least [**Insert Number of Days**] days subsequent to the due date for the Contractor's response. Should the Contractor fail to respond to such show cause notice, or if the Agency determines that the reasons provided by the Contractor for failure of the Contractor to fulfill its contractual obligations do not justify continuation of the contractual relationship, the Agency shall terminate the contract for default on the date indicated in the show cause notice. Should the Agency determine that the Contractor provided adequate justification that a termination for default is not appropriate under the circumstances, the Agency shall have a unilateral option to either continue the contract according to the original contract provisions or to terminate the contract for convenience. In the event that the Agency terminates the contract for default, all finished or unfinished deliverable items under this contract prepared by the Contractor shall, at the option of the Agency, become Agency property, and the Contractor shall be entitled to receive just and equitable compensation for any satisfactory work completed on such materials. Notwithstanding this compensation, the Contractor shall not be relieved of liability to the Agency for damages sustained by the Agency by virtue of any breach of this agreement, and the Agency may withhold any payment due the Contractor for the purpose of setoff until such time as the exact amount of damages due the Agency from such breach can be determined.*

*In case of default by the Contractor, the Agency may procure the services from other sources and hold the Contractor responsible for any excess cost occasioned thereby. The Agency reserves the right to require a performance bond or other acceptable alternative performance guarantees from the successor contractor without expense to the Agency.*

*In addition, in the event of default by the Contractor under this contract, the Agency may immediately cease doing business with the Contractor, immediately terminate for cause all existing contracts the Agency has with the Contractor, and debar the Contractor from doing future business with the Agency.*

*Upon the Contractor filing a petition for bankruptcy or the entering of a judgment of bankruptcy by or against the Contractor, the Agency may immediately terminate, for cause, this contract and all other existing contracts the Contractor has with the Agency, and debar the Contractor from doing future business with the Agency.*

*The Agency may terminate this contract for cause without penalty or further obligation at any time following contract execution, if any person significantly involved in initiating, negotiating, securing, drafting, or creating the contract on behalf of the Agency is at any time while the contract or any extension thereof is in effect, an employee or agent of any other party to the contract in any capacity or consultant to any other party of the contract with respect to the subject matter of the contract. Additionally, the Agency may recoup any fee or commission paid or due to any person significantly involved in initiating, negotiating, securing, drafting, or creating the contract on behalf of the Agency from any other party to the contract.*

This is the first of two termination clauses in the model services contract. This first termination clause provides that the agency may terminate the contract for default if the contractor materially breaches the contract provisions. The process involving the show cause notice as the first step in the default termination, and the contractor's response to the show cause notice, are also described. There is a sample show cause notice in Appendix L, "Sample Show Cause Letter." In the event that the contract is terminated for default, this clause provides that the agency may contract with another company for the services and hold the original contractor responsible for any excess costs, including the cost of a performance bond for the replacement contractor; terminate all other agency contracts with the contractor; and debar the contractor from doing future business with the agency. This clause further permits the agency, in the event of the contractor's bankruptcy, to terminate the contract and debar the contractor. And finally, the agency is permitted to terminate the contract for cause in the event that any of the stated conflicts of interest existed when the contract was secured, and to recoup any fees or commissions paid to individuals involved in the enumerated conflicts of interest.

## 9.1.3 Force Majeure

*Neither party shall be deemed to be in default of its obligations hereunder if and so long as it is prevented from performing such obligations by any act of war, hostile foreign action, nuclear explosion, riot, strikes, civil insurrection, earthquake, hurricane, tornado, or other catastrophic natural event or act of God. Should there be such an occurrence that impacts the ability of either party to perform their responsibilities under this contract, the nonperforming party shall give immediate written notice to the other party to explain the cause and probable duration of any such nonperformance.*

Force majeure provisions typically provide a list of reasons that excuse the contractor's or agency's failure to complete their responsibilities on time. The reasons included in this suggested provision are fairly typical. However, each agency may determine that more or fewer reasons are included. In this suggested provision, the reasons for delay are applicable to both the agency and the contractor. This mutual application of the force majeure provisions is recommended to provide parity between the agency's and the contractor's rights and responsibilities with respect to excusable delays. There is also a requirement to provide notice whenever there is the occurrence of an event that delays completion of the contractor's or the agency's responsibilities.

### 9.1.4 *Liquidated Damages*

*The parties acknowledge and agree that the damages that are to be expected as a result of a material breach of contract by Contractor may be uncertain in amount and very difficult to prove. In that event, the parties do intend and in fact now agree, if necessary, to liquidated damages in advance and stipulate that the amount set forth in this section is reasonable and an appropriate remedy as liquidated damages and not as a penalty. If the Contractor materially breaches the contract, then the Contractor shall pay the Agency [**Insert Dollar Amount**] per day for the duration of the delay.*

Liquidated damages pertain to reimbursement of costs incurred by the agency should the contractor fail to complete its contractual obligations on time due to a material breach of contract.

### 9.1.5 *Termination for Convenience*

*Either party to this contract may terminate this contract at any time without cause by providing the other party with sixty (60) days advance notice in writing. In the event of termination for any reason, all finished or unfinished deliverable items prepared by the Contractor under this contract shall, at the option of the Agency, become the Agency's property. If the contract is terminated by the Agency as provided herein, the Contractor shall be paid for services satisfactorily completed, less payment or compensation previously made.*

*The Contractor shall continue to perform the services described in the scope of work during the [**Insert Number of Days**]-day period following notice of termination for convenience and the Agency shall continue to pay the Contractor for services* *performed during such period in accordance with the compensation provisions contained herein.*

This second termination clause allows either party to terminate the contract without cause. In this case, there is a 60-day notice rather than the 15-day notice provided in the termination for cause provision. The agency has considerable discretion regarding the number of days' notice that is provided in this clause. It is not unusual to have a range from 10 days to 90 days for convenience termination notices. The contractor is required to continue performing services until the termination date, and the agency is required to continue paying the contractor for performing those services, regardless of which party initiated the termination. In certain cases, the party that constructs the contract may provide rights for itself to terminate the contract without cause, but provide no such rights for the other party to the contract. Of course, such one-sided provisions may be challenged, thus leading to the negotiation of more equitable provisions regarding termination for convenience. In the case where the agency has the right to termination for cause and to termination for convenience, the agency may feel that the other party committed a material breach of contract but may not be able to substantiate such material breach. In such cases, the agency may elect to terminate the contract for convenience to avoid the potential time and expense generally associated with a confrontation over the alleged material breach.

## 9.1.6 Termination Transition

*During the fifteen (15) calendar day period prior to termination of the contract, the Contractor shall provide reasonable cooperation in the transition of its responsibilities to the replacement Contractor selected by the Agency to perform the tasks described in the scope of work and formerly performed by the Contractor for this contract. The Contractor for this contract shall accept no additional tasks with respect to the scope of work after the effective date of the termination.*

This clause requires the contractor to cooperate with the replacement contractor during the transition, regardless of which party initiated the termination and regardless of whether the termination was for cause or convenience. There is also a provision that restricts the contractor from accepting additional tasks after the termination date. Awarding agencies should also consider the effectiveness of certain provisions of the contract following termination or completion of the contract. There are certain clauses that would be appropriate for continuation in the contract following contract termination or completion. Clauses that might be continued following contract termination or completion might include confidentiality, inspections, contractor evaluations, and audits. Such continued clauses would continue to be effective until completion of the retention period and destruction of the contract file.

## 9.1.7 Contractor Reimbursement

*The work shall be performed for the Fixed Price, Annual Price, Monthly Price, or Hourly Rate as indicated above in the variable information table, but shall not exceed the Not-to-Exceed Price if included in the variable information table. Reasonable expenses are authorized in addition to the Hourly Rate if both the Hourly Rate block and the block authorizing Reasonable Expenses are checked in the variable information table. Payment shall be made after the Agency's project manager or designee reviews and approves the work and after submittal of an invoice by the Contractor.*

The provisions of the reimbursement clause provide clarification of the variable information contained in the variable information table as it relates to the type of contract and whether reasonable expenses are authorized in addition to the hourly rates. The rationale for writing a contract wherein the contractor is not authorized to be paid for reasonable expenses in addition to the hourly rates is that some contractors build such expenses into their hourly rates. There is also a provision that requires approval of the work by the agency's project manager prior to reimbursement of the contractor. Requiring such approval of the work prior to payment is a prudent decision to ensure that payment is not made for work that the project manager considers incomplete or unacceptable.

## 9.1.8 Payment Terms

*Payment terms are indicated in the Variable Information Table. The due date indicated is based upon the number of days following receipt of a correct invoice(s) or acceptance of services, whichever is later. Invoices may not be submitted more frequently than once monthly. The using Agency is responsible for all payments to the Contractor under the contract. Payment by some agencies may be made by procurement card and they shall be accepted by the Contractor for payment if the Contractor accepts that card (Visa, MasterCard, etc.) from other customers. If payment is made by procurement card, then payment may be processed immediately by the Contractor.*

"Payment Terms" describe the timeframe wherein the agency is obligated to pay invoices received from the contractor. In this provision, the contractor is also limited to submitting invoices on a monthly basis.

## 9.1.9 Set-Off

*In the event that the Contractor owes the Agency any sum under the terms of this contract, any other contract, pursuant to any judgment, or pursuant to any law, the Agency may set-off the sum owed to the Agency against any sum owed by the Agency to the Contractor at the Agency's sole discretion, unless otherwise required by law. The Contractor agrees that this provision constitutes proper and timely notice.*

The set-off provisions are included in the event that the agency has paid the contractor all or virtually all the costs due under the contract when it is determined that the contractor is not entitled to the full amount remitted. The set-off provisions permit the agency to withhold funding from other agency contracts to recover the excess payments. In some cases, agencies have a retention provision in their contract wherein the agency withholds a certain percentage (say 5 or 10 percent) of the amount earned to ensure that there is funding available should it be determined that the contractor is not entitled to full reimbursement under the contract. Fund retention provisions are commonplace in construction contracts but were not found in any of the services contract templates submitted in support of the project to develop a best practices services contract.

### 9.1.10  Agency Project Manager

*The Agency's project manager or designee for this undertaking who will receive payment invoices and answer questions related to the coordination of this undertaking is identified above in the variable information table.*

The purpose of the agency project manager clause is to describe the role and responsibilities of the agency's project manager. Should this clause be adopted as a standard provision in a state or local government's contracts, a term such as "County," "City," or "District" would normally be substituted for the term "Agency."

### 9.1.11  Key Personnel

*The Contractor shall not substitute key personnel assigned to the performance of this contract without prior written approval by the Agency's project manager. The individuals designated as key personnel for purposes of this contract are those listed below:*

The key personnel provisions are intended to give the agency some control over the substitution of contractor personnel assigned to a particular project. Some unscrupulous contractors may be inclined to identify their best employees in all the proposals that they submit in response to RFPs. In this event, the contractor may attempt to substitute lesser-qualified employees once the contract has been awarded. There is also a more legitimate reason for substituting employees identified in a proposal, such as when a particular employee resigns to accept a position with another contractor. In either event, this provision gives the agency some control over such personnel substitutions.

### 9.1.12  Independent Contractor

*The Contractor shall be considered to be an independent contractor and as such shall be wholly responsible for the work to be performed and for the supervision of its employees.*

*The Contractor represents that it has, or will secure at its own expense, all personnel required in performing the services under this agreement. Such employees shall not be employees of, or have any individual contractual relationship with, the Agency. The Contractor shall be exclusively responsible for payment of employees and subcontractors for all wages and salaries, taxes, withholding payments, penalties, fees, fringe benefits, professional liability insurance premiums, contributions to insurance and pension or other deferred compensation, including but not limited to Workers' Compensation and Social Security obligations, and licensing fees, etc. and the filing of all necessary documents, forms, and returns pertinent to all the foregoing.*

The independent contractor clause is essential to help establish the fact that the contractor is an independent contractor as opposed to having employee status. Should it be determined, normally in a court of law, that a contractor's employee is actually an employee of the agency, the awarding agency may be required to provide full employee benefits to the contractor's employee (or employees) who performed services for the state or local government agency. The benefits awarded to the contractor's employee (or employees) could include retirement, employer's share of social security payments, health and medical insurance, vacation, holidays, and any other benefits provided for the contracting agency's employees. This clause, on its own however, does not entirely protect the contracting agency from providing benefits if the relationship between the contracting agency and the employee is determined to be that of an employer/employee. If the contractor's employee is actually supervised by an employee of the contracting agency, it may be determined that a contract employee working under the provisions of the contract is actually an employee of the contracting agency and therefore entitled to the full package of state or local agency employee benefits. Other factors that could lend to a court's decision to classify a contract employee as a contracting agency employee include state or local government agency establishment of work hours, work location, supervision, work tools, or other agency influence over the contractor's conduct of its performance that could establish an employer/employee relationship.

### 9.1.13 Confidentiality and Ownership

*The Agency retains the exclusive right of ownership to the work, products, inventions and confidential information produced for the Agency by the Contractor, and the Contractor shall not disclose any information, whether developed by the Contractor or given to the Contractor by the Agency.*

The confidentiality and ownership clause ensures that the contracting agency does not pay the contractor to develop products, inventions, and confidential information that are then wholly owned by the contractor and the contractor can then sell such work products that should rightfully belong to the contracting agency. The confidentiality and ownership clause is likely to be rejected by contractors that have developed substantial proprietary information or products that are included in the final product or service provided to the state or local government agency. A prime example of a company that would likely not accept this confidentiality and ownership clause is a computer software company that developed extensive proprietary property in the form of computer programs that are merely adapted for use by the contracting agency. State or local government agencies are likely required to accept contract provisions proposed by their computer software provider. Although the computer software company's terms and conditions may be required, this does not mean that the contracting agency cannot negotiate changes to the more onerous of the contractor's terms and conditions.

## 9.1.14 Indemnification

*The Contractor shall indemnify, defend, and hold harmless the Agency and its officers, representatives, agents, employees, successors, and assigns from and against any and all (1) claims arising directly or indirectly, in connection with the contract, including the acts of commission or omission (collectively, the "Acts") of the Contractor or Contractor Parties; and (2) liabilities, damages, losses, costs, and expenses, including but not limited to, attorneys' and other professionals' fees arising, directly or indirectly, in connection with claims, Acts, or the contract. The Contractor shall use counsel reasonably acceptable to the Agency to carry out its obligations under this section. The Contractor's obligations under this section to indemnify, defend, and hold harmless against claims includes claims concerning confidentiality or the proprietary nature of any part of all of the proposal or any records, any intellectual property rights, other proprietary rights of any person or entity, copyrighted or uncopyrighted compositions, secret processes, patented or unpatented inventions, articles or appliances furnished or used in the performance of the contract. The Contractor shall reimburse the Agency for any and all damages to the real or personal property of the Agency caused by the Acts of the Contractor or any Contractor parties. The Agency shall give the Contractor reasonable notice of any such claims. The Contractor's duties under this section shall remain fully in effect and binding in accordance with the terms and conditions of the contract, without being lessened or compromised in any way, even where the Contractor is alleged or is found to have merely contributed in part to the Acts giving rise to the claims and/or where the Agency is alleged or is found to have contributed to the Acts giving rise to the claims. The rights provided in this section for the benefit of the Agency shall encompass the recovery of attorney's and other professionals' fees expended in pursing a claim against a third party. This section shall survive the termination, cancellation, or expiration of the contract, and shall not be limited by reason of any insurance coverage.*

Indemnification provisions are often referred to as "hold harmless" clauses. Hold harmless is certainly more descriptive of the purpose of this clause, which provides that one party shall be held harmless for negligent acts or omissions or willful misconduct by the other party in the performance of the contract. The above indemnification clause holds the agency harmless for the negligent acts or omissions or willful misconduct of the contractor. Contractors oftentimes request that the indemnification provisions be modified to mutually hold both parties harmless for negligent acts or omissions or willful misconduct by the other party.

## 9.1.15 Insurance

*Contractor shall procure and maintain for the duration of this contract, insurance against claims for injuries to persons or damages to property which may arise from, or be in connection with, the performance of the work hereunder by Contractor, Contractor's agents, representatives, employees, and subcontractors. At the very least, Contractor shall maintain the insurance coverages, limits of coverage, and other insurance requirements as described in Attachment I to this contract.*

The Model Services Contract in Appendix F includes the above insurance requirements clause in addition to Attachment I ("Standard Insurance Requirements"), which provides a detailed description of the contractor's requirement to maintain the specified insurance coverage during the course of the contract. The above insurance requirements clause merely requires the contractor to procure and maintain, during the term of the contract, the insurance coverage described in Attachment I ("Standard Insurance Requirements").

## 9.1.16 Amendments

*This contract may be amended only by written amendments duly executed by the Agency and the Contractor.*

This clause is included in the contract in an attempt to prevent unwritten changes to the contract. These provisions do not necessarily prevent oral amendments. To further guard against oral amendments, it is recommended that agency personnel be trained to not give any oral direction to contractors unless necessitated by an actual emergency that threatens life, property, or the continuation of essential government operations. It is possible that the agency or contractor finds it necessary to waive some of the provisions of the terms and conditions. In the event that the agency or contractor actually does waive some provisions of the terms and conditions or other provisions of the contract, the "Waiver of Rights" clause below prevents such waiver (or waivers) from applying to other provisions of the contract.

## 9.1.17 Waiver of Rights

*It is the intention of the parties hereto that from time to time either party may waive any of their rights under this contract unless contrary to law. Any waiver by either party hereto of rights arising in connection with this contract shall not be deemed to be a waiver with respect to any other rights or matters.*

The above "Waiver of Rights" clause permits the agency or the contractor to waive one or more rights without waiving any other rights.

## 9.1.18 Compliance with Laws

*The Contractor shall comply with all laws, ordinances, codes, rules, regulations, and licensing requirements that are applicable to the conduct of its business, including those of federal, state, and local agencies having jurisdiction and/or authority.*

This is an all-encompassing provision that requires the contractor to comply with all applicable laws, rules, and regulations. The clause then names some specific jurisdictions without excluding any others.

## 9.1.19 Americans with Disabilities Act

*By signing this contract, Contractor assures the Agency that it will comply with the Americans with Disabilities Act (ADA) of 1990, (42 U.S.C. 12101 et seq.), which prohibits discrimination on the basis of disability, as well as all applicable regulations and guidelines issued pursuant to the ADA.*

The Americans with Disabilities Act (ADA) is a federal law designed to prevent discrimination against persons with disabilities. Federally funded contracts are likely to require flow-down of ADA contract provisions to contractors and subcontractors. State laws regarding nondiscrimination in contracting, treatment of employees and job applicants, as well as provisions regarding fair housing may be required flow-down charges when the state wholly funds or partially funds the contract. Due to the difficulty of tracking every contract that is funded through a state or federal agency, one efficient approach to ensure that provisions flow down properly is to include such provisions in standard terms and conditions that are incorporated in all state or local government agency contracts.

## 9.1.20 Health Insurance Portability and Accountability Act

*If the Contractor is a Business Associate under the Health Insurance Portability and Accountability Act of 1996 ("HIPAA"), the Contractor shall comply with all terms and conditions of the separate HIPAA agreement. If the Contractor is not a Business Associate under HIPAA, this HIPAA provision does not apply to this contract.*

The Health Insurance Portability and Accountability Act (HIPAA) is also a provision that occasionally needs to flow down. Agencies should consider keeping this provision in their standard terms and conditions because it is a self-deleting provision when it is not required. Keeping a self-deleting provision in the standard terms and conditions simplifies the work of agency personnel and does not impact the overall contract provisions when the provisions are not applicable.

## 9.1.21 Nondiscrimination

*During the performance of this contract, the Contractor and its Subcontractors shall not deny the Contractor's benefits to any person on the basis of religion, color, ethnic group identification, sex, age, physical or mental disability, nor shall they discriminate unlawfully against any employee or applicant for employment because of race, religion, color, national origin, ancestry, physical or mental disability, medical condition, marital status, age (over 40), or sex. Contractor shall ensure that the evaluation and treatment of employees and applicants for employment are free of such discrimination. Contractor and its Subcontractors shall comply with the provisions of all applicable state and federal laws regarding employment rights.*

The above nondiscrimination clause is oftentimes a flow-down clause required by state or federal agencies when the agency's contract is funded, or partially funded, by such state or federal agencies. The wording of the nondiscrimination clause evolves over time to remain in conformance with nondiscrimination laws. Although the Americans with Disabilities Act (ADA) substituted the words "disable" and "disabled" for the words "handicap" and "handicapped" well over a decade past, some government agencies continue to use the obsolete terminology. When challenged on the use of "handicapped" in lieu of "disabled," most government agencies readily change the terminology in their contracts and standard terms and conditions. This is especially true if the basis for this change in terminology is cited when challenging the use of "handicap" or "handicapped."

## 9.1.22 Drug-Free Workplace

*The Contractor shall provide a drug-free workplace in accordance with the Drug-Free Workplace Act of 1988 and all applicable regulations. The Contractor shall execute the certification regarding a drug-free workplace attached to the solicitation and provide the original certificate to the Agency when it executes this contract. Contractor agrees to abide by the terms of the certification. The certification is a material representation of fact upon which the Agency relied when making or entering into this contract and any extension or renewal thereof.*

The drug-free workplace certification applies to federal contractors and grantees.

## 9.1.23 Workers' Compensation

*Contractor affirms that it is aware of the provisions of the state labor laws that require every employer to be insured against liability for workers' compensation or to undertake self-insurance in accordance with the provisions of state labor laws, and Contractor affirms that it will comply with such provisions before commencing the performance of the work under this contract. Contractors shall require their subcontractors to be aware of this provision and determine that they have complied with it before commencing work on their subcontracts.*

By executing a contract with the above workers' compensation clause, the contractor states that it is aware of the state's workers' compensation laws and agrees to comply with such laws and to maintain the required workers' compensation insurance. The contractor also states that it will require subcontractors to comply with workers' compensation laws.

### 9.1.24 Contractor's Standard of Care

*The Agency has relied upon the professional ability and training of the Contractor as a material inducement to enter into this contract. Contractor hereby warrants that all of Contractor's work shall be performed in accordance with generally accepted and applicable professional practices and standards as well as the requirements of applicable federal, state, and local laws, it being understood that acceptance of Contractor's work by Agency shall not operate as a waiver or release.*

The contractor's standard of care clause states that the awarding agency relied upon the professional ability and training of the contractor when it selected the contractor for this project. By executing this contract with this clause, the contractor warrants that its work will be performed professionally and will be in compliance with professional practices and standards as well as the requirements of all applicable laws.

### 9.1.25 Care of Property

*The Contractor agrees that it shall be responsible for the proper custody and care of any property furnished it for use in connection with the performance of this contract or purchased by it for this contract and will reimburse the Agency for loss of or damage to such property.*

The care of property provisions are included in the Model Services Contract in the event that the contractor may obtain custody and responsibilities for care of agency property, and the agency wishes to impose responsibility for proper custody and care of any such agency property.

### 9.1.26 Advertising

*The Contractor shall not refer to sales to the Agency for advertising or promotional purposes, including, but no limited to, posting any material or data on the Internet, without the Agency's prior written approval.*

The inclusion of provisions for approval of advertising copy is to ensure that the contractor does not include the agency in an advertising campaign that could prove embarrassing to the agency. In this suggested clause, the agency retains final approval authority over any advertising copy related to the work performed under the contract.

## 9.1.27 Performance Evaluation

*The Contractor's performance under this project may be evaluated after completion of this contract.*

The agency may routinely evaluate the performance of all contractors following contract completion. Some awarding agencies may elect to evaluate contractor performance on a case-by-case basis following contract performance. The inclusion of this clause in all contracts ensures that, in either case, the agency has the right to evaluate contractor performance following contract completion.

## 9.1.28 Inspection of Work and Project Site

*The Agency shall have the right to inspect the work being performed at any and all reasonable times during the term of the contract. This right shall extend to any subcontracts, and Contractor shall include provisions ensuring such access in all their contracts or subcontracts entered into pursuant to this contract.*

*The Agency shall have the right to inspect the project site at any and all reasonable times after completion of the contract to ensure compliance with the "Contractor's Standard of Care" and the "Nondiscrimination" provisions of this contract.*

This clause permits the agency to inspect the work being performed by the contractor and subcontractor. However, caution should be exercised when dealing with subcontractors because the contracting agency does not have privity of contract with subcontractors. When it is absolutely necessary to deal with subcontractors, the contractor should always be invited to participate in any such contact. Inviting the contractor is necessary because the agency would not have privity of contract with subcontractors. The agency's legal counsel should be notified in advance of any proposed contact with subcontractors by agency employees. The agency's legal counsel should be notified because of the possibility of a legal issue developing over the fact that the agency does not have privity of contract with the subcontractor. Not having privity of contract means that the agency is not a party to the contract between the contractor and the subcontractor. The second part of this clause gives the agency the right to inspect the project site to ensure compliance with the "contractor's standard of care" and the "nondiscrimination" provisions of the contract. The agency can designate any specific clauses within this provision. Of course, contract provisions constructed by the agency are subject to negotiation by prospective contractors. Prospective contractors, however, rarely initiate negotiation of any terms and conditions. This tendency to accept the agency's standard terms and conditions is most pronounced when the provisions are evenly balanced with respect to responsibilities and rights afforded to both parties to the contract.

### 9.1.29 Applicable Law and Forum

*This contract shall be construed and interpreted according to the laws of the state of the awarding government agency.*

State or local government agencies have no flexibility with respect to the applicable law and forum. State or local government agencies are generally prohibited from subjecting themselves to the laws of a state other than their own. Some such provisions also indicate the name of the county where actions must be heard. The county where cases may be heard, however, is negotiable if the agreed-to county is within the local government agency's state.

### 9.1.30 Successors and Assigns

*This contract and all of its provisions shall apply to and bind the successors and assigns of the parties hereto. No assignment or transfer of this contract or any part hereof, rights hereunder, or interest herein by the Contractor shall be valid unless and until it is approved in writing by the awarding agency and made subject to such reasonable terms and conditions as the Agency may impose.*

This clause prevents the contractor from transferring or assigning the contract to another contractor for performance unless the agency approves such transfer or assignment in writing and in advance of the transfer. If the contract is assigned or transferred, the contract and all its provisions shall apply to the new contractor.

### 9.1.31 Subcontracting

*Work proposed to be performed under this contract by the Contractor or its employees shall not be subcontracted without prior advance written approval of the Agency's project manager. Acceptance of a prospective contractor's proposal shall include any subcontractor(s) specified therein. Substitution of subcontractors may be made if the Agency's project manager approves such substitution in advance in writing. The Contractor shall include provisions in its subcontracts requiring its subcontractors to comply with the applicable provisions of this contract, to indemnify the Agency, and to provide insurance coverage for the benefit of the Agency in a manner consistent with this contract. The Contractor shall cause its subcontractors, agents, and employees to comply with applicable federal, state, and local laws, regulations, ordinances, guidelines, permits and requirements, and will adopt such review and inspection procedures as are necessary to assure such compliance.*

Subcontracting is often a criterion for source selection. This clause restricts the contractor from making changes, without prior agency written approval, to the subcontracting approach presented in the proposal. When the agency's selection of a particular contractor is based, at least partially, on the subcontracting program outlined in its proposal, it is logical to expect that the subcontracting program cannot be changed after contract award without pre-approval from the agency. Certain subcontracting provisions in this clause also flow from the contractor to its subcontractors.

## 9.1.32 Unallowable Costs

*The Contractor shall not claim reimbursement for any of the following costs unless disclosed in the Contractor's Certification of Cost or Pricing Data that was submitted with the Contractor's proposal and reimbursement for the following costs had been approved, in writing, in advance by the Agency:*

- *Costs of fines or penalties paid to any government agency*
- *Contingency fees paid to obtain award of this contract*
- *Subcontractor profits for goods or services provided by Contractor's subsidiaries*
- *Gifts or gratuities paid to employees of the Agency or any other government agency*

Inclusion of provisions for unallowable costs in services contract templates, submitted in support of this project, were virtually nonexistent. The costs identified as unallowable in this suggested provision are extremely limited when compared to the costs that are unallowable in federal government contracts. However, most agencies would likely agree that they would not wish to reimburse contractors for the costs identified in this suggested clause. State and local government agencies should give serious consideration to inclusion of provisions similar to this unallowable cost clause in their standard terms and conditions. A provision similar to the unallowable cost clause could prevent the contractor from invoicing the agency for inappropriate expenses, and insulate the agency from such inappropriate contractor practices. Agencies that develop a more comprehensive list of unallowable costs are encouraged to share that information with other agencies.

## 9.1.33 Audit, Employee Interviews, and Document Retention

*Contractor agrees that the Agency, or its designated representative, shall have the right to review and to copy any records and supporting documentation and have access to Contractor personnel pertaining to the performance of this contract. Contractor agrees to maintain such records for possible audit for a minimum of three years after final payment, unless a longer period of records retention is stipulated. Contractor agrees to allow the Agency's auditor(s) access to such records during normal business hours and to allow interviews of any employees who might reasonably have information related to such records. Further, Contractor agrees to include a similar right to the Agency to audit and interview staff in any subcontract related to performance of this contract. If at any time the Agency determines that a cost for which payment has been made is a disallowed cost, such as overpayment, the Agency shall notify the Contractor in writing of the disallowance or claim for unallowable costs. The Agency shall also state the means of correction, which may be, but shall not be limited to, adjustment of any future claim submitted by the Contractor by the amount of the disallowance, or to require repayment of the disallowed amount by the Contractor.*

Audit clauses often apply only to the contractor and require the contractor to maintain records relating to the performance of the contract for a specific period of time, and to be subject to audit by the agency during that same time period. This particular clause also requires subcontractors to maintain records and be subject to audit for the same period of time. The requirements and responsibilities placed on the agency would likely be the result of flow-down provisions required due to the receipt of federal or state funding.

## 9.1.34 Remedies Not Exclusive

*The use by either party of any remedy specified herein for the enforcement of this contract is not exclusive and shall not deprive the party using such remedy of, or limit the application of, any other remedy provided by law.*

This clause merely states that if either party elects to use one remedy to enforce the provisions of the contract that it does not prevent that party from using another remedy concurrently or at some later date.

## 9.1.35 Conflict of Interest

■ *Current Employees or Officers of the Agency:*
  - *No current employee or officer of the Agency shall engage in any employment, activity, or enterprise from which the officer or employee receives compensation or has a financial interest and which is sponsored or funded by the Agency unless the employment, activity, or enterprise is required as a condition of the regular employment with the Agency.*
  - *No current employee or officer of the Agency shall contract on his or her own behalf as an independent contractor with any department of the Agency to provide goods or services.*
■ *Former Employees or Officers of the Agency:*
  - *For a period of two years following the termination of employment with the Agency, no former employee or officer of the Agency may enter into a contract in which he or she engaged in any of the negotiations, transactions, planning,*

> *arrangements, or any part of the decision-making process relevant to the contracts while employed in any capacity by the Agency.*
> – *For a period of twelve (12) months following the termination of employment with the Agency, no former employee or officer of the Agency may enter into a contract with any department of the Agency if he or she was employed by that Agency department in a policy-making position in the same general subject area as the proposed contract within the  twelve-month period prior to his or her terminating employment with the Agency.*

This clause differentiates between current and former employees and officers of the agency:

■ Current agency employees and officers, in this example, are prohibited from participating in any agency-sponsored or -financed activity if their participation results in compensation or financial rewards, unless the activity is required as a condition of the regular employment with the agency. Additionally, current employees and officers shall not contract with his or her agency as an independent contractor.

■ Former employees and officers, in this example, are prohibited, for a two-year period from the termination date from the agency, from engaging in any negotiations, transactions, planning arrangements, or any part of the decision-making process related to the contracts they were involved with as an agency employee. Former employees are also prohibited from entering into a contract with any department of the Agency if they were employed during the past twelve-month period in a policy-making position on matters included in the proposed contract.

The specific restrictions and time periods in the above provisions may vary greatly from contracting agency to contracting agency. It is a good practice to limit the contracting opportunities of current and former employees. However, the actual limits could vary greatly from those in this example yet effectively discourage actual or perceived conflicts of interest. Agencies should consider establishing a process for exceptions to these limitations in the event that the agency has an urgent need to engage a former employee or retired employee on a consulting basis. Without provisions for such an exception, the agency may be prevented from contracting with the former or retired employee.

### 9.1.36  *Contractor Integrity*

■ *For the purposes of this clause only, the words or phrases "proprietary information," "consent," "Contractor," "financial interest," and "gratuity" shall have the following definitions:*

- *Proprietary Information means information that is company confidential, a trade secret, or otherwise not public knowledge, disclosure of which would give an unfair, unethical, or illegal advantage to another entity or individual desiring to contract with the Agency.*
- *Consent means written permission signed by a duly authorized officer or employee of the Agency, provided that the material facts have been disclosed, in writing, by prequalification, proposal, or contractual terms.*
- *Contractor means the individual or entity that has entered into the contract with the Agency, including directors, officers, partners, managers, key employees, and owners for more than a five percent ownership of the Contractors' firm, subsidiaries, or parent companies.*
- *Financial Interest means: (a) ownership of more than a five percent interest in any business; or (b) holding a position as an officer, director, trustee, partner, employee, or the like, or holding any position of management.*
- *Gratuity means any payment of anything of monetary value in the form of cash, travel, entertainment, gift, meal(s), lodging, loans, subscriptions, conference fees, advances, deposits of money, services, employment or promises of employment, contracts of any kind, or any other article or intellection having present or future pecuniary benefit.*

■ *The Contractor shall maintain the highest standards of integrity in the performance of the contract and shall take no action in violation of state or federal laws, regulations, or other requirements that govern contracting with the Agency.*

■ *The Contractor shall not disclose to others any confidential or proprietary information gained by virtue of the contract.*

■ *The Contractor shall not, in connection with this or any other agreement with the Agency, directly, or indirectly, offer, confer, or agree to confer any pecuniary benefit on anyone as consideration for the decision, opinion, recommendation, vote, other exercise of discretion, or violation of a known legal duty by any officer or employee of the Agency.*

■ *The Contractor shall not, in connection with this or any other agreement with the Agency, directly, or indirectly, offer, give, or agree or promise to give to anyone any gratuity for the benefit of or at the direction or request of any officer or employee of the Agency.*

■ *Except with the written consent of the Agency, neither the Contractor nor anyone in privity with him or her shall accept or agree to accept from, or give or agree to give to, any person, any gratuity from any person in connection with the performance of the Contract except as provided herein.*

■ *Except with the advance written consent of the Agency, the Contractor shall not have a financial interest in any other contractor, subcontractor, or supplier providing services, labor, or material on this project.*

■ *The Contractor, upon being informed that any violation of these provisions has occurred or may occur, shall immediately notify the Agency in writing.*

■ *The Contractor, by execution of this contract and by the submission of any bills or invoices for payment pursuant thereto, certifies, and represents that she or he has not violated any of these provisions.*

■ *The Contractor, upon the inquiry or request of the Agency or any of the Agency's agents or representatives, shall provide, or if appropriate, make promptly available for inspection or copying, any information of any type or form deemed relevant by the Agency to the Contractor's integrity or responsibility, as those terms are defined by the Agency's statutes, regulations, or management directives. Such information may include but shall not be limited to, the Contractor's business or financial records, documents or files of any type, or form that refer to or concern the contract. Such information shall be retained by the Contractor for a period of three years beyond the termination of the contract unless otherwise provided by law.*

■ *For violation of any of the above provisions, the Agency may terminate this and any other contract with the Contractor, claim liquidated damages in an amount equal to the value of anything received in breach of these provisions, claim damages for all expenses incurred in obtaining another Contractor to complete performance hereunder, and debar or suspend the Contractor from doing business with the Agency. These rights and remedies are cumulative, and the use or non-use of any one shall not preclude the use of all or any other. These rights and remedies are in addition to those the Agency may have under law, statute, regulation, or otherwise.*

This contractor integrity clause imposes business practices standards on the contractor to discourage the practice of providing gratuities or similar rewards to individuals who may have influence over the award and administration of agency contracts. This suggested clause provides for significant contractor penalties for nonconformance with these provisions.

## 9.1.37  Political Contribution Disclosure

*The Contractor shall comply with election laws requiring entities or persons entering into contracts, leases, or other agreements with the state, county, city, or their agencies in the aggregate amount requiring such disclosure to file a statement disclosing a contribution(s) in excess of $500 in the aggregate during any calendar year.*

The above provision requires modification to comply with state election laws, modified if the state election laws include a threshold other than $500 or deleted if the state does not have an equivalent election law.

## 9.1.38  Assignment of Antitrust Claims

*The Contractor and the Agency recognize that, in actual economic practice, overcharges by the Contractor's suppliers resulting form violation of state or federal antitrust laws are in fact borne by the Agency. As part of the consideration for the award of the contract, and intending to be legally bound, the Contractor assigns to the Agency all rights, title, and interest in and to any claims the Contractor now has, or may acquire, under state or federal antitrust laws relating to the services or any products that are, or that may become, the subject of this contract.*

The assignment of antitrust claims provisions ensures that proceeds from claims for excess costs that are in fact borne by the agency due to violation of antitrust laws are assigned to the agency.

## 9.1.39 Payment of Taxes

*By execution of this contract, the Contractor certifies that it and all of its affiliates, if applicable, collect all appropriate taxes and remit them to the applicable state or local government agency.*

The above provision requires adjustment to comply with state and local government agency tax laws.

## 9.1.40 Officials Not to Prosper

*No members of the governing body of the state or local public agency, and no other officer, elected or appointed official, employee, or agent of the state or local public agency who exercise any functions or responsibilities in connection with the carrying out of the project to which this contract pertains, shall have any personal interest direct or indirect, in this contract. No member of the governing body of the locality in which the project area is situated, or other public official of such locality, who exercises any functions or responsibilities in the review or approval of the carrying out of the work to which this project pertains, shall have any personal interest, direct or indirect, in this contract. No state official, Member of or Delegate to the Congress of the United States, and no Resident Commissioner, shall be admitted to any share or part of the contract or to any benefit to arise herefrom.*

One would think that the inclusion of provisions prohibiting officials from prospering from the award of public contracts would not be necessary. The vast majority of public officials would not expect to prosper personally from the award of a contract to the agency they represent. However, weekly summaries of media stories concerning state and local government agencies almost invariably include one or more accounts of corruption involving a government official. This provision is intended to discourage such behavior by government officials and contractor representatives by prohibiting agency officials from benefiting from the award of agency contracts.

## 9.1.41 Copyrights

*Where copyrights are an essential element of performance under this contract, Contractor certifies that it has appropriate systems and controls in place to ensure that Agency funds will not be used in the performance of this contract for acquisition, operation, or maintenance of literature or computer software in violation of copyright laws.*

The copyrights provision above simply states that the contractor certifies that it has taken measures to ensure that the agency's funds will not be used to purchase, operate, or maintain products that are in violation of copyright laws. Copyright provisions may be considerably more extensive and may include provisions requiring the agency to notify the contractor in a timely manner if it learns of an alleged copyright infringement associated with the product or services provided by the contractor. Such provisions normally require the contractor to defend against copyright infringement suits, and the agency to cooperate in the defense of such claims. Copyright provisions occasionally require the contractor to pay all fees associated with copyright infringements, provide alternative products or services that do not infringe on copyrights, and terminate the contract at no cost to the agency.

## 9.1.42 Budget Contingency

*It is mutually agreed that if the approved budget for the current year and/or any subsequent years covered under this contract does not appropriate sufficient funds for the project, this contract shall no longer be in force and effect. In this event, the Agency shall have no liability to pay any funds whatsoever to Contractor or to furnish any other consideration under this contract, and Contractor shall not be obligated to perform any provisions of this contract. If funding for any fiscal year is reduced or deleted by the approved budget for purposes of this project, the Agency shall have the option to either: cancel this contract with no liability occurring to the Agency, or offer a contract amendment to the Contractor reflecting the reduced amount.*

The budget contingency provision permits the agency to terminate the contract without any liabilities should there be insufficient appropriations to fund the project under contract. Alternatively, the agency and contractor may agree to reduce the scope of the contract if a lesser amount of funding is available.

## 9.1.43 Counterparts

*The parties to this contract agree that this contract has been or may be executed in several counterparts, each of which shall be deemed an original and all such counterparts shall together constitute one and the same instrument.*

The provisions in agency contracts to provide numerous original copies of each contract are essential if the agency and the contractor are both to be provided with original versions of the contract.

### 9.1.44 Severability

*If any provision of this contract is held invalid or unenforceable by any court of final juris-diction, it is the intent of the parties that all other provisions of this contract be construed to remain fully valid, enforceable, and binding on the parties.*

The severability provisions guard against the possibility that the entire contract may be held invalid or unenforceable merely because one or a few of the provisions are determined to be invalid or unenforceable.

### 9.1.45 Notices

*For any notice applicable to the contract to be effective, it must be made in writing and sent to the Contractor or Agency representative at the address indicated in the variable information table unless such party has notified the other party, in accordance with the provisions of this section, of a revised mailing address. Such notices shall be sent via certified mail or an alternative mode that requires a signature by the recipient. This notice requirement does not apply to any notices that this contract expressly authorizes to be made orally.*

The provision regarding notices is routinely included in contracts to ensure that notices regarding contractual matters are sent to the appropriate address.

### 9.1.46 Titles, Headings, or Captions

*This contract includes titles, headings, and captions appearing herein; they are for con-venience only, and such titles, headings, and captions shall not affect the contractual interpretation or meaning of this contract.*

The titles provisions in the MSC prevent attempts to interpret the provisions of contracts based on the title of various sections of the contract. This is essen-tial to avoid extended discourse regarding what provisions should or should not be included in a section of the contract with a particular section title.

### 9.1.47 Entire Agreement and Survival of Provisions beyond the Contract Term

*This contract and any documents incorporated specifically by reference or attachment represent the entire agreement between the parties and supersede all prior oral or written statements or agreements.*

*All promises, requirements, terms, conditions, provisions, representations, guarantees, and warranties contained herein shall survive the contract expiration or termination date unless specifically provided otherwise herein, or unless superseded by applicable federal or state statutes of limitation.*

The entire agreement provision ensures that neither party to the contract can claim that prior oral or written statements or agreements are a part of this contract. This is an essential provision because it eliminates the inclusion of information included in the contractor's proposal, previous agreements, or oral representations unless they are specifically incorporated in the contract in writing. Otherwise, the contractor may be able to claim that unacceptable provisions in their proposal or earlier representations are included in the contract. If the agency does not have any reservations concerning the contractor's proposal or other representations and wishes to have them made a part of the contract, such proposals or representations may be incorporated in the agency's contract.

The second part of this clause provides that all contract conditions survive the contract expiration or termination date. However, there are also some stated exceptions regarding the survival of contract conditions.

## 9.2 Conclusion

The terms and conditions presented in this chapter were accumulated from the terms and conditions provided by state and local government agencies that participated in the best practices research project. All agencies are invited to adopt these terms and conditions as presented, modify or delete certain provisions, and supplement these terms and conditions with agency-specific provisions that are required for their services contracts.

## Chapter 10

# Short-Form Contracts, Short-Form RFPs, Emergencies, and Letter Contracts

## Chapter Objectives

This chapter provides readers with information and guidance on an abridged version of the Best Practices Model Services Contract (MSC) that may be used when relatively low contract prices and agency risks do not justify the more expansive MSC discussed in previous chapters. An abridged version of the Best Practices Request for Proposals (RFP) for use in conjunction with the abridged MSC is also presented to the readers. A discussion concerning advance planning for emergency operations is provided as it relates to contracting for services required during actual emergencies. A recommendation is made to award contracts in advance of emergencies to facilitate contracting for services during actual emergencies that threaten lives, property, and the continuance of essential government services. Additionally, there is a discussion and recommended solution for awarding contracts during actual emergencies for needed services that were not anticipated during the advance planning for emergency operations.

The abridged version of the Best Practices MSC shall be referred to as the short-form contract, and the abridged version of the Best Practices RFP shall be referred to as the short-form RFP. The short-form contract is more appropriate for use by state and local government agencies when the lengthier MSC is not justified because of the relatively low risk and low dollar value of the proposed contract. Owing to the close relationship between the content of the contract that a particular agency intends to award and the solicitation for proposals leading to the award of such contracts, an abridged RFP was developed and is provided for use in conjunction with the short-form contract. The discussion of the short-form contract and RFP includes the following topics:

- Conditions under which an abridged version of the Model Services Contract (MSC) template is appropriate
- Why a short-form RFP should be used in conjunction with a short-form contract
- Considerations for establishing a dollar threshold or characterizing the nature of services provided that would distinguish between the appropriate use of the standard templates or short-form templates
- Recommend a template for the short-form RFP and short-form MSC
- Describe the rationale for each modification to the RFP, MSC, and terms and conditions to achieve the short-form versions of the contract and RFP

State and local government agencies must be continuously prepared to deal with emergencies that threaten lives, property, or the continued provision of essential government services. Private-sector contractors may contribute to the agency's efforts to deal with such emergencies. Just as agencies plan in advance to employ government resources to deal with emergencies, they need to plan in advance for engaging private-sector contractors during actual emergencies. Failure to plan in advance for participation by non-government entities in reaction to emergencies could result in delays in the award of needed contracts or in the award of agreements that are lacking in cost effectiveness as the result of hasty decision making. Readers are introduced to several measures involving both contracts made in advance of emergencies and letter contracts awarded during actual emergencies. Although this book is concerned with contracting for services by state and local government agencies, the contracting tools described to provide services during emergencies are also applicable to the provision of needed commodities during emergencies. The discussion of contracting for emergencies and letter contracts include the following topics:

- The need to conduct advance planning for contracting during emergencies
- An overview of the need to award contracts for services in advance of actual emergencies that pose an imminent threat to life, property, or the continuation of essential government services

- Description of how letter contracts can be used during an actual emergency to contract for those services that were not anticipated during the advance planning for emergencies
- Discuss a process to obtain services needed during an emergency through the competitive process to minimize costs and maximize the probability of obtaining needed services in a timely manner
- Provide a letter contract template and describe features of letter contracts used during emergencies

## 10.1 Short-Form Contracts and RFPs

The Best Practices MSC discussed in Chapters 8 and 9 is appropriate for high-dollar-value and high-risk contracts. However, numerous provisions in the MSC are included primarily to protect the agency from consequences associated with high-dollar-value contracts and risks associated with the highly sensitive nature of some contracts for services. Therefore, when the anticipated contract is for a relatively low dollar value with nominal risks, a less elaborate contract template is appropriate. Use of abridged solicitation and contract documents simplifies the agency's contracting effort and increases the willingness of contractors to accept government contracts. Agencies need to decide on an appropriate dollar value threshold when the standard RFP and MSC are used and when it is acceptable to use the short-form RFP and contract. The RFP content is closely related to the contract text; therefore, when it is appropriate, due to the existence of lesser risk or cost, to use a shortened version of the contract format, it is also appropriate to use a shortened version of the RFP. Just as with the Best Practices RFP, a model contract in the form expected to be awarded by the contracting agency should be included with the RFP. Failure to include a short-form contract in the abridged RFP, along with a statement regarding the agency's intention to award a contract essentially in the form of the attached short-form contract, would likely result in prospective contractors proposing their own contract format including their version of terms and conditions favoring the contractor's rights and responsibilities over the agency's rights and responsibilities. To facilitate academic exercises and agency operations involving contracting for low-dollar-value and low-risk services, a short-form RFP with an attached short-form contract is provided in Appendix G, "Short-Form RFP with Short-Form Contract," and on the CD accompanying this book.

In addition to simplifying the contracting efforts for the agency when using simplified documentation, contractors are more likely to contract with the agency when the documentation is simplified. This is especially important when considering the fact that small businesses are more likely to be qualified to perform under low-dollar-value, low-risk contracts and that small contractors are more likely than large contractors to balk at dealing with the more complex expanded versions of the standard RFP and MSC.

Contractor certifications and contract provisions based on flow-downs from federal contracts or grants are normally triggered by dollar thresholds established by the federal government. Therefore, when contracting for services that are funded entirely or partially by the federal government, it is necessary to use the standard RFP and MSC when the dollar value of the resultant contract is expected to exceed the federal government's threshold for certifications and contract provisions contained in the standard RFP and MSC.

There is also a relationship between the threshold for selecting the standard version over the short-form RFP and MSC and an agency's budget. This relationship can be explained by the tendency for agencies to use a formula such as an 80/20 rule for establishing such thresholds. The 80/20 rule implies that agencies attempt to use the simplified documentation for 80 percent of their contracts and restrict the more complex documentation to the top 20 percent of their contracts representing the largest-dollar-value or high-risk contracts.

The threshold established by the federal government for certifications and flow-down contract provisions are periodically adjusted for inflation. Due to the relationship between an agency's budget and its thresholds, there could be a wide variance established for thresholds between states with large contracting budgets and agencies with significantly lower budgets such as counties, cities, and special districts. This text does not include a recommendation for a dollar value where the standard or short-form templates should be used because of the periodic adjustments to federal thresholds and the wide variations between various state and local government budgets. There could essentially be significant differences in the threshold established between the larger and smaller states, as well as between the larger and smaller local government agencies. Just as there are adjustments to federal thresholds for inflation, state and local governments are likely to make inflationary adjustments to their thresholds for use of the standard or short-form templates as well. Such anticipated changes to state and local government agency thresholds therefore constitute one additional reason for not recommending a threshold in this text for differentiating between standard and short-form templates.

The standard template might be considered for some contracts below the threshold if the nature of the services provided is considered high risk. Services that might be considered high risk are those that impact the provisioning of essential government services, safety and security, or physical and mental health services.

The short-form RFP with the short-form contract provided in Appendix G is approximately half the length of the Best Practices RFP with the standard MSC. The changes made to shorten the RFP and MSC are merely suggested. Individual agencies may elect to reinstate certain deleted provisions or delete certain retained provisions of the templates provided in Appendix G to arrive at their own version of short-form templates.

The rationale for making the changes to shorten the RFP and contract templates is provided below.

## 10.1.1 *Simplification of the RFP*

Changes made to simplify the RFP are described below. The removal of the majority of RFP provisions were justified by the fact that lower-dollar-value, low-risk contracts do not require the agency's insulation against the risk avoidance afforded by the provisions that were removed. Provisions involving federal contract clauses and certifications were removed because their application is determined by dollar thresholds that would not be exceeded when contracting with the short-form contract template.

1. The notice to prospective contractors was condensed to reduce the overall length of the text without removing material that, given the lower dollar and reduced risk, was essential for the contracting process.
2. The RFP introduction was shortened by removing the example of an introductory statement.
3. The description of the contractor selection process was simplified by deleting references to material discussed elsewhere in the solicitation, such as the process for posing questions regarding the RFP, the fact that the agency may accept late proposals if that would be in the agency's best interests, and that there is no public opening of the proposals. The need for prospective contractors to submit a CD-ROM version of their proposal along with paper copies was eliminated.
4. The contractor selection process was further simplified by removing the description of the color-coded rating system and ranking scheme, collaboration by members of the proposal evaluation committee, certain details of the life cycle cost proposal, details of the combined weighted scoring technique, simplifying the weighted criteria explanation, reducing the number of proposal evaluation criteria, and reducing the number of sections required in proposals.
5. The prospective contractor's certification was simplified to reflect the lower dollar value and lessened risk to the contracting agency.
6. Because the certifications required due to federal funding become mandatory when the contract exceeds a certain specified total price for the contract, a determination was made to remove the certifications regarding lobbying; compliance with the Pro-Children Act of 1994; debarment, suspension, and ineligibility and voluntary exclusion — lower-tier covered transactions.
7. The certification of cost or pricing data was not included in the abridged RFP and MSC templates because this certification, also, is normally required for high-dollar-value contracts.
8. The proposal preparation instructions were simplified by removing the references to the fact that the agency would not consider data provided external to the RFP when evaluating proposals. The restriction against elaborate proposals was deleted because it was determined that the page limits on the individual sections of the proposals would eliminate the possibility of excessively

long proposals. The statement regarding the agency's preference for recyclable materials in proposals, historically underutilized businesses, and accommodations for disabled persons were removed because it was determined that these instructions were not needed for low-dollar-value, low-risk contracts.

9. The table of contents was removed because the 50 percent overall reduction in the length of the text simplifies the task of locating information within the RFP and MSC to the extent that a table of contents is no longer necessary.

## 10.1.2 Simplification of the MSC

In certain instances it was determined that simplification of particular elements of the MSC would not be appropriate despite the lower dollar value or reduced risk. The elements that were not changed, as well as those that were changed, are discussed below.

1. The one-page contract format was not changed because the information contained in this format is considered essential regardless of the dollar value of the contract or the risk associated with awarding the contract. However, because it is appropriate to delegate authority to sign contracts below some certain dollar threshold to an individual at a lower organizational level, the short-form contract template made available to department personnel could reflect a signature block indicating the name of the person to whom contract signing has been delegated while the longer version of the contract would reflect the signature block of the official authorized to execute large-dollar-value contracts. Additionally, the information in the variable information table, as shown in Figure 10.1, facilitates population of the database for computer software used to manage contracts and to monitor the performance of contractors.

2. Attachment I, "Insurance Provisions," likewise is not modified because insurance coverage is required regardless of the contract price or associated risks. However, it is appropriate to consider reducing the amount of insurance coverage for low-dollar-value or lower-risk contracts. The agency's risk manager is normally the official who makes the decision to increase or decrease the insurance coverage from the level of coverage reflected on the agency's standard contractual insurance requirements.

3. Attachment II, "Scope of Work," was simplified significantly due to the expectation that work performed by the contractor on lower-priced or lower-risk contracts could be described in a more straightforward manner than work on higher-priced or higher-risk contracts. Agencies that populate their computer database for managing contracts concurrently with the preparation

| VARIABLE INFORMATION TABLE | | | | |
|---|---|---|---|---|
| | | Contract Number | | |
| **Term of This Contract** (Complete Dates in Just One of the Following Three Shaded Rows) | | | | |
| √Below | **Term Begins** | | **Term Completion Date** | |
| | On Following Date | | On Following Date | |
| | Upon Receipt of Notice to Proceed | | Calendar Days Following Notice to Proceed | |
| | Upon Execution by Agency | | Calendar Days Following Agency Contract Execution | |
| | Agency Department | | FOB Point | |
| Terms | | **Basis of Price (Do Not√ More Than One of the Following Four Blocks)** | | |
| Price | | Fixed Price | Annual Price | Monthly Price | Hourly Rate |
| Not-to-Exceed Price | | √ If Reasonable Expenses Authorized in Addition to Hourly Rate | | |
| **Contractor Contact Information** | | **Agency Contact Information** | | |
| Contractor | | Project Manager | | |
| Address | | Address | | |
| City, State & ZIP | | City, State & ZIP | | |
| Telephone | | Telephone | | |
| Facsimile | | Facsimile | | |

**Figure 10.1   Variable information table.**

of contractual documents, and that track deliverables and milestones, need to maintain the scope of work feature that provides a format, as depicted in Figure 10.2, for the entry of information on meetings, milestones, and deliverables.

| Meetings/Milestones/Deliverables | | |
|---|---|---|
| Item No. | Meeting/Milestone/Deliverable Title | Due Date |
|  |  |  |
|  |  |  |
|  |  |  |
|  |  |  |
|  |  |  |
|  |  |  |
|  |  |  |
|  |  |  |
|  |  |  |
|  |  |  |
|  |  |  |
|  |  |  |

**Figure 10.2  Meetings/milestones/deliverables.**

## 10.1.3 Simplification of the Terms and Conditions

Lower-dollar-value and lower-risk contracts do not necessarily require the extensive terms and conditions such as those in the standard MSC. The modifications made to the standard MSC terms and conditions to arrive at the terms and conditions for the short-form contract are described below:

1. *Term.* The provision regarding the term of the agreement was simplified by removing the provisions for continuation of the contract and for price escalation.
2. *Termination for Default.* The termination for default provisions were simplified by deleting:
   − Details on continuation of the contract
   − Provisions for contracting with an alternative contractor
   − Provisions for termination of all other agency contracts and debarring the contractor
   − Termination provisions in the event of the contractor's bankruptcy

3. *Liquidated Damages.* The liquidated damages provisions were deleted because this is not considered necessary for relatively low-dollar-value, low-risk contracts.

4. *Termination for Convenience.* The termination for convenience provision was simplified by removing details of the provision regarding services performed but not yet paid.

5. *Termination Transition.* The termination transition provision was deleted because it is not considered necessary for relatively low-dollar-value, low-risk contracts.

6. *Key Personnel.* The key personnel provision was deleted because it is not considered necessary for relatively low-dollar-value, low-risk contracts.

7. *Americans with Disabilities Act.* The ADA provision was deleted because it is not considered necessary for relatively low-dollar-value, low-risk contracts.

8. *Health Insurance Portability and Accountability Act.* This provision was deleted because it is not considered necessary for relatively low-dollar-value, low-risk contracts.

9. *Drug-Free Workplace.* The drug-free workplace provision was deleted because it is not considered necessary for relatively low-dollar-value, low-risk contracts.

10. *Workers' Compensation.* This provision was deleted because the insurance provisions with respect to workers' compensation coverage are considered adequate for low-dollar-value, low-risk contracts.

11. *Advertising.* The advertising provision was deleted because it is not considered necessary for relatively low-dollar-value, low-risk contracts.

12. *Subcontracting.* The subcontracting provision was deleted because it is not considered necessary for relatively low-dollar-value, low-risk contracts.

13. *Unallowable Costs.* This provision was deleted because unallowable costs are not applicable for relatively low-dollar-value, low-risk contracts.

14. *Remedies Not Exclusive.* This provision was deleted because it is not considered necessary for relatively low-dollar-value, low-risk contracts.

15. *Contractor Integrity.* The provisions for contractor integrity were simplified by removing the definitions.

16. *Political Contribution Disclosure.* This provision was deleted because it is not considered necessary for relatively low-dollar-value, low-risk contracts.

17. *Assignment of Antitrust Claims.* This provision was deleted because it is not considered necessary for relatively low-dollar-value, low-risk contracts.

## 10.2 Amendments to Short-Form Contracts

The amendment template for the MSC includes spaces to check in the event that full-page exhibits to modify the contractor/agency meeting schedule, project milestone schedule or contract reports, and other deliverables are attached to the contract amendment. With respect to the short-form contract, however, changes to such dates would most likely be possible by including spaces for such changes on the amendment template as shown in Figure 10.3 — The Short-Form Contract Amendment.

| SHORT-FORM CONTRACT AMENDMENT | | | | | |
|---|---|---|---|---|---|
| **Contract No.** | | **Amendment No.:** | | **Amendment Date:** | |

| VARIABLE INFORMATION TABLE | | | |
|---|---|---|---|
| **Term of This Contract** (Complete Dates in Just One of the Following Three Rows) | | | |

| √ Below | **Term Begins** | | **Term Completion Date** | |
|---|---|---|---|---|
| | On Following Date | | On Following Date | |
| | Upon Receipt of Notice to Proceed | | Calendar Days Following Notice to Proceed | |
| | Upon Execution by Agency | | Calendar Days Following Agency Contract Execution | |
| | Agency Department | | FOB Point | |

| Terms | | Basis of Price (**Do Not √ More Than One of the Following Four Blocks**) | | | | |
|---|---|---|---|---|---|---|
| Price | | | Fixed Price | Annual Price | Monthly Price | Hourly Rate |
| Not-to-Exceed Price | | | √ if Reasonable Expenses authorized in addition to Hourly Rate | | | |

| **Contractor Contact Information** | | **Agency Contact Information** | |
|---|---|---|---|
| Contractor | | Project Manager | |
| Address | | Address | |
| City, State & ZIP | | City, State & ZIP | |
| Telephone | | Telephone | |
| Facsimile | | Facsimile | |

**Figure 10.3  The short-form contract amendment.**

| Meetings/Milestones/Deliverables | | |
|---|---|---|
| Item No. | Meeting/Milestone/Deliverable Title | Due Date |
| | | |
| | | |
| | | |

| ACCOUNT INFORMATION | | |
|---|---|---|
| Account Number | Project Name | Funding |
| | | $_____ |
| | | $_____ |

| NARRATIVE |
|---|
| |

AGENCY                           CONTRACTOR

By_____        By_____

Name_____        Name_____

Title_____        Title_____

**Figure 10.3 (continued)   The short-form contract amendment.**

## 10.3 Contracting for Services to be Provided during Emergencies

State and local government agencies have experienced situations when it was necessary to declare an actual emergency and activate their emergency operations center (EOC) due to an imminent threat to life, property, or the continuation of essential agency services. Exercises are also conducted regularly in the EOC to ensure that personnel assigned to the EOC are well trained and that plans continue to be current for future emergencies. Although private-sector contractors are not likely required to provide services or commodities during an exercise, it is most likely necessary to obtain both services and commodities from private-sector companies to support agencies during an actual emergency. When the services required during future emergencies or exercises can be determined in advance, agencies should consider the award of a contract or contracts in advance of the emergency with provisions (such as contract activation upon receipt by the contractor of a notice-to-proceed from the agency) to begin contract performance when the services are needed. Awarding contracts in advance of actual emergencies decreases the time required to employ private-sector services during actual emergencies when time is such a precious resource. Additionally, placing contracts in advance of the emergency, in the absence of pressure to place the contracts with minimal lead-time, permits agencies to ensure that contractors were selected on the basis of fair and reasonable pricing from private-sector organizations that are able to provide adequate services in a timely manner. Agencies may also wish to consider similar contracts for ordering supplies needed during an emergency.

When contracts are awarded in advance of an emergency, the lack of pressure for dealing with an ongoing emergency concurrently with award of contracts permits the agency to deal with the contract award in a more routine manner and permit time for more discretion when developing the list of firms to be solicited, scope of work, preparation of a written solicitation, selection of the best contractor (or contractors) based on detailed analyses of competitive proposals and development of terms and conditions that are agreed upon in advance of the emergency. In fact, the contracts that are activated during an emergency can be awarded routinely just as described for non-emergency contracts described in previous chapters.

Contracts placed in advance of emergencies should be reviewed periodically to ensure that the contract provisions have not become obsolete over time. When such a review reveals obsolete provisions, the contracts may be updated by amendment or it may be necessary to award replacement contracts. The extent of the changes needed to update the contract provisions could conceivably necessitate certain agencies to solicit new proposals for another competitive selection of contractors. One reason that the new round of competitive solicitations could be required is the discovery that the existing contracts are scheduled to expire in the near future.

# 10.4 Letter Contracts

## 10.4.1 Award of Letter Contracts due to Unanticipated Needs during an Emergency

Once the emergency has occurred or appears to be imminent, there is insufficient time to follow the procedures described above for award of contracts to private-sector companies or individuals. However, agencies still can plan in advance for dealing with an emergency by establishing procedures for awarding contracts in a timely manner during emergencies. Just as in the situation where it is possible to place contracts in advance for activation during an emergency, letter contracts too need not be limited to those emergencies involving threats to lives or property, but can also be awarded to ensure the continuation of essential government services.

Agencies can develop a letter contract template, such as the one provided in Appendix K, "Sample Letter Contract," in advance for award during an emergency. Development of a letter contract, containing provisions to minimize the agency's exposure to risk yet which can be awarded in time to address most emergencies, is recommended to minimize the agency's risks when it is necessary to award a contract and there is insufficient time to award a fully staffed contract.

In the absence of a template for awarding letter contracts during an actual emergency, the need for the agency to act in haste may result in awarding contracts without considering basic good contracting practices such as selecting contractors on a competitive basis whenever possible, including a scope of work that permits the agency to mitigate risks, to include some element of control over the costs incurred during the emergency, and inclusion of terms and conditions to protect the rights of the agency and the interests of the constituency.

## 10.4.2 Competitive Emergency Contracting

For many readers, the term "competitive emergency contracting" may constitute an oxymoron. There are, however, good arguments for using competition not only to achieve optimal pricing, but also to obtain earlier commencement of service delivery or the provision of more comprehensive services as well. Although most agencies are authorized to use relaxed contracting procedures during emergencies, the relaxed procedures may not relax the need to obtain competition for certain high-dollar-value projects. To award a contract, even in an emergency, it is necessary to advise prospective contractors of the agency's needs and to request the prospective contractor (or contractors) to respond by describing how they can meet the agency's needs. Although the agency's inquiries to prospective contractors are informal (and possibly oral), it is, in fact, a solicitation, and the contractors' responses (although informal) are, in fact, proposals. Such an informal solicitation can be delivered to more than one prospective contractor in essentially the same timeframe that it can be delivered to just one contractor. Likewise, the solicitation can indicate a mandatory response time to ensure that proposals are received in a timely manner. Should the transmittal of such a solicitation be limited to one contractor, the agency may be disappointed by both the delay before the contractor can commence service delivery and the level of service proposed. However, had multiple contractors been solicited, one or more of the added contractors may have included an earlier service delivery commencement date or a superior level of service, or both. It may also prove to be in the agency's best interests to award multiple contracts for the same service.

When communicating such solicitations for services to be ordered via letter contract during an emergency, the prospective contractors should be advised of the agency's criteria for selecting the successful contractor (or contractors). Advising contractors of the selection criteria is a basic tenet in government contracting, as discussed in Chapter 3. One would expect the criteria to be heavily weighted on the basis of (1) the timeline for commencing service delivery and (2) the level of service proposed. Most agencies minimize the importance of the price criterion for contractor selection during an emergency. Depending on the nature of the emergency and communication alternatives available to the agency, the solicitation may be communicated via e-mail, facsimile, telephone, in person, or any other accelerated alternative available to the agency. By soliciting competitive proposals in this manner, the agency can choose between multiple proposals available in essentially the same time period that it would have obtained one noncompetitive proposal. If the contractor that would have been solicited on a noncompetitive basis submitted a proposal for a delayed commencement of service delivery and a disappointing service level, the agency may have no option but to accept their minimalist proposal. Had the agency obtained multiple proposals, however, they likely would have had the opportunity to contract with a company or individual proposing an earlier service delivery commencement and a superior service level. Although the contractor submitting the more attractive proposal may have included a higher price, the agency would be able to award the contract based on the more critical selection criteria mentioned in their solicitation. Agencies that are not presently authorized to contract in this manner during actual emergencies need to have their contracting authority modified and procedures permitting these actions established in advance to make these options available when dealing with future emergencies.

### 10.4.2.1 Scope of Work

The agency should consider the inclusion of a template for a scope or work in their letter contract template. Providing a letter contract template with a scope of work helps to ensure that contractors are obligated to provide the needed services through scope-of-work terminology that includes the word (or words) that most compel the contractor to perform. A template containing the framework for a complete scope of work, wherein the agency personnel completing the scope of work need only fill in blanks for the work to be performed by the contractor, helps to ensure that the contractor is obligated to perform the emergency services when needed.

### 10.4.2.2 Cost Control

Although letter contracts are used in emergency conditions or in other cases when the time remaining before award of the contract precludes the availability of a fully executed definitive contract, this does not imply that the agency awarding the letter contract cannot include a fixed price, hourly rate, or not-to-exceed price. The agency's informal solicitation would normally require the prospective contractors to include proposed pricing based on a fixed price or a not-to-exceed (NTE) price. As mentioned above, the need for early service delivery commencement may require selection of other than the lowest-priced contractor. However, the NTE pricing provides an element of cost control despite selection of a contractor that did not propose the lowest pricing.

### 10.4.2.3 Terms and Conditions

The agency's standard terms and conditions are familiar to all contractors that provide goods or services during non-emergency time periods. It is very likely that those same contractors are included on the list of firms solicited to provide services during an emergency. Because those firms are familiar with the agency's terms and conditions, including insurance and indemnification provisions, such letter contracts with standard terms and conditions should be able to be awarded without experiencing delays.

## 10.4.3 Authority to Award Letter Contracts

State and local government agencies routinely have regulations in place for the award of high-value emergency contracts by an official who would not have the authority to award a non-emergency contract at the same price level. However, those same regulations also routinely require ratification, within some timeframe certain, of the contract by the official, board, or commission that has authority to award high-value contracts during non-emergency periods. The timeframe established for ratification is normally the next meeting of the commission or board when time permits placement of the contract ratification on the agenda.

## 10.4.4 Definitization of Letter Contracts

A letter contract typically has a limited effective time period and requires replacement by a definitive contract. A definitive contract is a fully staffed contract in the form described earlier for the Best Practices MSC or short-form contracts executed by an agency official authorized to approve contracts at the stated dollar value during non-emergency time periods. The expiration date of the letter contract should be clearly defined in the text of the letter contract, and there should be a statement to the effect that it is the intent of the agency to replace the letter contract with a definitive contract on or before the expiration of the letter contract. Inclusion of the expiration date and need to replace the letter contract with a definitive contract clearly informs the contractor of these agency requirements and reinforces the need to seek ratification by agency personnel involved in award of the letter contract. Agency regulations typically specify the length of time, such as 30, 60, or 90 days following contract award; when the letter contract expires; and requires definitization through the award of a standard agency contract. In the event that a definitive contract cannot be approved prior to expiration of the letter contract, the official, commission, or board responsible for approval of the definitized contract may extend the letter contract expiration date.

## 10.5 Conclusion

The best practices services contract developed on the basis of the research project conducted in preparation for writing this book was designed to accommodate the needs for high-dollar-value and high-risk contracts. However, state and local government agencies often award routine low-dollar-value contracts without extraordinary risks. Because many of the features in the Best Practices RFP and MSC were designed to lessen the risks faced by the agency, and because relatively low-dollar-value and low-risk contracts require fewer risk avoidance measures by state and local government agencies, abridged RFPs and MSCs are appropriate for low-dollar-value, low-risk contracts. Additionally, federal flow-down contract clauses and certification requirements are needed only when contracts exceed fairly high-dollar-value thresholds. Based on the lessened risk and federal contracting thresholds, it is reasonable for state and local government agencies to use short-form RFPs and contracts for relatively low-risk, low-dollar-value contracts.

Templates for short-form RFPs and contracts were prepared for the convenience of agencies that wish to simplify the process for selecting contractors, awarding contracts, and administering those contracts absent high risks and high dollar values that necessitate more complex solicitations and services contracts. These templates are also suited for academic exercises that involve relatively low-dollar-value, low-risk contracts. The rationale for making the template modifications was discussed in this chapter and the templates are provided in Appendix G, "Short-Form RFP with Short-Form Contract."

When state and local government agencies are faced with emergencies involving an imminent threat to life, property, or the provision of essential government services, time does not permit formal solicitations, sophisticated proposal evaluation processes, and the full staffing that is normally afforded services contracts awarded during non-emergency periods. Yet it is important to seek competitive pricing combined with high-quality, timely service delivery despite the existence of emergencies. Hasty contracting decisions may be necessitated by the failure to plan in advance for these services. Excessive pricing and less than optimal quality and timely commencement of service delivery are the likely results of contracting decisions made in haste. Two approaches to planning for contracted services during an emergency are to place contracts in advance of emergencies for services that can be anticipated, and to provide for a contract instrument that can be awarded expeditiously during an emergency when the need for certain services cannot be anticipated.

When services that are required during an emergency can be anticipated, agencies can release competitive solicitations for the selection of contractors and award of contracts in the usual fashion without the time constraints present during an actual emergency. Such contracts can be drafted such that they become effective upon receipt of a notice to proceed from the agency. During an emergency, the agency can quickly provide written direction to proceed via e-mail or a facsimile transmission. When such contracts have been in place for an extended period of time, say one year, it would be appropriate to review the contracts to determine whether the contract provisions are current and the contractors continue to be prepared to provide the services according to contract provisions.

When the services required during an emergency cannot be anticipated, agencies should be prepared to select contractors and place contracts while expending minimal time and effort yet while achieving competitive pricing and ensuring that quality and commencement of service delivery are not sacrificed. The contractual instrument suggested for award during actual emergencies is the letter contract. Letter contracts are intended for award in an emergency situation when there is not sufficient time to seek formal proposals, conduct sophisticated proposal evaluations, and obtain approval of the official who would normally approve such contracts at the required dollar value. Letter contracts are not intended as long-term contracting instruments, and they do require ratification from the official or governing body that would normally be required to approve such contracts awarded during non-emergency periods. Letter contracts also require replacement by a definitive contract that is fully staffed and written on the agency's standard contract template.

# Chapter 11

# Contract Review, Execution, and Audit

## Chapter Objectives

This chapter introduces readers to the timing, security, and additional issues involved in the execution of contracts by contractors. The agency's contract review and execution process is normally conducted following execution by the contractor and is discussed in that sequence in this text; however, there is also a discussion of potential revisions to this sequence resulting from the capability for conducting the agency's contract review function more efficiently using computer networking technology.

The extent of contract review prior to presenting contracts to agency officials for execution is thoroughly explored in this chapter. Readers are introduced to a form used as a contract cover sheet during the review and execution process. The form was designed to ensure conformance with agency policy regarding contractor selection and pricing. The various aspects of contract reviews performed by state and local government agencies include:

- Contract review by contract management staff
- Contract review by financial management staff
- Contract review by legal counsel
- Online contract review
- Hard copy contract review

There is also a discussion of contract characteristics that should be considered by elected and appointed officials as well as career civil servants who execute contracts for state and local government agencies, actions that should be considered when fully executed contracts are distributed to the contractor and various agency departments, and the need for follow-up contract audits and features to build into a contract audit program.

## 11.1 Contract Execution by Contractor

Ideally, the contractor executes the document before it is sent through the contracting agency's review process in preparation for execution by the agency. The primary reason for obtaining the contractor's execution prior to the internal agency review is that review and execution by the contracting agency typically requires considerably more time than the contractor's review and execution. Should the contractor take exception to any terms and conditions following the possibly lengthy contracting agency internal review and execution process, that entire process would need to be repeated following the contractor revisions, thus nearly doubling the time and effort required to obtain a fully executed contract.

Immediately following contract negotiations, the contract template can normally be modified to incorporate the negotiated changes. Once those changes have been completed, the negotiated contract document can be printed. If the negotiations were conducted on a face-to-face basis, at the agency's facilities, and with a contractor representative with authority to execute the contract for the contractor, the contractor representative could then sign the negotiated contract. The contract could then begin its journey through the agency's contract review and execution process. If negotiations were conducted by telephone, e-mail, or a combination of the two, the final contract document can be sent to the contractor as an e-mail attachment for printing and execution by the contractor. When the signed contract is returned to the agency, it should be reviewed once again to ensure that there were no unauthorized changes. When a contract document is sent to a contractor for execution, it is no longer in the agency's control, and page substitutions or other changes could be made to the contract version sent to the contractor. If the agency elects to send a contract to a contractor as an e-mail attachment, consideration should be given to sending it as a .pdf file or in some alternative format that cannot readily be changed. Should an easily alterable electronic version of the document be sent to the contractor, an unscrupulous contractor could make a change that would be difficult to detect. Therefore, the agency should consider this possibility when establishing practices for electronic contract document transmittal.

Once the contract has been printed and executed by the contractor, the document can be mailed or transmitted overnight to the contracting agency for execution. If the contracting agency accepts facsimile or electronic signatures on contracts, full executing can be further expedited by faxing or e-mailing a contractor-executed contract to the contracting agency.

## 11.2 Contract Review

If the Model Services Contract (MSC) attached to the Request for Proposals (RFP) had been reviewed by agency staff prior to release of the RFP, then the contract review prior to execution may be limited to the changes to the MSC since release of the RFP. If the RFP and MSC are based on the agency's templates, the insurance requirements and terms and conditions would be standard agency boilerplate; and if the scope of work had been prepared from the agency template, then legal counsel and finance would likely not need to review the RFP prior to release. If the RFP is for an ongoing project with an established scope of work, the contract management staff would likely not need to review the RFP prior to release. However, when newly drafted contract documents are incorporated in the MSC attached to the RFP, the contract management staff and other relevant agency staff should be required to review the RFP prior to its release. This contract document review conducted prior to RFP release is necessary to correct potential contract anomalies at this early stage of the procurement process. The early correction of errors is intended to avoid delays associated with error correction following review of the MSC by prospective contractors. The balance of the discussion in this chapter is based on the assumption that if newly drafted materials are included in the MSC, they are reviewed by the appropriate agency staff prior to release of the RFP.

The objective of the contract review is to ensure that the contractor was selected in compliance with agency practices, the pricing is fair and reasonable, the required funding is available, and the contract was drafted in proper legal form. The contract review is also used to ensure that the agency's risks are addressed, the contractor's responsibilities are clearly specified, there are no internal inconsistencies in the contractual documentation, the understanding of the contracting parties is clearly described, and the contract was prepared in conformance with the agency's contracting practices. The availability of funding is normally verified by the financial staff while review as to legal form is normally verified by in-house legal counsel. The financial staff and legal counsel are referred to as support staff during the discussion of the contract review and execution process. All aspects of the contract review process, other than fund availability and legal form, are normally performed by agency officials, directors, executive-level personnel, or contracts professionals. Contracting professionals may be tasked with reviewing contracts for the agency officials prior to executing contracts.

Contract review prior to execution may be conducted differently, depending on internal agency organization, policy, and practices. The contract management staff function may be centralized or decentralized to various departments. Although the departments participating in contract review may vary depending on internal practices, the remainder of this discussion is based on the assumption that contract management, legal counsel, and finance are the support departments that review contracts prior to execution by the agency representative responsible for final approval of contracts. Although certain state and local government agencies undoubtedly use personnel in other functions to conduct the contract review, all the review functions described below should be completed prior to contract execution. Failure to complete all the review functions can subject the agency to unnecessary risk assumption.

## 11.2.1 Contract Review by Contract Management Staff

The contract management staff is normally responsible for review of all matters relating to the solicitation, source selection, contract negotiation, and drafting of the contractual documents. To facilitate and document the contract management review, as well as the financial and legal counsel reviews and contract execution, agencies are encouraged to adopt a contract cover sheet essentially in the format of Figure 11.1. This cover sheet would then accompany the contract as it progresses through the review and execution process. This discussion regarding Figure 11.1 assumes that contract review is conducted on hard-copy contracts. A variation of this process involving an online contract review process is discussed later in this chapter.

For contracts based on agency templates and selection of the contractor through free and open competition, a relatively routine review process should be expected. Other than the contract document, the only other documents that are required to complete the review are a completed contract review and execution request, and a summary of the competition results as required by footnote 3 on the contract review and execution request (Figure 11.1). The existence of free and open competition greatly simplifies the justification of both contractor selection and price reasonableness. It is generally not necessary to spend considerable time evaluating contractor selection and price reasonableness when the contractor was selected through free and open competition, unless other than the low-priced contractor was selected. In this event, it would be prudent to evaluate the proposal evaluation criteria, weighted criteria, if applicable, and proposal evaluation calculations to verify that contractor selection was accurate.

Contract review also requires verification that entries in the variable information table correspond to the information on the contract review and execution request and the summary of competitive results. The insurance requirements and terms and conditions should be reviewed to determine that the standard templates were not modified. Any exceptions, including the incorporation of contractor terms and conditions, require review to determine that contractor provisions are acceptable or if they require modification or deletion. The scope of work is checked to ensure that it is clear, complete, and that the word "shall" (or other word considered most compelling) is used whenever contractor tasks are mandatory. Mathematical calculations are verified as well during this review by the contract management staff.

| CONTRACT REVIEW AND EXECUTION | | | | | | | |
|---|---|---|---|---|---|---|---|
| **CONTRACTOR** | | | **CONTRACT** | | | | |
| Contractor | | | Number | | | | |
| Address 1 | | | Project | | | | |
| Address 2 | | | Price | | | | |
| Telephone | | | Type[1] | | FP | NTE | Other |
| Facsimile | | | Account[2] | | | | |
| Email | | | Department | | | | |
| Proj Manager | | | Proj Manager | | | | |
| Basis for Price Reasonableness | | Adequate Competition[3] | | | Other[4] | | |
| Basis for Source Selection | | Adequate Competition[2] | | | Other[5] | | |
| Remarks: | | | | | | | |

The undersigned department head or designee hereby certifies that the attached contract was solicited and the contractor was selected in complete conformance with agency policy and all applicable laws. Consideration was given to agency policy regarding conflicts of interest, scrutiny of non-agency contract provisions, source selection, price reasonableness and adequacy of the scope of work. All exceptions are noted in Remarks or described in an attached document.

| Typed or Printed Name | Signature | Date |
|---|---|---|
| | | |
| Contract Management Review | | |
| Financial Management Review | | |
| Legal Counsel Review | | |
| Executed By | | |

[1]Check "FP" for fixed price contract. Check "NTE" for fixed price contract with not-to-exceed ceiling price. Check "Other" for any other type of contract and explain in Remarks or attach explanation.
[2]Explain multiple account numbers in Remarks.
[3]Attach summary of results from competition.
[4]Explain in Remarks or attach price analysis.
[5]Explain in Remarks if price is $5,000 or less. Attach sole source approval if price exceeds $5,000.

**Figure 11.1   Contract review and execution form.**

If time permits, the added analyses described in the audit section of this chapter, just prior to the chapter conclusion would also be performed prior to contract execution. However, state and local government agencies generally do not enjoy the availability of resources needed to review all contracts to this extent. As described in the audit section of this chapter, certain contracts are selected after they have been awarded for a more thorough review to identify ongoing problems in the agency's contracting process.

## 11.2.2 Contract Review by Financial Management Staff

The timing of the financial review may vary, depending on internal policy and procedure. In some organizations, financial review is completed prior to contract execution while in other organizations, financial review is completed following contract execution. Verification of account number (or numbers) and availability of funding combined with encumbrance of the funds required to compensate the contractor normally constitute the minimum elements of the financial review. Verification of other financial features depends on agency policy.

## 11.2.3 Contract Review by Legal Counsel

Contract review by the agency's in-house legal counsel is ideally accomplished immediately prior to execution by the chief elected official or head of the governing body or her or his designated representative. In-house counsel often reviews the contract to the extent necessary to determine that it meets legal form. More time may be expended on contract provisions, such as indemnification, which could impede future legal actions if improperly drafted.

## 11.2.4 Online Contract Review

Reviews conducted on hard-copy contracts may be recorded by original signatures by reviewing officials on the contract documents, one of which is provided to the contractor following full execution of the contract. Alternatively, the support department review may be memorialized on a separate document maintained internally to document the support department review. Signatures on the contract review and execution request form could serve as this separate record of the contract review.

As an alternative to reviewing hard-copy contract documents, some organizations post contracts on shared computer servers, thus permitting access to the document by the various departments participating in the contract review process. Internal contract review can be facilitated by storing an electronic version of the contract document where it can be accessed by multiple departments, such as on a shared server. Ideally, the contractor finds the contracting agency's standard terms and conditions and insurance requirements acceptable. In this event, analyses may be limited to variable information table entries and the scope of work. Due to the variations between contract reviews conducted online and reviews of hard-copy contractual documents, separate discussions are provided for each alternative.

For online reviews conducted prior to contractor execution, this function is facilitated when the "track changes" feature of Microsoft Word or other word processing program is employed. The "track changes" feature highlights text changes through differing font colors and underlining, and identifies the author of text changes. Highlighted changes can be made to the contract document on the shared server while discussion of the changes is conducted by e-mail or telephone. Alternatively, documents with highlighting of the proposed changes that are not on a shared server may be attached to an e-mail for consideration by all reviewing parties. Either method of online review of contracts avoids the delays associated with making hard-copy changes and forwarding the actual document to the next reviewing or executing official. The online review process also avoids delays associated with changes made subsequent to review completion by another official. An example of this type of delay would be a change to a hard-copy contract made by legal counsel following completion of the contract management and financial reviews. In this event, it would be necessary for contract management and financial management staffs to review the contract again.

When the online review is conducted after the contractor executes the contract, it may not be possible to use the "track changes" function; however, the contract document may be scanned and posted to a shared server or attached to an e-mail and sent to all contract reviewers. Once the contract is made available to all concerned, comments can be made via e-mail or conferencing options until agreement is reached on any changes required. If changes are necessary following contractor execution, it may be possible to make insignificant changes in handwriting and have both the agency and contractor executing officials initial the changes. Naturally, changes to information used to populate a computer database would require correction and reprinting of the contract, or an amendment to the contract that is executed concurrently with the contract to permit the needed update to the computer database. When the contract is corrected and reprinted to correct information collected to populate the computer database, or to correct other significant errors, the contractor needs to execute the revised version of the contract.

Regardless of the method used to conduct the online contract review, completion of the review may be documented by printing copies of e-mails indicating a satisfactory review or by submittal of a form similar to the one depicted in Figure 11.1.

## 11.2.5 Hard-Copy Contract Review

Review of hard-copy contracts generally requires considerably more time than an online review process. This is due primarily to the need to physically move the hard-copy documents from one office to another to conduct the reviews sequentially. Furthermore, should a reviewer determine that a change is required following the approval of an earlier reviewer, the earlier reviewer must be provided another opportunity to review the contract following changes made since her or his most recent review. This process can be time consuming when the reviews are conducted on hard copies. It is necessary to physically send documents from office to office, gather the reviewers together for a face-to-face meeting or closed-circuit conference, or attempt to discuss the proposed changes by telephone or e-mail. Posting the contract on a shared server that all reviewers can access provides the most expedient solution for reviewers to coordinate the changes and develop a contract document that is acceptable to all concerned. Participation in negotiations by representatives from the reviewing departments would help facilitate contract review; however, staffing levels in the reviewing departments often makes this level of negotiation participation impractical.

Regardless of what parties participated in the contract review or negotiations, however, it is necessary to determine that no unauthorized changes have been made to the standard boilerplate documents prior to any facilitated or expedited contract review. Although the availability of word processing programs has greatly simplified the preparation of contract documents, this technology has also facilitated the potential for difficult-to-detect illicit changes to standard documents. Two methods to help ensure that there have been no such unauthorized changes are (1) the use of distinctive offset printed documents that cannot be duplicated through word processing or (2) a certification from the department originating the contracts that no unauthorized changes have been made. Whenever there is any doubt about the possibility of unauthorized changes, however, the standard contract templates should be read along with the other contract documents as a routine practice in the contract review process. This added precaution helps to further guard against unauthorized changes to the contract document.

Another technique for ensuring that pages have not been substituted in reviewed and executed hard-copy contracts is to provide a space on each page for the reviewing and executing officials to initial each page after reviewing them.

# 11.3 Contract Execution by Contracting Agency

Contract execution refers to the signing of a contract by an individual duly authorized to bind and commit her or his company or organization to the provisions of the contract being signed. Signature by staff personnel such as legal counsel to indicate concurrence that a contract is sufficient as to form does not constitute execution of a contract. A contract that is executed by all parties to the contract is considered *fully executed*. Ratification of contracts refers to the approval of contracts that were originally awarded by an individual who did not have the authority to execute the contract. In certain cases, the contract may have been appropriately awarded during an actual emergency to help protect lives, property, or the continuation of essential government services. In other instances, the official, board, or commission with authority to award the contracts may have been asked to ratify a contract that had been inappropriately awarded by an individual who lacked the required authority to execute the contract.

As mentioned earlier, depending on contracting agency policy, the financial review may be conducted prior to or following contract execution. However, legal counsel review should always be accomplished prior to execution by the contracting agency. Legal counsel review is essential to ensure that the contract is constructed in legal form prior to being presented to the agency official who is responsible for execution of that contract.

The novice agency official, executive, or employee may feel confident in executing a contract, even if she or he was not involved in the negotiations, based on the fact that the contract was previously reviewed by legal counsel and a finance professional. However, the limited scope of those reviews must be considered prior to executing the contract for the agency or recommending approval of the contract by the chief elected official or governing body. Astute agency representatives read every page of a contract prior to execution or making a recommendation for approval and execution. It is also prudent for senior agency officials to read the provisions of the contract prior to applying their signatures. At this point it is relevant to remind contract professionals and agency officials to take heed of the old axiom, "Read the contract."

A critical reading of the contract is especially called for prior to execution if the contract was prepared and negotiated by department personnel with little or no input from employees outside their department. Key considerations in reviewing the contract include:

- Contractor selection consistent with contracting agency policies
- Fair and reasonable pricing
- Contract provisions make good business sense
- Accurate mathematical calculations
- Each word, sentence, and paragraph is reviewed to ensure internal consistency
- All tasks expected of the contractor are included in the scope of work
- Consistency between the number and description of contractor tasks throughout the scope of work
- Most compelling word such as "shall" requiring contractor to perform
- Scope-of-work specifies party responsible for performing tasks
- Troublesome terms and conditions (as discussed in Chapter 7) not included in the contract

- Absence of evergreen clauses
- Conformance with grant requirements

Several of the above considerations, such as contractor selection and price reasonableness, cannot be determined solely by reading the contract. However, a review of the department's explanation for source selection and price reasonableness on a form such as the one provided in Figure 11.1, and other documentation that accompanies the contract when it is forwarded for execution, addresses these considerations.

Ensuring that the contract provisions make good business sense is normally not especially challenging when the agency prepared the scope-of-work and the contract provisions are limited to the agency's standard boilerplate. However, when the contractor prepares the scope-of-work and other contract provisions, or makes modifications to agency-prepared documents, the contractual documents need to be carefully scrutinized. Contractor-prepared documents, or modifications to agency documents, are generally made to limit the contractor's risks. Oftentimes, such reductions in the risks to the contractor are limited to the point where the contractor's commitment is negligible. Department personnel, contracting professionals, and other agency officials and employees need to evaluate the level of contractor commitment and determine whether a positive cost/benefit relationship still exists after the contractor's changes are incorporated in the contract.

Calculations should be verified to ensure that the dollar, quantity, and all other mathematical calculations reflected in the contract were properly performed. Failure to verify the mathematical calculations could result in errors in the contract document that could prove costly or troublesome to the agency.

In addition to verification that each word in the contract is correct, it is necessary to evaluate the contract provisions at the level of the sentences, paragraphs, and entire contract document to ensure that the document is internally consistent. Internal consistency problems usually occur when a contract document for another contractor or another project is modified for the present project. Internal inconsistencies also tend to occur when a previous year's contract for the same services is modified and changes are made in some sections but missed in others. Occasionally, some dates are modified but others are missed, resulting in nonsensical scheduling. Therefore, while ensuring that individual words, sentences, and other subparts of the contract document are accurate, the reviewer also needs to pay particular attention to the overall document to ensure internal consistency throughout the document.

During an actual contract review, conducted shortly before the contract was to be presented for execution, a highly significant inconsistency was detected. One reviewer noted that an address in one section of the contract did not exactly match the address in another section of the contract. Because the contract was for the demolition of a house that had been declared a health hazard, failure to detect that inconsistency could have resulted in the demolition of the wrong house.

There may also be consistency problems related to mismatching quantities in the contract documents and specifically in the scope of work. For example, one statement may indicate that the contractor is responsible for the four tasks described below. However, there may be just three tasks described in the text following that declaration.

Contract documents, and especially the scope-of-work, are likely to begin with statements to the effect that a contractor "shall" perform a particular task. However, further into the document the person drafting the document may elect to use a supposed synonym such as "may" or "should," which does not compel the contractor to perform that particular task.

A common, recurring problem found in numerous scope-of-work documents is a statement near the beginning of the document stating that a contractor shall perform a number of specific tasks, followed by a statement that the agency shall perform one or more tasks and, finally, a statement that one or more additional tasks are performed, but with no indication of which party to the contract is responsible for performing the additional tasks.

Terms and conditions, especially those prepared by the contractor, should be carefully reviewed to ensure that there are no provisions that would prove disadvantageous to the agency. Examples of such potentially unfavorable terms can be found in Chapter 7 in the section entitled "Objectionable or Unacceptable Contract Provisions."

Should the executed contract include an evergreen clause, a termination letter should be sent to the contractor at the time of contract execution or shortly thereafter. If there is a delay in sending the termination letter to the contractor, there is the possibility that sending the termination letter is overlooked and that the contract is, therefore, unexpectedly extended against the wishes of the agency. It is highly recommended that termination notices, as well as other critical contract correspondence, be sent via certified mail with a return receipt requested. When the termination letter (or other significant letter) cannot be sent in this manner, consideration should be given to obtaining a signed receipt for a hand-carried letter, proof of delivery for overnight letters, or printing a transmittal report for documents sent via facsimile. If the agency does not have proof that critical contract correspondence was delivered to the contractor, there is the possibility that the contractor either did not receive the correspondence or that the contractor denies receiving the correspondence.

If an agency official reviewing a contract prior to execution determines that contract changes are required prior to execution, this concern should be communicated to the contract preparer or negotiator immediately following complete contract review when all such concerns are known. Because the discovery of significant errors at this point in the contract review and approval process can result in a catastrophic delay in contract approval, department personnel preparing or negotiating contracts that vary from the contracting agency's standard template should be encouraged to coordinate such deviations as soon as the need to vary from the standard template becomes known. Coordination of such deviations should be completed with the agency official who ultimately executes the contract or recommends approval and execution by the chief elected official or governing body. Because agency staff undoubtedly expended considerable time and resources developing standard contract templates, it is necessary to analyze template modifications to ensure that the changes do not expose the agency to unacceptable risk. The agency official, in consultation with a contracts professional if needed, may then determine whether it is also necessary to coordinate the deviations with legal counsel or other agency representatives.

Should the contract fail to conform to the contracting agency's standards when immediate execution of the contract is required and it is not possible to make a correction or issue a concurrent amendment, consideration should be given to the issuance of a letter contract as discussed in Chapter 10. The use of a letter contract permits expedited execution of a contract to permit commencement of service delivery while providing the agency with more time to develop a definitive contract that conforms to the agency's standards.

## 11.4 Distribution of Fully Executed Contracts

Once the agreement is fully executed, standard contract distribution should be accomplished. Service delivery may not commence until the contractor receives the fully executed contract, and agency departments involved in contracting activities during the contract term may need a copy of the contract to properly perform their contracting responsibilities. Contracting agency practices may call for distribution to be made by the executing party, the department that prepared the contract, or the combined effort of both. In some cases, the executing party may make internal agency distribution but send the contractor's copy to the department along with the department's copy of the contract. Upon receipt of the fully executed contract, the department would normally keep one wet-signed contract for its files. The department normally prepares a transmittal letter to forward another wet-signed contract to the contractor. "Wet-signed contract" is the term used to describe a contract with original signatures. Due to the excellent quality of modern copying equipment, it is recommended that contracts printed in black be signed in blue, and that copies of original contracts not be made on color copiers. The transmittal letter would normally state that the fully executed contract for the named project and agreed-to pricing is enclosed. The letter should also advise the contractor to proceed with the work upon receipt of the contract or provide an alternative start date. Although contractors normally commence performance under the contract once they receive the fully executed contract, including advice to the contractor to proceed removes the possibility of a misunderstanding regarding the time to commence contract work. The agency could also use this letter as an opportunity to outline its expectations from the contractor and make reference to the next or next few milestones or contractual requirements. It is customary to include a statement to the effect that the agency official or contracting professional looks forward to working with the contractor through completion of the project.

When it is essential to have the contractor commence work before it is possible to get the fully executed contract to the contractor, the agency may send a notice of contract award via facsimile, e-mail, or some other expedited method. The notice of contract award should be addressed to the contractor's project manager and fully describe the contract to include the contract number, project, solicitation number, contract price, and any other relevant information to identify the contract. Failure to address the notice of contract award in this manner and to provide this identifying information could lead to confusion regarding the contract that was approved. It is recommended that the notice of contract award indicate the date to commence work and the fact that the fully executed contract will be sent in the near future.

## 11.5 Contract Audit

Although the contract review conducted prior to execution of the contract evaluated the reasonableness of the action taken by agency personnel preparing the contract documents, time constraints normally do not permit verification of the information supporting contractor selection, price reasonableness, and other functions performed to complete the contract documents. To compensate for the lack of time needed for such thorough analyses of all contracts prior to execution, agencies typically elect to audit a sample of the contracts that were executed during some recent time period, such as a fiscal year. Sampling would likely be based on the selection for audit of 100 percent of the highest-priced contracts, a lower percentage (e.g., 40 percent) of the mid-priced contracts, and a considerably lower percentage (e.g., 10 percent) of low-priced contracts.

Contract audits should be conducted by contracts professionals and should include review of all aspects of the contract and the contracting process as described later in this chapter. Contract audits by financial or legal professionals likely ensure that the financial or legal aspects of the contract are proper; however, financial professionals and legal counsel normally conduct a 100 percent review of contracts prior to contract execution. Audits by financial auditors are not normally required unless the contracts are selected for periodic financial audits or there is some subsequent indicator of a problem with a contract or contract review process.

The reason for reviewing the contractor selection process is to determine whether the committee members complied with the description of the source selection process described in the solicitation, to ensure that the committee evaluated the proposals according to the criteria in the solicitation, to determine whether weighted criteria were properly applied (if applicable), to determine whether the committee members used proportional scores for the life cycle cost or proposed price (as applicable), as well as to check for consistency between the instructions given to committee members and the record of the proposal evaluation process. In the event that the contractor was selected without the benefit of competition, the sole source justification should be reviewed to ensure that only one contractor was qualified and available for award of the contract. Department personnel preparing sole source justifications are prone to overlooking the existence of competitors of the contractor being recommended for a sole source contract. An example of checking the facts could be in the case where the sole source contract was justified on the basis that the contractor was the only known company capable of providing the services being contracted out. A routine Internet search often results in the identification of a number of competitors for virtually all contractors. In addition to ensuring that the justification is written in a convincing manner, relevant facts should be checked when possible.

Just as with justifying the source selection, the fairness and reasonableness of the pricing is simplified when the contractor is selected on a competitive basis. When the contractor is selected without the benefit of competition, justification of pricing becomes more difficult. Departments often attempt to justify pricing on noncompetitive contracts by the fact that the pricing from the previous year has either not increased at all or that any increase was consistent with inflation. However, if the previous price was based on a sole source contract without adequate price or cost analysis, then more justification would be required to determine that present pricing is fair and reasonable. If a department prepared a truly independent estimate of the pricing for the service prior to receipt of the proposals, then that independent estimate may be used to justify contract pricing. However, if that "independent" price estimate was prepared merely by contacting the contractor and asking for their estimated price prior to releasing the RFP, then that "independent" estimate would not be acceptable. Catalog or published pricing may be used to justify the pricing if the contractor does not routinely grant steep discounts that were not matched for the agency on the immediate contract. Pricing paid by other agencies for the same or similar services may be used to justify contract pricing if the other agency established their pricing on the basis of competition, or another method acceptable to the agency.

Time permitting, the actions included in the contract review by the contract management staff prior to contract execution should be repeated during the contract audit. This repeat of contract features reviewed prior to contract execution assists in the identification of problems with the contracting process and the contract review process as well. An audit of features reviewed prior to contract execution would be most appropriate for high-dollar-value contracts.

If the audit reveals potential problems associated with the source selection, the auditor might consider a more intensive investigation of the source selection process as described in Chapter 6.

The periodic audit of the contracting function should also audit the contract administration phase of the contract that begins immediately following contract award. The contract administration function is discussed in Chapter 12. Audit of the contract administration function can usually be conducted by reviewing the agency's policies and procedures with respect to the administration of contracts, and then reviewing the contract administration records, including contract amendments and their associated documentation, to confirm that this function is being performed in conformance with applicable policies and procedures.

## 11.6 Conclusion

The application of information technology may introduce efficiencies and facilitate the agency's review of contract documents. Posting contracts on a server that can be accessed by all parties that review contracts permits a more efficient concurrent review by all interested parties rather than the traditional sequential review of contracts. This concurrent review could also be facilitated and expedited following contractor execution by scanning the executed contract and placing it online for review by agency staff.

Contractors have traditionally executed contracts prior to the internal agency contract review and execution. An alternative approach to traditional contract reviews that deserves consideration by state and local government agencies is for the contracting and finance staff as well as legal counsel to review RFPs with MSCs prior to release of RFPs to prospective contractors. This initial review of the MSC prior to RFP release helps avoid the traditional problem associated with the discovery of nonconforming contracts following contractor execution. Contract anomalies discovered subsequent to contractor execution require negotiations with the contractor and revisions to the contract that would have been accomplished more efficiently if completed earlier in the contracting cycle. The review of the contract prior to release of the RFP would not eliminate the need for contract review again prior to execution by the agency; however, it could surface contract anomalies that could be corrected at this more opportune time.

A cover sheet, Figure 11.1, was proposed to facilitate the contract review and to ensure evaluation of agency policies and procedures, conformance with respect to contractor selection, price reasonableness, conflicts of interest, nonstandard contract provisions, and the adequacy of the scope of work.

Contract reviews are conducted to ensue that the contract documents, process for selecting contractors, and determination of price reasonableness are consistent with agency policy before the contracts are executed. Reading the contract, reviewing the contract review and execution request form, when combined with reading the other documentation accompanying the contract, provide the official responsible for executing the contract with sufficient information to determine that the contract was or was not prepared in conformance with agency policies and procedures.

Once contracts are fully executed, wet-signed copies are provided to the agency department that initiated the contracting action and to the contractor. Copies of the contract are distributed to other interested parties as needed.

Because time does not permit verification of all the actions taken during contractor selection, negotiation, and award of the contract, contracts are normally selected on a sampling basis for audit of the actions taken through award of the contract. Contract administration activities should also be subject to audit. Contract audits are performed to verify that the contracting process was conducted according to agency policies and procedures. The sampling process would normally select all high-dollar-value contracts for audit, as well as a decreasing percentage of contracts, correlated with the contract dollar value, for the mid-priced and low-priced contracts.

# Chapter 12

# Contract Administration and Closeout

## Chapter Objectives

This chapter provides the readers with an introduction to the contract administration and contract closeout functions, definitions for terminology applicable to these final phases of the contracting cycle, and specific information on contract administration and closeout functions.

The specific information on contract administration functions covers the following topics:

- Approval of contractor billings
- Managing contractor cost and schedule performance
- Contract amendments
- Managing completion of milestones and deliverables
- Reacting to substandard contractor performance

The specific information on contract closeout functions covers the following topics:

- Contractor performance reports
- Relief of financial encumbrances
- Records retention

## 12.1 Contract Administration

Contract administration involves monitoring the contractor's performance during the term of the contract to ensure that contractor obligations are met, schedules are adhered to, all conditions with respect to deliverables are met, and billings are accurate and timely. Contract amendments are, necessarily, made after award of the contract and are considered a function of contract administration. Contractors do not invariably encounter problems during the term of the contract; however, addressing these problems when they do occur is also a function of contract administration.

Thoughtful structuring of the scope of work during the advance procurement planning phase to completely describe the contractor's responsibilities, schedules, and contract deliverables proves beneficial when it is time to perform the contract administration functions. Project management software should be used to monitor the contractor's milestones and deliverables for large contracts with numerous milestones and deliverables. Such software programs are readily available, more efficient, and less labor intensive than manually tracking contractor responsibilities, schedules, and deliverables. Less complex contracts might be monitored less formally with a spreadsheet or by merely annotating future delivery dates on an electronic calendar. However, once project management software has been implemented, it should be used to track all active contracts regardless of contract complexity. When project management software is being used to track major contracts, it can be used to also track less complex contracts with the same efficiencies afforded large complex contracts, and using the same software to track both large and less complex contracts avoids the inconvenience of using separate tracking systems. Contractor prepared reports depicting schedule performance are also useful to ensure that the contractor and the agency have a mutual understanding of the schedule status.

Once the contractor's schedule is being monitored electronically, the project manager, contract administrator, or other individual responsible for monitoring the contractor's performance can concentrate more on the quality of the contractor's work product. Despite the fact that the contractor's schedule performance may be monitored electronically, however, monitoring contractor performance all too frequently is assigned a lower priority than most other contract management responsibilities. Minimizing one's concentration on monitoring a contractor's performance consistently results in considerable added workload if substandard contractor performance is not discovered until the problems have compounded and successful completion of the contractual work has been compromised.

### 12.1.1 Approval of Contractor Billings

Ensuring that the unit prices, price extensions, and subtotals on the invoice are totaled correctly for the amount claimed is the most basic element of invoice evaluation prior to approval. However, there are additional factors to consider when approving contractor payments. Contractors may submit an invoice for milestone completion, for the percentage of completion for some task, or some other billable item in anticipation of completing that milestone by the time the invoice is reviewed. However, the contractor could have been overly optimistic and may not have completed all the work claimed when the project manager reviews the invoice. Rather than placing complete trust in the contractor's reporting of schedule progress, the project manager should verify milestone completions, status of deliverables, and other billable costs prior to approval of the invoice. If the invoice includes the billing for a deliverable, the invoice review should include verification not only that the deliverable was received, but also that it is acceptable. Occasionally, contractors use an erroneous billing rate such as the incorrect hourly rate for a specific position title. While these are assumed to be honest errors, experience indicates that the errors are almost invariably in the contractor's favor. If anomalies are discovered during the invoice review process, the contractor should be requested to submit a revised invoice. Significant errors on invoices are normally corrected by canceling the invoice and issuing a revised invoice; however, minor pen-and-ink corrections to the invoice are permitted if acceptable to the contractor and if this practice is consistent with agency policy.

If there is sufficient information available on the invoice to compare the amount of contract funding available to the percentage of completed work, that comparison should be made. If the contractor is spending funds at a rate faster than the work is being completed, then the contracting agency should be concerned that the contractor may be in danger of realizing a loss in the event of a fixed-price or not-to-exceed (NTE) contract or an overrun in the event of a cost-reimbursement contract. In either event, the detection of a spend rate in excess of the contractor's work progress should be addressed with the contractor to ensure that financial considerations do not interfere with successful contract completion.

Overrun of cost occurs when the contractor expends funds in excess of the original target cost in the absence of a change in the scope of work. See the definition of cost growth below to differentiate between these two terms. Target cost is the cost associated with a cost-reimbursement contract that the contracting agency and contractor agree to as the expected cost for completion of the work described in the scope of work. This cost is normally determined through cost analysis and subsequent negotiation of the cost proposal submitted by the contractor. Underrun of cost is the exact opposite of overrun of cost. Cost growth occurs when a change in scope results in an amendment to the contract that increases the target cost and fee. Such a change in scope agreed to by both parties to the contract is considered cost growth and not cost overrun. By contrast, an overrun would occur when the contractor expends funds in excess of the target cost without an associated change in scope.

Change in scope occurs when the work to be performed by the contractor is modified from the original scope of work by agreement of the parties to the contract. The details of the change in scope, and possibly associated changes to the price or schedule, are normally negotiated by the contracting parties and formalized through a written contract amendment.

"Amendment" is the term used for the most formal type of a bilateral modification to a contract. Amendments are normally staffed, reviewed, and executed in the same manner as contracts. However, some agencies permit limited staffing and execution at a lower organizational level for amendments below a certain dollar value or percentage of the total contract price.

"Modification" is the generic term for any alteration to a contract. Modifications are generally limited to amendments and change orders. Bilateral refers to signing, or executing, a contract or modification thereto by both parties to the contract. Unilateral changes to a contract are those changes that are made with the signature of just one party to the contract: the government. State or local agency contracts and modifications thereto normally require bilateral agreements.

Change orders may be issued when there is an urgency to change the scope of work. Staff review is not normally required when a project manager issues a change order to a contractor. Change orders in state and local government contracting are normally limited to construction contracts, and can normally be approved, within certain price parameters, at a lower organizational level than the original contract. Certain state or local government agencies require the less formal change orders to be formalized at some subsequent time by an amendment. In this case, several change orders may normally be formalized by a single amendment.

### 12.1.2 Managing Contractor Cost and Schedule Performance

Agencies may wish to perform in-depth analyses of the expenditure rate and schedule performance for high-dollar-value contracts to determine if the contractor is expected to complete the contract work without exceeding the NTE price or experiencing an overrun. To ensure that the agency is able to perform a sophisticated analysis of the contractor's cost/schedule performance, consideration should be given, when the contract is first drafted, to making information needed for such an analysis available by including payment provisions and contractor reporting requirements that provide sufficient information to compare the percent of contract completion to the contractor's expenditure rate. Although the agency might consider the evaluation of this information at the total contract price level, schedule performance at this level is difficult to verify and it does not isolate the specific tasks where a problematic expenditure rate is imminent. Ideally, when the agency has a vested interest in monitoring the contractor's expenditure rate, the contract cost and invoices are broken out for analysis at the individual task level. When the agency structures the contract such that it knows the estimated costs for each task and the contractor is required to invoice at the task level, it is possible to require the contractor to report on the percentage of completion for each of the priced tasks and compare that percentage to the percentage of funds expended. This comparison can then be used to forecast the funds required to complete the tasks and the funds required to complete the entire contract. The resultant forecast of funds required to complete the tasks can be compared with the funds budgeted for that task to determine whether the spend rate is favorable or unfavorable. A tool and a formula for making an estimate of expenditures at completion at both the task level and at the contract level are presented below.

State and local government agencies should track the cost and schedule performance on all cost-reimbursement contracts. A comparison of the rate of expenditures to schedule progress permits the agency to determine in advance whether or not the contractor is expected to experience a cost overrun. Consideration should also be given to tracking cost and schedule performance on NTE contracts when they are for high-dollar-value contracts or for challenging projects, or if they were placed with contractors lacking excellent financial strength. If a contractor with a high-dollar-value contract or without excellent financial strength is in danger of having its expenditures exceed the NTE ceiling, contract completion could be jeopardized. When it is decided to track cost and schedule performance, that decision should be made prior to completion of the Request for Proposals (RFP). The decision to track the contractor's cost and schedule performance can be implemented subsequent to issuance of the RFP; however, incorporating the reporting requirements into the contract following release of the RFP becomes problematic. When the decision to track cost and schedule performance is made prior to release of the solicitation, the RFP can include instructions for the contractors to break out their pricing at the task level, prepare invoices at that same task level, and provide periodic reports on their schedule performance at the task level.

The calculation for making this estimate at completion is to divide the invoiced price by the percent of completion and then multiply the result by 100. This formula is based on the assumption that the contractor's spend rate continues in relationship to its progress from the date of the analysis through task completion. For example, the formula assumes that if $750,000 was invoiced to complete 75 percent of a particular task, one could project that the remaining 25 percent of the task would be invoiced at the same spending rate, or for an additional $250,000. The estimate at completion for this task, therefore, would be $1,000,000. This estimate at completion would be favorable if the task had been budgeted at $1,000,000 or more. However, the estimate would be unfavorable if the task had been budgeted below $1,000,000.

A more complete example using a template for calculating the estimate to complete is provided in Figure 12.1, Estimate at Completion, and a blank template is provided in Appendix N and on the CD accompanying this book. However, the accuracy of the estimate at completion depends on the accuracy of the contractor's estimate of the percent completion for each task. Agencies should consider having one of their employees or consultants monitor the contractor's progress to verify the percentage of completion reports submitted by the contractor. Due to the tendency for contractor personnel to be optimistic with respect to their on-time and

| ESTIMATE AT COMPLETION | | | | | |
|---|---|---|---|---|---|
| Contractor: | | Contract Number: | | Project: | |
| Task | Contract Price | Total Invoiced | Percent Invoiced | Percent Complete | Estimate to Complete |
| A | $500,000 | $250,000 | 50 | 50 | $500,000 |
| B | $2,500,000 | $1,500,000 | 75 | 80 | $1,875,000 |
| C | $3,000,000 | $2,000,000 | 67 | 65 | $3,076,923 |
| D | $6,000,000 | $5,000,000 | 83 | 70 | $7,142,857 |
| E | $2,000,000 | $1,000,000 | 50 | 50 | $2,000,000 |
| F | $500,000 | $300,000 | 60 | 60 | $500,000 |
| Total Project | $14,000,000 | $10,050,000 | 72 | 67 | $15,000,000 |

### Instructions for Completion of Estimate at Completion

1. The "Task" column is completed by listing the separately priced tasks in the scope of work with the "Total Project" at the bottoms of this column.
2. The "Contract Price" column is completed by listing the price for each task in the scope of work followed by the total contract price.
3. The "Total Invoiced" column is completed by listing the cumulative amount invoiced for each task in the scope of work followed by the total amount invoiced for the entire contract.
4. The "Percent Invoiced" column is completed by listing the percent of the cumulative amount invoiced for each task in the scope of work followed by the cumulative amount invoiced for the entire contract.
5. The "Percent Complete" column is completed by listing the contractor supplied (and agency verified) percentage of completion for each task in the scope of work followed by the percentage of completion for the entire contract.
6. The "Estimate to Complete" is calculated by dividing the "Total Invoiced" by "Percent Complete" and multiplying by 100.

**Figure 12.1  Estimate at completion form.**

under-budget performance, a critical in-house evaluation of their cost and schedule performance is likely to reflect more accurate results. Significant differences in the contractor's percentages and the agency's percentages for task completion should be discussed with the contractor. The objective of these discussions is to resolve the differences in task completion percentages. When the differences are not critical, the discussions may be delayed until the next periodic project meeting. If there is an impasse during these discussions, the agency should consider placing the contractor on notice via certified letter regarding the accuracy of the contractor's progress reporting. Documenting disagreements regarding schedule performance as they occur is essential should it prove necessary to address future issues regarding contractor schedules.

The estimate to complete is a good tool for forecasting the contractor's final cost performance at the completion of the contract; however, the contractor may have justification for challenging the agency's estimate. For example, some contractor tasks may have relied on higher billing rates at the beginning of the project and lower billing rates as the project nears completion. If this is true, the contractor could have acceptable justification for lowering the estimate at completion. To avoid this problem associated with changes in the predominant billing rates at different stages for project tasks, the agency could require the contractor to estimate expenditures on a monthly basis to compensate for the distortion created when billing rates are higher at the beginning of a project and are phased down as contract completion approaches. However, this added level of sophistication may not be justified for relatively low-dollar-value contracts or when calculating a precise estimate at completion is not critical. In the event that ever more highly sophisticated cost and schedule reporting is desired, agencies may wish to consider the guidelines in ANSI/EIA Standard 748 or evaluate the alternatives available through an Internet search on "cost/schedule-control-system."

As an alternative to requiring the contractor to provide the percentage of completion at the task level for use in the agency's estimate at completion, the agency could require the contractor to submit a periodic report in the format contained in Figure 12.1. Should the agency elect to have the contractor submit the estimate at completion in this format, the percentage of completion should be verified by an agency employee or consultant just as if the contractor had reported solely on the percentage of completion for each of the tasks and for the entire contract. The reason for this need to verify the percentage of completion is, again, due to the contractor's tendency to be optimistic with respect to cost and schedule performance. The interpretation of the data in Figure 12.1 is provided in Figure 12.2.

## 12.1.3 Contract Amendments

Changes to the contract, generally through amendments for services contracts, are considered part of the contract administration effort. Although some organizations have personnel who concentrate their efforts on contract administration, most state and local agencies rely on the employees responsible for selecting the contractor to also administer the contract. Therefore, contract amendments are normally processed by the same individual or team responsible for award of the original contract.

Amendments to contracts should include a description of the changes to the contract, describe any change in pricing, and any impact on the schedule. Including price and schedule impacts from amendments is a good practice because it

| Analysis of Estimate at Completion |
| --- |
| 1. Tasks A, E & F have all been invoiced at the same percentage as the percentage of task completion. Therefore, the estimate at completion for these three tasks is equal to the contract price and no overrun or underrun is anticipated. |
| 2. Task B has a completion percentage less than the invoiced percentage. Therefore, it is expected that there will be a cost underrun for this particular task. |
| 3. Tasks C & D and the Project completion percentages are all less than the invoiced percentage. Therefore, it is expected that there will be a cost overrun for these two tasks and the overall contract. |
| 4. Since the total contract price is $14,000,000 and the estimate at completion is $15,000,000, it is expected that there will be a total contract overrun of $1,000,000. NOTE: The total project estimate at completion is calculated without considering the percent invoiced for individual tasks; therefore, it is unlikely that the addition of the individual estimates at completion for the tasks indicated in the right hand column will exactly equal the project estimate to complete. |

**Figure 12.2  Analysis of estimate at completion.**

avoids the possibility that the contractor might subsequently claim that the amendment entitles the contractor to schedule relief or a price increase. When there is no impact on schedule or price, mentioning that fact on the amendment also avoids the possibility of subsequent price or schedule disputes relating to the amendment. Amendments also need to include the same essential requirements as contracts. Because these requirements are assumed to have been met when the original contract was awarded, one would assume that there would be no concern about continuing to meet these requirements when changing the contract. Although it is unlikely that illegal purposes, parties ineligible for entering into a contract, or other essential elements of a contract would be introduced through an amendment, there is the possibility that a contract amendment may fail to include consideration. For example, a contractor that cannot meet its scheduled completion date may request an extension. If that extension is granted without obtaining something of value to the agency in exchange for granting the schedule extension, then that amendment would lack consideration. The consideration could be a reduction in price. However, other valuable consideration could be substituted for a price reduction. For example, helpful additional information on future reports, expanded performance of a task in the scope of work, an additional task added to the scope of work, or any other item of value to the contracting agency could be accepted as consideration for the schedule extension.

When there are numerous amendments to a contract, it may be possible to encounter difficulty in tracking the total price or the pricing of individually priced

| SUMMARY OF PRICE CHANGES | | |
|---|---|---|
| **TASK** | **PREVIOUS PRICE** | **REVISED PRICE** |
| A | $100,000.00 | $100,000.00 |
| B | $100,000.00 | $100,000.00 |
| C | $202,753.00 | $181,131.00 |
| | Previous Total Contract Price | $402,753.00 |
| | Price Change This Amendment | ($21,622.00) |
| | | $381,131.00 |

**Figure 12.3  Summary of pricing changes.**

tasks in the scope of work. A good practice to avoid encountering this difficulty is to include a summary of the pricing changes on each contract amendment. This can be accomplished by including a summary as shown in Figure 12.3. If there is no change in price, this fact should either be reflected in the amendment using the above format and showing the same pricing for both the previous total contract price and revised total contract price with zero in the space for "Price Change This Amendment" in Figure 12.3 or simply by including a statement to the effect that that there is no change in contract pricing as a result of this amendment. As discussed above, the objective of this practice is the avoidance of future disputes regarding the price impact from the amendment.

The boilerplate templates for virtually all state and local government contracts include provisions that require all contract changes to be made in advance, in writing, and signed by all parties to the contract. While this is representative of good contract management practice, it does not ensure that verbal (or constructive) contract changes are not enforceable. Generally, whenever a government employee verbally instructs a contractor to perform work beyond that included in the scope of work, that verbal change is honored if the agency employee had the apparent authority to make such a change. The determination of which government employees have such apparent authority has historically been interpreted liberally. Therefore, complete reliance cannot be placed on contract provisions for "written-only contract changes" to protect the agency from constructive changes. Training employees to refrain from making constructive changes to contracts is highly recommended.

### 12.1.4 Managing Completion of Milestones and Deliverables

Although agencies with a small contract workload may feel content managing key contract dates manually, contract management software should be considered by agencies with moderate to large contract workloads. Contract management software generally improves the contract management function while reducing the reliance on human resources for this effort. Adopting contract and contract amendment templates with variable information tables and other tables for entering other key dates can facilitate database population for milestones and deliverables tracking software. Incorporating these features in contract documents permits collection of data required to populate the milestones and deliverables tracking database concurrently with the preparation of contract documents. This capture of key reporting data during the preparation of the contract and amendments eliminates the need to perform subsequent data entry and avoids the problems associated with information in the contract differing from the milestones and deliverables tracking database. Problems discovered while tracking the contractor's contract milestones and deliverables performance, as well as any other contractor performance issues, should be addressed according to the following section on reacting to substandard contractor performance. Failure to address performance problems regarding contractor milestones and deliverables is likely to lead to a worsening of the problem, while timely intervention ensures that the contractor devotes more attention to correcting the problems.

Agencies that opted for automated tracking of the contractor's milestones and deliverables performance and capture of key data concurrently with the preparation of contract documents need to update the database when that information changes through contract amendments. The information needed to update the database as a result of contract amendments can also be obtained concurrently with preparation of the contract amendment document if the variable information table and tables for key schedule dates are also included on the contract amendment document. A suggested template to accomplish this update is provided in the Contract Amendment in Figure 12.4. This template includes spaces for variable contract information and key schedule dates. There is also a space for a narrative explanation of the changes to the contract. A template for this contract amendment format is provided in Appendix O and on the CD accompanying this book.

If the agency is not tracking prices at the task level or collecting information to populate the milestones and deliverables computer database, it is unnecessary to include space for this information on the Contract Amendment form. However, in the absence of these tables used to collect milestones and deliverables tracking information concurrently with the preparation of contract documents, the agency should alternatively provide the summary of price changes as shown in Figure 12.3. Providing the summary of price changes in this format ensures that the agency is managing the total contract cost, but not needlessly expending effort to format information not used to populate a database.

| CONTRACT AMENDMENT | | | |
|---|---|---|---|
| **Amendment No.:** | | **Amendment Date:** | |
| **VARIABLE INFORMATION TABLE** | | | |
| **Term of This Contract** (Complete Dates in Just One of the Following Three Rows) | | | |
| √ Below | **Term Begins** | | **Term Completion Date** | |
| | On Following Date | | On Following Date | |
| | Upon Receipt of Notice to Proceed | | Calendar Days Following Notice to Proceed | |
| | Upon Execution by Agency | | Calendar Days Following Agency Contract Execution | |
| Agency Department | | FOB Point | |
| Terms | | Basis of Price (**Do Not** √ **More Than One of the Following Four Blocks**) | |
| Price | | Fixed Price | Annual Price | Monthly Price | Hourly Rate |
| Not-to-Exceed Price | | √ if Reasonable Expenses Authorized in Addition to Hourly Rate | |
| **Contractor Contact Information** | | **Agency Contact Information** | |
| Contractor | | Project Manager | |
| Address | | Address | |
| City, State & ZIP | | City, State & ZIP | |
| Telephone | | Telephone | |
| Facsimile | | Facsimile | |

**Figure 12.4   Contract amendment form.**

Traditional cost/schedule tracking systems are restricted to providing notification after a key date has passed and the contractor may be delinquent. However, when key dates are included in a computer database, it is possible to send reminders to the agency staff and the contractor in advance (one or two weeks, for example) prior to the due dates to ensure that the upcoming dates are not overlooked.

| Milestone No. | Milestone Description | Due Date |
|---|---|---|
| | | |
| | | |
| | | |
| | | |

| Item No. | Deliverable Item Description | Due Date |
|---|---|---|
| | | |
| | | |
| | | |

| NARRATIVE |
|---|
| |

AGENCY                                    CONTRACTOR

By_____          By_____

Name_____          Name_____

Title_____          Title_____

**Figure 12.4 (continued)    Contract amendment form.**

## 12.1.5 Reacting to Substandard Contractor Performance

When the individual responsible for managing a particular contract has other pressing responsibilities, it is likely that substandard contractor performance may eventually be recognized, but that rebukes, if any, communicated to the contractor regarding its lackluster performance are limited to verbal admonishments. In such a scenario, the contractor's performance may eventually deteriorate to the point where agency management may wish to immediately terminate the contract for default. However, the lack of attention paid to contract administration up to that point would likely find the contracting agency lacking the basis for an immediate default termination.

State and local government agencies must notify contractors when contractor performance is not satisfactory, and meticulous records of contractor performance must be maintained from the commencement of the contract. Without such contractor notifications and record keeping, the agency cannot effect a termination for default in a timely manner despite the fact that the contractor is not qualified or not willing to perform its contractual obligations.

"Default termination" is the term used to describe the termination of a contract by one party to a contract due to the other contracting party's failure to perform its contractual obligations. Ideally, the services contract outlines the steps needed to terminate a contract for default. Typically, the party that is considering taking action to terminate a contract for default notifies the other party of this intent by providing a show cause notice that includes a period of time for the party in default to show cause why the contract should not be terminated. Should the party receiving the show cause letter fail to respond within the time period stated in the letter, the contract may be terminated for default. Should the other party to the contract respond by describing the actions it plans to take to cure its failure to perform contractual obligations, the party issuing the show cause letter would then evaluate the merits of the plan to cure the failure. If the plan is accepted, contract performance would continue. If the plan is determined to be inadequate, the contract would be terminated for default. If the party that initiated the default termination by issuing a show cause notice does not feel confident that its default termination can be sustained or if agency officials are reluctant to incur the costs associated with pursuing a default termination, that party may elect to terminate the contract for convenience.

Convenience terminations are made to discontinue work on a contract when one party to the contract has not defaulted. Absent a convenience termination clause in a contract, one party cannot normally terminate a contract for convenience without the consent of the other party. Provisions for convenience terminations may be constructed to provide this option to just one or to both of the contracting parties.

Although it may be appropriate to give verbal rebukes to a contractor for its first one or two failures to meet contractual obligations, the contract file should be annotated to create a record of those failures and the verbal admonishments. This permits the agency to reference the earlier verbal admonishments if the contractor continues to fail to meet contractual obligations and it becomes necessary to notify the contractor in writing. The agency may elect to send such written communications via e-mail. When the contractor is admonished via e-mail, the agency should document the file with a printout of the e-mail, as well as any response from the contractor. The documentation is needed to support the agency's position in the event that the contractor's performance continues to deteriorate or fails entirely. The preferred method for communicating with contractors that are failing to meet their contractual obligations is via certified mail with a return receipt requested. The return receipt represents credible evidence that the contractor received the letter placing it on notice for substandard contract performance. To ensure that the admonishment is not unduly delayed when sent via certified mail, the agency may elect to also send a copy of the letter to the contractor as an e-mail attachment.

When the contract includes provisions for liquidated damages, the agency may pursue collection of the amount due from the contractor when completion dates are missed. When it is apparent that liquidated damages are due, the agency's initial contact with the contractor could be to ask if the contractor prefers to deduct the amounts due the agency for liquidated damages from future invoices, or if the contractor would prefer that the agency deduct the amounts due from invoices.

When efforts to obtain satisfactory performance from the contractor appear to be failing and there is a distinct possibility that the contract should be terminated for default, a show cause letter should be sent to the errant contractor. It is essential that the agency have proof that the contractor received the show cause letter to avoid the possibility that the contractor challenges a termination for default based on non-receipt of a show cause letter. A sample show cause letter is provided in Appendix L and on the CD. Citing all earlier infractions and agency admonishments regarding previous substandard contractor performance is a good practice. It is also good practice to fully describe the immediate infraction (or infractions) giving rise to the show cause letter. The show cause letter should reference the termination for default provisions of the contract and advise the contractor that the agency intends to terminate the contract for default unless the contractor can show cause (provide justification) by a date certain why the contract should not be terminated. Including the contract provision in the show cause letter reinforces the agency's rights with respect to default termination, and indicating the date certain for the response clearly identifies this critical date. In addition to the date when the contractor's response is due, the letter should also include a termination date (either the date the response is due or some subsequent date) in the event that the contractor fails to satisfactorily show cause why the contract should not be terminated. This date is also critical because it establishes the date when the contract is terminated for default if the contractor does not respond or provides an unsatisfactory response to the show cause letter. A contractor's failure to respond to the show cause notice is the equivalent of not providing adequate cause why the contract should not be terminated for default.

The justification provided by the contractor for continued performance under the contract would normally consist of the contractor's differing version of the performance cited as unacceptable, a description of the contracting agency's contribution to the performance considered unacceptable, a promise to improve future performance, or a combination of two or all three of these reasons.

In certain cases, the contractor may not contest the termination for default; however, in most cases, contractors vigorously challenge a termination for default because a default termination results in a blemish on the contractor's record that could damage its opportunities for obtaining future contracts from the contracting agency that awarded the contract or from other government agencies. If the contractor does contest the default termination, there are three alternative reactions for consideration by the contracting agency.

The first alternative (although not presented in any particular sequence) would be to keep the contract in force and permit the contractor to perform under the contract. This alternative would likely be chosen if agency personnel do not dispute the contractor's version of the performance failure or agency officials are convinced that there was contracting agency complicity in the contractor's substandard performance. Another reason for continuing to keep the contract in force would be a determination by the contracting agency that it is satisfied with the contractor's promise to improve its future performance.

The second alternative is to terminate the contract for default despite the fact that the contractor has contested such a termination. Because the contractor would have the option to bring this matter to litigation if the agency elects to continue to pursue the default termination, this option should be selected only if the agency has documented justification that it is certain would survive a court challenge and the contracting agency is willing to expend the time and funds required to support the default termination in court. Otherwise, the agency is likely to face a time-consuming, costly court case that could be unsuccessful.

The third alternative is to terminate the contract, but to terminate for convenience rather than for default. This alternative would likely be chosen if the agency can afford the added time needed for the convenience termination, does not wish to risk the time and funds required should the contractor elect to contest the default termination through litigation, or determines that there is some chance that the agency's justification for default termination or documentation of the contractor's unsatisfactory performance is not sufficient to survive the potential court challenge.

Regardless of the alternative selected, once the decision is made, the agency should advise the contractor in writing of its decision. The letter may serve as the agency's documentation of its decision. If the second or third alternative is selected, the contractor's notification should be sent via certified mail with a return receipt requested. The signed return receipt provides credible evidence that the contractor received written notice of the default or convenience termination.

The process of terminating a contract for default is time consuming. If the effort to terminate the contract for default is abandoned after considerable time had elapsed and the agency subsequently elects to pursue a termination for convenience, an exorbitant amount of time would be consumed before the contract is eventually terminated. Therefore, prior to initiating a termination for default, the contracting agency should consider the probability of a successful termination for default before sending the show cause letter. If it is determined that the contractor is likely to contest the default termination and the contracting agency is likely to react to such a challenge by abandoning the default termination in favor of a convenience termination, then the contracting agency should initially pursue a termination for convenience despite the fact that the contractor is not meeting its contractual obligations. Electing the convenience termination initially, in this situation, minimizes the time and effort expended by the agency in resolving this problem, and may result in an opportunity to terminate the contract sooner.

## 12.2 Contract Closeout

The tasks typically performed during contract closeout are preparation of the report on the contractor's performance, relief of any financial encumbrances, records retention, and eventually destruction of the records.

### 12.2.1 Contractor Performance Report

A report of the contractor's performance on the recently completed contract is recommended to document the quality of the contractor's performance in the event that the agency considers the contractor for future contracts. It is recommended that the report be completed immediately upon contract completion while the memories of the agency representatives are fresh. The availability of information contained in such a contractor's performance report becomes useful if and when the contractor is competing for, or otherwise being considered for, another contract at a later date or if another department or agency is checking references for a subsequent contract award. Three measures of a contractor's performance that are relevant for inclusion in performance reports are (1) cost management, (2) quality of the service that was provided, and (3) adherence to the schedule. A sample report is provided in the Contractor Performance Report in Appendix M.

Contract completion occurs when all the tasks required by the contractor, including final reports, have been completed, and all tasks required by the contracting agency, including final payment, have been completed. This differs from a notice of completion that is typically issued upon completion of the contractor's portion of the work for construction contracts, and final payment is normally withheld until a specified number of days following the notice of completion.

The availability of financial information applicable to the contractor's performance and significance of that information to the contracting agency depends on the type of contract. For example, very little information might be available to the contracting agency if a firm-fixed-price contract was awarded and there was no feedback on the contractor's profit or losses. However, under a cost-reimbursement contract, the contracting agency obtains far more insight into the contractor's management of costs. The performance report format should include a space for the type of contract, and the cost management report should include consideration of the contract type. Under a firm-fixed-price contract with no profit or loss feedback to the contracting agency, the report on cost management might be restricted to a statement to the effect that the contractor's cost management could not be evaluated because it was awarded a firm-fixed-price contract. The contracting agency's project manager is able to provide the information on the quality of the contractor's performance regardless of contract type. If the contractor's overall performance was considered satisfactory, excellent, or outstanding, it should be reported accordingly. Accurate reporting of the contractor's performance is beneficial in the event that the contractor is considered for future contracts. However, if there were any quality issues that required resolution during the term of the contract, the facts surrounding those issues should be discussed in the report. This information proves useful should there be subsequent warranty problems or in the event that the contractor is considered for future contracts.

The contracting agency's project manager and any other employees involved in the contract administration effort should be asked for feedback on the contractor's schedule adherence. Obtaining feedback from all those involved in the contract administration effort contributes to the completeness of the resultant contractor performance report. In addition to reporting on completion of the overall contract according to schedule, the report should include schedule performance with respect to intermediate milestones, report submittals, and all deliverables. Although completion of the end milestone dates are the most significant, completion of intermediate milestones also reflect on the acceptability of the contractor's performance.

Contractor performance reports should always include a question regarding the reporting official's recommendation to award a similar contract to the contractor in the future. This is relevant because willingness or not to use the contractor for similar contracts is one of the best indicators of the acceptability of a contractor's performance. It is recommended that rather than report a mere yes or no, that the reporting official be asked to report the reason for the recommendation, regardless of whether the recommendation is favorable or unfavorable.

Although a copy of the contractor performance report would normally be filed in the completed contract file, placing a copy of the report in a central depository (as well as a shared database) where all affected parties can gain access to the performance reports for the agency's contractors is an additional good practice for advising other agency personnel who may subsequently consider the contractor for similar projects.

## 12.2.2 Relief of Financial Encumbrances

Contracting agencies typically encumber funds upon contract award, and the process for encumbering funds on newly awarded contracts generally works well. However, numerous agencies do not have such an efficient process for removing excess encumbrances from completed contracts. In addition to the fact that it is a good contract management practice to remove excess funding from a contract when there is no chance of further expenditures, it is possible, especially in tight budget periods, that availability of the excess funding is essential to ensure the continued provisioning of agency services. To ensure that excess funds are removed from the contract, the contracting agency might consider either developing a contract closeout checklist or including a space on the contractor performance report to indicate that excess funding has been returned to the general fund or the applicable department.

### 12.2.3 Records Retention

Contract records should be maintained for a period of time following contract completion in the event that a question, dispute, litigation, or other matter arises following contract completion. State and local government agencies establish the time period for retention of completed contract files; however, a retention period that is frequently established is seven years following contract completion. Upon completion of the contract, all relevant contract documents are accumulated and inserted into the contract file. Agencies frequently maintain the completed contract files where they can be easily accessed during the first year following completion when it is most likely that contract questions are raised. After the first year, completed contract files are often removed to a more distant records storage area. Although most agencies have procedures requiring a destruction date on records sent to a central records storage area, those contracting offices that do not have such a policy should ensure that completed contract files sent to a central records storage facility do have a document destruction date clearly indicated on the file box. The failure to indicate the destruction date on records in central records storage can lead to retention of the contract records for an excessive time period. If storing records for an excessive time period is a common practice for the agency, it is likely that they are providing expensive floor space for storing obsolete records.

As an alternative to maintaining hardcopy records on completed contracts, some agencies have converted to the storage and maintenance of electronic records. Electronic storage requires significantly less space and also simplifies access to historical contract records.

## 12.3 Conclusion

The agency's responsibility with respect to contracts for services changes abruptly upon award of the contract. At this stage in the contracting cycle, the contractor begins to perform according to its contractual responsibilities. The agency's role changes from selecting a contractor and awarding a contract to evaluating and approving contractor billings, monitoring the contractor's performance, negotiating and approving contract amendments, managing the completion of milestones and contract deliverables, and reacting to any instances of substandard contractor performance.

Although it is important to verify that contractor invoices do not have mathematical errors, considerably more verification actions are required prior to approving an invoice. When the contractor is reimbursed on the basis of billing rates, it is necessary to ensure that the invoiced rates match the contractual rates. For contracts that base the amount of payment on the completion of milestones or percentage completion of milestones, complete reliance on the contractor's determination of milestone completion or percentage of milestone completion is not recommended. Because there is an element of subjectivity regarding the completion or percentage completion of milestones and because there can be a question regarding the acceptability of the completed milestones, agencies have a responsibility for verifying contractors' assertions regarding milestone completions prior to approving payments.

Agencies may wish to evaluate the contractor's performance with respect to its expenditure rate compared to its progress with respect to contractual responsibilities. Such evaluations could be critical should the contract involve a high-dollar-value project, a high-risk project, or if the contractor does not possess adequate financial strength. The decision to evaluate the contractor's performance in this manner should be made early in the contracting cycle. Ideally, there are provisions in the RFP and in the contract that require the contractor to provide reporting that facilitates tracking of the contractor's cost/schedule performance. Deciding to evaluate the contractor's cost/schedule performance at this early stage permits the agency to require schedule and financial information during the term of the contract that facilitates such an evaluation. When the agency decides to perform this evaluation, the contractor is required to report on the percentage completion of various tasks in the scope of work and invoice the agency based on actual expenditures for the same tasks used for tracking percentage completion. A template, Figure 12.1 — Estimate at Completion, is provided for the readers to use this information to calculate the estimate of costs to project completion. Use of the Figure 12.1 template permits the agency to determine if the contractor is able to complete the project without experiencing an overrun that might threaten project success. Although considerable reliance is placed on the contractor's input with respect to its reporting of progress on milestones and expenditure rate, it is prudent to have agency personnel or consultants verify the contractor's input.

Contract amendments are negotiated and approved during the contract administration phase of the contracting cycle. Amendments must meet all the essential elements of contracts. This is generally not an issue, however, except in the case of consideration. When either the agency or the contractor receives some benefit from the provisions of the amendment, the other party requires consideration. When an agency grants schedule relief or some other benefit to the contractor, the agency must be compensated for the relief it granted. Compensation may be in the form of a price reduction or additional work performed without compensation, or with compensation below the reasonable price for that work. When the agency is managing contracts or tracking milestone completions with computer software, there must be a process for updating the database for amendments that affect relevant computer database information. If the agency had elected to populate its contract management software database concurrently with the preparation of contract documents, then the logical approach for updating the database would be to use a contract amendment form that would automatically update the database during the preparation of the contract amendment. Readers are provided a template, Figure 12.4 — Contract Amendment Form, that was designed to facilitate automatic updates to computer software databases during preparation of the amendment.

Agencies with a relatively small number of contracts may find that tracking contract milestones and deliverables manually or through desktop applications such as the scheduling feature on desktop computers may not require automated tracking of contract milestones and deliverables. However, large to medium sized agencies with a relatively large volume of contracts may require an automated system to ensure that contractors are meeting their contract milestones and deliverables responsibilities. Just as with the need to prepare in advance for monitoring a contractor's cost/schedule performance, timely preparation for automated tracking of contract milestones and deliverables also benefits the agency. Contract and amendment templates can be designed to populate the computer database and respectively update the computer database with information needed to track contract milestones and deliverables. Should the agency discover that the contractor is not meeting its milestones and deliverables responsibilities, this problem needs to be addressed with the contractor to realize improved performance and avoid continued deterioration of contractor performance.

It is important for agency personnel to react to substandard performance when it is first detected. Failure to react to the first sign of substandard performance invites continued substandard performance or even a further deterioration of the contractor's performance. Should the agency delay its reaction until the performance has deteriorated to the point that the agency wishes to immediately terminate the contract for default, there is likely to be a delay in the termination until the agency can establish documentation of the contractor's substandard performance or pursue a termination for convenience in lieu of the default termination. Initial contractor rebukes may be verbal; however, a record of such verbal rebukes should be maintained to permit reference to the earlier agency actions in the event that it becomes necessary to escalate the rebukes to written contractor notifications. The recommended method for making written notifications is through letters sent via certified mail with a return receipt requested. This method provides the agency with written proof of delivery. Maintaining records of the contractor's substandard performance and the agency's reaction is important in the event that the contractor's performance deteriorates to the point that the agency wishes to terminate the contract. If liquidated damages provisions are in the contract, it is recommended that the agency pursue collection of such liquidated damages from the contractor.

If the agency does not have a strong case for terminating the contract for default, it may elect to terminate for convenience. Should the agency elect to pursue termination of the contract for default, the initial notification to the contractor is a show cause letter. If the contractor's response to the show cause letter presents a strong case supporting the fact that a default termination is not justified or that agency personnel were complicit with respect to the substandard performance, the agency may choose to permit the contractor to continue performance on the contract or to terminate the contract for convenience. Termination for default should not be pursued unless the agency has a strong case that is well documented. Contractors are likely to challenge default terminations, and a resultant court case could prove lengthy and costly.

Contract closeout commences after the contractor has performed all its contractual responsibilities except records retention, which is likely to continue for three to seven years following contract completion. The agency's actions during contract closeout are straightforward. Agency representatives normally prepare a contractor performance report to advise future advance contract planning teams of the acceptability of the contractor's performance. When there is no further expectation of revenues or expenditures with respect to the contract, then all remaining funds should be disencumbered. This action makes the funds available for use on other contracts or other agency needs. The contract records should be retained for about one year where they are readily available in case there is a need to access the contract records. There is likely to be little need to access the contract files one year or more following contract completion; therefore, the files can normally be sent to a central records storage area from that date until the records destruction date arrives. The records destruction date should be clearly marked on the records storage container to prevent storage of the records for an excessive time period.

# *Appendix A*

# Glossary of Terms

A clear understanding of terms used in the contracting field is essential to ensure that state and local government officials and employees maintain exacting communications between themselves and their internal customers, contractors, and prospective contractors. For example, to ensure that improper use of contracting terms does not result in confusion leading to such avoidable problems, this appendix provides definitions for contracting terms used throughout the book. Relatively brief definitions are provided in this appendix; however, a thorough discussion of the more significant topics is provided in the text.

**Acceptance:** The communication of the final, unqualified assent to an offer.

**Addendum:** The term used to describe the instrument used to make changes to an RFP or any other type of solicitation after the solicitation has been sent to prospective contractors and before contractor responses are due.

**Affirmative action programs:** Such programs can be differentiated from equal opportunity programs in that contractors that are targeted for a particular affirmative action program may be awarded a contract despite the fact that competing non-targeted companies may have proposed lower pricing, higher quality services, or earlier project completion.

**Agency official:** A term used to describe any government agency elected or appointed official or employee who is involved in the contracting process or has been designated to review or execute contracts.

**Agreement:** A term that is occasionally used as a synonym for contract.

**Allocable costs:** Those costs that pertain to the contracting agency's contract or project. Costs that are expended to support one contract would not be allocable to another contract.

**Allowable costs:** (*See* unallowable costs.)

**Amendment:** The term used for the most formal type of modification to a contract. Amendments are normally staffed, reviewed, and executed in the same manner as contracts. However, some agencies permit limited staffing and execution at a lower organizational level for amendments below a certain dollar value or percentage of the total contract price. Some state or local government agencies require the less formal change orders to be formalized at some subsequent time by an amendment. In this case, several change orders may normally be formalized by a single amendment.

**BAFO:** (*See* best and final offer.)

**Best and final offer (BAFO):** The term used to describe a basic approach to negotiations in which the agency asks one or more of the prospective contractors to submit a revision to their proposal that will not be subject to further negotiations. In some cases, the agency may provide a revised scope of work or other contract changes that should be considered when the contractor (or contractors) prepares their BAFOs.

**Bids:** Responses received from prospective contractors or suppliers in response to IFBs released by state or local government agencies. Similar to quotations or quotes, bids are typically prepared by completing blanks on a bid form prepared by the contracting agency. The information provided by the prospective contractors on the bid form is similar to the information provided for quotations or quotes; however, it may include added information that is required based on high-dollar-value projects solicited via IFBs as opposed to low-dollar-value projects solicited via RFQs. Unlike proposals, statements of qualifications and quotations or quotes, bids are opened publicly and the prices are read aloud for all to hear. Bids are normally recorded on a spreadsheet and copies of the spreadsheets are also considered public information that can be provided to anyone who submits a request or provides a self-addressed stamped envelope.

**Bilateral:** Signing, or executing, a contract or modification thereto by both parties to the contract. In state or local government agency contracting, all contracts and modifications thereto are normally required to be bilateral documents.

**Billing rates:** In not-to-exceed price contracts or cost reimbursement contracts, billing rates are typically hourly rates for each applicable employee classification; an amount certain for each mile driven (such as $0.50 per mile) or reimbursement at the then-current rate allowed by the Internal Revenue Service; meals and hotel expenses could be reimbursed at a per-diem rate such as $50.00 per day for meals and $150 per day for hotels or at actual cost. When certain rates are based on actual costs, it is possible to include a ceiling cost to ensure that contractor employees do not select luxury accommodations and expensive restaurants.

**Boilerplate:** (*See* contract boilerplate.)

**Cash discounts:** Frequently offered by contractors to ensure that invoices are paid in a timely manner. An example of payment terms when a cash discount is offered is "2% 15, Net 45." This indicates that the contracting agency may deduct 2 percent from the invoiced price if payment is made within 15 days of receipt of the invoice and products and services; and that if the payment is not made within 15 days, the full amount of the invoice is due within 45 days of receipt of the invoice and products or services.

**Change in scope:** Occurs when the work to be performed by the contractor is modified from the original scope of work by the parties to the contract. The details of the change in scope, and possibly associated changes to the price or schedule, are normally negotiated by the contracting parties and formalized through a written contract amendment.

**Change order:** A type of modification to a contract that is normally used to authorize a change in the scope of work required to become effective sooner than would be possible with the more formal contract amendment. Change orders in state and local government contracting are normally limited to construction contracts, and can normally be approved, within certain price parameters, at a lower organizational level than the original contract.

**Chief elected official:** The term to describe the ranking elected official for a particular jurisdiction, such as the governor of a state or the mayor of a city.

**Competent parties:** Implies that all the parties to the contract are mentally competent and of legal age.

**Consideration:** Consideration is established when each party is bound by their promises that constitute a bargain for exchange. However, being bound to perform some preexisting promise does not constitute consideration.

**Contract:** The term used for an agreement that is legally enforceable and reflects the relationship between two or more parties for a specific time period. Contracts should be crafted to identify potential risks and describe how these risks will be mitigated. There must be a meeting of the minds wherein there is no ambiguity with respect to the understanding of the parties regarding the nature of the agreement. Contracts must include an offer, acceptance, consideration, competent parties, and a legal purpose.

**Contract boilerplate (or boilerplate):** Refers to standard terminology that does not normally vary, regardless of the nature of the services for which proposals are being solicited. Standard terms and conditions are an example of boilerplate.

**Contract completion:** Occurs when all the tasks required by the contractor, including final reports, have been completed, and all tasks required by the contracting agency, including final payment, have been completed. This differs from a Notice of Completion that is typically issued upon completion of the contractor's portion of the work for construction contracts, and final payment is normally withheld until a specified number of days following the Notice of Completion.

**Contract execution:** Refers to the signing of a contract by an individual duly authorized to bind and commit her or his company or organization to the provisions of the contract being signed. Signature by staff personnel such as legal counsel to indicate concurrence that a contract is sufficient as to form does not constitute execution of a contract. A contract that is executed by all parties to the contract is considered to be fully executed.

**Contract term (period of performance):** The phrase used to indicate the beginning and ending dates of the work to be performed by the contractor.

**Contracting agency:** Synonymous with state or local government agency.

**Contractors:** Private-sector companies or individuals who provide services to state or local government agencies on a contract basis.

**Convenience terminations:** Convenience terminations are made to discontinue work on a contract when one party to the contract has not defaulted. Absent a convenience termination clause in a contract, one party cannot normally terminate a contract for convenience without the consent of the other party. Provisions for convenience terminations may be constructed to provide this option to just one or to both of the contracting parties.

**Cost elements:** In not-to-exceed price contracts or cost reimbursement contracts typically, cost elements include hourly rates that may be charged for various employee classifications such as senior analyst or administrative support personnel, mileage rates for vehicles, or per-diem rates for meals and hotel expenses. Cost elements in firm-fixed-price contracts could be fixed payments paid for milestone completion or a fixed periodic payment that is invoiced monthly during the term of the contract.

**Cost growth:** Occurs when a change in scope results in a bilateral amendment to the contract that increases the target cost and fee. Such a change in scope agreed to by both parties to the contract is considered cost growth and not a cost overrun. By contrast, an overrun would occur when the contractor expends funds in excess of the target cost without an associated change in scope or contract amendment.

**Cost-plus-a-percentage-of-cost (CPPC) contracts:** CPPC contracts are unlawful in federal contracting and in some states as well. The American Bar Association (ABA) also recommends the prohibition of CPPC contracts. CPPC contracts provide for reimbursement to the contractor for allowable and allocable costs plus a predetermined percentage of those costs. A cursory analysis of CPPC contracts might conclude that they are not significantly different from CPFF contracts. However, there is a significant difference between CPPC and CPFF contracts. When CPFF contractors overrun their contracts, the fee remains fixed. Therefore, the CPFF contractor's fee as a percentage of the costs is reduced when the contractor experiences a cost overrun and this reduction in the fee as a percentage of actual costs acts as an incentive to control costs. Contrast this with a CPPC contract wherein greater contractor expenditures result in higher fees, and thus higher profits.

**Cost-plus-award-fee (CPAF) contracts:** CPAF contracts are similar to CPIF contracts except that they do not use an exact formula for determining the amount of the fee. CPAF contracts typically include goals or criteria on which the award fee is based. The award fee factors may be established at the inception of the contract for the first phase of the period of performance, which could be, for instance, the first six months of the contract term. Long-term CPAF contracts typically provide for adjustments to the factors on which the award fee is based. At the end of each award period, the contractor submits a document that supports the award fee at the level at which the contractor feels it deserves. The contracting agency typically reviews the contractor's submittal, evaluates the contractor's performance with respect to the award fee factors, and then unilaterally determines the amount of the award fee.

**Cost-plus-fixed-fee (CPFF) contracts:** CPFF contracts provide for reimbursement of the contractor for allowable and allocable costs plus a fixed fee determined at the inception of the contract. Should the contractor overrun the target cost, the fixed fee is not decreased. Likewise, should the contractor underrun the target cost, the fixed fee is not increased. However, if the contract is amended due to a change in scope, the fixed fee is normally increased or decreased in proportion to the increase or decrease in the target cost. The fee normally established for federal contracts cannot exceed 10 percent of the estimated cost for CPFF contracts; however, the maximum is 15 percent for experimental, developmental, or research, and 6 percent of estimated construction costs for architect-engineering CPFF contracts.

**Cost-plus-incentive-fee (CPIF) contracts:** CPIF contracts provide for reimbursement to the contractor for allowable and allocable costs plus an incentive fee that is based on a formula determined at the inception of the contract. The incentive should always include cost containment, and may include other factors such as technical characteristics.

**Cost-reimbursement contracts:** Unlike fixed-price contracts, cost-reimbursement contracts reimburse the contractor based on predetermined rates for services that are priced on the basis of real or expected efforts to support completion of requirements specified in the contract. Just as with the fixed-price contracts, the definitions for cost-reimbursement contracts are generally based on the definitions for contract types contained in the FAR. Cost-reimbursement contracts should not be used by contracting agencies unless they are prepared to employ considerably more resources during contract negotiations and contract administration than they normally employ for fixed-price contracts. Additionally, cost-reimbursement contracts should not be awarded to contractors that do not have sophisticated accounting systems that provide the capability to track costs at the contract or project level. The FAR also includes an extensive list of unallowable costs. Some examples of costs that are unallowable according to the FAR include entertainment, advertising, taxes, interest, labor relations, and losses on other contracts. Including provisions for unallowable costs in contracts will necessitate more than a mere listing of costs that are unallowable. For example, advertising costs that would be considered unallowable would likely be limited to product advertising, while advertising to recruit employees or to announce upcoming procurement opportunities should be allowable. State and local government agencies that permit cost-reimbursement contracts should seriously consider establishing categories of costs that will or will not be reimbursed. If unallowable costs are not defined in cost-reimbursement contracts, agencies may be embarrassed by some categories of costs that they may reimburse.

**Counter-offer:** The party receiving the offer expresses an interest in accepting the offer with conditions. However, the existence of the conditions actually constitutes a rejection of the offer that was received and the expression of a new offer. Should the party making that counter-offer have his or her counter-offer rejected, he or she cannot then merely accept that original offer. The original offer that was rejected by the counter-offer can no longer be considered. Of course, the party that had its counter-offer rejected may then indicate that it now would accept the original offer. Should the party that had made the original offer agree to acceptance of its original offer without further condition, then acceptance has occurred.

**Debarred:** Refers to contractors that have been excluded from government contracting and government-approved subcontracting for a specified time period.

**Default termination:** The term used to describe the termination of a contract by one party to a contract due to the other contracting party's failure to perform its contractual obligations. Ideally, the services contract will outline the steps needed to terminate a contract for default. Typically, the party that is considering taking action to terminate a contract for default will notify the other party of this intent by providing a show cause notice that includes a period of time for the contractor in default to show cause why the contract should not be terminated. Should the party receiving the show cause letter fail to respond within the time period stated in the letter, the contract may be terminated for default. Should the other party to the contract respond by stating the actions they plan to take to cure their failure to perform their contractual obligations, the party issuing the show cause letter would then evaluate the merits of the plan to cure the failure. If the plan is accepted, contract performance would continue. If the plan is determined to be inadequate, the contract would be terminated for default. If the party that initiated the default termination by issuing a show cause notice does not feel confident that its default termination will be upheld or is reluctant to incur the costs associated with pursuing a default termination, that party may elect to terminate the contract for convenience.

**Definitive contract:** A term used to describe a fully executed, fully staffed contract that incorporates all the elements of a contract, including a complete understanding of the risks and responsibilities assumed by the parties to the contract. A definitive contract is generally used as the successor for a letter contract that was intended to remain effective for a limited time period. Fully staffed contracts awarded routinely when there are not the time constraints that result in award of a letter contract are also considered as definitive contracts; however, that term is normally not used in this case unless the definitive contract is intended as a replacement for a letter contract.

**Equal opportunity programs:** These programs involve outreach efforts to discover prospective contractors that historically have had less than full access to state or local government contracting opportunities. Contractors may be included in equal opportunity programs because they are small, minority-owned, woman-owned, veteran-owned, or belonging to any other category for which an equal opportunity program has been established. Equal opportunity programs usually provide outreach efforts to identify such companies and offer them the opportunity to compete with traditional contractors, but do not afford any competitive advantage with respect to price, quality, or schedule adherence. Equal opportunity programs are normally established on the assumption that management of small, minority-owned, woman-owned, or other identified categories of contractors is not inherently less qualified to compete with more traditional contractors in a capitalistic environment. Therefore, to succeed as state or local government contractors, they only need be given the opportunity to compete. They do not require a competitive advantage that might be considered unfair by traditional contractors and the citizenry.

**Evaluation criteria (or selection criteria):** The factors considered for evaluation of proposals to select the successful contractor from among the competing contractors. Evaluation criteria should be described in the solicitation to permit the prospective contractors to understand the basis for selecting the successful contractor by the contracting agency. When evaluating proposals, it is essential to base the selection of the successful contractor solely on the evaluation criteria stated in the solicitation. Therefore, great care should be taken to ensure that the evaluation criteria included in the solicitation measures significant and relevant attributes for a contractor with the desired attributes. In the event that an unsuccessful contractor protests the contract award or recommendation for award, selection committee records that indicate strict adherence to evaluation criteria in contractor selection will help defend the contractor selection being challenged by an unsuccessful contractor.

**Execution:** (*See* contract execution)

**Fair pricing:** Refers to pricing that enables a contractor to recover its allowable and allocable direct and indirect costs and earn a reasonable profit.

**Firm-fixed-price (FFP) contracts:** Those contracts wherein payment is based on completion of milestones or all the tasks in the scope of work without providing performance or other types of incentives developed to encourage the contractor to provide a product or service that exceeds the minimal specifications developed by the contracting agency or for delivery in advance of the contractual delivery date.

**Fixed-price contracts:** Those contracts wherein payment to the contractor is based on a fixed price to be paid to the contractor for completion of specific elements of the scope of work or for completion of the entire contract requirements.

**Fixed-price incentive (FPI) contracts:** These contracts are similar to firm-fixed-price (FFP) contracts with the exception that the contract terms may include monetary incentive payments should the contractor exceed the specifications or deliver the described service by some stated date certain.

**Flow-down terms and conditions:** Flow-down terms and conditions may be required if the contracting agency is awarding a contract in support of a grant or contract awarded by a state to a county, city, or district, or awarded by a federal agency to a state, county, city, or district. Oftentimes, grants, state contracts, and federal contracts include terms and conditions that are required to flow down to all state or local government agency contracts awarded in support of that grant or contract.

**Fully executed contract:** A term used to describe a contract that has been signed for all parties to the contract by representatives authorized to commit their respective organizations.

**Governing body:** The phrase used to describe the county board of supervisors, city council, district board, or any other entity that governs a particular local government agency.

**Incorporation:** The incorporation of documents in addition to the contract itself is essential to ensure that documents accompanying or attached to the contract are enforceable. Merely attaching additional documents to a contract does not make the provisions of those attachments enforceable upon the contractor. To ensure that the provisions of the attachments are enforceable, the attachments should be incorporated in the contract by identifying the attachment by attachment number, title, date, or other identifying information and then following that description with phraseology similar to "which is attached to and incorporated in this contract." A contractor's proposal is sometimes incorporated in a contract. This can be beneficial because it renders all the contractor's promises in their proposal to be a part of the contract. However, there can also be detrimental effects because undesirable provisions of the proposal also become a part of the contract. Hopefully, the detrimental effects will be minimized by placing the proposal lowest in precedence in the event of conflicts between contract provisions. However, an undesirable provision that does not conflict with other contract provisions becomes a part of the contract regardless of the precedence assigned to the contractor's proposal if the proposal is incorporated in the contract.

**Incorporation by reference:** This is similar to the incorporation defined above, with the exception that the actual document is not attached to the contract. Documents cannot be incorporated by reference unless they are readily available to all parties to the contract. The phraseology for incorporating documents by reference should be similar to "which is incorporated in this contract by reference."

**Indemnification:** Indemnification provisions typically require one or both parties to a contract to accept responsibility for loss or damage to a person or entity, and to compensate the other party for losses or expense incurred that arise out of, or in connection with, the other party's negligence or willful misconduct.

**Insurance:** Insurance provisions typically describe the types of insurance coverage and limits of liability for insurance policies that must be maintained by the contractor during the entire term of the contract. Typical types of required insurance coverage are general liability, automobile coverage, and workers' compensation. Professional liability coverage is also required if the contractor is expected to provide professional services such as legal, engineering, architectural, accounting, or the services of similarly trained professionals.

**Internal Customers:** Other employees of the contracting agency who rely on the contract professional to provide guidance in contracting matters.

**Invitation for Bids (IFB):** A formal solicitation normally used to solicit bids for high-dollar-value capital equipment or construction work. IFBs are normally not used to solicit bids for services. However, there are certain grants that require solicitation for services with IFBs. If solicitation by IFB is a condition of a grant, then compliance with grant terms will require adherence with the need to use an IFB to solicit bids for the specified services. IFBs solicit bids that are opened publicly, and result in award of a contract to the responsive, responsible contractor with the lowest price. When grants require solicitation through an IFB, an IFB template is normally provided by the granting agency for use by the state or local government agency.

**Legal purposes:** The nature of the services being contracted can be performed legally in the jurisdiction where the contract shall be construed and interpreted.

**Letter contract:** The term used for an agreement that must be executed prior to the time required for a formal contract to be staffed through normal channels. Letter contracts should include all the features (such as terms, start and end dates, and a not-to-exceed price) that the parties can agree to at the time the letter contract is executed. Letter contracts normally include provisions that cause them to expire after a certain specified time period with the expectation that they will be replaced by a definitive contract on or before the expiration date.

**Life cycle cost:** The initial price as adjusted during the term of the contract, plus all other agency costs associated with the project, such as the incremental cost of personnel, training, materials, project phase-out, or any other applicable project costs not included in the contract.

**Local government agency:** The phrase used to describe the county, city, or district that contracts with private-sector companies or individuals to perform services for the local government agency.

**Model Services Contract (MSC):** The term used to describe a contract that is included in the solicitation and is identified as the contract document essentially in the form of the one that the contracting agency intends to award to the successful contractor. MSCs ideally include the contracting agency's standard terms and conditions, insurance requirements, and the scope of work. Including a MSC in the solicitation and advising the prospective contractors that the contracting agency intends to award a contract essentially in the form of the MSC helps to derail the contractors' attempts to enter into a contract in their format with their terms and conditions. Contractors' terms and conditions often favor the contractor and may require extensive negotiations to render them acceptable to the contracting agency. The MSC should include all the essential elements of the contract awarded to the successful contractor such as offer, acceptance, consideration of competent parties, and a legal purpose.

**Modification:** The generic term for any alteration to a contract. Modifications are generally limited to amendments and change orders.

**Negotiations:** Negotiations are considered to be undertaken when the contracting agency enters into discussions with a prospective contractor or successful contractor to attempt to modify the price, schedule, terms, and conditions or any other element of the contractors' proposal or resultant contract. Solicitations often include a statement by the contracting agency to advise prospective contractors that the contracting agency may enter into negotiations or to award a contract based on the initial proposal without conducting negotiations. When such a statement is included in the solicitation, the prospective contractors are normally advised that they should include their best pricing and other terms and conditions in their initial proposal.

**Nondiscrimination clauses:** Nondiscrimination clauses may flow down from federal or state contracts or grants, and may be included in the state or local government agency's standard terms and conditions. The categories of characteristics that cannot be subject to discrimination in providing services or in employment practices typically include race, color, national origin, religion, age, sex, and physical or mental disability. Early, obsolete versions of nondiscrimination clauses referred to disabilities as handicaps. However, the terms "handicap," handicapped," and "handicaps" should never be included in state or local government contracts. There is an admonishment against use of such terms in the *Code of Federal Regulations* (CFR) as such terms are considered to be "overlaid with stereotypes" or invoke "patronizing attitudes and other emotional attitudes."

**Not-to-exceed (NTE) price:** Refers to a ceiling price that cannot be exceeded except when the contract has been amended to increase the NTE price.

**NTE:** (*See* not-to-exceed price.)

**Offer:** The communication of one party's willingness to enter into a contract that shall be binding if accepted by the party to which the offer was made.

**Offeror:** The term used to describe a person or organization making an offer.

**Overrun of cost:** Overrun of cost occurs when the contractor expends funds in excess of the original target cost in the absence of a change in the scope of work. See the definition of "cost growth" to differentiate between these two terms.

**Payment terms:** Payment terms in contracts typically describe the frequency with which the contractor may submit invoices, the cost elements and billing rates at which costs may be invoiced for not-to-exceed price and cost-reimbursement contracts, the time in which the contracting agency must pay the invoices, and cash discounts that may be taken if payments are made expeditiously. However, the payment terms may be less complex and merely indicate that the full contract price will be paid upon completion of the contract work. When no cash discount is offered by the contractor, payment terms are typically expressed as "Net 30," which indicates that the full amount of the invoice is due 30 days after the invoice and products or services are received by the contracting agency.

**Preamble:** The first section of the contract that identifies the contracting parties and their intent to enter into a contract. The effective date of the contract is often included in the preamble.

**Price:** The initial contract price paid to the contractor. This price may be increased or decreased through contract amendments based on changes in the scope of work. Price does not normally include agency personnel costs, training or materials not provided by the contractor, contract phase-out, or other miscellaneous project costs not included in the contract.

**Private sector:** The private sector includes companies, corporations, partnerships, sole proprietorships, individuals, consultants, or other non-government entities.

**Professional services contract:** The term for an agreement for the furnishing of professional services. Professional services are those services provided by an engineer, architect, attorney, accountant, professor, consultant, or a professional in another field that requires equivalent education and experience.

**Proposal format:** The term used to describe the contracting agency's prescribed organization of proposals submitted in response to an RFP. Specification of topics presented in the proposal that have a direct relationship to the evaluation criteria will simplify the work of the selection committee and will likely help ensure that the prospective contractors are treated equally. Specifying the sequence of the presentation of topics will also simplify the efforts of the selection committee. Placing a limit on the number of pages for each topic presented is highly recommended to prevent voluminous proposals that require an inordinate amount of time to read and evaluate.

**Proposals:** Responses to Requests for Proposals (RFPs) from prospective contractors that describe the approach that the contractor intends to employ to meet the services needs of the state or local government agency that released the RFP. Proposals also typically describe the prospective contractor's experience and qualifications to perform such services, as well as their proposed pricing and any other information requested in the RFP.

**Proprietary or trade secret:** These terms are used to describe company confidential information that may be included in a proposal but cannot ever be released to the proposing contractor's competitors or to the public. Although virtually all other information in proposals may be released after the contract has been awarded or recommended for award, proprietary or trade secret information must remain protected as confidential by the agency until it is destroyed or until the contractor that provided the information advises the agency that the material is no longer proprietary or a trade secret.

**Prospective contractors:** Those contractors that are believed to be qualified to deliver the required service to the state or local government agency and that, therefore, are included on the list of contractors solicited through the Request for Proposals (RFP) or other form of solicitation.

**Protest:** The term used to describe a challenge to the solicitation, procedure for selecting a contractor, recommendation to award a contract, or actual contract award. Protests are generally initiated by an unsuccessful contractor (or contractors). Defining the method for handling protests in the contracting agency's published policies and procedures, as well as in the solicitation, may help to keep protests manageable; however, contracts that are approved by the contracting agency's governing body or chief elected official may be protested at a public meeting of the governing body.

**Quotations (or quotes):** Responses to RFQs received from prospective contractors or suppliers in response to RFQs released by state or local government agencies. Quotations, or quotes, are typically prepared by completing blanks on a quotation form that was prepared by the contracting agency. The information provided by the prospective contractors on the quotation form may be limited to pricing, delivery time promised, payment terms, identifying company information, and a signature from a contractor representative.

**Quotes:** (*See* quotations.)

**Ratification:** Ratification of contracts refers to the approval of contracts that were originally awarded by an individual who did not have the authority to execute the contract. In some cases, the contract may have been awarded during an actual emergency to help protect lives or property. In other instances, the official, board, or commission with authority to award the contracts may have been asked to ratify a contract that had been improperly awarded by an individual who lacked the required authority to execute the contract.

**Reasonable pricing:** Refers to pricing that provides the contracting agency with the receipt of services at a price that does not exceed the reasonable value of the services received.

**Recitals:** Refers to the section of a contract that normally follows the preamble and describes the rationale for the parties entering into a contract. This section often includes the basis for consideration.

**Request for Contractor Qualifications (RFCQ):** The RFCQ is similar to the RFP except that its use is limited to obtaining information on the qualifications of various private-sector entities that may be qualified to perform the service. Prospective contractors, in response to the RFCQ, submit a statement of qualifications to the contracting agency. The contracting agency, in turn, evaluates the contractors' qualifications to determine which firms or individuals are qualified. Once a list of qualified contractors is developed, an RFP is normally sent to all the firms that were determined to be qualified through the RFCQ process. The RFCQ is a type of solicitation that is normally not used when the contracting agency is familiar with the prospective contractors for the service to be contracted. RFCQs are also not normally used when time is of the essence for placing the service under contract, because the need to follow through with an RFP after the list of qualified contractors is developed will significantly extend the time required to obtain proposals. Some agencies refer to RFCQs merely as Requests for Qualifications (RFQs) or Requests for Information (RFIs). However, use of the term "Request for Qualifications" (RFQ) can lead to confusion between requests for quotations and requests for qualifications, and a Request for Information (RFI) is not sufficiently descriptive of the nature of the solicitation.

**Request for Proposals (RFP):** The type of solicitation normally used to solicit proposals for services provided by private-sector contractors. RFPs typically include a short introduction of the state or local government agency soliciting proposals; background of the service to be contracted, to include the present manner in which the service is being provided; a description of the service to be provided; evaluation criteria to be used in selecting the successful contractor; rights reserved by the contracting activity; format for preparing proposals along with page limitations when appropriate; and a copy of a model contract that includes the terms and conditions, required insurance coverage, and scope of work. Chapter 3, "Solicitation Documents: Information for Prospective Contractors," includes an extensive discussion of RFPs and Appendix E, "Best Practices Request for Proposals (RFP)," includes a Best Practices RFP that should prove useful to state or local government contracting agencies.

**Request for Quotations (RFQ):** An informal solicitation normally used to solicit quotes for low-dollar-value merchandise that is easily described. RFQs are normally not used to solicit quotations for services.

**Responsible contractors:** Those contractors that meet the contracting agency's standards with respect to a reasonable expectation that the contractor has the management, technical, financial, equipment, and human resources available to ensure adequate performance of the work described in the solicitation. Agencies may have established a policy that specifies certain criteria that contractors must meet to be considered responsible. Those criteria could include companies that have not been debarred or suspended, not convicted of certain offenses, or that have not had a contract terminated for default, all within certain specified time periods.

**Responsive contractors:** Those contractors that provide a proposal satisfactorily addressing all requirements specified in the RFP. Because proposals, unlike bids, are subject to negotiation, certain omissions or variances should be resolved through negotiations to make the proposal responsive. An example of an omission or variance that could be resolved is a proposed period of performance that would not result in completion of the work within the required timeframe. Should negotiation with the contractor result in an adjustment to the period of performance that will result in completion with the required timeframe, the proposal then may be deemed "responsive."

**RFCQ:** (*See* Request for Contractor Qualifications.)

**RFI:** (*See* Request for Contractor Qualifications.)

**RFQ:** (*See* Request for Quotations and Request for Contractor Qualifications.)

**Rights reserved by contracting agency:** The rights of the contracting agency that are enumerated in the solicitation. They typically include the right to cancel the solicitation, modify the provisions of the solicitation, refrain from awarding a contract, engage in negotiations with prospective contractors, or any other rights that the contracting agency wishes to enumerate in the solicitation.

**Scope of work:** The title of the document that describes the work to be performed by the contractor. The scope of work may also include additional information such as certain aspects of the work that will be performed by the contracting agency. Some contracting agencies also include billing rates in the scope of work for not-to-exceed price or cost-reimbursement contracts. To ensure that the contractor is accountable for performance of the tasks listed in the scope of work, the scope of work should have a preamble that includes a statement to the effect that "the contractor shall provide all labor, materials, equipment, supplies, transportation, and pay all required taxes and fees to complete the following tasks." In jurisdictions where a word other than "shall" is used to compel a contractor to perform services, that word should be substituted for "shall" in the preamble to the scope of work. Jurisdictions that do not use "shall" to compel a contractor to perform work generally use "must" or "will."

**Selection committee membership:** Selection committee membership is typically comprised of employees from the contracting agency's department that requires the services of the contractor. In some cases consultants, who themselves are on contract, may also serve on the selection committee. Contracts or Purchasing personnel are also frequently members of selection committees. The departments participating on the selection committee are normally identified in the solicitation. A chairperson is typically designated for each selection committee. The selection committee opens the proposals, evaluates the proposals based on the evaluation criteria, and either selects the successful contractor or recommends a contractor to the governing body or chief elected official for approval and award of the contract.

**Services contract:** The term for an agreement for the furnishing of all services, including professional services. Services in addition to professional services include janitorial, pest control, landscaping, trash collection, security guards, or any other services not included in the definition for professional services. (*See also* Model Services Contract.)

**Set-asides:** The term used to describe procurements for which solicitations are sent only to a targeted class of contractors (such as small businesses or disabled veteran-owned businesses) and responses to the solicitation will not be considered unless the responding companies are members of the targeted class of contractors.

**Socioeconomic programs:** Equal opportunity or affirmative action programs that promote social or economic goals based on the award of contracts to targeted companies. Such programs encourage the award of contracts to contractors that fit certain criteria, such as a maximum number of employees or ownership of and management by women, minorities, veterans, or disabled persons.

**Solicitation:** The generic term used to describe documents sent to prospective contractors to advise them that a state or local government agency is seeking proposals, quotations, or bids for services provided by the private sector. Examples of solicitations traditionally used in state or local government contracting are Requests for Proposals (RFPs), Requests for Contractor Qualifications (RFCQs), Requests for Quotations (RFQs), and Invitations for Bids (IFBs).

**Statement of qualifications:** The response to an RFCQs from prospective contractors. It describes the contractor's qualifications to perform the services to be provided to the state or local government agency that released the RFCQ. A statement of qualifications does not normally include pricing.

**Successful contractor:** A successful contractor might intuitively be considered as a contractor that successfully completes the work described in a contract. However, for the purposes of this discussion, the successful contractor is the contractor selected for award of a particular contract.

**Supplier:** Another term often used to describe a contractor; however, this term is most often reserved for companies that provide materials rather than services.

**Suspended:** Refers to contractors that have been proposed for debarment, debarred, excluded, or otherwise disqualified for government contracting and government-approved subcontracting.

**Target cost:** The cost associated with a cost reimbursement contract that the contracting agency and contractor agree to as the expected cost for completion of the work described in the scope of work. This cost is normally determined through cost analysis and subsequent negotiation of the cost proposal submitted by the contractor.

**Targeted company:** The generic term used for companies that an agency targets for increased contracting opportunities through the agency's socioeconomic contracting program. Examples of targeted companies include small businesses, minority-owned small businesses, women-owned businesses, veteran-owned businesses, and disabled veteran-owned businesses.

**Terms and conditions:** Provisions that describe the rights and responsibilities of all parties to the contract. Typical examples of terms and conditions include payment, term of the contract, indemnification, termination, insurance, contract modifications, independent contractor, and other terms and conditions such as those included in the model contract in the Appendix E, "Best Practices Request for Proposals (RFP)." Ideally, terms and conditions are balanced to provide equivalent rights to all parties to the contract. An example of a termination clause that is imbalanced is one wherein one party has the right to terminate the contract for either convenience or for cause, while the other party merely has the right to terminate for cause. Contractors that propose their own versions of terms and conditions often include provisions that favor their companies over the rights and responsibilities afforded their customers.

**Types of contracts:** A term that refers primarily to the basis for payment by the contracting agency to the contractor. The definitions for types of contracts are generally based on contract types defined in the Federal Acquisition Regulations (FAR) because state or local agencies do not consistently define types of contracts.

**Unallowable costs:** Unallowable costs need to be defined by the contracting agency prior to contract award, and the rules for disallowance of unallowable costs need to be included in the contract. If costs such as those listed above in the definition for "cost-reimbursement contracts" are not designated as unallowable, the contracting agency could be obligated to reimburse the contractor for inappropriate costs. To ensure that unallowable costs are not reimbursed by the contracting agency, a contract clause permitting audit of the contractor's financial records should also be included in the contract terms and conditions.

**Underrun of cost:** Underrun of cost is the exact opposite of "overrun of cost."

**Unilateral changes to a contract:** Unilateral changes to a contract are those changes that are made with the signature of just one party to the contract. State or local agency contracts and modifications thereto normally require bilateral contracts and contract modifications.

**Unsuccessful contractor:** The term used to describe any contractor that submitted a proposal but was *not* selected for contract award.

**Vendor:** A term that is occasionally used to describe contractors; however, this term should be reserved for the limited number of companies that sell products through vending machines or from vending carts.

**Weighted evaluation criteria:** Identical to evaluation criteria, defined above, with the exception that weights are assigned to each of the criteria to differentiate between the importance of the various criteria. For example, if price has twice the importance of contractor's reputation, price might be assigned a weight of 40 while contractor's reputation is assigned a weight of 20. Although it is not essential, the sum of the weights assigned to the criteria typically equals 100. Weighted criteria should be considered when the contractor selection could potentially be contentious or controversial. Examples of weighted criteria are provided in Chapter 3, "Solicitation Documents: Information for Prospective Contractors," and Chapter 5, "Management of Pre-proposal Communications and Evaluation of Proposals."

**Wet signed contract:** The term used to describe a contract with original signatures. Due to the excellent quality of modern copying equipment, it is recommended that contracts printed in black be signed in blue, and that copies of original contracts not be made on color copiers.

# *Appendix B*

# Best Practices Research Project

In recognition of the potential for significant contributions to the body of knowledge for services contracting by state and local government agencies, representatives from fifty states, fifty cities, and fifty counties were invited to participate in a research project to develop best practices templates for a Request for Proposals (RFP) and for a Model Services Contract (MSC). A request for copies of an RFP and services contract templates and a short questionnaire (Figures B.1 and B.2, respectively) were sent to all fifty state governments as well as to the city governments in the capital cities and the county governments where the capitals are located. The number of questions posed to these agencies was limited; but more importantly, the agencies were asked to cooperate in the preparation of this text by permitting publication, in whole or in part, of the solicitation and contract templates they use for services contracting.

The solicitation and contract templates submitted for this project were requested to conduct a document review for selection of the best features from each document to incorporate in best practices templates for an RFP and an MSC that would be made available for use by all state and local government agencies. The solicitation templates for services contracts were predominately in the form of RFPs. The response from the states was considerably more complete and cooperative than anticipated. While the response from counties and cities was disappointing with respect to the number of such agencies that elected to participate, the responses revealed numerous excellent practices by the participating agencies. Although there was considerable disparity in the quality of solicitations and services contracts in use by the various state and local government agencies, it is gratifying to report that material from each of the templates was selected for incorporation in the best practices templates. The Acknowledgment

**William S. Curry**

**Street Address**

**City, State & ZIP+4**

August XX, 2006

Re: Request for Contract and Request for Proposal Templates to be Included in Book on
    Contracting for Services

Dear Sir or Madam:

I am in the process of writing of a book entitled, "Contracting for Services in State and Local
Government Agencies." The book includes chapters on solicitations and contractual documents,
as well as appendices that contain a sample request for proposals (RFP) and a sample contract for
services. Although the chapters on solicitations and contractual documents have been drafted and
the book is nearing completion, I have decided to write to all fifty states and the counties and cities
where the state capitols are located to request copies of RFP and contract templates that are
presently in use. The purpose of this request is to select the best features from all the documents
that are received to create a composite RFP and contract for inclusion in my book. The states,
counties and cities that provide copies of these documents, along with permission for publication
of the documents or portions thereof, will be recognized for their cooperation in the book and will
be provided with a copy of the composite RFP and contract. Please be assured that the book will
emphasize best practices, and that there will be no criticism of government agencies based on
documents provided in response to this request.

There is also a short questionnaire that is enclosed for completion by an individual in your
agency who is responsible for approval or recommendation for approval of contracts for services.
The responses to the questionnaire will be published only in the aggregate and responses from
individual government agencies will not be identified.

My qualifications for writing a book on contracting for services in state and local government
agencies include over thirty years of experience as a contracting professional in the federal
government, the private sector, and a local government agency; author of numerous published
articles on contracting matters; presenter of numerous seminars and workshops on contracts;
over thirty years membership in the National Contract Management Association (NCMA) and
designation by the NCMA as a Certified Professional Contracts Manager (CPCM) and a Fellow;
MBA from Ohio State University and BS in Business Management from Florida State University.

Sincerely,

William S. Curry, CPCM, Fellow

bnkcurry@sbcglobal.net

Enclosures

**Figure B.1   Request for copies of RFP and services contract templates.**

Contracting for Services Questionnaire State and Local Government Agencies

| Question Number | Question | Response | | |
|---|---|---|---|---|
| | | Yes | No | Don't Know |
| 1 | Are Cost-Plus-A-Percentage-of-Cost[1] contracts permitted in your jurisdiction? | | | |
| 2 | Is "shall" the word that most compels a contractor to perform tasks included in the contract Scope of Work? | | | |
| 3 | Is "must" the word that most compels a contractor to perform tasks included in the contract Scope of Work? | | | |
| 4 | Is some other word the one that most compels a contractor to perform tasks included in the contract Scope of Work? | | | |
| 5 | At what dollar threshold is it necessary to obtain sole source approval or competition to select contractors for service contracts? | $ | | |
| | | Remarks (if any) | | |

[1]Cost-Plus-a-Percentage-of-Cost contracts are not permitted in federal government contracting, because it has been determined that this contract type may provide an incentive for contractors to maximize reimbursable expenditures to increase their profit.

The results from this questionnaire may be published in a book with the title, "Contracting for Services in State and Local Government Agencies." Responses will be published only in the aggregate without identifying specific responses made by any government agency.

**Please mail the completed questionnaire to:**   William S. Curry
Street Address
City, State & ZIP+4

---

**Figure B.2   Questionnaire sent to state and local government agencies.**

in this book includes the author's appreciation to the states, counties, and cities that elected to participate in this project. The agencies that provided copies of or access to their solicitation and RFP templates included sixteen states, two counties, three cities, and one borough/city combination.

References throughout this book were made regarding the results of the document review performed on the solicitations and contracts and the resultant best-practices templates that were developed. The Best Practices RFP and MSC templates are included in other appendices and on the CD accompanying this book. There are also individual chapters devoted to describing the templates for the RFP, the MSC, and the MSC terms and conditions.

The MSC and Best Practices RFP should prove valuable to state and local government agencies that wish to improve the standard contract formats; however, there are some features of the MSC and RFP templates that may appeal to some, but not to all government agencies. In those cases where there are features that may have less-than-universal appeal, the features were included in the Best Practices MSC and RFP because it is a simpler matter to delete unwanted features than to provide a separate set of optional features for subsequent incorporation in the templates. Therefore, the templates provided for use by readers of this book contain certain features that may be deleted when contract and RFP formats are adopted for agency use. Likewise, some agencies may elect to revise the content of MSC and RFP features to comply with their agency's practices.

Results from the analysis of documents that were submitted in support of this project are contained in subsequent appendices dealing in activities where the best practices can be applied. Discussion of the research findings for each best practice is provided below. Verification, primarily from independent sources that support the selection of the particular practices as best practices, follows discussion of each of the research findings. Fourteen best practices are reflected in the Best Practices RFP template and four best practices are reflected in the MSC template.

# B.1 Best Practices Incorporated in the RFP Template

## B.1.1 Availability of an Agency Web Site

### B.1.1.1 Research Findings

Thirteen of the twenty-two RFPs (59 percent) provided by the participating state and local government agencies identified an agency Web site in their RFPs. Providing a Web site for prospective contractors is a desirable feature and is encouraged for implementation by state and local government agencies. The Web sites in the RFPs submitted for this project were provided for various reasons, including general information about the agency and its contracting program; announcement of active RFPs, Invitations for Bids (IFBs), and Requests for Quotations (RFQs) that had been released as competitive solicitations; for companies to register with the agency as prospective contractors; for prospective contractors to pose questions to the agency that would be posted to the Web site along with agency responses regarding active solicitations; and to announce the award of contracts for particular projects.

### B.1.1.2 Independent Verification

The National Purchasing Institute (NPI) criteria for the 2008 Achievement of Excellence in Procurement (AEP) award includes the availability of an Internet home page with a link to purchasing activities, online registration of prospective contractors, distribution of solicitations via the Internet, and electronic commerce.

## B.1.2 Web Site Provided for Management of Pre-Proposal Communications

### B.1.2.1 Research Findings

Seven of the twenty-two RFPS (32 percent) posted questions from prospective contractors regarding active RFPs and the agency's responses to those questions. This is a highly desirable feature for RFPs and is discussed in considerably more detail in Chapter 5, "Management of Pre-proposal Communications and Evaluation of Proposals." The short explanation for the desirability of this feature is that it facilitates equal treatment of prospective contractors by ensuring that all contractors receive the same information from the agency following release of the solicitation and prior to the due date for the receipt of proposals. The use of a Web site for this purpose also facilitates the timely availability of information on active solicitations.

Five of the RFPs (23 percent) permit the prospective contractors to submit questions regarding the solicitation directly to the Web site, while two of the RFPs (9 percent) require the contractors to submit their questions to the agency by e-mail. While slightly more agency effort is involved when contractors submit their questions via e-mail, because the contracting agency must post both the question and response on the Web site, this approach permits the agency more control over the information posted to its Web site.

The Best Practices RFP instructs prospective contractors to submit their questions regarding the solicitation via e-mail to the contracting agency, which in turn posts both the questions and responses on the Web site.

The fifteen participating agencies (68 percent) that did not provide a Web site for posting questions regarding the RFPs and agency responses did require submittal of the questions in writing. Just one agency permitted questions to be posed via telephone or in writing. Permitting contractors to pose questions via telephone, or in person, is considered an undesirable practice. When contractors pose questions by telephone or otherwise verbally, the agency representative who is the recipient of the questions must rely on her or his own note-taking skills or memory to ensure that the questions are transcribed correctly, that seemingly inconsequential as well as significant questions are recorded, and that all prospective contractors receive identical responses in the same timeframe. There is a distinct possibility that the agency representative may provide a verbal response to a verbal question that is regarded as inconsequential by the agency representative and, therefore, the agency representative may fail to advise the other prospective contractors of that particular question and response.

## B.1.2.2 Independent Verification

The original 1979 American Bar Association (ABA) *Model Procurement Code for State and Local Governments* includes eleven basic principles that have been preserved although there is now a *2000 Model Procurement Code for State and Local Governments*. The fifth basic principle from the 1979 code is "Equal Treatment of Bidders/Offerors." Posting questions regarding solicitations and agency responses to a Web site for all to see while prohibiting alternative methods for posing questions is an excellent practice that promotes equal treatment of prospective contractors.

The NPI's criteria for the 2008 AEP award regarding the availability of an Internet home page, as discussed in the independent verification for the previous best practices, further verifies this best practice as well.

## B.1.3 Dollar Threshold Where Sole Source Justification Is Required

### B.1.3.1 Research Findings

The questionnaire that was sent to states and local government agencies asked for the dollar threshold where it was necessary to obtain sole source justification for services contracts. Chapter 2, "Competition and Socioeconomic Contracting," stresses the importance of obtaining competition when selecting a contractor, and introduces a form that can be used to justify and approve sole source contracts when competition is not available. The responses from the state and local government agencies regarding the threshold where sole source justifications are required are summarized in Figure B.3.

### B.1.3.2 Independent Verification

The American Bar Association's (ABA) *2000 Model Procurement Code for State and Local Governments* includes, as one of its terms and conditions, §3-204, Small Purchases, indicating that procurements under an established dollar value threshold may be awarded on the basis of small purchase procedures. Small purchase procedures generally include the acceptability of sole source contracting. The *2000 Model Procurement Code for State and Local Governments* also includes §3-205, Sole Source Procurement, indicating that a contract may be awarded on a sole source basis only when the designated agency official determines in writing that there is only one source for the procurement.

| Response to: At what dollar threshold are sole source justifications required? | | |
|---|---|---|
| States | Local Agencies | Response |
| 0 | 1 | No dollar amount, but sole source must be proven |
| 1 | 1 | $1,000 |
| 2 | 0 | $2,500 |
| 3 | 1 | $3,000 to $3,100 |
| 3 | 2 | $5,000 |
| 0 | 1 | $10,000 |
| 2 | 0 | $50,000 |
| 1 | 0 | $62,600 |

**Figure B.3** **Response to: At what dollar threshold are sole source justifications required?**

## B.1.4 Preference Not Given to Local Contractors

### B.1.4.1 Research Findings

Four of the twenty-two RFPs (18 percent) described a preference given to local contractors in the proposal evaluation process. The chapter on solicitations discusses the prohibition against providing local preferences when federal funding is included in the project budget. Other objections to local and other types of socioeconomic preferences in the selection process are also included in the chapter on solicitations. Eight of the RFPs (36 percent) included socioeconomic preferences, other than for local contractors, to be applied in the selection process. The Best Practices RFP does not include any socioeconomic preferences that are employed in the selection process. However, the chapter on socioeconomic contracting programs does describe methods for establishing outreach programs to increase the participation from underrepresented categories of contractors.

### B.1.4.2 Independent Verification

The *Code of Federal Regulations* (CFR) states in 28 CFR PART 35, STATE AND LOCAL ASSISTANCE, Part 35.936-2, Grantee procurement systems; State or local law, subpart (C) Preference, states, State or local laws, ordinances, regulations or procedures which effectively give local or in-State bidders or proposers preference over other bidders or proposers shall not be employed in evaluating bids or proposals for subagreements under a grant. Similar prohibitions are also included in CFR Subpart 35.938-4, Formal advertising.

## B.1.5 The Words "Proposal" and "Bid" Are Not Used Synonymously

### B.1.5.1 Research Findings

Three of the twenty-two RFPs (14 percent) referred to the response requested from the prospective contractors exclusively as "proposal" while all the remaining RFPs (86 percent) used "bid" as a synonym for "proposal." The discussion in this text regarding the confidential opening of proposals and the acceptance of late proposals provides insight into just two of the distinctions between RFPs and IFBs. RFPs, IFBs, and RFQs are all distinct types of solicitation documents. While virtually all agencies have provisions for at least two if not all three types of solicitations, there is a widespread problem when agencies use an RFP wherein the response from the contractors should be restricted to proposals, yet the text of the RFP provides instructions for submittal of a bid. Because there are distinctions in the laws and agency policies between the processes for receipt and treatment of proposals and for the receipt and treatment of bids, RFPs should not use the term "bid" as a synonym for "proposal."

### B.1.5.2 Independent Verification

The ABA's *2000 Model Procurement Code for State and Local Governments* §3-202, Competitive Sealed Bidding, and §3-203, Competitive Sealed Proposals, point out the differences between the conditions for use of IFBs and RFPs and the differences between the treatment of "bids" in response to IFBs and "proposals" in response to RFPs. This difference in the treatment of bids and proposals is consistent with practices in federal contracting. Reading the descriptions of the treatment of bids and proposals in §3-203 should make it clear that the terms "bid" and "proposal" have distinctly differing definitions and should not be used interchangeably.

## B.1.6 Reference to Companies Solicited as "Contractors" or "Prospective Contractors"

### B.1.6.1 Research Findings

Four of the twenty-two RFPs (18 percent) referred to the companies solicited exclusively as contractors or prospective contractors. One reason why this is a good practice is that the contract awarded to the successful company, virtually without variation, refers to that company exclusively as "contractor" throughout the balance of the contract document. Three of the RFPs (14 percent) referred to the prospective contractors as "offerors." This is not a recommended practice because proposals received in response to an RFP are technically not offers. The remaining fifteen RFPs (68 percent) refer to the prospective contractors as vendors or a combination of terms other than contractor. The word "vendor" seems more fitting to small-scale proprietors such as street vendors, vendors at sporting events, or operators of vending machine companies rather than companies that provide services, and occasionally professional services, to government agencies. Because "vendor" and other alternatives to "contractor" conflict with the term "contractor" as used in the contract that is anticipated for award to the successful contractor, the Best Practices RFP refers to the companies solicited for submittal of a proposal exclusively as "contractor" or "prospective contractor."

## B.1.6.2 Independent Verification

The use of the term "vendor" and additional terms other than "contractor" and "prospective contractor" are often used by contracting professionals and other state and local government officials and employees to describe contractors. Discouraging use of the term "vendor" is not based on any legal requirement or standards developed by associations or other organizations, but on the fact that virtually all government contracts identify the legal name of the contractor early in their contract documents and then state that the term "contractor" shall subsequently be used in the contract document in lieu of the contractor's name. Additionally, a few of the synonyms for the word "vendor" listed in *Webster's Collegiate Thesaurus* are peddler, duffer, hawker, haggler, huckster, and roadman. Certainly, state and local government contractors are worthy of being characterized by a term with more dignity than "vendor."

## B.1.7 Word Used That Best Compels Contractors to Perform Tasks

### B.1.7.1 Research Findings

There is no wrong answer to the question posed to states and local government agencies regarding the word that most compels the contractor to perform its tasks. However, it is of interest to note the variations in the responses to this question from the state and local government agencies. Incidentally, the word used that best compels federal contractors to perform their tasks is "shall." Whatever word is used by an agency that best compels contractors to perform should be used consistently. An agency using "must" to compel contractors to perform should not state that

| Response to: What word most compels a contractor to perform tasks? | | |
|---|---|---|
| States | Local Agencies | Response |
| 6 | 1 | Shall |
| 1 | 0 | Must |
| 5 | 3 | Shall and Must |
| 0 | 1 | Shall, Must and Will |

**Figure B.4   Response to: What word most compels contractors to perform tasks?**

contractors "may" or "should" perform certain tasks unless those tasks are truly optional. The responses to the questionnaire regarding the word that best compels a contractor to perform its tasks are shown in Figure B.4.

## B.1.7.2 Independent Verification

Although the text indicates that there is no correct answer to the word that best compels a contractor to perform tasks, the term "shall" is used throughout federal contracting. Additionally, the ABA's *2000 Model Procurement Code for State and Local Governments* reflects the following as the definition for shall: "*Shall* denotes the imperative."

## B.1.8 Weighted Criteria Established for Evaluation of Proposals

### B.1.8.1 Research Findings

Ten of the RFPs (45 percent) identified proposal evaluation criteria that would be used and identified weights assigned to each criterion. When agencies decide to use weighted criteria in the proposal evaluation process, the weighted criteria should always be identified in the RFP. The use of weighted criteria is appropriate when larger dollar value contracts are anticipated, or for those projects where there is aggressive competition by contentious contractors that are predisposed to protesting when the contract is awarded to their competitors. Although the evaluation of proposals for the majority of selection criteria, other than pricing or life cycle-cost, tends to be subjective, the introduction of weighting to the selection criteria increases the level of objectivity into the proposal evaluation process. The chapter on the evaluation of proposals (Chapter 5) provides considerable detail on the use of weighted criteria in the evaluation of proposals. The use of weighted evaluation criteria can result in narrowing the proposal evaluation committee's result to a single number that is calculated strictly in accordance with a selection process as fully disclosed in the RFP. When this level of objectivity is introduced into the contractor selection process, the chances of receiving a protest from one or more of the unsuccessful contractors are lessened. The agency also is better positioned to defend against any protests that are received when it discloses the process for evaluating proposals in the RFP and when the proposal evaluation committee actually conforms to that process.

### B.1.8.2 Independent Verification

The ABA's *2000 Model Procurement Code for State and Local Governments* includes, as one of its terms and conditions, §3-203(5), Evaluation Factors, indicating that the RFP "shall state the relative importance of price and other factors and subfactors." The only known way to reflect the "relative importance" of the various evaluation factors would be some scheme to assign weights to each of the criteria.

## B.1.9 Price Stated as One Criterion for Evaluation of Proposals

### B.1.9.1 Research Findings

Eight of the RFPs (36 percent) specified price as a criterion for evaluating proposals. However, it is suspected that all the agencies consider pricing in their proposal evaluation process but just failed to include that information in their RFPs. The Best Practices RFP specifies life cycle cost, as an alternative to contract price, as one of the selection criteria. Life cycle cost, which considers all contract costs plus all other agency project costs over a specified number of years, is considered superior to consideration of cost to the agency that is limited to contract pricing. As an example of the superiority of the life cycle cost evaluation, consider one proposal for a three-year contract with annual pricing of $4,000,000 that requires the addition of three agency employees to manage the project at a cost to the agency of $60,000 per employee per year. If a competing proposal includes a three-year contract with annual pricing of $4,050,000 and requires just one additional agency employee to manage the project at $60,000 per year, the company with the higher contract cost has a life cycle cost that is lower than their competitor's life cycle cost by $70,000 per year.

### B.1.9.2 Independent Verification

The ABA's *2000 Model Procurement Code for State and Local Governments* includes, as one of its terms and conditions, §3-203(7), Award, which states that the award shall be made on the basis of "price and the evaluation factors set forth in the Request for Proposals" as well as the statement "No other factors or criteria shall be used in the evaluation." This recommended contract provision clearly indicates that price is an evaluation factor that shall be set forth in the RFP, and the factors set forth in the RFP shall be used to evaluate proposals.

## B.1.10 Format Specified for Proposals

### B.1.10.1 Research Findings

Sixteen of the twenty-two RFPs (73 percent) specified the format for proposals submitted in response to the RFP. Another three RFPs (14 percent) included limited direction on the organization for proposals. The remaining three RFPs (14 percent) provided no directions for the format or organization of the proposals. The Best Practices RFP includes specific instructions for organizing proposals. The receipt of numerous proposals that are organized however the prospective contractors determine as most advantageous for their company creates an unnecessary burden for the agency's proposal evaluation committee. When prospective contractors are not instructed as to what to include in their proposals, they tend to omit coverage of their self-perceived weaknesses and elaborate of their strengths. Even more importantly, however, is the fact that the material concerning a particular selection criterion could be discussed by one contractor in the beginning of the proposal, discussed near the center of another contractor's proposal, and possibly even discussed in several different locations in a third contractor's proposal. This lack of uniformity in the format for the proposals greatly increases the time required for and effort expended by the agency's proposal evaluation committee. Lack of proposal uniformity also increases the possibility that material relating to one of the selection criteria for one or more prospective contractors may be overlooked. The receipt of proposals that are organized identically, and in a manner relating to the proposal evaluation criteria, greatly simplifies the task of the proposal evaluation committee and likely improves the quality of the committee's proposal evaluation.

### B.1.10.2 Independent Verification

Although there is neither any known statutory requirement nor is this a criterion established by an association or agency, the majority of agencies participating in the research project elected to reap the benefits of this practice. Homogeneous proposals facilitate increased efficiency in the evaluation of proposals by the agency's proposal evaluation committee and simplify the task of correlating the contractors' qualifications to the criteria. These features promote efficiency in use of the evaluation committee's time and promote equal treatment of prospective contractors.

## B.1.11  Page Limit Established for Proposals

### B.1.11.1  Research Findings

Just one of the RFPs (5 percent) contained a page limitation for proposals. While a page limit is not nearly as essential as the specification of the proposal format, it is considered a best practice to include a page limitation. The Best Practices RFP specifies proposals that are organized in separate sections that relate to the proposal evaluation criteria and contains a page limit for each section of the proposal. One objective of imposing a page limitation is to eliminate needlessly verbose proposals that require excessive time to read and evaluate. More importantly, however, is that when a page limit is established for each section, contractors tend to prepare their proposals with exactly the maximum number of pages for each section. Therefore, the proposals are organized in exactly the same manner and with the same number of pages in each section. This greatly simplifies the evaluation task of the proposal evaluation committee and contributes to a more equitable proposal evaluation.

### B.1.11.2  Independent Verification

Although just one of the RFPs submitted in support of the research project includes a page limit for proposals, this practice is actually a logical extension to the preceding practice of specifying the format for proposals. The impact of proposals with a more uniform length overall, as well as uniform lengths for the individual sections, further increases efficiency in the evaluation of proposals and further ensures the equal treatment of contractors. The page limitation helps restrict the capability of big business to gain excessive advantage over its competitors through the submittal of elaborate proposals that would be cost prohibitive to all but the largest corporations.

## B.1.12  Model Contract Included in RFP

### B.1.12.1  Research Findings

Seventeen of the twenty-two RFPs (77 percent) included a copy of the agency's standard contract format in the solicitation. Three of the five RFPs that did not include a copy of the agency's standard services contract, however, did include a copy of their terms and conditions. It was rare to find a statement in the RFP that the agency intended to award a contract that was substantially in the format of the MSC in the RFP. The Best Practices RFP does include an MSC and a statement to the effect that the agency intends to award a contract substantially in the format of the MSC. The primary resultant problem if an agency does not include a copy of its standard services contract in its solicitations is that this practice encourages prospective contractors to submit their own versions of a contract along with their proposals. Contractors are prone to drafting terms and conditions that favor the rights and risks of the contractor over the rights and risks of the agency. Additionally, when contractors submit their own contracts, there is less consistency between risks and rights for the competing contractors. This inconsistency results in one additional element that decreases the probability of evaluating the proposals on an equivalent basis.

### B.1.12.2 Independent Verification

Including a model contract in the RFP as a best practice is based primarily on the nearly universal practice among state and local government agencies that participated in the research project, and the logic behind the practice of including a copy of the agency's standard contract that it intends to award to the contractor to avoid the strong possibility, in the absence of this practice, that prospective contractors propose their standard contracts. Contractor standard provisions generally include provisions that are less than favorable to the government agency. The discussion of this best practice adds the author's recommendation that the RFP include a statement to the effect that the agency intends to award a contract substantially in the form of the attached model contract.

## B.1.13 Late Proposals May Be Accepted if in the Best Interests of the Agency

### B.1.13.1 Research Findings

None of the RFPs (0 percent) indicated that the agency had the option to accept late proposals. However, there were two RFPs (9 percent) that did not eliminate the possibility for accepting late proposals. Twenty of the RFPs (91 percent) indicated that late proposals were unacceptable. Unlike bids in response to an IFB where late bids must be rejected, contracting agencies have more flexibility for accepting late proposals in response to an RFP. Because bids are opened publicly, it is absolutely unfair to permit the acceptance of a bid after the competitors submitted their bids on time and their pricing became public knowledge. A proposal that is submitted a minute, hour, or possibly a day or two late could include pricing and other features that would greatly benefit the contracting agency. Because the competing proposals have been held in confidence during that time period, the company submitting the late proposal would not have any apparent advantage over the competitors that submitted their proposals on time. If a contracting agency elects to accept late proposals, however, they should include a statement in their RFP to the effect that late proposals may be accepted prior to contract award if such acceptance would be in the best interests of the contracting agency. The Best Practices RFP includes provisions for accepting late proposals if they are in the best interests of the contracting agency; however, it is understood that all agencies may not wish to incorporate this provision in their RFPs, and their policy of rejecting late proposals may be maintained.

## B.1.13.2 Independent Verification

State and local statutes, ordinances, and policies and procedures generally require that bids in response to IFBs be opened publicly. However, the opening of proposals in response to RFPs is generally not addressed. In the absence of restrictions against accepting late proposals, this practice would be acceptable; however, the RFP should advise prospective contractors that late proposals are acceptable if they are in the agency's best interests, but that contractors should submit their proposals on time because the agency maintains the right to reject late proposals. Although the rules for handling proposals are universally less stringent than for handling bids, there was an interesting court case (*Power Systems Analysis, Inc.* v. *City of Bloomer*, 541 N.W.2d 214 (Wisc. App. Ct. 1995)) involving the acceptability of a late bid by City of Bloomer, Wisconsin, and Power Systems Analysis, Inc. In that court case, it was decided that because State of Wisconsin Statute §62.15 is silent regarding receipt of late bids, the City was permitted to accept a late bid after other bids had been opened because that practice permitted the City to secure the best work at the best practicable price.

## B.1.14  Proposals Opened in Confidence

### B.1.14.1  Research Findings

Seven of the twenty-two RFPs (32 percent) provided for a confidential opening of the proposals. However, there were an additional seven RFPs (32 percent) that did not indicate whether or not the proposals would be opened confidentially or publicly. There were eight RFPs (36 percent) that announced a public opening of the proposals; however, two of the agencies announcing a public opening also indicated that the proposed pricing would be treated confidentially. Unlike bids in response to an IFB, proposals in response to an RFP should be treated as confidential until the contract is awarded or recommended to the governing board or chief elected official for approval and award. The rationale for treating the proposals as confidential is that the proposals, unlike bids, are subject to negotiation. If the companies that submitted proposals know the proposed pricing or other features of their competitors' proposals, they become capable of unfairly adjusting their own proposals or negotiating changes to their proposals to make their organization more competitive. Therefore, the Best Practices RFP does not provide for a public opening of the proposals and does indicate that the proposals are treated as confidential until the contract is awarded or recommended for award.

### B.1.14.2 Independent Verification

The ABA's *2000 Model Procurement Code for State and Local Governments* §3-203(4), Receipt of Proposals, states that proposals are to be opened so as to avoid disclosure of contents and made available for public disclosure following contract award.

# B.2 Best Practices Incorporated in the RFP Template

## B.2.1 One Page Contract Format with Incorporated Attachments

### B.2.1.1 Research Findings

Five of the twenty-two contracts (23 percent) provided by participating agencies included a one-page contract format with most of the essential contract information on the same page as the executing signatures. The Best Practices MSC is a one-page contract containing a preamble that identifies the contracting parties, the agency's project manager, contract price, type of contract, identification of documents that are incorporated in the contract either by attachment or by reference, recitals that briefly describe the contractor's qualifications, the agency's decision to obtain the services through contracting, and the signatures that represent full execution of the contract. There are several advantages to providing this information on a single page. The essential contract information for the seventeen contracts that were not in this one-page format had that essential information distributed throughout numerous pages of those contract documents. In some cases there was virtually nothing but the executing signatures on the execution page of the contracts that were not in the one-page format. An individual who signs such a contract that has virtually no contract information on the signature page may feel that she or he is being asked to sign the equivalent of a blank check. Another disadvantage of the traditional multi-page contract format is that there is a greater possibility that differing essential contract information may be introduced into the contract through page substitutions made following contract execution. The page substitutions may be accidental or intentional. The use of the one-page contract format provides considerable protection from unintentional or unauthorized page substitutions. Another distinct advantage of the one-page contract format is that it facilitates the incorporation of a variable information table such as the one in the MSC or a similar arrangement for the variable information, which greatly simplifies the collection of contract data during the preparation of the contract document on a computer. The information thus collected can be used to populate the database for computer software programs designed to report on financial information for contracts and also for reports in support of subsequent contract administration efforts.

## B.2.1.2 Independent Verification

The number of state and local government agencies that provided one-page contract formats was in the minority. However, the advantages of using such a one-page format become obvious when comparing them to traditional contracts. The author's professional experience following the transition from traditional multi-page contracts to one-page contracts resulted in a significant reduction in errors from the previous practice of making updates to earlier traditional contract document texts when drafting new contracts. Overlooking variable information that was imbedded throughout the text in traditional contracts resulted in carryover of some inappropriate variable information from the earlier contract to the more recent contract. The inclusion of all the variable contract information in a variable information table, as shown in Figure B.5, in the one-page contract virtually eliminated this class of error that was frequently found in traditional contracts. Additionally, the one-page format facilitates the completion of the contract document on a computer and the simultaneous populating of computer software databases used for subsequent managing and administering contracts. The one-page contract format provides for virtually all variable contract information on the one-page contract and a scope of work. This arrangement also permits the inclusion of all contract boilerplate on easily recognizable and unalterable documents that require just a cursory reading prior to reviewing or executing contracts, rather than the laboriously word-for-word reading of the entire contract boilerplate text. This practice also lessens the possibility that unauthorized or erroneous material is included in the contract boilerplate.

## B.2.2 Cost Plus a Percentage of Cost Prohibited

### B.2.2.1 Research Findings

It was also extremely rare to find any limitation on the reimbursement of cost-plus-a-percentage-of-costs (CPPC) contracts. The questionnaire sent to the state and local government agencies included a question regarding the allowability of CPPC contracts. Despite a footnote indicating that such contracts were not permitted in federal contracting and were discouraged by the American Bar Association (ABA), some questionnaire respondents indicated that CPPC arrangements were acceptable. The reason that CPPC contracts are prohibited in federal contracts and discouraged by the ABA is that including CPPC provisions in contracts tends to motivate certain contractors to maximize the expenditure of funds in support of the CPPC contracts

| VARIABLE INFORMATION TABLE | | | |
|---|---|---|---|
| | Contract Number | | |
| **Term of This Contract** (Complete Dates in Just One of the Following Three Shaded Rows) | | | |
| √ Below | **Term Begins** | **Term Completion Date** | |
| | On Following Date | On Following Date | |
| | Upon Receipt of Notice to Proceed | Calendar Days Following Notice to Proceed | |
| | Upon Execution by Agency | Calendar Days Following Agency Contract Execution | |
| Agency Department | | FOB Point | |
| Terms | | Basis of Price (**Do Not √ More Than One of the Following Four Blocks**) | |
| Price | | Fixed Price / Annual Price / Monthly Price / Hourly Rate | |
| Not-to-Exceed Price | | √ if Reasonable Expenses authorized in addition to Hourly Rate | |

| Contractor Contact Information | | Agency Contact Information | |
|---|---|---|---|
| Contractor | | Project Manager | |
| Address | | Address | |
| City, State & ZIP | | City, State & ZIP | |
| Telephone | | Telephone | |
| Facsimile | | Facsimile | |

**Figure B.5  Variable information table.**

because that tactic maximizes corporate profit at the expense of the government and the taxpayers.

The summary in Figure B.6 reflects the responses to the question on the questionnaire, "Are cost-plus-a-percentage-of-cost contracts permitted in your jurisdiction?"

| Response to: Are Cost-Plus-a-Percentage-of-Cost Contracts Permitted? | | |
|---|---|---|
| **States** | **Local Agencies** | **Response** |
| 3 | 1 | Yes |
| 1 | 0 | Yes, but not used |
| 1 | 0 | Yes, but rare |
| 6 | 4 | No |
| 1 | 0 | Don't know |
| 0 | 1 | No response |

**Figure B.6   Response to: Are cost-plus-a-percentage-of-cost contracts permitted?**

## B.2.2.2 Independent Verification

Numerous states have statutes prohibiting CPPC contracts. The ABA's *2000 Model Procurement Code for State and Local Governments* includes, as one of its terms and conditions, §3-501, Types of Contracts, which includes a prohibition against the use of CPPC contracts. The FAR, Subpart 16.1, Selecting Contract Types, also prohibits the use of CPPC provisions in federal contracts.

## B.2.3   Unallowable Costs Specified

### B.2.3.1 Research Findings

It was extremely rare to find any limitation on costs that could be claimed by contractors either in the RFPs or in the contracts. When there are no limitations to the costs that can be claimed by contractors, the agency could inadvertently reimburse a contractor for highly questionable expenditures. Readers can use their own imaginations to develop examples of contractor expenditures reimbursed by their agency that would not be appropriate for reimbursement by their agency or that might prove embarrassing if reported in the media. The MSC includes a clause that prevents certain categories of costs from being reimbursed by the agency unless they were disclosed in the contractor's proposal and reimbursement was approved in advance, in writing by the agency.

## B.2.3.2 Independent Verification

The ABA's *2000 Model Procurement Code for State and Local Governments* includes, as one of its terms and conditions, §7-101, Cost Principles Regulations Required; it was not necessarily designed to exclude costs that might not meet the headline test.[1] However, it is written such that it would be appropriate for an agency to include provisions for excluding costs such as fines, entertainment, advertising, and other costs that most government employees and taxpayers may not consider appropriate for reimbursement by government agencies. The Federal Acquisition Regulations (FAR) include an entire section on unallowable costs that provides an expanded list of unallowable costs and definitions therefor.

## B.2.4 State and Local Government Agency Standard Terms and Conditions

### B.2.4.1 Research Findings

There is a detailed discussion of the terms and conditions that were incorporated in the MSC discussed in Chapter 8, Contract Document. However, Figure B.7 provides a summary of the incidence that each of the MSC terms and conditions appeared in the contracts provided by the participating state and local government agencies. Other features of contracts submitted by state and local government agencies are discussed below, along with information on the number of participating agencies that had these features in the contracts they provided for this project.

### B.2.4.2 Independent Verification

The 47 individual terms and conditions included in the text (see Figure 1.1 and Chapter 1) were all taken from the terms and conditions submitted by the state and local government agencies participating in the research project. Terms and conditions included in any agency's standard terms and conditions are typically drafted by the agency's contracting professionals, in-house legal counsel, or borrowed from other government agencies. None of the participating government agencies included all forty-seven of those contract provisions in their own standard terms and conditions. All forty-seven were included in the recommended standard terms and conditions for consideration of inclusion in the standard terms and conditions by all state and local government agencies. Naturally, agencies may elect to modify or delete a portion of the terms and conditions, or to supplement the template with additional provisions.

Incidence of Inclusion of Provisions in State and Local Government Terms & Conditions

| No. | Title of Provision | Incidence | |
|---|---|---|---|
| | | Number | Percent |
| 1 | Term | 21 | 100% |
| 2 | Termination for Default | 19 | 90% |
| 3 | Force Majeure | 9 | 43% |
| 4 | Liquidated Damages | 2 | 10% |
| 5 | Termination for Convenience | 17 | 81% |
| 6 | Termination Transition | 2 | 10% |
| 7 | Contractor Reimbursement | 21 | 100% |
| 8 | Payment Terms | 21 | 100% |
| 9 | Set-Off | 5 | 24% |
| 10 | Agency Project Manager | 7 | 33% |
| 11 | Key Personnel | 3 | 14% |
| 12 | Independent Contractor | 13 | 62% |
| 13a | Confidentiality | 10 | 48% |
| 13b | Ownership | 10 | 48% |
| 14 | Indemnification | 18 | 86% |
| 15 | Insurance | 13 | 62% |
| 16 | Amendments | 18 | 86% |
| 17 | Waiver of Rights | 7 | 33% |
| 18 | Compliance with Laws | 14 | 67% |
| 19 | Americans with Disabilities Act | 3 | 14% |
| 20 | Health Insurance Portability and Accountability Act | 1 | 5% |
| 21 | Nondiscrimination | 17 | 81% |
| 22 | Drug Free Workplace | 5 | 24% |
| 23 | Workers' Compensation | 13 | 62% |
| 24 | Contractor's Standard of Care | 10 | 48% |
| 25 | Care of Property | 3 | 14% |
| 26 | Advertising | 4 | 19% |
| 27 | Performance Evaluation | 1 | 5% |

**Figure B.7** Incidence of inclusion of provisions in state and local government terms and conditions.

| 28 | Inspection of Work and Project Site | 2 | 10% |
|-----|-----------------------------------------------|-----|------|
| 29 | Applicable Law and Forum | 18 | 86% |
| 30 | Successors and Assigns | 16 | 76% |
| 31 | Subcontracting | 17 | 81% |
| 32 | Unallowable Costs | 1 | 5% |
| 33a | Audit & Employee Interviews | 15 | 71% |
| 33b | Document Retention | 16 | 76% |
| 34 | Remedies Not Exclusive | 3 | 14% |
| 35 | Conflict of Interest | 13 | 62% |
| 36 | Contractor Integrity | 7 | 33% |
| 37 | Political Contribution Disclosure | 5 | 24% |
| 38 | Assignment of Antitrust Claims | 3 | 14% |
| 39 | Payment of Taxes | 9 | 43% |
| 40 | Officials Not to Prosper | 6 | 29% |
| 41 | Copyrights | 7 | 33% |
| 42 | Budget Contingency | 12 | 57% |
| 43 | Counterparts | 3 | 14% |
| 44 | Severability | 11 | 52% |
| 45 | Notices | 7 | 33% |
| 46 | Titles, Headings, or Captions | 4 | 19% |
| 47a | Entire Agreement | 9 | 43% |
| 47b | Survival of Provisions beyond the Contract Term | 7 | 33% |

**Figure B.7 (continued)    Incidence of inclusion of provisions in state and local government terms and conditions.**

# Note

1. The headline test refers to basing one's decision to make some certain decision based on how that person would feel should the result of that decision appear in the local newspaper's headline.

# Appendix C

# Advance Contract Planning Topics Not Included in Best Practices

Chapter 1, "The Contracting Cycle and Advance Contract Planning," includes a discussion of topics normally addressed during advance contract planning. However, that discussion is restricted to topics included among the best practices. Other relevant topics normally addressed during advance contract planning are discussed below.

## C.1 Develop a List of Prospective Contractors

Developing of a list of prospective contractors should be initiated early in the planning process, or possibly as early as the initial meeting of the advance contract planning team. Early development of a list of prospective contractors is recommended because preparation of the list is normally a time-consuming effort and a delay in the availability of this list of contractors delays both the release of the solicitation and commencement of the project. Planning team members are generally aware of at least one prospective contractor that has experience in providing the needed service for state or local government agencies. The benefits of selecting the contractor on a competitive basis, and the policy of most government agencies that emphasize the importance of competition when selecting a contractor, compel the advance contract planning team members to consider free and open competition during source selection. The list of companies or individuals to be solicited is an essential document to facilitate a competitive source selection. Identification of individuals or companies to be solicited may begin with listing those prospective contractors known by the team members. Additional companies may be identified through contact with other state or local government agencies, Internet searches, professional directories, or even telephone directories. The criticality of contracting for services on a competitive basis is of such great importance that there is extensive coverage in Chapter 2 dedicated to the competitive process.

## C.2 Establish Required Proposal Content

Once development of the scope of work is well underway, consideration should be given to enumerating subjects that need to be addressed by the contractors in their proposals. Directing prospective contractors to address all the relevant subjects in their proposals contributes to relatively homogeneous proposals, thereby achieving greater efficiencies during the proposal evaluation process. The tasks enumerated in the scope of work are necessarily related closely to subject matter that needs to be addressed in the contractors' proposals. Therefore, there is a need for consistency between the contractor's responsibilities described in the scope of work and in the proposal content proscribed in the Request for Proposals (RFP). There is, however, added information that is normally requested for inclusion in the proposals to facilitate the evaluation of each competing contractor's reputation and financial strength.

Contracting agency RFP templates contribute to the likelihood that information concerning the contractor tasks, reputation, and financial strength is requested for inclusion in the solicitation. The availability of this information in proposals contributes to selection of the superior contractor. The use of agency RFP templates also contributes to the submittal of proposals in an organized manner to facilitate proposal evaluation and a page limitation to avoid excessive time spent evaluating extraneous documentation.

The required proposal content should also be consistent with the proposal evaluation criteria. Inconsistencies between the required proposal content and the proposal evaluation criteria virtually guarantee proposals that do not address the criteria that need to be evaluated. Descriptions of proposal content and contractor responsibilities for inclusion in the scope of work assist the advance contract planning team in developing the proposal evaluation criteria. Although development of detailed proposal evaluation criteria may be delayed until RFP drafting is underway, consideration should be given to developing evaluation criteria at this early stage of the project.

## C.3 Develop the Scope of Work

Once the project background and objectives have been stated, the planning team is prepared to start developing the scope of work. If the contracting agency has a standard template for a scope of work, such as the one included in the Appendix G, "Short-Form RFP with Short-Form Contract," such a template provides an excellent beginning for preparation of the scope of work. Elements of a scope of work typically include an introductory statement indicating that the contractor shall[1] provide all labor, materials, supervision, tools, equipment, transportation, taxes, and any other resources needed to perform the tasks enumerated in the scope of work; and a description of the contractor responsibilities such as specific tasks, project milestones, meetings, progress reports, reports of findings, and other deliverables. The scope of work could also include the basis for reimbursement of the contractor for not-to-exceed price contracts and the contracting agency's responsibilities, if any, during the term of the contract. The scope of work is such a critical element of the services contract that considerable effort and thought should be devoted when developing this essential document. Meetings that stress the need for team member discussions, and possibly brainstorming, are helpful to ensure the development of a comprehensive scope of work. A follow-up meeting held after sufficient time has elapsed to permit incubation of ideas developed during brainstorming normally results in further refinement of the scope of work.

The criticality of a well-crafted scope of work underscores the need for contracting agencies to develop a scope of work training program for contracting professionals and department personnel who are expected to be involved in the contracting process.

## C.4 Establish Criteria for Responsibility and Responsiveness

One universally accepted concept in government contracting is that contractors' replies (proposals, quotations, or bids) to solicitations (RFPs, Requests for Quotations [RFQs], or Invitations for Bids [IFBs]) must be responsive to the particulars of the solicitation and the contractor submitting the replies must be responsible. If any reply to a solicitation is not responsive and not from a responsible contractor, that reply shall be rejected. However, nonresponsive proposals, unlike bids, may be modified through negotiations to render them responsive. Responsiveness is achieved if the contractor's reply to the solicitation addresses all the project requirements specified in the RFP without taking significant exceptions or making significant deviations. Responsibility should be specified in the solicitation. Contractors must be made aware of the criteria for evaluating their responsibility because failure to meet the responsibility criteria normally results in a summary rejection of their proposal. Lack of responsibility is generally defined as a default termination, conviction for fraud, or for making kickbacks all within a specified number of years. Agencies may elect to omit one or more of the previously stated reasons for declaring that a contractor is not responsible, or agencies may elect to include additional reasons for declaring that a contractor is not responsible.

## C.5 Establish Proposal Scoring Scheme

A discussion of various scoring schemes, including numerical schemes such as a range of 1 to 10, adjective scales, color-coding schemes, or ranking schemes is included in Chapter 5 on the evaluation of proposals and selection of contractors. Advance planning committee members who are not familiar with the various scoring schemes should read this chapter prior to establishing a proposal scoring scheme. The chapter on the evaluation of proposals provides valuable information on the advantages and disadvantages of a number of possible scoring schemes.

## C.6 Establish Strategy for Dealing with Possible Budget Shortfall

It is always gratifying when the proposed prices are lower than the amount budgeted for the project. However, there is also the possibility that the proposed prices exceed the amount budgeted for the contract. Because proposals are valid for a limited number of days certain, it is prudent to develop contingency plans in the event that the proposed prices exceed the amount budgeted.

One of the alternatives to consider is conducting negotiations to reduce the pricing. An oftentimes successful negotiation technique is to advise all prospective contractors of the budgetary limitations and to ask them to submit a best and final offer (BAFO). Should this approach be taken, some of the BAFOs may include a scaled-back scope of work. To avoid the situation where there are competing BAFOs with inconsistent scaled-back work scopes, the contingency planning may include substitution of a scope of work scaled back by the contracting agency as a part of the request for BAFOs. When all the BAFOs are based on a scaled back scope of work, the problem with inconsistent scopes of work is avoided. If it is not possible to scale back the scope of work, consideration should be given to including an alternative for seeking additional project funding.

## C.7 Use of Proposal Evaluation Criteria in Evaluating Proposals

The proposal evaluation team must evaluate the proposals strictly in accordance with the criteria described in the RFP. The advance contract planning committee should take measures to ensure that proposals are evaluated solely on the basis of the evaluation criteria. Evaluating proposals on criteria that were not included in the solicitation is tantamount to inviting protests. Additionally, it is difficult to react to protests when the agency did not adhere to its own criteria when evaluating the proposals. Proposal evaluation instructions that highlight the need to adhere to the evaluation criteria should be included in the proposal evaluation guidelines. This provides guidance to the proposal evaluation team members on the importance of evaluating proposals solely based on the evaluation criteria contained in the RFP. Additionally, a proposal evaluation spreadsheet that includes the evaluation criteria combined with an admonishment on the spreadsheet to adhere to the criteria further ensures that the proposal evaluation team limits its evaluation to the criteria stated in the RFP when evaluating proposals.

## C.8 Use of Proposal Scoring Procedure in Evaluating Proposals

In addition to the importance of conforming to the requirement to evaluate proposals according to the criteria in the RFP, the advance contract planning committee should take similar measures to ensure that the proposal evaluation committee also conforms to the scoring procedure outlined in the RFP. This action helps prevent protests from aggrieved contractors and the resultant administrative burden and possible project commencement delays.

## C.9 Contractor Presentations

During the evaluation of proposals, the proposal evaluation committee may realize that it needs a presentation from the contractors to ensure that it selects the best-qualified contractor. However, a mere review of the proposals may permit the committee to identify the best-qualified contractor without contractor presentations. To permit the proposal evaluation committee the flexibility to schedule contractor presentations on an as-needed basis, the advance contract planning committee should consider placing the possibility of contractor presentations in the RFP at the option of the agency.

## C.10 Describing the Option for Debriefings and Process for Filing Protests in the RFP

The advance contract planning committee should consider placing a description of the option for offering debriefings and process for filing protests in the RFP. The advantages and disadvantages to including this information in the RFP are described in Chapter 6, Protests. Advance contract planning committee members who are not familiar with this topic should read the chapter on protests to prepare for making this decision. The chapter on protests provides valuable information for advance planning committee members who are not familiar with the benefits of including information on debriefings and filing of protests in the RFP.

## C.11 Procedure for Managing Protests

The advance contract planning committee should review the agency's procedure for managing protests and communicate instructions for managing protests to all personnel who may be involved in the protest process. If agency employees become involved in the protest process without being familiar with the procedures for managing protests, they are likely to further complicate the disruption inherent with the receipt of a protest.

## C.12 Managing Contractor Performance

Although the advance contract planning team is normally disbanded at about the time of the contract award, this team's planning should include consideration of contract administration and monitoring of the successful contractor's performance. Contract administration and contractor monitoring are essential tasks that benefit from preplanning by the advance contract planning committee. This task can be accomplished through development of a quality surveillance plan. The quality surveillance plan requires tools and strategies for monitoring the contractor's performance. The strategies that should be considered include periodic progress meetings, critical milestones, deliverable reports of findings, and contract status meetings. These are all tools that provide the agency with insight into the quality and progress of the contractor's performance. Once these tools and strategies are developed, relevant meetings, milestones, and contractor reporting responsibilities can be incorporated in the scope of work that is included in the model contract sent to the prospective contractors along with the solicitation.

## Note

1. Although some state and local government agencies use a word other than "shall" to most compel a contractor to perform a particular task or tasks, the word "shall" is used for that purpose throughout this book. Agencies using a word or words other than "shall" to compel contractor performance, should substitute their most compelling word when using the templates provided with this book.

# *Appendix D*

# Instructions for Completion of the Sole Source Justification/ Approval Form

Figure D.1 provides a sole source justification/approval form.

Items 1–4: The first four spaces to identify the contractor recommended for the sole source contract are self-explanatory.

Item 5: The contract price is significant because higher-dollar-value contracts normally require stronger justification than low-dollar-value contracts. Additionally, the contract price may also dictate the party authorized to approve the contract on a sole source basis. In this example, the spaces at the bottom of the form (16) for approval or disapproval of the sole source contract indicate that the agency official has authority to approve or disapprove sole source contracts up to some certain dollar value, while the agency official merely recommends approval or disapproval by the chief elected official or governing body for contracts that exceed his or her authority for sole source contracting. The dollar threshold for approving sole source requests normally mirrors the state or local government official's dollar threshold for executing contracts.

Item 6: The general description of services to be provided is for further identification of the nature of the contract.

| 1 | Contractor Name: | | | |
|---|---|---|---|---|
| 2 | Street Address: | | | |
| 3 | City/State/ZIP: | | | |
| 4 | Telephone: | | 5 | Contract Price: |
| 6 | General Description of Services to be Provided: | | | |
| | | | | |

INSTRUCTIONS: Please initial all entries below that apply to the proposed contract. Attach additional information or support documentation if needed. More than one entry will apply to most sole source justifications.

| **1 SOLE SOURCE JUSTIFICATION** | | |
|---|---|---|
| INITIALS | | JUSTIFICATION |
| 7 | | Contract is required from only the original service provider. If this item is initialed, Item 10 below must also be initialed. |
| 8 | | Contract is required from only an authorized representative of the original service provider. If this item is initialed, Item 10 below must also be initialed. |
| 9 | | The services provided by this contractor are proprietary and no other contractor provides an equivalent service. If this item is initialed, please explain below (attach additional sheet if needed). |
| 10 | **Explanation:** | |
| 11 | | This is the only known service that will meet the specialized needs of this department or perform the intended function. If this item is initialed, please explain below (attach additional sheet if needed). |
| 12 | **Explanation:** | |

**Figure D.1  Sole source justification/approval form.**

Item 7: If the department requesting the sole source procurement is basing its justification on the fact that only the original provider can provide this service, then Item 7 should be initialed. When Item 7 is initialed, the department is instructed to complete Item 10 as well and to provide a written explanation of why the recommended contractor is the "only" contractor that can provide this service. The form can be designed to automatically expand to accommodate lengthy text when necessary to fully justify sole source procurement.

| 13 | | None of the above applies. A detailed justification for this sole source contract is provided below (attach additional sheet if needed). | |
|---|---|---|---|
| 14 | **Detailed Justification:** | | |
| 15 | On the basis of the foregoing, I recommend that competitive procurement procedures be waived and that the service in the referenced contract by procured on a sole source basis. I understand that I may be required to provide a detailed cost estimate since price reasonableness will not be established through the competitive process. | | |
| 16 | **DEPARTMENT NAME** | **AUTHORIZED SIGNATURE** | **DATE** |
| | | | |
| 17 | **3 APPROVAL/DISAPPROVAL/RECOMMENDATION BY [AGENCY OFFICIAL]** | | |
| Based on the above justification: | | | |
| | I hereby approve the waiver of the competitive process for the services in the referenced contract. | | |
| | I recommend that the Governing Body approve this purchase on a sole source basis. | | |
| | I disapprove the waiver of the competitive process for this contract based on the reason attached hereto. | | |
| | I recommend that the Governing Body disapprove the waiver of the competitive process for this contract for the reason attached hereto. | | |
| 18 | **Signature** | | **Date** | |
| 19 | **Name** | | **Title** | |

**Figure D.1 (continued)   Sole source justification/approval form.**

Item 9: If the department is requesting that sole source procurement is basing its justification on the fact that the service provided by the contractor is proprietary and no other contractor provides an equivalent service, then Item 9 should be initialed. When Item 9 is initialed, the department is instructed to complete Item 10 as well and to provide a brief written explanation of why the recommended contractor is the "only" contractor that has a proprietary service for which no other contractor offers an equivalent service.

Item 10: If the department is requesting the sole source procurement based on Items 7, 8, or 9, then Item 10 should be completed.

Item 11: If the justification for sole source is based on the fact that the contractor provides the only known service that will meet the specialized needs of the department or perform the intended function, this block should be initialed.

Item 12: The explanation for justifying the sole source procurement based on the fact that the contractor provides the only known service that will meet the specialized needs of the department or perform the intended function should be entered in this space. If there is insufficient room to provide the justification, a separate sheet containing the balance of the justification may be attached.

Item 13: Whenever the department is requesting the sole source procurement based on a reason that is not included above, Item 13 should be initialed.

Item 14: The detailed justification for a sole source procurement based on a reason that is not included in any of the above blocks should be entered in this block.

Item 15: There is a statement following the "Detailed Justification" block indicating that the department head, or designated representative, recommends that competitive procedures be waived and that a detailed cost estimate may be required to establish the reasonableness of pricing in the absence of competition.

Item 16: The three blocks in this section provide spaces for the name of the department, signature of the department representative, and date that the justification was signed.

Item 17: The Approval/Disapproval/Recommendation block for the agency official to approve or disapprove waiving the competitive process for contracts that are estimated to be priced within his or her authority for executing services contracts. There are also blocks for recommending that the chief elected official or governing body approve or disapprove waiving the competitive process for contracts priced above the dollar threshold wherein the agency official has authority to execute contracts.

Item 18: The agency official checks one of the four blocks and then signs and dates in the spaces provided. If the agency official disapproves or recommends disapproval of a waiver of the competitive process, then an explanation of the rationale for the disapproval or disapproval recommendation shall be attached to the form.

Item 19: Enter the printed or typed name of the approving official and the approving official's title.

## *Appendix E*

# Best Practices Request For Proposals (RFP)

*[AGENCY NAME]*

***REQUEST FOR PROPOSALS (RFP) #:***_____

***PROJECT TITLE:*** _____

*USING AGENCY:* _____

*CONTRACTING AGENCY:*_____

*AGENCY PROJECT MANAGER:* _____

*PROJECT MANAGER E-MAIL ADDRESS:* _____

*AGENCY MAILING ADDRESS:* _____

*AGENCY INTERNET SITE:*_____

*RFP ISSUE DATE:* _____

*DUE DATE FOR RECEIPT OF QUESTIONS*
*REGARDING THIS RFP:*_____

# Table of Contents

# Notice to Prospective Contractors

Prospective contractors should carefully review this solicitation for defects and questionable or objectionable matter. Comments concerning defects and questionable or objectionable matter must be made to the agency project manager at the e-mail address on the cover page, and must be received by the agency prior to the deadline for written questions also shown on the Request for Proposals (RFP) cover page. Questions concerning the specifications must be posed through the same e-mail address provided on the cover page. The date limitation for posing questions will permit this agency to issue any necessary corrections and/or addenda to this RFP in time for all prospective contractors to react by adjusting, if needed, their proposals. A summary of all questions from prospective contractors and agency responses to those questions will be posted by RFP number on the agency's Internet site, which is also provided on the cover page.

*Prospective contractors are prohibited from communicating directly with any agency employee except as specified in this RFP, and no agency employee or representative other than the agency's project manager is authorized to provide any information or respond to any question or inquiry concerning this RFP. Prospective contractors may contact the agency's project manager solely via e-mail.*

The project manager may provide reasonable accommodations, including the provision of informational material in an alternative format, for qualified prospective contractors with a disability. Prospective contractors requiring accommodation shall submit requests in writing, with supporting documentation justifying the accommodation, to the project manager. The project manager reserves the right to grant or reject any request for accommodation.

Proposals will be treated confidentially until either the contract is awarded or recommended for award. Late proposals may be considered if that would be in the best interest of the agency. Errors in the proposals or nonresponsive proposals may be corrected during the negotiation process. However, prospective contractors are advised that they should endeavor to submit responsive, error-free proposals on time because failure to do so may result in rejection of their proposals.

Prospective contractors that receive this RFP from the agency Web site or from any source other than the project manager, and wish to assure receipt of any addenda or additional materials related to this RFP, should immediately contact the project manager and provide their contact information so that RFP addenda and other communications related to this procurement can be sent to them.

Receipt of sealed proposals for furnishing the services described herein is due **no later than [*Time*] p.m., [*Date (month, day, year)*].**

SEND ALL PROPOSALS DIRECTLY TO THE CONTRACTING AGENCY ADDRESS AS SHOWN IN FIGURE E.1:

| DELIVERED BY U.S. POSTAL SERVICE | DELIVERED BY ANY OTHER MEANS |
|---|---|
| RFP NO. | RFP NO. |

**Figure E.1   Address format.**

IMPORTANT NOTE: Indicate ("Technical Proposal" or "Cost Proposal") (if applicable), and the RFP number on the front of each sealed proposal envelope or package, along with the date for receipt of proposals in response to this RFP.

There will be no public opening of the proposals. Proposals will be treated as confidential until the contract is awarded or recommended for award.

Any question submitted in response to this RFP via telegraph, facsimile (FAX) machine, or telephone is not acceptable. Prospective contractors are required to make all inquiries concerning this RFP via e-mail to: [***Insert E-mail Address***]

Prospective contractors that do not have access to e-mail may make written inquiries to the following address: [***Insert Address***]

It is the prospective contractor's responsibility to assure that all addenda have been reviewed and, if need be, signed and returned or noted in the proposal.

A copy of all inquiries along with the agency response will be posted at the agency's Internet site indicated below:

Internet Site: [***Insert Internet Address***]

## Introduction

Make an introductory statement, provide guidance regarding the intent to use the agency's standard contact, and refer to the scope of work for a description of the work to be performed.

An example of the information that might be provided in an introductory statement is provided below in bold:

**The agency is seeking a firm to develop a [*Name of Project*] for the [*Name of Agency*], [*Department*]. The agency intends to award a contract to a firm that will meet agency qualification criteria and has successfully performed services on similar projects in the past. The successful firm will be required to enter into a contract with the agency for the services requested in this RFP within a reasonable time after award. A firm submitting a proposal must be prepared to use the agency's standard contract form rather than its own contract form. The contract will include terms appropriate for this project. Generally, the terms of the contract will include, but are not limited to: (1) completion of the project within the timeframe provided; (2) no additional work authorized without prior approval; (3) no payment without prior approval; (4) funding availability; (5) termination of the contract under certain conditions; (6) indemnification of the state or local government agency; (7) approval by the state or local government agency of any subcontractors; and (8) minimum appropriate insurance requirements. A Model Services Contract is attached as Attachment I to this RFP. The state or local government agency intends to award a contract substantially in the form of the attached Model Services Contract to the selected contractor.**

## Background

Describe how the services fit into the using agency's function, legislation, or new initiatives that necessitate these services, other solutions tried in the past, etc. Reference to attachments may be helpful here.

## Scope of Work

The scope of work describes the work to be performed by the contractor, and is contained in "Attachment II — Scope of Work" in the Model Services Contract included in this RFP.

# Contractor Selection Process

The following is a general description of the process by which a contractor will be selected for award of a contract to perform the services described in this RFP:

1. Request for Proposals (RFP) is released to prospective contractors.
2. To help ensure that all prospective contractors are treated consistently during the selection process, all questions regarding this RFP, as well as the agency's responses to the questions, will be posted on the agency's Web site. A deadline for the receipt of written questions has been established. (See the cover sheet of this RFP for deadline date.) After issuance of an RFP by the agency and prior to the date and time for receipt of proposals, persons or entities who intend to respond to such RFP by submission of a competitive proposal may wish to pose questions, objections, or requests for information, request clarification, or ask for an interpretation regarding terms, provisions, or requirements of the RFP. In this event, prospective contractors shall not attempt to communicate with, in writing, electronically, or orally with any agency official or employee other than the agency's project manager. The project manager may be reached at her or his e-mail address on the RFP cover page. Prospective contractors shall not contact any other agency officials in an attempt to gather information regarding this RFP, or in an attempt to influence the agency's consideration of its proposal. All inappropriate communications with agency officials or employees will be forwarded to the agency's project manager as well as the proposal evaluation committee. Inappropriate communications by a prospective contractor may, at the discretion of the project manager, constitute grounds for disqualification of that prospective contractor's proposal. Alternatively, the evaluation committee may, at its discretion, consider such inappropriate communications when evaluating and scoring proposals.
3. Proposals in one original and [at least two] copies are required in a sealed envelope or package from each prospective contractor. Each original proposal shall be signed and dated by an official authorized to bind the contractor. Unsigned proposals may be rejected. In addition to the paper copies of the proposal, prospective contractors shall submit one **complete and exact** copy of the technical proposal on CD-ROM in Microsoft Office or Microsoft Office-compatible format. A prospective contractor shall make no other distribution of its proposal to other agency officials or consultants. Each proposal page shall be numbered for ease of reference.
4. All proposals must be received by the issuing agency no later than the date and time specified on the cover sheet of this RFP. Late proposals may be considered if that would be in the best interests of the agency. However, the agency may elect to reject any proposal that is received after the due date and time.

5. Following the date and time when proposals are due, the envelopes or packages containing the proposals from each responding firm will be opened by agency personnel. **The opening of the proposals is not open to prospective contractors or the public.** Proposals are subject to change, clarification, and negotiation following the receipt date; therefore, the proposals will be treated as confidential until the resultant contract is awarded or when a recommendation is made to award the contract.

6. The agency's Proposal Evaluation Committee expects to take the following actions to determine the relative merits of the proposals that are submitted:

   a. Review the proposals to determine whether they are responsive to the RFP and that they were submitted by responsible companies.

   b. If there are six or more responsive proposals from responsible companies, the agency will review the proposals, according to the criteria included in this RFP, and assign scores to each criterion using a color-coded scheme, with green being assigned to proposals that are among the best of the proposals, yellow for the average proposals, and red for the marginal proposals. This color-coded rating system will be used to narrow the number of proposals to five or fewer.

   c. The five, or fewer, finalists will then be subjected to a more stringent evaluation that will require individual members of the Proposal Evaluation Committee to rank each criterion with the exception of life cycle cost. Life cycle cost will be scored proportionally rather than ranked. In the event that there are four proposals among the finalists for the ranked criteria, each committee member will assign a 4 to the highest ranked proposal, 3 to the next highest ranked proposal, 2 to the penultimate ranked proposal, and 1 to the lowest ranked proposal.

   d. The committee members will then meet to discuss their rankings and the rationale therefor. Following this meeting, the committee members may elect to modify their rankings based upon those discussions. The committee members will then turn in their evaluation sheets.

   e. The individual committee member rankings will then be averaged to provide a single combined score for each of the finalist prospective contractors.

   f. The single combined scores will then be adjusted according to the weights assigned to the criterion to obtain combined weighted scores.

   g. The life cycle cost figures will be evaluated separately. The lowest net life cycle cost to the agency will receive a score that is equal to the weight assigned to the life cycle cost criterion. To obtain weighted life cycle cost criteria scores for the higher dollar value life cycle cost proposals, each higher-dollar-value life cycle cost proposal will be assigned a score that is proportionally lower based on the net life cycle cost to the agency.

   h. *The combined weighted scores for the criteria, other than life cycle cost, will be added to the weighted life cycle cost criterion scores to obtain a final score for each prospective contractor. The contractor with the highest score will then be awarded the contract or recommended to the governing board or chief elected official for award of the contract.*

7. At the option of the Proposal Evaluation Committee, the evaluators may request oral presentations, discussions, or negotiations with any or all prospective contractors for the purpose of clarification or to amplify the materials presented in any part of the proposal, or make adjustments to the details of the proposals. The evaluators may also request best and final offers (BAFOs) from one or more prospective contractors. However, prospective contractors are cautioned that the evaluators are not required to request clarification or conduct negotiations and may award a contract based on the original proposal. Therefore, all proposals should be complete and reflect the contractor's most favorable terms.

8. Prospective contractors are cautioned that this is a request for proposals, not a request to contract, and the agency reserves the unqualified right to reject any and all proposals when such rejection is deemed to be in the best interest of the agency.

9. Proposals will be evaluated according to the criteria indicated in Figure E.2, and because the agency has determined that some criteria are more significant than others, Figure E.2 also reflects weights that have been assigned to the criteria to permit more emphasis being placed on the more significant criteria.

10. **Debriefing:** Any company that submitted a proposal and feels that its proposal was not given adequate consideration or given a fair evaluation may request a debriefing from the agency proposal evaluation committee.

11. **Protests:** Any company that received a debriefing but continues to feel that its proposal was not given adequate consideration or a fair evaluation may wish to protest the procedures for selection or the actual selection of a particular contractor. Contractors wishing to file a protest should abide by the following procedures. Failure to follow these procedures may result in a summary rejection of the protest:

    a. Any actual or prospective contractor that is aggrieved in connection with the solicitation or award of a contract may protest to the [*Title of Agency Official*]. The protest shall be submitted in writing to the [*Title of Agency Official*] within seven (7) working days after such aggrieved person or company knows or should have known of the facts giving rise thereto.

    b. Upon receipt of such a protest, the [*Title of Agency Official*] shall issue a written determination within ten (10) working days following receipt of the protest. The determination shall:
       i. State the reason for the action taken;
       ii Inform the protesting company that a request for further administrative appeal of an adverse decision must be submitted in writing to the [*Organization or Agency Official Who Will Consider Any Appeal of the Determination*] within seven (7) working days after receipt of the determination by the [*Title of Agency Official Making Determination*].

| PROPOSAL EVALUATION CRITERIA AND CRITERIA WEIGHTING | |
|---|---|
| *Criteria* | Weight |
| **Past Performance** | 10 |
| ☐ Corporate experience with similar projects<br>☐ Feedback from references regarding qualifications to succeed on this project | |
| **Financial Stability** | 10 |
| ☐ Evaluation of contractor's financial stability based on analysis of most recent financial statements or similar evidence | |
| **Risk Assessment** | 20 |
| ☐ Identification of risks to the agency associated with this project<br>☐ Evaluation of the prospective contractor's proposed approach to reducing, mitigating or eliminating these risks | |
| **Project Plan** | 20 |
| ☐ Evaluation of the prospective contractor's plan for accomplishing the tasks outlined in the scope of work<br>☐ Determination of contractor's understanding of the problem based on the contractor's description of each project task, contract deliverables and the project schedule submitted by the prospective contractor<br>☐ Evaluation of contractor's proposed staffing, deployment and organization of personnel to be assigned to this project as well as minimum qualifications such as education, certification, and experience on similar projects for personnel in key positions<br>☐ Evaluation of contractor's qualifications and experience of all executive, managerial, legal, and professional personnel to be assigned to this project<br>☐ Evaluation of contractor's proposed project schedule and methodology for monitoring performance according to the schedule milestones | |
| **Outsourcing** | 10 |
| ☐ Evaluation of risks associated with reliance on subcontractors located outside the United States<br>☐ Evaluation of subcontractor qualifications<br>☐ Evaluation of risks associated with over reliance on subcontracted work | |
| **Life Cycle Cost** | 30 |
| ☐ Evaluation of all agency costs associated with acceptance of the contractor's proposal.<br>Life cycle costs include the contract price plus all other project costs borne by the agency including the need for added personnel, equipment, space, training, disposal of equipment or chemicals, eventual contract closeout, and any other costs associated with the contract. | |
| **Proposal Score** | 0–100 |

**Figure E.2   Proposal evaluation criteria and criteria weighting.**

12. The agency reserves the right to:
    a. Reject any or all submittals;
    b. Request clarification of any submitted information;
    c. Waive any informalities or irregularities in any proposal;
    d. Not enter into any contract;
    e. Not select any firm;
    f. Cancel this process at any time;
    g. Amend this process at any time;
    h. Interview firms prior to award;
    i. Enter into negotiations with one or more firms, or request a best and final offer (BAFO) or BAFOs;
    j. Award more than one contract if it is in the best interests of the agency;
    k. Issue similar solicitations in the future; or
    l. Request additional information from prospective contractors.
13. The response to this RFP shall consist of a completed Prospective Contractor Certification (included in this solicitation), a cover letter limited to a maximum of two pages including an executive summary of the proposal. The cover letter shall indicate whether or not the contractor had any contract terminated for default in the past five years. If no such termination for default has been experienced by the prospective contractor in the past five years, this fact shall be stated in the cover letter. Proposals shall be divided into six sections in the same sequence, and with the same titles, shown below. Proposals shall be prepared on 8 1/2 × 11 paper; however, larger foldouts are acceptable for milestone charts and similar documentation. The font size shall be 10 point or larger.

| Section | Title | Page Limitation |
| --- | --- | --- |
| A. | Past Performance | 6 |
| B. | Financial Stability | 4 |
| C. | Risk Assessment | 8 |
| D. | Project Plan | 8 + Resumes |
| E. | Outsourcing | 4 |
| F. | Life Cycle Cost | 8 |

## A. Past Performance

This section shall be limited to a maximum of six pages, shall include background information on the organization and provide details on company experience with similar projects. A list of references (including contact persons, organizations, e-mail and regular mail addresses, and telephone numbers) for each of the above similar projects shall be included.

If the prospective contractor's past performance with the agency requires response to Items 1 through 4 below, such responses shall be on a separate sheet and shall be excluded from the maximum number of pages indicated above:

1. If the prospective contractor or any prospective subcontractor contracted with the agency during the past 24 months, indicate the name of the agency, contract price, the contract number and project description, and other information available to identify the contract.

2. If the prospective contractor or prospective subcontractor has a staff member who was an employee of the agency during the past 24 months, or is currently an agency employee, identify the individual by name, the agency previously or currently employed by, job title or position held, and separation date from the agency.

3. If the prospective contractor has had a contract terminated for default in the past five years, describe each such incident. Termination for default is defined as a notice to stop performance due to the prospective contractor's non-performance or poor performance and the issue of performance was either:
   a.  Not litigated due to inaction on the part of the prospective contractor, or
   b.  Litigated and such litigation determined that the prospective contractor was in default.

4. Submit full details of the terms for default, including the other party's name, address, and telephone number. The agency will evaluate the facts and may, at its sole discretion, reject the proposal on the grounds of the prospective contractor's past experience. If no such termination for default has been experienced by the prospective contractor in the past five years, state so in the cover letter.

## B.  Financial Stability

This section shall be limited to a maximum of four pages, and shall include the prospective contractor's most recent audited financial statement or similar evidence of financial stability.

## C.  Risk Assessment

This section shall be limited to a maximum of eight pages, and must identify all risks to the agency that must be addressed should the agency enter into a contract in furtherance of this project. The prospective contractors shall also identify measures that will be taken by the contractor or should be taken by the agency to mitigate the risks.

## D.  Project Plan

This section shall be limited to a maximum of eight pages (not including resumes), and shall include a thorough description of the prospective contractor's approach to accomplishing the tasks outlined in the scope of work. This section shall include the proposed staffing, resumes for key staff members, deployment, and organization of personnel to be assigned to this project. A description of each task and contractor deliverables shall be included in this section along with a schedule for accomplishing all contract milestones.

## E. Outsourcing

This section shall be limited to a maximum of four pages, and shall include a description of the work (including the percentage of the total contract effort) performed by company employees, subcontracted resources, as well as any work performed outside the United States by company employees or subcontractors. The proposal shall also include the percentage of work to be performed by specific subcontractors, evaluation of subcontractor qualifications, and identification of the geographical area where all work will be performed.

## F. Life Cycle Cost

Contract Price: The lifecycle cost proposal shall be limited to a maximum of eight pages, and shall be submitted in a separate, sealed envelope or package and marked accordingly. The agency prefers to contract on a firm-fixed-cost basis whenever permitted by the nature of the work. However, it is understood that in some instances the proposal must be based on incurred expenses. In this latter case, the proposal shall include the following contractor costs:

1. Personnel costs (including job titles, hourly rates, and total hours)
2. Travel and subsistence expenses
3. Subcontractor costs (if any)
4. Other costs (e.g., office expenses) shall be identified by the nature of the costs
5. Not-to-exceed price (A total not-to-exceed [NTE] price representing the maximum amount for all work to be performed by the contractor and any subcontractors must be clearly indicated under this heading.)

Incremental Agency Costs: The contractors' proposals shall include, in addition to contract costs, all incremental agency costs associated with entering into the contract. Agency costs generally include the costs of required additional personnel to support the contracted effort, training, equipment, and facilities, as well as any other incremental costs associated with award and administration of the contract for the term of the contract, or a period of five years, whichever is longer. No contract costs are to be included in incremental agency costs.

Life Cycle Costs: The life cycle cost is the total of the contract price plus the incremental agency costs. This information should be depicted in the proposal on a monthly basis for the first year of the project and on an annual basis for the duration of the project.

A life cycle cost proposal format has been provided as Figure E.3. All prospective contractors shall include all contract life cycle costs, including the NTE cost or incremental agency costs to the agency should a particular proposal be accepted, or risk the possibility of having their proposal declared to be nonresponsive.

The required certifications, identified below, do not count against the page limitations.

| LIFE CYCLE COST PROPOSAL FORMAT | | | | | |
|---|---|---|---|---|---|
| **CONTRACT PRICE** | | | **ANNUAL PRICE** | | |
| **Cost Category** | **Units/Yr** | **Unit Cost** | **Year 1** | **Year 2** | **Year 3** |
| Job Title One | | | | | |
| Job Title Two | | | | | |
| Job Title Three | | | | | |
| Travel and Subsistence | | | | | |
| Subcontractor Costs | | | | | |
| All Other Contract Costs | | | | | |
| TOTAL NOT-TO-EXCEED CONTRACT PRICE | | | | | |
| **INCREMENTAL AGENCY COST** | | | **ANNUAL COST** | | |
| **Cost Category** | **Units/Yr** | **Unit Cost** | **Year 1** | **Year 2** | **Year 3** |
| Job Title One | | | | | |
| Job Title Two | | | | | |
| Job Title Three | | | | | |
| Training | | | | | |
| Equipment | | | | | |
| Facilities | | | | | |
| All Other Incremental Agency Costs | | | | | |
| TOTAL ESTIMATED AGENCY INREMENTAL COSTS | | | | | |
| TOTAL LIFE CYCLE COST | | | | | |

**Figure E.3  Life cycle cost proposal format.**

## Prospective Contractor Certification

By submitting this proposal, the prospective contractor certifies the following:

The contractor representative who signs below certifies that she/he has carefully read and understands the provisions of the solicitation and associated documents attached thereto, and hereby submits the attached proposal to perform the work specified therein, all in accordance with the true intent and meaning thereof. The contractor representative further understands and agrees that by signing this certification, all of the following information in the certification is true and accurate to the best of her or his knowledge. If this certification cannot be made unequivocally, a written description of all instances wherein the prospective contractor cannot unequivocally make this certification is provided with this proposal:

Prospective contractor is:

☐ Sole Proprietor    ☐ Partnership    ☐ Corporation*    ☐ Joint Venture

☐ Other_____

* State of Incorporation _____

Other entities or individuals shall not be allowed to perform work or take data outside the United States without express advance written authorization from the agency's project manager.

All personnel provided for work under this contract, who are not U.S. citizens, will have executed a valid I-9 form, Employment Eligibility Form, and presented valid employment authorization documents.

This proposal is signed by a representative who is authorized to commit the prospective contractor.

The company identified below is the prime contractor.

The prospective contractor's insurance carrier(s) can provide insurance certificates as required within 10 calendar days following notice of award.

The proposed costs have been arrived at independently, without consultation, communication, or agreement for the purpose of restricting competition as to any matter relating to such process with any other organization or with any competitor.

Unless otherwise required by law, the costs proposed have not been knowingly disclosed by the prospective contractor on a prior basis directly or indirectly to any other organization or to any competitor.

No attempt has been made, or will be made, by the prospective contractor to induce any other person or firm to submit or not to submit a proposal for the purpose of restricting competition.

The cost and availability of all equipment, materials, and supplies associated with performing the services described, including associated indirect costs and profit, herein have been determined and included in the proposed cost. All labor costs, direct and indirect, and profit have been determined and included in the proposed cost. The incremental costs expected to be incurred by the agency, should it enter into this contract, have also been estimated to the best ability of the prospective contractor. It is understood that the life cycle cost includes the total of the contract cost plus the estimated costs to be incurred by the agency should it enter into this contract.

The prospective contractor can and shall provide the specified performance bond or alternate performance guarantee (if applicable).

In submitting its proposal, the prospective contractor agrees not to discuss or otherwise reveal the contents of the proposal to any source outside the using or contracting agency, government or private, until after the award of the contract. Prospective contractors not in compliance with this provision may be disqualified, at the option of the agency, from contract award. Only discussions authorized in advance and in writing by the contracting agency are exempt from this provision.

The prospective contractor hereby certifies that it and all of its affiliates collect appropriate taxes and remit them as provided by law.

The prospective contractor certifies that all insurance policies required by this contract shall remain in full force and effect during the entire term of this contact. All insurance policies and any extensions or renewals thereof shall not be canceled or amended except with the advance written approval of the agency. The contractor agrees to submit certificates of insurance, which indicate coverage and notice provisions as required by this contract, to the agency upon execution of this contract. The insurance certificates shall be subject to approval by the agency. The insurance certificates shall include a statement in the certificate that no cancellation of the insurance shall be made without at least thirty (30) calendar days' prior written notice to the agency. Approval of the insurance certificates by the agency shall not relieve the contractor of any obligation under this contract.

The prospective contractor has read and understands the conditions set forth in this RFP and agrees to them with no exceptions. (If exceptions are taken, attach a written description of each exception to this certification.)

The prospective contractor warrants, represents, and certifies that no elected or appointed official or employee of the agency has, or will, personally or indirectly benefit financially or materially from this contract.

Any contract and/or award arising from this RFP may be terminated by the agency if it is determined that gratuities of any kind were either offered to, or received by, any of the aforementioned officials or employees from the prospective contractor, the prospective contractor's agent(s), representative(s), or employee(s). Any contract and/or award arising from the RFP may also be terminated if it is determined that the contract and/or award was obtained by fraud, collusion, conspiracy, or other unlawful means, or if the contract and/or award conflicts with any statutory or Constitutional provision of the State of [***Insert State***] or of the United States.

Therefore, in compliance with this Request for Proposals, and subject to all conditions herein, the undersigned offers and agrees, that if this proposal is accepted within [***Insert Number of Days***] from the date of the opening, to furnish the subject services for a Firm Fixed/Not-to-Exceed (delete "Firm Fixed" or "Not-to-Exceed") Contract Price of $_____.

The following addenda have been received, and considered in the preparation of this proposal:

_____

I further affirm that: neither I, nor to the best of my knowledge, information, and belief, the business identified below, or any of its officers, directors, partners, or any of its employees directly involved in obtaining or performing contracts with public bodies has been convicted of, or has had probation before judgment imposed pursuant to criminal proceedings, or has pleaded *nolo contendere* to a charge of bribery, attempted bribery, or conspiracy to bribe in violation of any state or federal law, **except as indicated on the attachment** [indicate the reasons why the affirmation cannot be given and list any conviction, plea, or imposition of probation before judgment with the date, court, official, or administrative body, the sentence or disposition, the name(s) of person(s) involved, and their current positions and responsibilities with the business]:

## Attachments to Prospective Contractor Certification

☐ A description of a potential instance(s) of collusion or violation is attached.
☐ A list of exceptions to the RFP is attached.
☐ A description of instances involving bribery, attempted bribery, or conspiracy to bribe in violation of any state or federal law is attached.

The agency may initiate proceedings to debar a contractor or subcontractor from participation in the proposal process and from contract award if it is determined that the contractor has refused to disclose or has falsified any information provided in its proposal.

Because federal funds are included in the revenue that funds this contract, the agency included the following additional certifications, which are attached hereto if applicable, and which shall be completed by all prospective contractors, and returned to the agency with the proposal:

Exhibit __: Certification Regarding Lobbying
Exhibit __: Certification of Compliance with Pro-Children Act of 1994
Exhibit __: Certification Regarding Debarment, Suspension, Ineligibility and Voluntary Exclusion — Lower Tier Covered Transactions

PROSPECTIVE CONTRACTOR NAME:_____

BUSINESS STREET ADDRESS: _____

CITY, STATE, AND ZIP+4: _____

PAYMENT ADDRESS (IF DIFFERENT): _____

CITY, STATE, AND ZIP+4: _____

TELEPHONE NUMBER: _____  FAX: _____

FEDERAL EMPLOYER IDENTIFICATION NUMBER: _____

E-MAIL: _____

BY: _____  TITLE: _____

(SIGNATURE)

DATE: _____

_____

(TYPED OR PRINTED NAME)

Unsigned certifications may result in a determination that the proposal is nonresponsive.

# Exhibit __

## *Certification Regarding Lobbying*

The undersigned certifies, to the best of his or her knowledge and belief, that:

A. No federal appropriated funds have been paid or will be paid on behalf of the sub-grantee to any person for influencing or attempting to influence an officer or employee of any federal agency, a member of the Congress, an officer or employee of the Congress, or an employee of a member of Congress in connection with the awarding of any federal contract, the making of any federal grant, the making of any federal loan, the entering into of any cooperative agreement, or the extension, continuation, renewal, amendment, or modification of any federal contract, grant, loan, or cooperative agreement.

B. If any funds other than federal appropriated funds have been paid or will be paid to any person for influencing or attempting to influence an officer or employee of any federal agency, a member of the Congress, or an employee of a member of Congress in connection with this contract, grant, loan, or cooperative agreement, the applicant shall complete and submit Standard Form-LLL, "Disclosure Form to Report Lobbying," in accordance with its instructions.

C. The contractor shall require that the language of this certification be included in the award documents for all sub-awards at all tiers (including subcontracts, sub-grants, and contracts under grants, loans, and cooperative agreements) and that all sub-recipients shall certify and disclose accordingly.

This certification is a material representation of fact upon which reliance was placed when this transaction was made or entered into. Submission of this certification is a prerequisite for making or entering into this transaction imposed by Section 1352, Title 31, U.S. Code. Any person who fails to file the required certification shall be subject to a civil penalty of not less than $10,000 and not more than $100,000 for each such failure.

Signature:_____

Typed or Printed Name: _____

Title: _____

Organization:_____

Date: _____

# Exhibit ___

## *Certification of Compliance with Pro-Children Act of 1994*

Contractors shall comply with Public Law 103-227, Part C Environmental Tobacco Smoke, also known as the Pro-Children Act of 1994 (Act). This Act requires that smoking not be permitted in any portion of any indoor facility owned or leased or contracted by an entity and used routinely or regularly for the provision of health, day care, education, or library services to children under the age of 18, if the services are funded by federal programs either directly or through state or local governments. Federal programs include grants, cooperative agreements, loans or loan guarantees, and contracts. The law also applies to children's services that are provided in indoor facilities that are constructed, operated, or maintained with such federal funds. The law does not apply to children's services provided in private residences; portions of facilities used for inpatient drug or alcohol treatment; service providers whose sole source of applicable federal funds is Medicare or Medicaid; or facilities (other than clinics) where WIC coupons are redeemed.

The contractor further agrees that the above language will be included in any sub-awards that contain provisions for children's services and that all sub-grantees shall certify compliance accordingly. Failure to comply with the provisions of this law may result in the imposition of a civil monetary penalty of up to $1000 per day.

Signature:_____

Typed or Printed Name: _____

Title: _____

Organization:_____

Date: _____

# Exhibit __

## Certification Regarding Debarment, Suspension, Ineligibility, and Voluntary Exclusion — Lower Tier Covered Transactions

By signing and submitting this proposal, the prospective contractor is providing the certification set out below:

1. The certification in this clause is a material representation of fact upon which reliance was placed when this transaction was entered into. If it is later determined that the prospective contractor knowingly rendered an erroneous certification, in addition to other remedies available to the federal government, the department or agency with which this transaction originated may pursue available remedies, including suspension and/or debarment.

2. The prospective contractor certifies that it has not and will not provide any gratuities to any agency elected or appointed official, employee, representative, or consultant in connection with the award or administration of the contract that is expected to result from this solicitation.

3. The prospective contractor shall provide immediate written notice to the person to whom this proposal is submitted if at any time the prospective contractor learns that its certification was erroneous when submitted or had become erroneous by reason of changed circumstances.

4. The terms "covered transaction," "debarred," "suspended," "ineligible," "lower tier covered transaction," "participant," "person," "primary covered transaction," "principle," "proposal," and "voluntarily excluded," as used in this clause, have the meaning set out in the Definitions and Coverage sections of rules implementing Executive Order 12549. You may contact the person to whom this proposal is submitted for assistance in obtaining a copy of those regulations.

5. The prospective contractor agrees by submitting this proposal that, should the proposed covered transaction be entered into, it shall not knowingly enter into any lower tier covered transaction with a person who is proposed for debarment under 48 CFR Part 9, Subpart 9.4, debarred, suspended, declared ineligible, or voluntarily excluded from participation in this covered transac-

tion, unless authorized by the department or agency with which this transaction originated.

6. The prospective contractor further agrees by submitting this proposal that it will include this clause title, "Certification Regarding Debarment, Suspension, Ineligibility, and Voluntary Exclusion — Lower Tier Covered Transaction," without modification, in all lower tier covered transactions and in all solicitations for lower tier covered transactions.

7. A participant in a covered transaction may rely upon a certification of a prospective participant in a lower tier covered transaction that it is not proposed for debarment under 48 CFR Part 9, Subpart 9.4, suspended, ineligible, or voluntarily excluded from covered transactions, unless it knows that the certification is erroneous. A participant may decide the method and frequency by which it determines the eligibility of its principals. A participant may, but is not required to, check the List of Parties Excluded from Federal Procurement and Non-procurement Programs.

8. Nothing contained in the foregoing shall be construed to require establishment of a system of records in order to render in good faith the certification required by this clause. The knowledge and information of a participant is not required to exceed that which is normally possessed by a prudent person in the ordinary course of business dealings.

9. Except for transactions authorized under Paragraph 4 of these instructions, if a participant in a covered transaction knowingly enters into a lower tier covered transaction with a person who is proposed for debarment under 48 CFR Part 9, Subpart 9.4, suspended, debarred, ineligible, or voluntarily excluded from participation in this transaction, in addition to other remedies available to the federal government, the department or agency with which this transaction originated may pursue available remedies, including suspension and/or debarment.

10. The prospective contractor certifies, by submission of this proposal, that neither it nor its principals, nor its prospective subcontractors are presently debarred, suspended, proposed for debarment, declared ineligible, or voluntarily excluded from participation in this transaction by any federal department or agency.

11. Where the prospective contractor is unable to certify to any of the statements in this certification, such prospective contractor shall attach an explanation to this proposal.

Signature:_____

Typed or Printed Name: _____

Title: _____

Organization:_____

Date: _____

# Exhibit __

## *Certification of Cost or Pricing Data*

The undersigned hereby certifies that the contract price is based upon:

- ☐ Established catalog prices (copies of the applicable catalog pages showing the established catalog prices are enclosed).
- ☐ Established market prices (the amounts of contract prices offered to other contractor customers and the name of the contractor customers are enclosed).
- ☐ Statute or regulation (the citation for the statute or regulation and the date and short description of its provisions are enclosed).
- ☐ Other (describe any other basis for pricing on a separate attached sheet signed by the signatory to this Certification of Cost or Pricing Data).

*Submitted cost or pricing data.* To the extent that the contract price is based upon submitted cost or pricing data, I certify, on behalf of the Contractor, that to the best of my knowledge and belief, the cost or pricing data submitted is accurate, complete, and current as of the date specified above.

I further certify, to the best of my knowledge and belief, that the costs payable by the agency do not include any of the following (unless full disclosure is attached on a separate sheet signed by the signatory to this Certification of Cost or Pricing Data):

- Costs of fines or penalties paid to any government agency
- Contingency fees paid to obtain award of this contract
- Subcontractor profits for goods or services provided by contractor subsidiaries
- Gifts or gratuities paid to employees of the agency or any other government agency

The contractor understands that in addition to any other remedies or criminal penalties, the contract price shall be adjusted to exclude any significant sums by which the agency finds that the price was increased because the cost or pricing data furnished by the contractor was inaccurate, incomplete, or not current as of the date specified above.

Signature:_____

Typed or Printed Name: _____

Title: _____

Organization:_____

Date: _____

# Proposal Preparation and Submittal Instructions for Prospective Contractors

## Proposal Preparation Instructions

1. **EXCEPTIONS:** The agency intends to award a contract substantially in the form of and including the provisions of the attached Model Services Contract (MSC). Contractors that take exception to the terms and conditions do so at the risk that their proposal may be declared to be nonresponsive and not considered for contract award. By signing the PROSPECTIVE CONTRACTOR CERTIFICATION included in this RFP, the representative of the prospective contractor certifies that no exceptions are taken to the form of the MSC or to the provisions therein, unless such exceptions are fully disclosed in a document attached to the PROSPECTIVE CONTRACTOR CERTIFICATION.

2. **ORAL EXPLANATIONS:** The agency shall not be bound by oral explanations or instructions given at any time during the competitive process or after award.

3. **REFERENCE TO OTHER DATA:** Only information that is received in response to this RFP will be evaluated; reference to information previously submitted shall not be evaluated.

4. **ELABORATE PROPOSALS:** Elaborate proposals in the form of brochures or other presentations beyond that necessary to present a complete and effective proposal are not desired. Proposals that do not conform to the page limitations or format prescribed in this RFP may be rejected by the agency as nonresponsive.

   **It is desirable that all responses meet the following requirements:**

   - All copies are printed **double sided**.
   - All submittals and copies are printed on **recycled paper with a minimum post-consumer content of 30 percent** and an endorsement in the proposal indicating the minimum post-consumer recycled content for the recycled paper.
   - Unless absolutely necessary, all proposals and copies should **minimize or eliminate use of non-recyclable or non re-usable materials** such as plastic report covers, plastic dividers, vinyl sleeves, and GBC binding. Three-ringed binders, glued materials, paper clips, and staples are preferred.
   - Materials should be submitted in a format that allows for **easy removal and recycling** of paper materials.

5. **COST FOR PROPOSAL PREPARATION:** Any costs incurred by prospective contractors in preparing or submitting proposals, as well as costs associated with any resultant presentations or negotiations, are the prospective

contractors' sole responsibility; the agency will not reimburse any prospective contractor for any costs incurred prior to contract award.

6. **TIME FOR ACCEPTANCE:** Each proposal shall state that it is a firm offer that may be accepted within a period of [**Insert at least 30**] days. Although the contract is expected to be awarded prior to that time, the longer validity period is requested to allow for unforeseen delays.

7. **RIGHT TO SUBMITTED MATERIAL:** All responses, inquiries, or correspondence relating to or in reference to the RFP, and all other reports, charts, displays, schedules, exhibits, and other documentation submitted by the prospective contractors shall become the property of the agency when received.

8. **PROSPECTIVE CONTRACTOR'S REPRESENTATIVE:** Each prospective contractor shall submit with its proposal the name, mailing address, e-mail address, and telephone number of the person(s) with authority to bind the firm and answer questions or provide clarification concerning the firm's proposal.

9. **SUBCONTRACTING:** Prospective contractors may propose to subcontract portions, but not all, of the work performed. However, prospective contractors shall clearly indicate in their proposals all the work they plan to subcontract and to whom it will be subcontracted. Prospective contractors shall also provide identifying information for each proposed subcontractor similar to the identifying information provided for the contractor submitting the proposal.

10. **PROPRIETARY INFORMATION:** Trade secrets or similar proprietary data that the prospective contractor does not wish disclosed to other than personnel involved in the proposal evaluation effort or post-award contract administration will be kept confidential to the extent permitted by the agency as follows. Each page shall be identified by the prospective contractor in bold-face text at the top and bottom as "PROPRIETARY." Any section of the proposal that is to remain confidential shall also be so marked in boldface text on the title page of that section. Cost information may not be deemed proprietary. Despite what is labeled as confidential, proprietary, or trade secret, the determination as to whether or not certain material is confidential, proprietary, or a trade secret shall be determined by law. If a prospective contractor designates any information in its proposal as proprietary pursuant to this provision, the prospective contractor must also submit one copy of the proposal from which the proprietary information has been excised. The proprietary material shall be excised in such a way as to allow the public to determine the general nature of the material removed and to retain as much of the content of the proposal as possible.

11. **HISTORICALLY UNDERUTILIZED BUSINESSES:** The agency invites and encourages participation in this procurement process by businesses owned by minorities, women, disabled business enterprises, disabled veterans, and non-profit work centers for the blind and severely disabled.

12. **ACCOMODATIONS:** Reasonable accommodations will be provided by the agency for prospective contractor personnel who need assistance due to a physical disability. However, the agency must have reasonable advance written notice prior to the pre-proposal conference (if any) or any other visit to the agency's facilities. The prospective contractor must contact [*Insert Agency Official Name*] at [*Insert Contact Information*] no later than the fifth working day prior to the scheduled date and time of the pre-proposal conference to arrange for reasonable accommodations.

[**NOTE: A Model Services Contract (such as in Appendix F) should be attached to this Sample Request for Proposals (RFP) when it is sent to prospective contractors.**]

*Appendix F*

# Model Services
# Contract (MSC)

### MODEL SERVICES CONTRACT

This Contract, dated as of the last date executed by the [*Insert Agency Name*] is between the [*Insert Agency Name*], hereinafter referred to as "Agency", and the Contractor indicated in the variable information table below, hereinafter referred to as "Contractor."

| VARIABLE INFORMATION TABLE | | | | |
|---|---|---|---|---|
| | | **Contract Number** | | |
| **Term of This Contract** (Complete Dates in Just One of the Following Three Shaded Rows) | | | | |
| √ Below | **Term Begins** | | **Term Completion Date** | |
| | On Following Date | | On Following Date | |
| | Upon Receipt of Notice to Proceed | | Calendar Days Following Notice to Proceed | |
| | Upon Execution by Agency | | Calendar Days Following Agency Contract Execution | |
| | Agency Department | | FOB Point | |
| Terms | | Basis of Price (**Do Not √ More Than One of the Following Four Blocks**) | | |
| Price | | Fixed Price | Annual Price | Monthly Price | Hourly Rate |
| Not-to-Exceed Price | | √ if Reasonable Expenses authorized in addition to Hourly Rate | | |
| **Contractor Contact Information** | | **Agency Contact Information** | | |
| Contractor | | Project Manager | | |
| Address | | Address | | |
| City, State & ZIP | | City, State & ZIP | | |
| Telephone | | Telephone | | |
| Facsimile | | Facsimile | | |

**Figure F.1  Model Services Contract (MSC).**

**WHEREAS**, Agency, through the Agency Department identified above, desires to have work described in the Attachment II–Scope of Work performed; and

**WHEREAS**, Contractor possesses the necessary qualifications to perform the work described herein.

**NOW THEREFORE BE IT AGREED** between the parties to this Contract that this Contract is subject to the provisions contained in the attachments which are incorporated in this Contract, and the provisions which are incorporated in this Contract by reference. Should there be a conflict between the provisions of this contract and any of the attachments, precedence shall be given first to the contract and then to the attachments in descending order by the numbers assigned to each attachment.

| Attachments Incorporated in Contract | Provisions Incorporated by Reference as if Attached Hereto |
|---|---|
| 1. Attachment III–Agency General Contract Terms and Conditions | 2. Agency Special Terms and Conditions available at the following Web Site: |
| 5. Attachment I–Contract Insurance Requirements | 3. Compliance with Federal Law available at the following Web Site: |
| 6. Attachment II–Scope of Work | 4. Following Contractor Certifications: |

**AGENCY**                                 **CONTRACTOR**

By_____          By_____

Name_____          Name_____

Title_____          Title_____

**Figure F.1 (continued)    Model Services Contract (MSC).**

## Attachment I: Contract Insurance Requirements

Before the commencement of work, Contractor shall submit Certificates of Insurance and Endorsements evidencing that Contractor has obtained the following forms of coverage and minimal amounts specified:

## A. Minimum Scope of Insurance

1. Commercial General Liability coverage (Insurance Services Office [ISO] "occurrence" form CG 0001 1185)
2. Automobile Liability Insurance — standard coverage offered by insurance carriers licensed to sell auto liability insurance in the State of *[Insert State]*.
3. Workers' Compensation Insurance as required by the Labor code and Employers Liability Insurance
4. Professional Liability Insurance (Delete if not contracting for professional services); when the contract involves professional services such as engineering architectural, legal, accounting, instructing, consulting, or other profession requiring a similar level of education or experience, professional liability insurance is required

## B. Minimum Limits of Insurance

1. **General Liability**: At least $1,000,000 combined single limit **per occurrence** coverage for bodily injury, personal injury, and property damage, plus an annual aggregate of at least $2,000,000. If a general aggregate limit is used, then either the general aggregate limit shall apply separately to this project/location, or the general aggregate limit shall be **twice** the required per-occurrence limit. The contractor or contractor's insurance carrier shall notify Agency in writing if incurred losses covered by the policy exceed 50 percent of the annual aggregate limit.
2. **Automobile Liability**: At least $100,000 to cover bodily injury for one person and $300,000 for two or more persons, and $50,000 to cover property damages. However, policy limits for construction projects shall be at least $1,000,000 combined single limit per accident for bodily injury and property damage for autos used by the contractor to fulfill the requirements of this contract, and coverage shall be provided for "Any Auto," Code 1 as listed on the Accord from Certificate of Insurance.
3. **Workers' Compensation and Employer's Liability:** Workers' Compensation insurance up to policy limits and Employer Liability insurance each with policy limits of at least $1,000,000 for bodily injury or disease.

4. **Professional Liability Insurance (Delete if not contracting for professional services):** Professional liability insurance covering professional services shall be provided in an amount of at least $1,000,000 per occurrence or $1,000,000 on a claims made basis. However, if coverage is written on a claims made basis, the policy shall be endorsed to provide at least a two-year extended reporting provision.

## C. Deductibles and Self-Insured Retentions

Any deductibles or self-insured retention must be declared on certificates of insurance and approved in writing by the Agency. At the option of the Agency, either the insurer shall reduce or eliminate such deductibles or self-insured retention as respects the Agency, its officers, officials, employees, agents, and volunteers, or the Contractor shall procure a bond guaranteeing payment of losses and related investigations, claims administration and defense expenses.

## D. Other Insurance Provisions

1. **General liability insurance policies shall be endorsed to state:**
   a. The Agency, its officers, officials, employees, agents, and volunteers are to be covered as insured as respects liability arising out of activities performed by or at the direction of the Contractor, including products and completed operations of the Contractor; premises owned, occupied, or used by the Contractor; or automobiles owned, leased, hired, or borrowed by Contractor. The coverage shall contain no special limitations on the scope of protection afforded to the Agency, its officers, officials, employees, agents, or volunteers.
   b. Contractor's insurance coverage shall be primary insurance as respects the Agency, its officers, officials, employees, agents, and volunteers. Any insurance or self-insurance maintained by the Agency, its officers, officials, employees, agents, or volunteers shall be in excess of the Contractor's insurance and shall not contribute with it.
   c. Contractor's insurance shall apply separately to each insured against whom claim is made or suit is brought, except with respect to the limits of the insurer's liability.

## E. Acceptability of Insurance Carriers

Insurance shall be placed with insurers who are licensed to sell insurance in the State of [***Insert State***] and that possess a Best's rating of no less than A–: VII. If the Contractor's insurance carrier is not licensed to sell insurance in the State of **[Insert State]**, then the carrier must possess a Best rating of at least A: VIII. (For Best ratings, go to http://www.ambest.com/)

## F. Verification of Coverage

Contractor shall furnish the Agency certificates of insurance and original endorsements affecting coverage required by this clause. All certificates of insurance and endorsements shall be received and approved in writing by the Agency before work under the contract begins. The Agency reserves the right to require complete, certified copies of all insurance policies required by this contract.

Certificates of insurance shall state that the insuring agency agrees to endeavor to mail to Agency written notice 30 days before any of the insurance policies described herein are cancelled. Contractor agrees to notify Agency within two working days of any notice from an insuring agency that cancels, suspends, or reduces in coverage or policy limits the insurance coverages described herein.

## G. Subcontractors

Contractor shall include all subcontractors as insured under its policies or require all subcontractors to be insured under their own policies. If subcontractors are insured under their own policies, they shall be subject to all the requirements stated herein, including providing the Agency with certificates of insurance and endorsements prior to beginning work under this contract.

# Attachment II: Scope of Work

Unless indicated otherwise herein, the Contractor shall furnish all labor, materials, transportation, supervision, and management, and pay all taxes required to complete the project described below:

*[The following paragraph headings are provided as tasks to consider for inclusion in the Scope of Work. If one or more of these paragraph headings are not applicable, they should be deleted from the Scope of Work. The text following each heading includes an explanation of material that would be included in that section. All the information in bold italics on this sample should be removed when the Scope of Work is finalized for inclusion in the contract.]*

## Contractor Responsibility

*[This section should include all the work that the Contractor will be required to complete during performance of the contract. When Contractor tasks are specified, they should be worded such that the Contractor "shall" perform. Words such as "must," "should," "will," or "may" are to be avoided as "shall" is the word used in contracts that most compels the contractor to complete tasks in the Scope of Work.]*

## Contractor Tasks

*[All Contractor tasks should be described in this section of the Scope of Work. Because the expertise of the Contractor's employees was likely a key criterion in selecting a particular contractor, the Agency should have assurance that the employee(s) named in the proposal (or at least a like-qualified employee) be assigned to work on the Agency's contract. This could be accomplished by designating an employee to each task in this section of the SOW. Because it is not always possible for a Contractor to guarantee the availability of a particular employee, provisions can be drafted requiring the replacement of a named employee with another individual with like qualifications if approved in advance, in writing, by the Agency.]*

## Contractor/Agency Meetings

| Check the block on the left side of the row below if an Exhibit I, Contractor/Agency Meeting Schedule, is attached |
|---|
| If block on left is checked, Exhibit I, Contractor/Agency Meeting Schedule, is attached and incorporated in this scope of work. |

**Figure F.2  Contractor/agency meetings.**

*[If there are certain regularly scheduled meetings between the Contractor and the Agency, requirements for those meeting should be reflected here (Figure F.2), and the schedule dates should be reflected in Exhibit I, Contractor/Agency Meeting Schedule (see Figure F.6). The preamble to the first sentence in this section should be "The Contractor shall."]*

## Milestones

| |
|---|
| Check the block on the left side of the row below if an Exhibit II, Project Milestone Schedule, is attached |
| If block on left is checked, Exhibit II, Project Milestone Schedule, is attached and incorporated in this scope of work. |

**Figure F.3   Milestones.**

*[If there are significant milestones (such as task completions), the requirements for those milestones should be reflected here (Figure F.3) and the dates should be reflected in Exhibit II, Milestone Schedule (see Figure F.7). The preamble to the first sentence in this section should be "The Contractor shall."]*

## Contractor Reports and Other Deliverables

| |
|---|
| Check the block on the left side of the row below if an Exhibit III, Contract Deliverables, is attached |
| If block on left is checked, Exhibit III, Contract Reports and other Deliverables, is attached and incorporated in this scope of work. |

**Figure F.4   Contractor reports and other deliverables.**

*[If there are reports such as periodic progress reports, draft studies, final reports, or other contractor deliverables, the requirements for those reports and other deliverables (Figure F.4) should be reflected here and the due dates should be reflected in Exhibit III, Contract Reports and Other Deliverables (see Figure F.8). The preamble to the first sentence in this section should be "The Contractor shall."]*

## Contractor Compensation

*[If the Contractor is to be paid on a Not-to-Exceed basis or otherwise based on reimbursable expenses, then the basis for reimbursing the Contractor should be indicated in this paragraph. If the Contractor is to be reimbursed on a Firm-Fixed-Price basis, this paragraph is not required. If the Contractor is to be reimbursed based on hours of work performed, then separate billing rates should be shown by job title or employee name. Mileage reimbursement may be based on the IRS rate or a specified rate per mile. In some cases, contractors are required to drive a vehicle that is more expensive to operate than an automobile. In this case, a mileage rate greater than the IRS rate may be appropriate. When rates are based on actual expenditures, departments should avoid paying the actual expenditure plus an additional percentage. The reason to avoid payment of a percentage over the actual expenditure is that this reimbursement method motivates the Contractor to spend excessively. If it is not possible to entirely eliminate the percentage paid in addition to the actual cost, a not-to-exceed cost should be negotiated for these expenditures.]*

*[The table below (Figure F.5) is provided to permit a single or multiple account numbers for funding the contract. By using this format, the information will become available for populating the database for the contract management system.]*

| ACCOUNT INFORMATION | | |
|---|---|---|
| Account Number | Project Name | Funding |
| | | $_____ |

Figure F.5    Account information.

## Agency Responsibility

*[If the Agency has some specific responsibilities to perform during the term of the contract, they can be described in this section of the Scope of Work. While it is the Agency's policy to faithfully perform the work described in this section, it is acceptable to use words such as "must," "should," "will," or "may" rather than "shall" to describe the work to be performed by the Agency.]*

| Exhibit I, Contractor/Agency Meeting Schedule | | |
|---|---|---|
| Item No. | Meeting Title | Due Date |
| 1 | February Meeting | Feb 18, XX |
| 2 | March Meeting | Mar 22, XX |
| 3 | April Meeting | Apr 19, XX |
| 4 | May Meeting | May 15, XX |
| 5 | June Meeting | Jun 17, XX |
| 6 | July Meeting | Jul 19, XX |
| 7 | August Meeting | Aug 20, XX |
| 8 | September Meeting | Sep 15, XX |
| 9 | October Meeting | Oct 18, XX |
| 10 | November Meeting | Nov 22, XX |
| 11 | December Meeting | Dec 17, XX |
| 12 | January Meeting | Jan 20, XX |

**Figure F.6   Exhibit I: Contractor/Agency Meeting Schedule.**

| Exhibit II, Project Milestone Schedule | | |
|---|---|---|
| Item No. | Milestone Title | Due Date |
| 1 | Task A Commencement | Feb 9, XX |
| 2 | Task A Completion | Mar 18, XX |
| 3 | Task B Commencement | Mar 9, XX |
| 4 | Task C Commencement | Mar 9, XX |
| 5 | Task B Completion | Jun 17, XX |
| 6 | Task D Commencement | Aug 9, XX |
| 7 | Task C Completion | Sep 7, XX |
| 8 | Task D Completion | Sep 15, XX |

**Figure F.7   Exhibit II: Milestone Schedule.**

| Exhibit III, Contract Reports and Other Deliverables | | |
|---|---|---|
| Item No. | Report or Other Deliverable Title | Due Date |
| 1 | Task A Report | Mar 25, XX |
| 2 | Task B Report | Jun 24, XX |
| 3 | Task C Report | Sep 14, XX |
| 4 | Task D Report | Sep 22, XX |

**Figure F.8  Exhibit III: Contract Reports and Other Deliverables.**

## Attachment III: Agency Services Contract Terms and Conditions

[NOTE: For "Agency", substitute "State," "Commonwealth," "Department," "University," "County," "City," "District," etc., as applicable.]

1. **TERM.** The term of this contract is reflected in the Variable Information Table. Should the Agency elect to continue to contract with the Contractor for a continuing period of time beyond the completion of the contract term reflected in the Variable Information Table, the Contractor shall agree to accept an extension of up to six weeks under the provisions of this contract to provide the Agency an opportunity to prepare and execute a formal amendment that includes any changed provisions or compensation rates. No later than ninety days prior to the expiration of a one-year contract, the Contractor may request, in writing, a cost adjustment for the second year of the contract. Any proposed increase in price shall not exceed the rate of inflation as determined by the Consumer Price Index for all urban consumers (CPI-U) U. S. City average all items 1982-84 + 100 published by the Bureau of Labor Statistics as the percent of change at the time of the request, from one year prior (the baseline index). The Agency reserves the right to accept the cost adjustment and extend the contract for one additional year; negotiate the cost adjustment, scope of work, length of the contract extension, or any other provisions of the contract; or to allow the contract to end at the completion of the period of performance.

2. **TERMINATION FOR DEFAULT.** If, through any cause, the Contractor shall fail to fulfill in a timely and proper manner the obligations under this contract, other than for the instances listed below due to "Force Majeure,"

the Agency shall thereupon have the right to terminate this contract by providing a written notice (show cause notice) to the Contractor requiring a written response due within ten days from receipt of the written notice as to why the contract should not be terminated for default. The Agency's show cause notice shall include a contract termination date at least [***Insert Number***] days subsequent to the due date for the Contractor's response. Should the Contractor fail to respond to such show cause notice, or if the Agency determines that the reasons provided by the Contractor for failure of the Contractor to fulfill its contractual obligations do not justify continuation of the contractual relationship, the Agency shall terminate the contract for default on the date indicated in the show cause notice. Should the Agency determine that the Contractor provided adequate justification that a termination for default is not appropriate under the circumstances, the Agency shall have a unilateral option to either continue the contract according to the original contract provisions or to terminate the contract for convenience. In the event that the Agency terminates the contract for default, all finished or unfinished deliverable items under this contract prepared by the Contractor shall, at the option of the Agency, become Agency property, and the Contractor shall be entitled to receive just and equitable compensation for any satisfactory work completed on such materials. Notwithstanding this compensation, the Contractor shall not be relieved of liability to the Agency for damages sustained by the Agency by virtue of any breach of this agreement, and the Agency may withhold any payment due the Contractor for the purpose of set-off until such time as the exact amount of damages due the Agency from such breach can be determined.

In case of default by the Contractor, the Agency may procure the services from other sources and hold the Contractor responsible for any excess cost occasioned thereby. The Agency reserves the right to require a performance bond or other acceptable alternative performance guarantees from the successor Contractor without expense to the Agency.

In addition, in the event of default by the Contractor under this contract, the Agency may immediately cease doing business with the Contractor, immediately terminate for cause all existing contracts the Agency has with the Contractor, and debar the Contractor from doing future business with the Agency.

Upon the Contractor filing a petition for bankruptcy or the entering of a judgment of bankruptcy by or against the Contractor, the Agency may immediately terminate, for cause, this contract and all other existing contracts the Contractor has with the Agency, and debar the Contractor from doing future business with the Agency.

The Agency may terminate this contract for cause without penalty or further obligation at any time following contract execution, if any person significantly involved in initiating, negotiating, securing, drafting, or creating the contract on behalf of the Agency is at any time while the contract or any extension thereof is in effect, an employee or agent of any other party to the contract in any capacity or consultant to any other party of the contract with respect to the subject matter of the contract. Additionally, the Agency may recoup any fee or commission paid or due to any person significantly involved in initiating, negotiating, securing, drafting or creating the contract on behalf of the Agency from any other party to the contract.

3. **FORCE MAJEURE.** Neither party shall be deemed to be in default of its obligations hereunder if and so long as it is prevented from performing such obligations by any act of war, hostile foreign action, nuclear explosion, riot, strikes, civil insurrection, earthquake, hurricane, tornado, or other catastrophic natural event or act of God. Should there be such an occurrence that impacts the ability of either party to perform their responsibilities under this contract, the nonperforming party shall give immediate written notice to the other party to explain the cause and probable duration of any such nonperformance.

4. **LIQUIDATED DAMAGES.** The parties acknowledge and agree that the damages that are to be expected as a result of a material breach of contract by Contractor may be uncertain in amount and very difficult to prove. In that event, the parties do intend and in fact now agree, if necessary, to liquidated damages in advance and stipulate that the amount set forth in this section is reasonable and an appropriate remedy as liquidated damages and not as a penalty. If the Contractor materially breaches the contract, then the Contractor shall pay the Agency $*[Insert Amount]* per day for the duration of the delay.

5. **TERMINATION FOR CONVENIENCE.** Either party to this contract may terminate this contract at any time without cause by providing the other party with sixty days' advance notice in writing. In the event of termination for any reason, all finished or unfinished deliverable items prepared by the Contractor under this contract shall, at the option of the Agency, become the Agency's property. If the contract is terminated by the Agency as provided herein, the Contractor shall be paid for services satisfactorily completed, less payment or compensation previously made.

The Contractor shall continue to perform the services described in the scope of work during the *[Insert Number of Days]*-day period following notice of termination for convenience, and the Agency shall continue to pay the Contractor for services performed during such period in accordance with the compensation provisions contained herein.

6. **TERMINATION TRANSITION.** During the fifteen calendar day period prior to termination of the contract, the Contractor shall provide reasonable cooperation in the transition of its responsibilities to the replacement Contractor selected by the Agency to perform the tasks described in the scope of work and formerly performed by the Contractor for this contract. The Contractor for this contract shall accept no additional tasks with respect to the scope of work after the effective date of the termination.

7. **CONTRACTOR REIMBURSEMENT**. The work shall be performed for the Fixed Price, Annual Price, Monthly Price, or Hourly Rate as indicated above in the Variable Information Table, but shall not exceed the Not-to-Exceed Price if included in the Variable Information Table. Reasonable expenses are authorized in addition to the Hourly Rate if both the Hourly Rate block and the block authorizing Reasonable Expenses are checked in the variable information table. Payment shall be made after the Agency's project manager or designee reviews and approves the work and after submittal of an invoice by the Contractor.

8. **PAYMENT TERMS.** Payment terms are indicated in the Variable Information Table. The due date indicated is based upon the number of days following receipt of a correct invoice(s) or acceptance of services, whichever is later. Invoices may not be submitted more frequently than once monthly. The using Agency is responsible for all payments to the Contractor under the contract. Payment by some agencies may be made by procurement card, and they shall be accepted by the Contractor for payment if the Contractor accepts that card (Visa, MasterCard, etc.) from other customers. If payment is made by procurement card, then payment may be processed immediately by the Contractor.

9. **SET-OFF.** In the event that the Contractor owes the Agency any sum under the terms of this contract, any other contract, pursuant to any judgment, or pursuant to any law, the Agency may set-off the sum owed to the Agency against any sum owed by the Agency to the Contractor at the Agency's sole discretion, unless otherwise required by law. The Contractor agrees that this provision constitutes proper and timely notice.

10. **AGENCY PROJECT MANAGER.** The Agency's project manager or designee for this undertaking who will receive payment invoices and answer questions related to the coordination of this undertaking is identified above in the Variable Information Table.

11. **KEY PERSONNEL.** The Contractor shall not substitute key personnel assigned to the performance of this contract without prior written approval by the Agency's project manager. The individuals designated as key personnel for purposes of this contract are those listed below:

12. **INDEPENDENT CONTRACTOR.** The Contractor shall be considered to be an independent contractor and as such shall be wholly responsible for the work to be performed and for the supervision of its employees. The Contractor represents that it has, or will secure at its own expense, all personnel required in performing the services under this agreement. Such employees shall not be employees of, or have any individual contractual relationship with, the Agency. The Contractor shall be exclusively responsible for payment of employees and subcontractors for all wages and salaries, taxes, withholding payments, penalties, fees, fringe benefits, professional liability insurance premiums, contributions to insurance and pension, or other deferred compensation, including but not limited to Workers' Compensation and Social

Security obligations, and licensing fees, etc., and the filing of all necessary documents, forms, and returns pertinent to all the foregoing.

13. **CONFIDENTIALITY AND OWNERSHIP.** The Agency retains the exclusive right of ownership to the work, products, inventions, and confidential information produced for the Agency by the Contractor, and the Contractor shall not disclose any information, whether developed by the Contractor or given to the Contractor by the Agency.

14. **INDEMNIFICATION.** The Contractor shall indemnify, defend, and hold harmless the Agency and its officers, representatives, agents, employees, successors, and assigns from and against any and all (1) claims arising directly or indirectly, in connection with the contract, including the acts of commission or omission (collectively, the "Acts") of the Contractor or Contractor Parties; and (2) liabilities, damages, losses, costs, and expenses, including but not limited to, attorneys' and other professionals' fees arising, directly or indirectly, in connection with claims, Acts, or the contract. The Contractor shall use counsel reasonably acceptable to the Agency to carry out its obligations under this section. The Contractor's obligations under this section to indemnify, defend, and hold harmless against claims includes claims concerning confidentiality or the proprietary nature of any part or all of the proposal or any records, any intellectual property rights, other proprietary rights of any person or entity, copyrighted or uncopyrighted compositions, secret processes, patented or unpatented inventions, articles or appliances furnished or used in the performance of the contract. The Contractor shall reimburse the Agency for any and all damages to the real or personal property of the Agency caused by the Acts of the Contractor or any Contractor parties. The Agency shall give the Contractor reasonable notice of any such claims. The Contractor's duties under this section shall remain fully in effect and binding in accordance with the terms and conditions of the contract, without being lessened or compromised in any way, even where the Contractor is alleged or is found to have merely contributed in part to the Acts giving rise to the claims and/or where the Agency is alleged or is found to have contributed to the Acts giving rise to the claims. The rights provided in this section for the benefit of the Agency shall encompass the recovery of attorneys' and other professionals' fees expended in pursing a claim against a third party. This section shall survive the termination, cancellation, or expiration of the contract, and shall not be limited by reason of any insurance coverage.

15. **INSURANCE.** Contractor shall procure and maintain for the duration of this contract, insurance against claims for injuries to persons or damages to property that may arise from, or be in connection with the performance of the work hereunder by Contractor, Contractor's agents, representatives, employees, and subcontractors. At the very least, Contractor shall maintain the insurance coverages, limits of coverage, and other insurance requirements as described in Attachment I to this contract.

16. **AMENDMENTS.** This contract may be amended only by written amendments duly executed by the Agency and the Contractor.

17. **WAIVER OF RIGHTS.** It is the intention of the parties hereto that from time to time either party may waive any of its rights under this contract unless contrary to law. Any waiver by either party hereto of rights arising in connection with this contract shall not be deemed a waiver with respect to any other rights or matters.

18. **COMPLIANCE WITH LAWS.** The Contractor shall comply with all laws, ordinances, codes, rules, regulations, and licensing requirements that are applicable to the conduct of its business, including those of federal, state, and local agencies having jurisdiction and/or authority.

19. **AMERICANS WITH DISABILITIES ACT.** By signing this contract, the Contractor assures the Agency that it will comply with the Americans with Disabilities Act (ADA) of 1990, (42 U.S.C. 12101 et seq.), which prohibits discrimination on the basis of disability, as well as all applicable regulations and guidelines issued pursuant to the ADA.

20. **HEALTH INSURANCE PORTABILITY AND ACCOUNTABILITY ACT.** If the Contractor is a Business Associate under the Health Insurance Portability and Accountability Act of 1996 ("HIPAA"), the Contractor shall comply with all terms and conditions of the separate HIPAA agreement. If the Contractor is not a Business Associate under HIPAA, this HIPAA provision does not apply to this contract.

21. **NONDISCRIMINATION.** During the performance of this contract, the Contractor and its subcontractors shall not deny the Contractor's benefits to any person on the basis of religion, color, ethnic group identification, sex, age, physical or mental disability, nor shall they discriminate unlawfully against any employee or applicant for employment because of race, religion, color, national origin, ancestry, physical or mental disability, medical condition, marital status, age (over 40), or sex. The Contractor shall ensure that the evaluation and treatment of employees and applicants for employment are free of such discrimination. The Contractor and its subcontractors shall comply with the provisions of all applicable state and federal laws regarding employment rights.

22. **DRUG-FREE WORKPLACE.** The Contractor shall provide a drug-free workplace in accordance with the Drug-Free Workplace Act of 1988 and all applicable regulations. The Contractor shall execute the certification regarding a drug-free workplace attached to the solicitation and provide the original certificate to the Agency when it executes this contract. The Contractor agrees to abide by the terms of the certification. The certification is a material representation of fact upon which the Agency relied when making or entering into this contract and any extension or renewal thereof.

23. **WORKERS' COMPENSATION.** The Contractor affirms that it is aware of the provisions of the state labor laws that require every employer to be insured against liability for workers' compensation or to undertake self-insurance in

accordance with the provisions of state labor laws, and the Contractor affirms that it will comply with such provisions before commencing the performance of the work under this contract. Contractors shall require their subcontractors to be aware of this provision and determine that they have complied with it before commencing work on their subcontracts.

24. **CONTRACTOR'S STANDARD OF CARE.** The Agency has relied upon the professional ability and training of the Contractor as a material inducement to enter into this contract. The Contractor hereby warrants that all of the Contractor's work shall be performed in accordance with generally accepted and applicable professional practices and standards as well as the requirements of applicable federal, state, and local laws, it being understood that acceptance of the Contractor's work by the Agency shall not operate as a waiver or release.

25. **CARE OF PROPERTY.** The Contractor agrees that it shall be responsible for the proper custody and care of any property furnished it for use in connection with the performance of this contract or purchased by it for this contract, and will reimburse the Agency for loss of or damage to such property.

26. **ADVERTISING.** The Contractor shall not refer to sales to the Agency for advertising or promotional purposes, including, but not limited to, posting any material or data on the Internet, without the Agency's prior written approval.

27. **PERFORMANCE EVALUATION.** The Contractor's performance under this project may be evaluated after completion of this contract.

28. **INSPECTION OF WORK AND PROJECT SITE.**
    - The Agency shall have the right to inspect the work being performed at any and all reasonable times during the term of the contract. This right shall extend to any subcontracts, and the Contractor shall include provisions ensuring such access in all its contracts or subcontracts entered into pursuant to this contract.
    - The Agency shall have the right to inspect the project site at any and all reasonable times after completion of the contract to ensure compliance with the "Contractor's Standard of Care" and the "Nondiscrimination" provisions of this contract.

29. **APPLICABLE LAW AND FORUM.** This contract shall be construed and interpreted according to the laws of the state of the awarding government agency.

30. **SUCCESSORS AND ASSIGNS.** This contract and all of its provisions shall apply to and bind the successors and assigns of the parties hereto. No assignment or transfer of this contract or any part hereof, rights hereunder, or interest herein by the Contractor shall be valid unless and until it is approved in writing by the awarding agency and made subject to such reasonable terms and conditions as the Agency may impose.

31. **SUBCONTRACTING.** Work proposed to be performed under this contract by the Contractor or its employees shall not be subcontracted without prior

advance written approval of the Agency's project manager. Acceptance of a prospective contractor's proposal shall include any subcontractor(s) specified therein. Substitution of subcontractors may be made if the Agency's project manager approves such substitution in advance in writing. The Contractor shall include provisions in its subcontracts requiring its subcontractors to comply with the applicable provisions of this contract, to indemnify the Agency, and to provide insurance coverage for the benefit of the Agency in a manner consistent with this contract. The Contractor shall cause its subcontractors, agents, and employees to comply with applicable federal, state, and local laws, regulations, ordinances, guidelines, permits, and requirements, and will adopt such review and inspection procedures as are necessary to assure such compliance.

32. **UNALLOWABLE COSTS.** The Contractor shall not claim reimbursement for any of the following costs unless disclosed in the Contractor's Certification of Cost or Pricing Data that was submitted with the Contractor's proposal and reimbursement for the following costs had been approved in writing, in advance by the Agency:
   - Costs of fines or penalties paid to any government agency
   - Contingency fees paid to obtain award of this contract
   - Subcontractor profits for goods or services provided by Contractor's subsidiaries
   - Gifts or gratuities paid to employees of the Agency or any other government agency

33. **AUDIT, EMPLOYEE INTERVIEWS, AND DOCUMENT RETENTION.** Contractor agrees that the Agency, or its designated representative, shall have the right to review and to copy any records and supporting documentation and have access to Contractor personnel pertaining to the performance of this contract. Contractor agrees to maintain such records for possible audit for a minimum of three years after final payment, unless a longer period of records retention is stipulated. Contractor agrees to allow the Agency's auditor(s) access to such records during normal business hours and to allow interviews of any employees who might reasonably have information related to such records. Further, Contractor agrees to include a similar right to the Agency to audit and interview staff in any subcontract related to performance of this contract. If at any time, the Agency determines that a cost for which payment has been made is a disallowed cost, such as overpayment, the Agency shall notify the Contractor in writing of the disallowance or claim for unallowable costs. The Agency shall also state the means of correction, which may be, but shall not be limited to, adjustment of any future claim submitted by the Contractor by the amount of the disallowance, or to require repayment of the disallowed amount by the Contractor.

34. **REMEDIES NOT EXCLUSIVE.** The use by either party of any remedy specified herein for the enforcement of this contract is not exclusive and shall

not deprive the party using such remedy of, or limit the application of, any other remedy provided by law.

## 35. CONFLICT OF INTEREST.
a.  Current Employees or Officers of the Agency:
- i. No current employee or officer of the Agency shall engage in any employment, activity, or enterprise from which the officer or employee receives compensation or has a financial interest and which is sponsored or funded by the Agency unless the employment, activity, or enterprise is required as a condition of the regular employment with the Agency.
- ii. No current employee or officer of the Agency shall contract on his or her own behalf as an independent contractor with any department of the Agency to provide goods or services.

b.  Former Employees or Officers of the Agency:
- i. For a period of two years following the termination of employment with the Agency, no former employee or officer of the Agency may enter into a contract in which he or she is engaged in any of the negotiations, transactions, planning, arrangements, or any part of the decision-making process relevant to the contracts while employed in any capacity by the Agency.
- ii. For a period of twelve months following the termination of employment with the Agency, no former employee or officer of the Agency may enter into a contract with any department of the Agency if he or she was employed by that Agency department in a policy-making position in the same general subject area as the proposed contract within the twelve-month period prior to his or her terminating employment with the Agency.

## 36. CONTRACTOR INTEGRITY.
a.  For the purposes of this clause only, the words or phrases "proprietary information," "consent," "Contractor," "financial interest," and "gratuity" shall have the following definitions:
- i. **Proprietary Information** means information that is company confidential, a trade secret, or otherwise not public knowledge, disclosure of which would give an unfair, unethical, or illegal advantage to another entity or individual desiring to contract with the Agency.
- ii. **Consent** means written permission signed by a duly authorized officer or employee of the Agency, provided that where the material facts have been disclosed, in writing, by prequalification, proposal, or contractual terms.
- iii. **Contractor** means the individual or entity that has entered into the contract with the Agency, including directors, officers, partners, managers, key employees, and owners for more than a five percent ownership of the Contractors' firm, subsidiaries, or parent companies.

    iv. **Financial Interest** means: (a) ownership of more than a five percent interest in any business; or (b) holding a position as an officer, director, trustee, partner, employee, or the like, or holding any position of management.

    v. **Gratuity** means any payment of anything of monetary value in the form of cash, travel, entertainment, gift, meal(s), lodging, loans, subscriptions, conference fees, advances, deposits of money, services, employment or promises of employment, contracts of any kind, or any other article or intellection having present or future pecuniary benefit.

b. The Contractor shall maintain the highest standards of integrity in the performance of the contract and shall take no action in violation of state or federal laws, regulations, or other requirements that govern contracting with the Agency.

c. The Contractor shall not disclose to others any confidential or proprietary information gained by virtue of the contract.

d. The Contractor shall not, in connection with this or any other agreement with the Agency, directly, or indirectly, offer, confer, or agree to confer any pecuniary benefit on anyone as consideration for the decision, opinion, recommendation, vote, other exercise of discretion, or violation of a known legal duty by any officer or employee of the Agency.

e. The Contractor shall not, in connection with this or any other agreement with the Agency, directly, or indirectly, offer, give, or agree or promise to give to anyone any gratuity for the benefit of or at the direction or request of any officer or employee of the Agency.

f. Except with the written consent of the Agency, neither the Contractor nor anyone in privity with him or her shall accept or agree to accept from, or give or agree to give to, any person, any gratuity from any person in connection with the performance of services under the contract except as provided herein.

g. Except with the written consent of the Agency, the Contractor shall not have a financial interest in any other contractor, subcontractor, or supplier providing services, labor, or material on this project.

h. The Contractor, upon being informed that any violation of these provisions has occurred or may occur, shall immediately notify the Agency in writing.

i. The Contractor, by execution of this contract and by the submission of any bills or invoices for payment pursuant thereto, certifies and represents that she or he has not violated any of these provisions.

j. The Contractor, upon the inquiry or request of the Agency or any of the Agency's agents or representatives, shall provide, or if appropriate, make promptly available for inspection or copying, any information of any type or form deemed relevant by the Agency to the Contractor's integrity or responsibility, as those terms are defined by the Agency's statutes, regulations, or management directives. Such information may include but shall not be limited to the Contractor's business or financial records, document, or files of any type or form that refers to or concern the contract. Such information shall be retained by the Contractor for a period of three years beyond the termination of the contract unless otherwise provided by law.

k.  For violation of any of the above provisions, the Agency may terminate this and any other agreement with the Contractor, claim liquidated damages in an amount equal to the value of anything received in breach of these provisions, claim damages for all expenses incurred in obtaining another Contractor to complete performance hereunder, and debar and suspend the Contractor from doing business with the Agency. These rights and remedies are cumulative, and the use or nonuse of any one shall not preclude the use of all or any other. These rights and remedies are in addition to those the Agency may have under law, statute, regulation, or otherwise.

**37. POLITICAL CONTRIBUTION DISCLOSURE.** The Contractor shall comply with election laws requiring entities or persons entering into contracts, leases, or other agreements with the state, county, city, or their agencies in the aggregate amount requiring such disclosure to file a statement disclosing a contribution(s) in excess of $500 in the aggregate during any calendar year.

**38. ASSIGNMENT OF ANTITRUST CLAIMS.** The Contractor and the Agency recognize that in actual economic practice, overcharges by the Contractor's suppliers resulting from violation of state or federal antitrust laws are in fact borne by the Agency. As part of the consideration for the award of the contract, and intending to be legally bound, the Contractor assigns to the Agency all rights, title, and interest in; and to any claims the Contractor now has, or may acquire, under state or federal antitrust laws relating to the services or any products that are, or which may become, the subject of this contract.

**39. PAYMENT OF TAXES.** By execution of this contract, the Contractor certifies that it and all of its affiliates, if applicable, collect all appropriate taxes and remit them to the applicable state or local government agency.

**40. OFFICIALS NOT TO PROSPER.** No members of the governing body of the state or local public agency, and no other officer, elected or appointed official, employee, or agent of the state or local public agency who exercise any functions or responsibilities in connection with the carrying out of the project to which this contract pertains, shall have any personal interest, direct or indirect, in this contract. No member of the governing body of the locality in which the project area is situated, or other public official of such locality, who exercises any functions or responsibilities in the review or approval of the carrying out of the work to which this project pertains, shall have any personal interest, direct or indirect, in this contract. No state official, Member of or Delegate to the

Congress of the United States, and no Resident Commissioner, shall be admitted to any share or part of the contract or to any benefit to arise therefrom.

41. **COPYRIGHTS.** Where copyrights are an essential element of performance under this contract, the Contractor certifies that it has appropriate systems and controls in place to ensure that Agency funds will not be used in the performance of this contract for acquisition, operation, or maintenance of literature or computer software in violation of copyright laws.

42. **BUDGET CONTINGENCY.** It is mutually agreed that if the approved budget for the current year and/or any subsequent years covered under this contract does not appropriate sufficient funds for the project, this contract shall no longer be in force and effect. In this event, the Agency shall have no liability to pay any funds whatsoever to Contractor or to furnish any other consideration under this contract and Contractors shall not be obligated to perform any provisions of this contract. If funding for any fiscal year is reduced or deleted by the approved budget for purposes of this project, the Agency shall have the option to either: cancel this contract with no liability occurring to the Agency, or offer a contract amendment to the Contractor reflecting the reduced amount.

43. **COUNTERPARTS.** The parties to this contract agree that this contract has been or may be executed in several counterparts, each of which shall be deemed an original and all such counterparts shall together constitute one and the same instrument.

44. **SEVERABILITY.** If any provision of this contract is held invalid or unenforceable by any court of final jurisdiction, it is the intent of the parties that all other provisions of this contract be construed to remain fully valid, enforceable, and binding on the parties.

45. **NOTICES.** For any notice applicable to the contract to be effective, it must be made in writing and sent to the Contractor or Agency representative at the address indicated in the Variable Information Table unless such party has notified the other party, in accordance with the provisions of this section, of a revised mailing address. Such notices shall be sent via certified mail or an alternative mode that requires a signature by the recipient. This notice requirement does not apply to any notices that this contract expressly authorizes to be made orally.

46. **TITLES, HEADINGS, OR CAPTIONS.** The titles, headings, and captions appearing in this contract are for convenience only, and such titles, headings, and captions shall not affect the contractual interpretation or meaning of this contract.

47. **ENTIRE AGREEMENT AND SURVIVAL OF PROVISIONS BEYOND THE CONTRACT TERM.** This contract and any documents incorporated specifically by reference or attachment represent the entire agreement between the parties and supersede all prior oral or written statements or agreements.

All promises, requirements, terms, conditions, provisions, representations, guarantees, and warranties contained herein shall survive the contract expiration or termination date unless specifically provided otherwise herein, or unless superseded by applicable federal or state statutes of limitation.

# Compliance with Federal Law

*[This document titled "Compliance with Federal Law" is not to be attached to the contract or included in the RFP; however, it shall be posted on the Agency's Web site and be incorporated by reference in this contract.]*

Where a contract involves the expenditure of federal assistance or contract grant funds, the successful contractor shall comply with such federal law and authorized regulations that are mandatorily applicable and that are incorporated in the contract by reference. Select federal laws requiring compliance by the Contractor are summarized below; however, this list should not be considered all inclusive:

1. All contracts awarded in excess of $10,000 by grantees and their contractors or subgrantees require compliance with Executive Order 11246, entitled "Equal Employment Opportunity," as amended by Executive Order 11375, and as supplemented in Department of Labor regulations (41 CFR Part 60).

2. All negotiated contracts (except those awarded by small purchase procedures) awarded by grantees provide that the grantee, the Federal grantor agency, the Comptroller General of the United States, or any of their duly authorized representatives, shall have access to any books, documents, papers, and records of the Contractor that are directly pertinent to this specific contract, for the purpose of making an audit, examination excerpts and transcriptions. Contractors are to maintain all required records for three years after grantees make final payments and all other pending matters are closed.

3. Contracts, subcontracts, and subgrants of amounts in excess of $100,000 require compliance with all applicable standards, orders, or requirements issued under Section 306 of the Clean Air Act (42 U.S. C 1857 (h)), Section 508 of the Clean Water Act (33 U.S.C. 1368), Executive Order 11738, and Environmental Protection Agency regulations (40 CFR Part 15), which prohibit the use under nonexempt federal contracts, grants, or loans of facilities included on the EPA List of Violating Facilities. This provision requires reporting of violations to the grantor agency and to the U.S. EPA Assistant Administrator for Enforcement.

4. Employees performing work under this contract shall be paid unconditionally and not less often than once a month without deduction or rebate on any account except only such payroll deductions as are mandatory by law or permitted by the applicable regulations issued by the Secretary of Labor pursuant to the "Anti-Kickback Act" of June 13, 1934, (48 Stat. 948; 62 Stat.

740, 63 Stat. 108; title 18 U.S.C., Section 874; and title 40 U.S.C. Section 276c). The Contractor shall comply with all applicable "Anti-Kickback" regulations and shall insert appropriate provisions in all subcontracts covering work under the Contract to ensure compliance by subcontractors with such regulations, and shall be responsible for the submission of affidavits required of subcontractors thereunder except as the Secretary of Labor may specifically provide for variations of or exemptions from the requirements thereof.

5. The requirements of the Federal Disadvantaged Business Enterprise (DBE) Program set forth in Title 49 Code of Federal Regulations Part 26 shall be adhered to. The Agency encourages participation by small disadvantaged businesses and socially disadvantaged businesses as prime contractors, joint ventures, and subcontractors.

Small Disadvantaged Businesses are small businesses that are owned or controlled by a majority of persons, not limited to members of minority groups, who have been deprived of the opportunity to develop and maintain a competitive position in the economy because of social disadvantages. The term includes:

a. Department of General Services Bureau of Minority and Women Business Opportunities (BMWBO)-certified minority business enterprises (MBEs) and women business enterprises (WBEs) that qualify as small businesses; and

b. United States Small Business Administration-certified small disadvantaged businesses or 8(a) small disadvantaged business concerns.

Small Businesses are businesses in the United States that are independently owned, are not dominant in their field of operation, employ no more than 100 persons, and earn less than $20 million in gross annual revenues ($25 million in gross annual revenue for those businesses in the information technology sales or service business).

Socially Disadvantaged Businesses are businesses in the United States that BMWBO determines are owned or controlled by a majority of persons, not limited to members of minority groups, who are subject to racial or ethnic prejudice or cultural bias, but which do not qualify as small businesses. For a business to qualify as "socially disadvantaged," the prospective contractor must include in its proposal clear and convincing evidence to establish that the business has personally suffered racial or ethnic prejudice or cultural bias stemming from the business person's color, ethnic origin, or gender.

# *Appendix G*

# Short-Form RFP with Short-Form Contract

*[AGENCY NAME]*

REQUEST FOR PROPOSALS (RFP) #: _____

PROJECT TITLE: _____

USING AGENCY: _____

CONTRACTING AGENCY: _____

AGENCY PROJECT MANAGER: _____

PROJECT MANAGER E-MAIL ADDRESS: _____

AGENCY MAILING ADDRESS: _____

AGENCY INTERNET SITE: _____

RFP ISSUE DATE: _____

DUE DATE FOR RECEIPT OF QUESTIONS
REGARDING THIS RFP:_____

PROPOSAL DUE DATE:_____

## Notice to Prospective Contractors

Prospective contractors should carefully review this solicitation. Comments concerning defects and questionable or objectionable matter must be made to the agency project manager at the e-mail address on the Request for Proposals (RFP) cover page, and must be received by the agency prior to the deadline for written questions also shown on the RFP cover page. Questions concerning the specifications must be posed through the same e-mail address provided on the cover page. The date limitation for posing questions will permit this agency to issue any necessary corrections and/or addenda to this RFP in time for all prospective contractors to react by adjusting, if needed, their proposals. A summary of all questions from prospective contractors and agency responses to those questions will be posted by RFP number on the agency's Internet site, which is also provided on the RFP cover page.

*Prospective contractors are prohibited from communicating directly with any agency employee except as specified in this RFP, and no agency employee or representative other than the agency's project manager is authorized to provide any information or respond to any question or inquiry concerning this RFP. Prospective contractors may contact the agency's project manager solely via e-mail.*

The project manager may provide reasonable accommodations, including the provision of informational material in an alternative format, for qualified prospective contractors with a disability. Prospective contractors requiring accommodation shall submit requests in writing, with supporting documentation justifying the accommodation, to the project manager. The project manager reserves the right to grant or reject any request for accommodation.

Proposals will be treated confidentially until either the contract is awarded or recommended for award. Late proposals may be considered if that would be in the best interest of the agency. Errors in the proposals or nonresponsive proposals may be corrected during the negotiation process. However, prospective contractors are advised that they should endeavor to submit responsive, error-free proposals on time because failure to do so may result in rejection of their proposal. There will be no public opening of the proposals.

Prospective contractors that receive this RFP from the agency Web site or from any source other than the project manager, and wish to assure receipt of any addenda or additional materials related to this RFP, should immediately contact the project manager and provide their contact information so that RFP addenda and other communications related to this procurement can be sent to them. It is the prospective contractor's responsibility to note receipt of addenda in the proposal.

Receipt of sealed proposals for furnishing the services described herein is due no later than **2:30 p.m.,** *[Insert Time Zone]*, on the date indicated on the RFP cover page.

SEND ALL PROPOSALS TO THE CONTRACTING AGENCY ADDRESS IN FIGURE G.1.

| DELIVERED BY U.S. POSTAL SERVICE | DELIVERED BY ANY OTHER MEANS |
|---|---|
| RFP NO. | RFP NO. |
| | |
| | |
| | |

**Figure G.1   Address format.**

# Introduction

[Make an introductory statement, provide guidance regarding the intent to use the agency's standard contract, and refer to the scope of work for a description of the work to be performed.]

# Background

[Describe how the services fit into the using agency's function, legislation, or new initiatives that necessitate these services, other solutions tried in the past, etc. Reference to attachments may be helpful here.]

# Scope of Work

The scope of work describes the work to be performed by the successful contractor and is contained in "Attachment II — Scope of Work" in the Model Service Contract in this RFP.

# Contractor Selection Process

1. Proposals in one original and [**at least two**] copies are required in a sealed envelope or package from each prospective contractor. Each original proposal shall be signed and dated by an official authorized to bind the contractor. Unsigned proposals may be rejected.
2. The agency will review the proposals to determine whether they are responsive to the RFP and that responsible companies submitted them.
3. At the option of the agency, the evaluators may request oral presentations, discussions, or negotiations with any or all prospective contractors for the purpose of clarification or to amplify the materials presented in any part of

the proposal, or make adjustments to the details of the proposals. The evaluators may also request best and final offers (BAFOs) from one or more prospective contractors. However, prospective contractors are cautioned that the evaluators are not required to request clarification or conduct negotiations and may award a contract based on the original proposal. Therefore, all proposals should be complete and reflect the contractor's most favorable terms.

4. Proposals will be evaluated according to the criteria indicated below, and because the agency has determined that some criteria are more significant than others, weights have been assigned to the criteria to permit more emphasis being placed on the more significant criteria.

| Criteria | Weight |
|---|---|
| Past Performance | 10 |
| Risk Assessment | 20 |
| Project Plan | 30 |
| Life Cycle Cost | 40 |
| TOTAL | 100 |

5. **Debriefing:** Any company that plans to submit a proposal or has submitted a proposal and feels that its proposal was not given adequate consideration or given a fair evaluation may contact the agency project manager to request a debriefing.

6. **Protests:** Companies that received a debriefing, but continue to feel that their proposal was not given adequate consideration or a fair evaluation, may wish to protest the procedures for selection or the actual selection of a particular contractor. Contractors wishing to file a protest should abide by the following procedures. Failure to comply with the following procedures may result in a summary rejection of their protest:

   a. Any actual or prospective contractor that is aggrieved in connection with the solicitation or award of a contract may protest to the [*Insert Title and Contact Information for Agency Official Making Determination*]. The protest shall be submitted in writing within seven (7) working days after such aggrieved person or company knows or should have known of the facts giving rise thereto.

   b. Upon receipt of such a protest, the [*Insert Title of Agency Official Making Determination*] shall issue a written determination within ten (10) working days following receipt of the protest. The determination shall:

      (1) State the reason for the action taken;

      (2) Inform the protesting company that a request for further administrative appeal of an adverse decision must be submitted in writing to the [*Insert Organization or Agency Official Who will Consider Any Appeal of the Determination*] within seven (7) working days after receipt of the determination by the [*Insert Title of Agency Official Making Determination*].

7. The agency reserves the right to:
    a. Reject any or all submittals;
    b. Request clarification of any submitted information;
    c. Waive any informalities or irregularities in any proposal;
    d. Not enter into any contract;
    e. Not select any firm;
    f. Cancel this process at any time;
    g. Amend this process at any time;
    h. Interview firms prior to award;
    i. Enter into negotiations with one or more firms, or request a best and final offer (BAFO) or BAFOs;
    j. Award more than one contract if it is in the best interests of the agency;
    k. Issue similar solicitations in the future; or
    l. Request additional information from prospective contractors.
8. The response to this RFP shall consist of a completed Prospective Contractor Certification (included in this solicitation), a cover letter limited to a maximum of two pages including an executive summary of the proposal. The cover letter shall indicate whether or not the contractor had any contract terminated for default in the past five years. If no such termination for default has been experienced by the prospective contractor in the past five years, this fact shall be stated in the cover letter. Proposals shall be divided into six sections in the same sequence, and with the same titles, shown below. Proposals shall be prepared on 8½ × 11 paper; however, larger foldouts are acceptable for milestone charts and similar documentation. The font size shall be 10 point or larger.

## A. Past Performance

This section shall be limited to a maximum of six pages, shall include background information on the organization and provide details on company experience with similar projects. A list of references (including contact persons, organizations, e-mail and regular mail addresses, and telephone numbers) for each of the above similar projects shall be included.

If the prospective contractor's past performance with the agency requires response to Items 1 through 4 below, such responses shall be on a separate sheet and shall be excluded from the maximum number of pages indicated above:

1. If the prospective contractor or any prospective subcontractor contracted with the agency during the past 24 months, indicate the name of the agency, contract price, the contract number and project description, or other information available to identify the contract.
2. If the prospective contractor or prospective subcontractor has a staff member who was an employee of the agency during the past 24 months, or is currently

an agency employee, identify the individual by name, the agency previously or currently employed by, job title or position held, and separation date from the agency.

3. If the prospective contractor has had a contract terminated for default in the past five years, describe each such incident. Termination for default is defined as a notice to stop performance due to the prospective contractor's non-performance or poor performance and the issue of performance was either:

   a. Not litigated due to inaction on the part of the prospective contractor, or

   b. Litigated and such litigation determined that the prospective contractor was in default.

4. Submit full details of the terms for default including the other party's name, address, and telephone number. The agency will evaluate the facts and may, at its sole discretion, reject the proposal on the grounds of the prospective contractor's past experience. If no such termination for default has been experienced by the prospective contractor in the past five years, state so in the cover letter.

## B. Risk Assessment

This section shall be limited to a maximum of eight pages, and must identify all risks to the agency that must be addressed should the agency enter into a contract in furtherance of this project. The prospective contractors shall also identify measures that will be taken by the contractor or should be taken by the agency to mitigate the risks.

## C. Project Plan

This section shall be limited to a maximum of eight pages (not including resumes), and shall include a thorough description of the prospective contractor's approach to accomplishing the tasks outlined in the scope of work. This section shall include the proposed staffing, resumes for key staff members, and deployment and organization of personnel to be assigned to this project. A description of each task and contractor deliverables shall be included in this section, along with a schedule for accomplishing all contract milestones.

## D. Life Cycle Cost

Contract Price: The Life Cycle Cost Proposal shall be limited to a maximum of eight pages, and shall be submitted in a separate, sealed envelope or package and marked accordingly. The agency prefers to contract on a firm fixed cost basis whenever permitted by the nature of the work. However, it is understood that in some instances the proposal must be based on incurred expenses. In this latter case, the proposal shall include the following contractor costs:

1. Personnel costs (including job titles, hourly rates, and total hours)
2. Travel and subsistence expenses
3. Subcontractor costs (if any)
4. Other costs (e.g., office expenses) shall be identified by the nature of the costs
5. Not-to-exceed price (A total not-to-exceed [NTE] price representing the maximum amount for all work to be performed by the contractor and any subcontractors must be clearly indicated under this heading.)

Incremental Agency Costs: The contractors' proposals shall include, in addition to contract costs, all incremental agency costs associated with entering into the contract. Agency costs generally include the costs of required additional personnel to support the contracted effort, training, equipment, and facilities, as well as any other incremental costs associated with award and administration of the contract for the term of the contract, or a period of five years, whichever is longer. No contract costs are to be included in incremental agency costs.

A Life Cycle Cost Proposal format has been provided as Enclosure A. All prospective contractors shall include all contract life cycle costs, including the NTE cost or incremental agency costs to the agency should a particular proposal be accepted, or risk the possibility of having their proposal declared nonresponsive.

## Prospective Contractor Certification

By submitting this proposal, the prospective contractor certifies the following:

The Contractor Representative who signs below certifies that she/he has carefully read and understands the provisions of the solicitation and associated documents attached thereto, and hereby submits the attached proposal to perform the work specified therein, all in accordance with the true intent and meaning thereof. The Contractor Representative further understands and agrees that by signing this certification all of the following information in the certification is true and accurate to the best of her/his knowledge. If this certification cannot be made unequivocally, a written description of all instances wherein the prospective contractor cannot unequivocally make this certification is provided with this proposal:

Prospective contractor is:

☐ Sole Proprietor   ☐ Partnership   ☐ Corporation*   ☐ Joint Venture

☐ Other_____

* State of Incorporation _____

Other entities or individuals shall not be allowed to perform work or take data outside the United States without express advance written authorization from the agency's project manager.

The prospective contractor's insurance carrier(s) can provide insurance certificates as required within ten (10) calendar days following notice of award.

The proposed costs have been arrived at independently, without consultation, communication, or agreement, for the purpose of restricting competition as to any matter relating to such process with any other organization or with any competitor.

Unless otherwise required by law, the costs proposed have not been knowingly disclosed by the prospective contractor on a prior basis directly or indirectly to any other organization or to any competitor.

No attempt has been made, or will be made, by the prospective contractor to induce any other person or firm to submit or not to submit a proposal for the purpose of restricting competition.

Any contract and/or award arising from this RFP may be terminated by the agency if it is determined that gratuities of any kind were either offered to, or received by, any of the aforementioned officials or employees from the prospective contractor, the prospective contractor's agent(s), representative(s), or employee(s). Any contract and/or award arising from the RFP may also be terminated if it is determined that the contract and/or award was obtained by fraud, collusion, conspiracy, or other unlawful means, or if the contract and/or award conflicts with any statutory or Constitutional provision of the State of [*Insert State*] or of the United States.

Therefore, in compliance with this Request for Proposals, and subject to all conditions herein, the undersigned offers and agrees, that if this proposal is accepted within [*Insert Number of Days*] from the date of the opening, to furnish the subject services for a Firm Fixed/Not-to-Exceed (delete "Firm Fixed" or "Not-to-Exceed") Contract Price of $_____.

I further affirm that: neither I, nor to the best of my knowledge, information, and belief, the business identified below, or any of its officers, directors, partners, or any of its employees directly involved in obtaining or performing contracts with public bodies has been convicted of, or has had probation before judgment imposed pursuant to criminal proceedings, or has pleaded *nolo contendere* to a charge of bribery, attempted bribery, or conspiracy to bribe in violation of any state or federal law, **except as indicated on the attachment** [indicate the reasons why the affirmation cannot be given and list any conviction, plea, or imposition of probation before judgment with the date, court, official, or administrative body, the sentence or disposition, the name(s) of person(s) involved, and their current positions and responsibilities with the business]:

## *Attachments to Prospective Contractor Certification*

☐ A description of a potential instance(s) of collusion or violation is attached.
☐ A list of exceptions to the RFP is attached.
☐ A description of instances involving bribery, attempted bribery, or conspiracy to bribe in violation of any state or federal law is attached.

PROSPECTIVE CONTRACTOR NAME:_____

BUSINESS STREET ADDRESS: _____

CITY, STATE, AND ZIP+4: _____

PAYMENT ADDRESS (IF DIFFERENT): _____

CITY, STATE, AND ZIP+4: _____

TELEPHONE NUMBER: _____ FAX: _____

FEDERAL EMPLOYER IDENTIFICATION NUMBER: _____

E-MAIL: _____

BY:_____ TITLE: _____
        (SIGNATURE)
                                       DATE:_____

_____
(TYPED OR PRINTED NAME)

Unsigned certifications may result in a determination that the proposal is nonresponsive.

# Proposal Preparation and Submittal Instructions for Prospective Contractors

## *Proposal Preparation Instructions*

1. **EXCEPTIONS:** The agency intends to award a contract substantially in the form of and including the provisions of the attached Model Services Contract (MSC). Contractors that take exception to the terms and conditions do so at the risk that their proposals may be declared nonresponsive and not considered for contract award. By signing the PROSPECTIVE CONTRACTOR CERTIFICATION included in this RFP, the representative of the prospective contractor certifies that no exceptions are taken to the form of the MSC or to the provisions therein, unless such exceptions are fully disclosed in a document attached to the PROSPECTIVE CONTRACTOR CERTIFICATION.

2. **ORAL EXPLANATIONS:** The agency shall not be bound by oral explanations or instructions given at any time during the competitive process or after award.

3. **COST FOR PROPOSAL PREPARATION:** Any costs incurred by prospective contractors in preparing or submitting proposals as well as costs associated with any resultant presentations or negotiations are the prospective contractors' sole responsibility; the agency will not reimburse any prospective contractor for any costs incurred prior to contract award.

4. **TIME FOR ACCEPTANCE:** Each proposal shall state that it is a firm offer that may be accepted within a period of **[Insert at least 30]** days.

5. **RIGHT TO SUBMITTED MATERIAL:** All responses, inquiries, or correspondence relating to or in reference to the RFP, and all other reports, charts, displays, schedules, exhibits, and other documentation submitted by the prospective contractors shall become the property of the agency when received.

6. **PROSPECTIVE CONTRACTOR'S REPRESENTATIVE:** Each prospective contractor shall submit with its proposal the name, mailing address, e-mail address, and telephone number of the person(s) with authority to bind the firm and answer questions or provide clarification concerning the firm's proposal.

7. **PROPRIETARY INFORMATION:** Trade secrets or similar proprietary data that the prospective contractor does not wish disclosed to other than personnel involved in the proposal evaluation effort or post-award contract administration will be kept confidential to the extent permitted by the agency as follows: Each page shall be identified by the prospective contractor in boldface text at the top and bottom as **"PROPRIETARY"**.

A Life Cycle Cost Proposal format has been provided as Enclosure A (Figure G.2). All prospective contractors shall include all contract life cycle costs, including the NTE contract cost and the estimated incremental agency costs should the contractor's proposal be accepted, or risk the possibility of having its proposal declared nonresponsive. The cost categories may be adjusted as needed to correlate with the contractor's proposal.

| LIFE CYCLE COST PROPOSAL FORMAT | | | | | |
|---|---|---|---|---|---|
| **CONTRACT PRICE** | | | **ANNUAL PRICE** | | |
| **Cost Category** | **Units/Yr** | **Unit Cost** | **Year 1** | **Year 2** | **Year 3** |
| Job Title One | | | | | |
| Job Title Two | | | | | |
| Job Title Three | | | | | |
| Travel and Subsistence | | | | | |
| Subcontractor Costs | | | | | |
| All Other Contract Costs | | | | | |
| TOTAL NOT-TO-EXCEED CONTRACT PRICE | | | | | |
| **INCREMENTAL AGENCY COST** | | | **ANNUAL COST** | | |
| **Cost Category** | **Units/Yr** | **Unit Cost** | **Year 1** | **Year 2** | **Year 3** |
| Job Title One | | | | | |
| Job Title Two | | | | | |
| Job Title Three | | | | | |
| Training | | | | | |
| Equipment | | | | | |
| Facilities | | | | | |
| All Other Incremental Agency Costs | | | | | |
| TOTAL ESTIMATED AGENCY INCREMENTAL COSTS | | | | | |
| **TOTAL LIFE CYCLE COST** | | | | | |

**Figure G.2   Life cycle cost proposal format.**

### SHORT FORM MODEL SERVICES CONTRACT

This Contract, dated as of the last date executed by the **[Insert Agency Name]** is between the **[Insert Agency Name]**, hereinafter referred to as "Agency", and the Contractor indicated in the variable information table below, hereinafter referred to as "Contractor."

| VARIABLE INFORMATION TABLE | | | | | |
|---|---|---|---|---|---|
| | | Contract Number | | | |
| Term of This Contract (Complete Dates in Just One of the Following Three Shaded Rows) | | | | | |
| √ Below | Term Begins | | Term Completion Date | | |
| | On Following Date | | On Following Date | | |
| | Upon Receipt of Notice to Proceed | | Calendar Days Following Notice to Proceed | | |
| | Upon Execution by Agency | | Calendar Days Following Agency Contract Execution | | |
| | Agency Department | | FOB Point | | |
| Terms | | Basis of Price (Do Not √ More Than One of the Following Four Blocks) | | | |
| Price | | Fixed Price | Annual Price | Monthly Price | Hourly Rate |
| Not-to-Exceed Price | | √ If Reasonable Expenses Authorized in Addition to Hourly Rate | | | |
| Contractor Contact Information | | | Agency Contact Information | | |
| Contractor | | | Project Manager | | |
| Address | | | Address | | |
| City, State & ZIP | | | City, State & ZIP | | |
| Telephone | | | Telephone | | |
| Facsimile | | | Facsimile | | |

**Figure G.3   Short-form Model Services Contract (MSC).**

**WHEREAS**, Agency, through the Agency Department identified above, desires to have work described in the Attachment II–Scope of Work performed; and

**WHEREAS**, Contractor possesses the necessary qualifications to perform the work described herein.

**NOW THEREFORE BE IT AGREED** between the parties to this Contract that this Contract is subject to the provisions contained in the attachments which are incorporated in this Contract, and the provisions which are incorporated in this Contract by reference. Should there be a conflict between the provisions of this contract and any of the attachments, precedence shall be given first to the contract and then to the attachments in descending order by the numbers assigned to each attachment.

| Attachments Incorporated in Contract | Provisions Incorporated by Reference as if Attached Hereto |
| --- | --- |
| 1. Attachment III–Agency General Contract Terms and Conditions | 2. Agency Special Terms & Conditions available at the following Web Site: |
| 5. Attachment I–Contract Insurance Requirements | 3. Compliance with Federal Law available at the following Web Site: |
| 6. Attachment II–Scope of Work | 4. Following Contractor Certifications: |

| AGENCY | CONTRACTOR |
| --- | --- |
| By_____ | By_____ |
| Name_____ | Name_____ |
| Title_____ | Title_____ |

**Figure G.3 (continued)   Short-form Model Services Contract (MSC).**

# Attachment I: Contract Insurance Requirements

**Before the commencement of work, Contractor shall submit Certificates of Insurance and Endorsements evidencing that Contractor has obtained the following forms of coverage and minimal amounts specified:**

## A. *Minimum Scope of Insurance*

1. Commercial General Liability coverage (Insurance Services Office [ISO] "occurrence" form CG 0001 1185).
2. Automobile Liability Insurance — standard coverage offered by insurance carriers licensed to sell auto liability insurance in the State of *[Insert State]*.
3. Workers' Compensation Insurance as required by the Labor code and Employers Liability insurance.
4. Professional Liability Insurance (Delete if not contracting for professional services) — when the contract involves professional services such as engineering, architectural, legal, accounting, instructing, consulting, or other profession requiring a similar level of education or experience, professional liability insurance is required.

## B. *Minimum Limits of Insurance*

1. **General Liability**: At least $1,000,000 combined single limit **per occurrence** coverage for bodily injury, personal injury, and property damage, plus an annual aggregate of at least $2,000,000. If a general aggregate limit is used, then either the general aggregate limit shall apply separately to this project/location, or the general aggregate limit shall be **twice** the required per occurrence limit. The Contractor or Contractor's insurance carrier shall notify Agency in writing if incurred losses covered by the policy exceed 50 percent of the annual aggregate limit.
2. **Automobile Liability**: At least $100,000 to cover bodily injury for one person and $300,000 for two or more persons, and $50,000 to cover property damages. However, policy limits for construction projects shall be at least $1,000,000 combined single limit per accident for bodily injury and property damage for autos used by the Contractor to fulfill the requirements of this contract, and coverage shall be provided for "Any Auto," Code 1 as listed on the Accord form Certificate of Insurance.
3. **Workers' Compensation and Employer's Liability:** Workers' Compensation insurance up to policy limits and Employer Liability insurance each with policy limits of at least $1,000,000 for bodily injury or disease.
4. **Professional Liability Insurance (Delete if not contracting for professional services):** Professional Liability insurance covering professional services shall

be provided in an amount of at least $1,000,000 per occurrence or $1,000,000 on a claims made basis. However, if coverage is written on a claims made basis, the policy shall be endorsed to provide at least a two-year extended reporting provision.

## C. Deductibles and Self-Insured Retentions

Any deductibles or self-insured retention must be declared on certificates of insurance and approved in writing by the Agency. At the option of the Agency, either the insurer shall reduce or eliminate such deductibles or self-insured retention as respects the Agency, its officers, officials, employees, agents, and volunteers, or the Contractor shall procure a bond guaranteeing payment of losses and related investigations, claims administration and defense expenses.

## D. Other Insurance Provisions

1. General liability insurance policies shall be endorsed to state:
   a. The Agency, its officers, officials, employees, agents, and volunteers are to be covered as insured as respects liability arising out of activities performed by or at the direction of the Contractor, including products and completed operations of the Contractor; premises owned, occupied, or used by the Contractor; or automobiles owned, leased, hired, or borrowed by Contractor. The coverage shall contain no special limitations on the scope of protection afforded to the Agency, its officers, officials, employees, agents, or volunteers.
   b. Contractor's insurance coverage shall be primary insurance as respects the Agency, its officers, officials, employees, agents, and volunteers. Any insurance or self-insurance maintained by the Agency, its officers, officials, employees, agents, or volunteers shall be in excess of the Contractor's insurance and shall not contribute with it.
   c. Contractor's insurance shall apply separately to each insured against whom claim is made or suit is brought, except with respect to the limits of the insurer's liability.

## E. Acceptability of Insurance Carriers

Insurance shall be placed with insurers who are licensed to sell insurance in the State of [*Insert State*] and that possess a Best's rating of no less than A-: VII. If the Contractor's insurance carrier is not licensed to sell insurance in the State of [*Insert State*], then the carrier must possess a Best rating of at least A: VIII. (For Best ratings, go to http://www.ambest.com/)

## F. Verification of Coverage

Contractor shall furnish the Agency **certificates of insurance** and original **endorsements** affecting coverage required by this clause. All certificates of insurance and endorsements shall be received and approved in writing by the Agency before work under the contract begins. The Agency reserves the right to require complete, certified copies of all insurance policies required by this contract.

Certificates of insurance shall state that the insuring agency agrees to endeavor to mail to Agency written notice 30 days before any of the insurance policies described herein are cancelled. Contractor agrees to notify Agency within two working days of any notice from an insuring agency that cancels, suspends, or reduces in coverage or policy limits the insurance coverages described herein.

## G. Subcontractors

Contractor shall include all subcontractors as insured under its policies or require all subcontractors to be insured under their own policies. If subcontractors are insured under their own policies, they shall be subject to all the requirements stated herein, including providing the Agency certificates of insurance and endorsements prior to beginning work under this contract.

## Attachment II: Scope of Work

Unless indicated otherwise herein, the Contractor shall furnish all labor, materials, transportation, supervision, and management, and pay all taxes required to complete the project described below:

| Meetings/Milestones/Deliverables | | |
|---|---|---|
| **Item No.** | **Meeting/Milestone/Deliverable Title** | **Due Date** |
| | | |
| | | |
| | | |
| | | |
| | | |
| | | |
| | | |
| | | |
| | | |
| | | |
| | | |
| | | |
| | | |
| **ACCOUNT INFORMATION** | | |
| **Account Number** | **Project Name** | **Funding** |
| | | $_____ |
| | | $_____ |

**Figure G.4    Meetings/milestones/deliverables and account information.**

## Attachment III: Agency Services Contract Terms and Conditions

[NOTE: For "Agency," substitute "State," "Commonwealth," "Department," "University," "County," "City," "District," etc., as applicable.]

1. **TERM.** The term of this contract is reflected in the Variable Information Table.

2. **TERMINATION FOR DEFAULT.** If, through any cause, the Contractor shall fail to fulfill in a timely and proper manner the obligations under this contract, other than for the instances listed below due to "Force Majeure," the Agency shall thereupon have the right to terminate this contract by providing a written notice (show cause notice) to the Contractor requiring a written response due within ten days from receipt of the written notice as to why the contract should not be terminated for default. Should the Contractor fail to respond to such show cause notice, or if the Agency determines that the reasons provided by the Contractor for failure of the Contractor to fulfill its contractual obligations do not justify continuation of the contractual relationship, the Agency shall terminate the contract for default on the date indicated in the show cause notice.

   In addition, in the event of default by the Contractor under this contract, the Agency may immediately cease doing business with the Contractor, immediately terminate for cause all existing contracts the Agency has with the Contractor, and debar the Contractor from doing future business with the Agency.

   Upon the Contractor filing a petition for bankruptcy or the entering of a judgment of bankruptcy by or against the Contractor, the Agency may immediately terminate, for cause, this contract and all other existing contracts the Contractor has with the Agency, and debar the Contractor from doing future business with the Agency.

   The Agency may terminate this contract for cause without penalty or further obligation at any time following contract execution, if any person significantly involved in initiating, negotiating, securing, drafting, or creating the contract on behalf of the Agency is at any time while the contract or any extension thereof is in effect, an employee or agent of any other party to the contract in any capacity or consultant to any other party of the contract with respect to the subject matter of the contract. Additionally, the Agency may recoup any fee or commission paid or due to any person significantly involved in initiating, negotiating, securing, drafting, or creating the contract on behalf of the Agency from any other party to the contract.

3. **FORCE MAJEURE.** Neither party shall be deemed to be in default of its obligations hereunder if and so long as it is prevented from performing such obligations by any act of war, hostile foreign action, nuclear explosion, riot,

strikes, civil insurrection, earthquake, hurricane, tornado, or other catastrophic natural event or act of God. Should there be such an occurrence that impacts the ability of either party to perform their responsibilities under this contract, the nonperforming party shall give immediate written notice to the other party to explain the cause and probable duration of any such nonperformance.

4. **TERMINATION FOR CONVENIENCE.** Either party to this contract may terminate this contract at any time without cause by providing the other party with sixty (60) days' advance notice in writing.

5. **CONTRACTOR REIMBURSEMENT.** The work shall be performed for the Fixed Price, Annual Price, Monthly Price, or Hourly Rate as indicated above in the variable information table, but shall not exceed the Not-to-Exceed Price if included in the variable information table. Reasonable expenses are authorized in addition to the Hourly Rate if both the Hourly Rate block and the block authorizing Reasonable Expenses are checked in the variable information table. Payment shall be made after the Agency's project manager or designee reviews and approves the work and after submittal of an invoice by the Contractor.

6. **PAYMENT TERMS.** Payment terms are indicated in the Variable Information Table. The due date indicated is based upon the number of days following receipt of a correct invoice (or invoices) or acceptance of services, whichever is later. Invoices may not be submitted more frequently than once monthly. The using Agency is responsible for all payments to the Contractor under the contract. Payment by some agencies may be made by procurement card and they shall be accepted by the Contractor for payment if the Contractor accepts that card (Visa, MasterCard, etc.) from other customers. If payment is made by procurement card, then payment may be processed immediately by the Contractor.

7. **SET-OFF.** In the event that the Contractor owes the Agency any sum under the terms of this contract, any other contract, pursuant to any judgment, or pursuant to any law, the Agency may set-off the sum owed to the Agency against any sum owed by the Agency to the Contractor at the Agency's sole discretion, unless otherwise required by law. The Contractor agrees that this provision constitutes proper and timely notice.

8. **AGENCY PROJECT MANAGER.** The Agency's project manager or designee for this undertaking who will receive payment invoices and answer questions related to the coordination of this undertaking is identified above in the variable information table.

9. **INDEPENDENT CONTRACTOR.** The Contractor shall be considered an independent contractor and as such shall be wholly responsible for the work to be performed and for the supervision of its employees. The Contractor represents that it has, or will secure at its own expense, all personnel required in performing the services under this agreement. Such employees

shall not be employees of, or have any individual contractual relationship with, the Agency. The Contractor shall be exclusively responsible for payment of employees and subcontractors for all wages and salaries, taxes, withholding payments, penalties, fees, fringe benefits, professional liability insurance premiums, contributions to insurance and pension, or other deferred compensation, including but not limited to Workers' Compensation and Social Security obligations, and licensing fees, etc. and the filing of all necessary documents, forms, and returns pertinent to all the foregoing.

10. **CONFIDENTIALITY AND OWNERSHIP.** The Agency retains the exclusive right of ownership to the work, products, inventions, and confidential information produced for the Agency by the Contractor, and the Contractor shall not disclose any information, whether developed by the Contractor or given to the Contractor by the Agency.

11. **INDEMNIFICATION.** The Contractor shall indemnify, defend, and hold harmless the Agency and its officers, representatives, agents, employees, successors and assigns from and against any and all (1) claims arising directly or indirectly, in connection with the contract, including the acts of commission or omission (collectively, the "Acts") of the Contractor or Contractor Parties; and (2) liabilities, damages, losses, costs, and expenses, including but not limited to, attorneys' and other professionals' fees arising, directly or indirectly, in connection with claims, Acts, or the contract. The Contractor shall use counsel reasonably acceptable to the Agency to carry out its obligations under this section. The Contractor's obligations under this section to indemnify, defend, and hold harmless against claims include claims concerning confidentiality or the proprietary nature of any part or all of the proposal or any records, any intellectual property rights, other proprietary rights of any person or entity, copyrighted or uncopyrighted compositions, secret processes, patented or unpatented inventions, articles or appliances furnished or used in the performance of the contract. The Contractor shall reimburse the Agency for any and all damages to the real or personal property of the Agency caused by the Acts of the Contractor or any Contractor parties. The Agency shall give the Contractor reasonable notice of any such claims. The Contractor's duties under this section shall remain fully in effect and binding in accordance with the terms and conditions of the contract, without being lessened or compromised in any way, even where the Contractor is alleged or is found to have merely contributed in part to the Acts giving rise to the claims and/ or where the Agency is alleged or is found to have contributed to the Acts giving rise to the claims. The rights provided in this section for the benefit of the Agency shall encompass the recovery of attorney's and other professionals' fees expended in pursuing a claim against a third party. This section shall survive the termination, cancellation, or expiration of the contract, and shall not be limited by reason of any insurance coverage.

12. **INSURANCE.** Contractor shall procure and maintain for the duration of this contract, insurance against claims for injuries to persons or damages to property that may arise from, or be in connection with the performance of the work hereunder by Contractor, Contractor's agents, representatives, employees, and subcontractors. At the very least, Contractor shall maintain the insurance coverages, limits of coverage, and other insurance requirements as described in Attachment I to this contract.

13. **AMENDMENTS.** This contract may be amended only by written amendments duly executed by the Agency and the Contractor.

14. **WAIVER OF RIGHTS.** It is the intention of the parties hereto that from time to time either party may waive any of their rights under this contract unless contrary to law. Any waiver by either party hereto of rights arising in connection with this contract shall not be deemed to be a waiver with respect to any other rights or matters.

15. **COMPLIANCE WITH LAWS.** The Contractor shall comply with all laws, ordinances, codes, rules, regulations, and licensing requirements that are applicable to the conduct of its business, including those of federal, state, and local agencies having jurisdiction and/or authority.

16. **NONDISCRIMINATION.** During the performance of this contract, the Contractor and its subcontractors shall not deny the Contractor's benefits to any person on the basis of religion, color, ethnic group identification, sex, age, physical or mental disability, nor shall they discriminate unlawfully against any employee or applicant for employment because of race, religion, color, national origin, ancestry, physical or mental disability, medical condition, martial status, age (over 40), or sex. Contractor shall ensure that the evaluation and treatment of employees and applicants for employment are free of such discrimination. Contractor and its subcontractors shall comply with the provisions of all applicable state and federal laws regarding employment rights.

17. **CONTRACTOR'S STANDARD OF CARE.** The Agency has relied upon the professional ability and training of the Contractor as a material inducement to enter into this contract. Contractor hereby warrants that all of Contractor's work shall be performed in accordance with generally accepted and applicable professional practices and standards as well as the requirements of applicable federal, state, and local laws, it being understood that acceptance of Contractor's work by Agency shall not operate as a waiver or release.

18. **CARE OF PROPERTY.** The Contractor agrees that it shall be responsible for the proper custody and care of any property furnished it for use in connection with the performance of this contract or purchased by it for this contract and will reimburse the Agency for loss of or damage to such property.

19. **PERFORMANCE EVALUATION.** The Contractor's performance under this project may be evaluated after completion of this contract.

**20. INSPECTION OF WORK AND PROJECT SITE.**
- The Agency shall have the right to inspect the work being performed at any and all reasonable times during the term of the contract. This right shall extend to any subcontracts, and Contractor shall include provisions ensuring such access in all its contracts or subcontracts entered into pursuant to this contract.
- The Agency shall have the right to inspect the project site at any and all reasonable times after completion of the contract to ensure compliance with the "Contractor's Standard of Care" and the "Nondiscrimination" provisions of this contract.

**21. APPLICABLE LAW AND FORUM.** This contract shall be construed and interpreted according to the laws of the state of the awarding government agency.

**22. SUCCESSORS AND ASSIGNS.** This contract and all of its provisions shall apply to and bind the successors and assigns of the parties hereto. No assignment or transfer of this contract or any part hereof, rights hereunder, or interest herein by the Contractor shall be valid unless and until it is approved in writing by the awarding agency and made subject to such reasonable terms and conditions as the Agency may impose.

**23. AUDIT, EMPLOYEE INTERVIEWS, AND DOCUMENT RETENTION.** Contractor agrees that the Agency, or its designated representative, shall have the right to review and to copy any records and supporting documentation and have access to Contractor personnel pertaining to the performance of this contract. Contractor agrees to maintain such records for possible audit for a minimum of three years after final payment, unless a longer period of records retention is stipulated. Contractor agrees to allow the Agency's auditor (or auditors) access to such records during normal business hours and to allow interviews of any employees who might reasonably have information related to such records. Further, Contractor agrees to include a similar right to the Agency to audit and interview staff in any subcontract related to performance of this contract. If at any time the Agency determines that a cost for which payment has been made is a disallowed cost, such as overpayment, the Agency shall notify the Contractor in writing of the disallowance or claim for unallowable costs. The Agency shall also state the means of correction, which may be, but shall not be limited to, adjustment of any future claim submitted by the Contractor by the amount of the disallowance, or to require repayment of the disallowed amount by the Contractor.

**24. CONFLICT OF INTEREST.**
- a. Current Employees or Officers of the Agency:
  - No current employee or officer of the Agency shall engage in any employment, activity, or enterprise from which the officer or employee receives compensation or has a financial interest and which is sponsored or funded by the Agency unless the employment, activity, or

enterprise is required as a condition of the regular employment with the Agency.

- No current employee or officer of the Agency shall contract on his or her own behalf as an independent contractor with any department of the Agency to provide goods or services.

b. Former Employees or Officers of the Agency:

- For a period of two years following the termination of employment with the Agency, no former employee or officer of the Agency may enter into a contract in which he or she engaged in any of the negotiations, transactions, planning, arrangements, or any part of the decision-making process relevant to the contracts while employed in any capacity by the Agency.

- For a period of twelve (12) months following the termination of employment with the Agency, no former employee or officer of the Agency may enter into a contract with any department of the Agency if he or she was employed by that Agency department in a policy-making position in the same general subject area as the proposed contract within the twelve-month period prior to his or her terminating employment with the Agency.

## 25. CONTRACTOR INTEGRITY.

a. The Contractor shall maintain the highest standards of integrity in the performance of the contract and shall take no action in violation of state or federal laws, regulations, or other requirements that govern contracting with the Agency.

b. The Contractor shall not disclose to others any confidential or proprietary information gained by virtue of the contract.

c. The Contractor shall not, in connection with this or any other agreement with the Agency, directly, or indirectly, offer, confer, or agree to confer any pecuniary benefit on anyone as consideration for the decision, opinion, recommendation, vote, other exercise of discretion, or violation of a known legal duty by any officer or employee of the Agency.

d. The Contractor shall not, in connection with this or any other agreement with the Agency, directly, or indirectly, offer, give, or agree, or promise to give to anyone any gratuity for the benefit of or at the direction or request of any officer or employee of the Agency.

e. Except with the written consent of the Agency, neither the Contractor nor anyone in privity with him or her shall accept or agree to accept from, or give or agree to give to, any person, any gratuity from any person in connection with the performance of under the Contract except as provided herein.

f. Except with the consent of the Agency, the Contractor shall not have a financial interest in any other contractor, subcontractor, or supplier providing services, labor, or material on this project.

g. The Contractor, upon being informed that any violation of these provisions has occurred or may occur, shall immediately notify the Agency in writing.

h. The Contractor, by execution of this contract and by the submission of any bills or invoices for payment pursuant thereto, certifies and represents that she or he has not violated any of these provisions.

i. The Contractor, upon the inquiry or request of the Agency or any of the Agency's agents or representatives, shall provide, or if appropriate, make promptly available for inspection or copying, any information of any type or form deemed relevant by the Agency to the Contractor's integrity or responsibility, as those terms are defined by the Agency's statutes, regulations, or management directives. Such information may include but shall not be limited to, the Contractor's business or financial records, document or files of any type, or form that refers to or concerns the contract. Such information shall be retained by the Contractor for a period of three years beyond the termination of the contract unless otherwise provided by law.

j. For violation of any of the above provisions, the Agency may terminate this and any other agreement with the Contractor, claim liquidated damages in an amount equal to the value of anything received in breach of these provisions, claim damages for all expenses incurred in obtaining another Contractor to complete performance hereunder, and debar and suspend the Contractor from doing business with the Agency. These rights and remedies are cumulative, and the use or nonuse of any one shall not preclude the use of all or any other. These rights and remedies are in addition to those the Agency may have under law, statute, regulation, or otherwise.

26. **PAYMENT OF TAXES.** By execution of this contract, the Contractor certifies that it and all of its affiliates, if applicable, collect all appropriate taxes and remit them to the applicable state or local government agency.

27. **OFFICIALS NOT TO PROSPER.** No members of the governing body of the state or local public agency, and no other officer, elected or appointed official, employee, or agent of the state or local public agency who exercise any functions or responsibilities in connection with the carrying out of the project to which this contract pertains, shall have any personal interest, direct or indirect, in this contract. No member of the governing body of the locality in which the project area is situated, or other public official of such locality, who exercises any functions or responsibilities in the review or approval of the carrying out of the work to which this project pertains, shall have any personal interest, direct or indirect, in this contract. No state official, member of or Delegate to the Congress of the United States, and no Resident Commissioner shall be admitted to any share or part of the contract or to any benefit to arise therefrom.

28. **COPYRIGHTS.** Where copyrights are an essential element of performance under this contract, the Contractor certifies that it has appropriate systems and controls in place to ensure that Agency funds will not be used in the performance of this contract for acquisition, operation, or maintenance of literature or computer software in violation of copyright laws.

29. **BUDGET CONTINGENCY.** It is mutually agreed that if the approved budget for the current year and/or any subsequent years covered under this contract does not appropriate sufficient funds for the project, this contract shall no longer be in force and effect. In this event, the Agency shall have no liability to pay any funds whatsoever to the Contractor or to furnish any other consideration under this contract, and Contractors shall not be obligated to perform any provisions of this contract. If funding for any fiscal year is reduced or deleted by the approved budget for purposes of this project, the Agency shall have the option to either cancel this contract with no liability occurring to the Agency, or offer a contract amendment to the Contractor reflecting the reduced amount.

30. **COUNTERPARTS.** The parties to this contract agree that this contract has been or may be executed in several counterparts, each of which shall be deemed an original and all such counterparts shall together constitute one and the same instrument.

31. **SEVERABILITY.** If any provision of this contract is held invalid or unenforceable by any court of final jurisdiction, it is the intent of the parties that all other provisions of this contract be construed to remain fully valid, enforceable, and binding on the parties.

32. **NOTICES.** For any notice applicable to the contract to be effective, it must be made in writing and sent to the Contractor or Agency representative at the address indicated in the variable information table unless such party has notified the other party, in accordance with the provisions of this section, of a revised mailing address. Such notices shall be sent via certified mail or an alternative mode that requires a signature by the recipient. This notice requirement does not apply to any notices that this contract expressly authorizes to be made orally.

33. **TITLES, HEADINGS, OR CAPTIONS.** This contract includes titles, headings, and captions appearing herein that are for convenience only, and such titles, headings, and captions shall not affect the contractual interpretation or meaning of this contract.

34. **ENTIRE AGREEMENT AND SURVIVAL OF PROVISIONS BEYOND THE CONTRACT TERM.** This contract and any documents incorporated specifically by reference or attachment represent the entire agreement between the parties and supersede all prior oral or written statements or agreements.

All promises, requirements, terms, conditions, provisions, representations, guarantees, and warranties contained herein shall survive the contract expiration or termination date unless specifically provided otherwise herein, or unless superseded by applicable federal or state statutes of limitation.

# *Appendix H*

# **Reference Checklist**

| REFERENCE CHECKLIST | |
|---|---|
| Contractor's Name | |
| Reference's Name | |
| Reference's Agency | |
| Reference's Telephone Number | |
| Referenced Project | |
| **Did the Contractor Perform Well on the Technical Requirements?** | |
| | |
| **Did the Contractor Meet the Schedule Requirements?** | |
| | |
| **Was the Project Completed within the Budget?** | |
| | |
| **Did the Contractor Provide Adequate Customer Service?** | |
| | |
| **Was the Contractor's Follow-Up After Project Completion Acceptable?** | |
| | |
| **Would You Use This Contractor Again for a Similar Project?** | |
| | |
| Signature & Date of Person Taking Reference | |
| Typed or Printed Name of Reference Taker | |

*Appendix I*

# Evaluation of Proposals in Response to RFP

| 1 Evaluation of Proposals in Response to RFP<br><br>[Project Name]<br><br>[NOTE: ENSURE THAT EVALUATION FACTORS MATCH EXACTLY THE<br>EVALUATION FACTORS IN THE RFP.] | | | |
|---|---|---|---|
| **EVALUATION FACTOR**<br>**(From RFP Selection Criteria)** | **PROPOSAL**<br>**A** | **PROPOSAL**<br>**B** | **PROPOSAL**<br>**C** |
| **Past Performance**<br><br>◊ Corporate experience with similar projects<br><br>◊ Feedback from references regarding qualifications<br>to succeed on this project | | | |
| **Financial Stability**<br><br>◊ Evaluation of contractor's financial stability based<br>on evaluation of most recent financial statements or<br>similar evidence | | | |
| **Risk Assessment**<br><br>◊ Identification of risks to the County associated with<br>this project<br><br>◊ Evaluation of the prospective contractor's proposed<br>approach to reducing, mitigating, or eliminating<br>these risks | | | |
| **Project Plan**<br><br>◊ Evaluation of the prospective contractor's plan<br>for accomplishing the tasks outlined in the<br>Scope of Work<br><br>◊ Determination of contractor's understanding of the<br>problem based on the contractor's description of each<br>project task, contract deliverables, and the project<br>schedule submitted by the prospective contractor<br><br>◊ Evaluation of contractor's proposed staffing,<br>deployment, and organization of personnel to be<br>assigned to this project as well as minimum<br>qualifications such as education, certification, and<br>experience on similar projects for personnel in key<br>positions<br><br>◊ Evaluation of contractor's qualifications and<br>experience of all executive, managerial, legal, and<br>professional personnel to be assigned to this project<br><br>◊ Evaluation of contractor's proposed project schedule<br>and methodology for monitoring performance<br>according to the schedule milestones | | | |

| | | | |
|---|---|---|---|
| **Outsourcing**<br><br>◊ Evaluate risks associated with reliance on subcontractors located outside the United States<br><br>◊ Evaluation of subcontractor qualifications<br><br>◊ Evaluate risks associated with over reliance on subcontracted work | | | |
| **Life Cycle Cost**<br><br>◊ Evaluation of all Agency costs associated with acceptance of the contractor's proposal. Life Cycle Costs include the contract price plus all other project costs including the need for added personnel, equipment, space, training, disposal of equipment or chemicals, eventual contract closeout, and any other costs associated with the contract. | | | |

# *Appendix J*

# Tables Used in Proposal Evaluation Process

The forms used in the example of a source selection using weighted evaluation factors in Chapter 5, "Management of Pre-Proposal Communications and Evaluation of Proposals," are provided in this Appendix J along with instructions for completing the forms. These forms are also included on the compact disc (CD) accompanying this book to give the reader an opportunity to download the tables and either use them as-is, adapt them for use in evaluating proposals in the actual work environment, or adapt them for use in an academic exercise. Although the forms in Chapter 5 contained proposal scoring data, the forms in this appendix are blank, and they are provided in the sequence that one would expect them to be completed during an actual proposal evaluation situation. To maximize the clarity of the instructions for completing the forms, the forms are on one dedicated page and the instructions for completing that form are on the opposite dedicated page without consideration of the fact that neither all the forms nor instructions require an entire page.

## Instructions for Completing Information in Form Used in Evaluation of Proposals Using Weighted Criteria

The form in Figure J.1 may be used in the evaluation of proposals when the contracting agency has elected to use weighted criteria. Weighted criteria are generally used whenever the contracting professional or project manager makes the determination that one or more of the criteria are more important than another criterion or other criteria. The difference in importance of one criterion over another, or others, is reflected by the weights assigned to the individual criterion.

Whenever weighted criteria are to be used in evaluating proposals, this fact, along with full details on the weighting, should be included in the Request for Proposals (RFP). Great care should be taken to ensure that the selection criteria, or proposal evaluation criteria, provided in the RFP, or other form of solicitation document, is repeated exactly in the "Criterion" section of the form. Should the individual who drafts the solicitation use a standard solicitation template provided by the contracting agency and elect to make changes to selection criteria provided in the solicitation template, the exact changes must also be made to the criteria on this form.

The weights included in the "Weight" column should reflect the importance of each criterion. Should it be determined that a contractor's risk assessment is twice as important as their past performance, while past performance is twice as important as outsourcing, then risk assessment might be assigned a weight of 40, past performance assigned a weight of 20, and outsourcing assigned a weight of 10. Traditionally, the total of weights for all the criteria equals 100. The weights used by the proposal evaluation committee should exactly equal the weights described in the solicitation.

Should there be a deviation between the criteria or the weights in the solicitation and the criteria or the weights used by the proposal evaluation committee, there could be serious consequences should there be a protest over the selection of the successful contractor. The individual designated to investigate the complaints in the protest and the actual practices of the proposal evaluation committee may feel compelled to make a determination that the selection decision be changed in response to the protest.

**Weighted Criteria:** The local government agency has elected to assign weights to the above evaluation criteria. The weights assigned to each of the criterion are indicated in the table below:

| Criterion | Weight |
|---|---|
| Past Performance | |
| Financial Stability | |
| Risk Assessment | |
| Project Plan | |
| Outsourcing | |
| Life Cycle Cost | |
| TOTAL WEIGHT | 100 |

**Figure J.1   Weighted criteria used to evaluate proposals.**

## Instruction for Calculating Weighted Life Cycle Cost Score

Calculation of the weighted life cycle cost score is accomplished as follows:

1. Enter the name of the contractor submitting each of the proposals in the column headed, "Proposal."
2. Enter the life cycle cost proposed by each of the contractors in the column entitled "Proposed Life Cycle Cost."
3. Calculate the percentage of the proposed life cycle cost by adding all the proposed life cycle costs in the "Proposed Life Cycle Cost" column and dividing that sum by the proposed life cycle cost for each contractor, and then enter the quotient for each contractor in the column entitled "Percentage of Total Life Cycle Cost."
4. The inverse is calculated by subtracting the percentage of the total life cycle cost from 100. This is a necessary step to adjust the weighted life cycle cost score to obtain a weight wherein the high score is advantageous to the contracting agency. Enter the difference in the "Inverse" Column.
5. The weighted life cycle cost score (WLCC) is equal to the weight (W) for the lowest life cycle cost proposal. To calculate the weighted score for the higher life cycle cost proposals, it is necessary to divide the weight (W) by the inverse (I) for the lowest life cycle cost proposal (W ÷ I = WLCC) and then multiplying the inverse for the higher life cycle cost proposals by the quotient. Enter the result for each contractor in the "Weighted Life Cycle Cost Score" column.

| WEIGHTED LIFE CYCLE COST SCORE TABLE | | | Weight (W) | |
|---|---|---|---|---|
| Proposal | Proposed Life Cycle Cost | Percentage of Total Life Cycle Cost | Inverse (I) | Weighted Life Cycle Cost Score (WPS) |
| | | | | |
| | | | | |
| | | | | |

**Figure J.2   Weighted life cycle cost score table.**

## Instructions for Calculating Weighted Scores for Factors other than Life Cycle Cost

Calculation of weighted scores for factors other than cost is accomplished as follows:

1. Enter the possible weights (other than for pricing) in the weight column, ensuring that the number of rows equals the number of proposals being ranked. In this example, there are three rows (representing three proposals) for each of three possible weights. In this example, the weights used are limited to: 5, 10, and 20.

2. The multiplier is calculated by dividing the weight by the highest possible ranking. In this example, the weight of 5 is divided by the ranking of 3 to calculate the multiplier of 1.67. The multiplier of 1.67 is used for all rankings with a corresponding weight of 5. The remaining multipliers are calculated in the same manner, resulting in a multiplier of 3.33 calculated by dividing 10 by 3, and a multiplier of 6.67 calculated by dividing 20 by 3.

3. The rankings are merely the possible rankings of 1, 2, and 3 resulting from the ranking of three proposals.

4. The weighted score is calculated by multiplying the ranking by the multiplier and rounding to the first decimal place.

| WEIGHTED FACTOR SCORE TABLE | | | |
|---|---|---|---|
| Weight | Multiplier | Ranking | Weighted Score |
| 5 | 1.67 | 3 | 5.0 |
| 5 | 1.67 | 2 | 3.3 |
| 5 | 1.67 | 1 | 1.7 |
| 10 | 3.33 | 3 | 10.0 |
| 10 | 3.33 | 2 | 6.7 |
| 10 | 3.33 | 1 | 3.3 |
| 20 | 6.67 | 3 | 20.0 |
| 20 | 6.67 | 2 | 13.3 |
| 20 | 6.67 | 1 | 6.7 |

**Figure J.3   Weighted factor score table.**

## Instructions for Completing Form Used by an Individual Evaluation Committee Member to Record the Ranking of Proposals at the Criteria Level

Completion of the form used by an individual Evaluation Committee member to record the ranking of proposals at the criteria level is accomplished as follows:

1. Enter the name of the Evaluation Committee member to the right of the cell labeled "Name of Evaluator."
2. Evaluate each proposal at the criteria level according to the criteria in the solicitation that have been duplicated exactly in the "Criteria" column of this form.
3. The ranking of the highest ranked proposal, for each criterion, is equal to the number of proposals evaluated.
4. The ranking of the second highest ranked proposal, for each criterion, is equal to the number of proposals evaluated minus one.
5. The ranking of each of the next highest ranked proposals, for each criterion, is equal to the number of proposals evaluated minus the number of proposals that were ranked higher.
6. The ranking of the lowest ranked proposal, for each criterion, is the number one.
7. Enter the ranking for each criterion in the appropriate column for the proposing contractor and the row for the applicable criterion.

## Second Form for Recording the Weighted Scores for Each Proposal by Evaluation Committee Member based on Weighted Criteria and Ranked Proposals

A separate table is required for each member of the evaluation committee.

| | Name of Evaluator | | |
|---|---|---|---|
| CRITERIA | PROPOSAL A | PROPOSAL B | PROPOSAL C |
| Past Performance | | | |
| Financial Stability | | | |
| Risk Assessment | | | |
| Project Plan | | | |
| Outsourcing | | | |
| TOTAL SCORES | | | |

Figure J.4   First form for individual evaluation.

## Instructions for Recording the Weighted Scores for Each Proposal by Evaluation Committee Member Based on Weighted Criteria and Ranked Proposals

Completion of the form used to record the weighted scores for each proposal by Evaluation Committee member based on weighted criteria and ranked proposals is accomplished as follows:

1. Enter the name of the Evaluation Committee member to the right of the cell labeled "Name of Evaluator."
2. Enter [**Contractor Name**] to the right of the cell labeled "CONTRACTOR" for each applicable contractor that submitted a proposal that was evaluated.
3. Enter the ranking for each criterion, for each contractor under the applicable contractor name.
4. Enter the weight for each criterion, which is identical for each contractor, in the "Weight" column.
5. Calculate the "Weighted Score" for each criterion, for each contractor, by multiplying the ranking for that criterion by the "Weight." Enter the product in the "Weighted Score" column for each criterion, for each contractor.
6. Calculate the "Total Weighted Score" for each contractor by adding the "Weighted Score" for each criterion for the applicable contractor, and enter the sum in the space to the right of the cell labeled "Total Weighted Score" for each of the applicable contractors.

| WEIGHTED SCORES BY EVALUATOR | | | |
|---|---|---|---|
| | Name of Evaluator | | |
| **CONTRACTOR** | | | |
| **CRITERIA** | **RANKING** | **WEIGHT** | **WEIGHTED SCORE** |
| Past Performance | | | |
| Financial Stability | | | |
| Risk Assessment | | | |
| Project Plan | | | |
| Outsourcing | | | |
| Proposed Life Cycle Cost | | | |
| | | TOTAL WEIGHTED SCORE | |
| **CONTRACTOR** | | | |
| **CRITERIA** | **RANKING** | **WEIGHT** | **WEIGHTED SCORE** |
| Past Performance | | | |
| Financial Stability | | | |
| Risk Assessment | | | |
| Project Plan | | | |
| Outsourcing | | | |
| Proposed Life Cycle Cost | | | |
| | | TOTAL WEIGHTED SCORE | |
| **CONTRACTOR** | | | |
| **CRITERIA** | **RANKING** | **WEIGHT** | **WEIGHTED SCORE** |
| Past Performance | | | |
| Financial Stability | | | |
| Risk Assessment | | | |
| Project Plan | | | |
| Outsourcing | | | |
| Proposed Life Cycle Cost | | | |
| | | TOTAL WEIGHTED SCORE | |

**Figure J.5    Weighted scores by evaluator.**

## Instructions for Summarizing the Weighted Scores from All the Proposal Evaluation Committee Members for All Proposals

Completion of the form used to record the combined weighted scores for each proposal by all the Evaluation Committee members based on weighted criteria and ranked proposals is accomplished as follows:

The combined weighted scores are calculated by determining the mean average of all the evaluators' weighted scores for each criterion and for each proposal. For example, the Past Performance for Proposal A is calculated by adding the weighted score for Past Performance for Proposal A assigned by each evaluator (10.0 + 6.7 + 10.0 = 26.7) and then dividing the sum by the number of evaluators (26.7 ÷ 3 = 8.9). The combined weighted score for Past Performance for Proposal A is then entered in the cell immediately to the right of "Past Performance" and immediately below "Proposal A" in Figure J.6.

1. The remaining combined weighted scores are calculated in the same manner and entered into the appropriate box in the table for the Combined Weighted Scores (Figure J.6). The calculation of one additional example is provided to illustrate this process. The combined weighted score for capability and availability of staff for Proposal B is calculated by adding the weighted score for capability and availability of staff for Proposal B assigned by each evaluator (20.0 + 6.7 + 6.7 = 33.4) and then dividing the sum by the number of evaluators (33.4 ÷ 3 = 11.1).

2. The Weighted Scores in the bottom row of the Combined Weighted Scores (Figure J.6) are calculated by adding the weighted scores in the cells in the row immediately above the bottom row. For example, the weighted score of 80.6 for Proposal A is determined by calculating 8.9 + 15.3 + 15.6 + 3.3 + 1.7 + 35.8 = 80.6.

| COMBINED WEIGHTED SCORES | | | |
|---|---|---|---|
| CRITERIA | [CONTRACTOR NAME] PROPOSAL A | [CONTRACTOR NAME] PROPOSAL B | [CONTRACTOR NAME] PROPOSAL C |
| Past Performance | | | |
| Financial Stability | | | |
| Risk Assessment | | | |
| Project Plan | | | |
| Outsourcing | | | |
| Weighted Life Cycle Cost Score | | | |
| WEIGHTED SCORES | | | |

**Figure J.6 Combined weighted scores.**

# Appendix K

# Sample Letter Contract

[*Insert Agency Letterhead*]

Contractor Contact Name and Address                    Date

Re: Letter Contract for [*Project Name*]

Dear: [*Contractor Contact Name*]

It is the policy of [**Agency Name**] to award contracts for the duration or cost of the referenced project only after the contract has been approved by [**Governing Body, etc.**]. However, in emergency situations, when it is necessary to award a contract before it is possible to obtain [**Governing Body, etc.**] approval, a letter contract with a definite expiration date and not-to-exceed price may be prepared by [**Agency Department**] for approval by *the* [**Governing Body, etc.**]. An emergency exists when it is necessary to obtain goods and/or services immediately to avoid a substantial hazard to life or property or to avoid a serious interruption in the operation of a/an [**Agency**] department.

This letter contract authorized your company to proceed with the work described in the Enclosure 1, Scope of Work.

This letter contract is valid for work performed through [**Date about Three Months in the Future**]. Unless an extension is granted in writing by the [**Governing Body, etc.**], this letter contract shall expire no later than [**Repeat Above Date**]. In the event that *the* [**Governing Body, etc.**] approves completion of this contractual effort, a/an [**Agency**] contract, essentially in the format of Enclosure 2, will be used to definitize this letter contract.

The not-to-exceed price for the work to be performed to complete the entire contract, including the work performed per this letter contract and the work performed under the definitized contract, is [$___,___]. This not-to-exceed contract price may be changed, by mutual consent of both parties, when the agreement to definitize the agreement is consummated.

Should the [***Governing Body, etc.***] fail to definitize this letter contract, the contractor shall be paid for the actual work performed during the term of this letter contract. The price to be paid by the [***Agency***], should this letter contract expire on [***Repeat Above Date***], shall not exceed [$___,___].

Sincerely,

[***Signature of Agency Official***]

[***Name of Agency Official***]

# Appendix L

# Sample Show Cause Letter

[*Insert Agency Letterhead*]

[*Insert Contractor Name and Address*]                    [*Insert Date*]

Re: Show Cause Notice for [*Project Name*]

Dear [*Insert Contractor Contact Name*]:

Agency Contract Number was awarded to [*Contractor Name*] for [*Project Name*]. The contract was awarded in response to RFP [*Number*]. Your proposal indicated project completion in ninety (90) days following contract award. The contract was awarded on [*Date*] and there has been no apparent progress on this project despite the fact that over ninety (90) days have elapsed since the contract was awarded. Repeated telephone calls to your project manager and follow up letter on [Date] and [*Date*] have failed to result in any improvement in your company's performance on this project.

In light of your company's failure to show any progress on this project, [*Agency*] considers this lack of progress to be a material breach of contract. It is the intention of [*Agency*] to terminate this contract for default and award a replacement contract to another company. If you do not respond to this letter by [*Date*] to **SHOW CAUSE** why this contract should not be terminated, contract [*Number*] will be terminated for default on [*Date*]. If you do respond to this letter on time, [*Agency*] will make a determination, based on the justification in our response, to continue or terminate this contract.

A termination for default may be a consideration in the decision to remove a particular contractor from solicitation lists for future projects.

Sincerely,

[*Agency*]

[*Signature*]

[*Typed Name*]

[*Title*]

*Appendix M*

# Sample Contractor Performance Report

| CONTRACTOR PERFORMANCE REPORT | | | |
|---|---|---|---|
| Contractor Name | | | |
| Contractor Number | | | |
| Contractor Contact Name | | | |
| Street Address | | | |
| City, State ZIP + 4 | | | |
| Telephone | | | |
| Facsimile | | | |
| Email | | | |
| Project Name | | | |
| Project Completion Date | | | |
| Contract Number | | Contract Type | |
| Agency Department | | Project Manager | |
| Cost Management | | | |
| | | | |
| Quality | | | |
| | | | |
| Adherence to Schedule | | | |
| | | | |
| Recommendation for Future Similar Projects | | | |
| | | | |
| Report Completed By | | | |
| Signature | | | |
| Date | | | |

Figure M.1  Contractor performance report.

# *Appendix N*

# Estimate at Completion

| | ESTIMATE AT COMPLETION | | | | |
|---|---|---|---|---|---|
| **Contractor:** | | **Contract Number:** | | **Project:** | |
| **Task** | **Contract Price** | **Total Invoiced** | **Percent Invoiced** | **Percent Complete** | **Estimate to Complete** |
| | | | | | |
| | | | | | |
| | | | | | |
| | | | | | |
| | | | | | |
| | | | | | |
| **Total Project** | | | | | |

**Instructions for Completion of Estimate at Completion**

1. The "Task" column is completed by listing the separately priced tasks in the scope of work followed by "Total Project."

2. The "Contract Price" column is completed by listing the price for each task in the scope of work followed b the total contract price.

3. The "Total Invoiced" column is completed by listing the cumulative amount invoiced for each task in the scope of work followed by the total amount invoiced for the entire contract.

4. The "Percent Invoiced" column is completed by listing the percent of the cumulative amount invoiced for each task in the scope of work followed by the cumulative amount invoiced for the entire contract.

5. The "Percent Complete" column is completed by listing the contractor supplied (and agency verified) percentage of completion for each task in the scope of work followed by the percentage of completion for the entire contract.

6. The "Estimate to Complete" is calculated by dividing the "Total Invoiced" by "Percent Complete" and multiplying by 100.

**Figure N.1   Contractor's estimate at completion.**

# *Appendix O*

# Contract Amendment

| CONTRACT AMENDMENT | | | | | |
|---|---|---|---|---|---|
| **Contract No.** | | **Amendment No.:** | | **Amendment Date:** | |

| VARIABLE INFORMATION TABLE |
|---|

| Term of This Contract (Complete Dates in Just One of the Following Three Rows) | | | |
|---|---|---|---|
| √ Below | **Term Begins** | | **Term Completion Date** |
| | On Following Date | | On Following Date | |
| | Upon Receipt of Notice to Proceed | | Calendar Days Following Notice to Proceed | |
| | Upon Execution by Agency | | Calendar Days Following Agency Contract Execution | |

| Agency Department | | FOB Point | |
|---|---|---|---|

| Terms | | Basis of Price (**Do Not** √ More Than One of the Following Four Blocks) | | | |
|---|---|---|---|---|---|
| Price | | Fixed Price | Annual Price | Monthly Price | Hourly Rate |
| Not-to-Exceed Price | | √ if Reasonable Expenses authorized in addition to Hourly Rate | | | |

| Contractor Contact Information | | Agency Contact Information | |
|---|---|---|---|
| Contractor | | Project Manager | |
| Address | | Address | |
| City, State & ZIP | | City, State & ZIP | |
| Telephone | | Telephone | |
| Facsimile | | Facsimile | |

**Figure O.1   Contract amendment.**

| Check One or More of the Blocks Below on the Left if a Replacement Exhibit (s) Is Applicable to This Amendment |
| --- |
| Exhibit I, Contractor/Agency Meeting Schedule |
| Exhibit II, Project Milestone Schedule |
| Exhibit III, Contract Reports and other Deliverables |

| NARRATIVE |
| --- |
| |

**AGENCY**                    **CONTRACTOR**

By_____        By_____

Name_____        Name_____

Title_____        Title_____

**Figure O.1 (continued)    Contract amendment.**

## *Appendix P*

# Short-Form Contract Amendment

| SHORT-FORM CONTRACT AMENDMENT | | | | | |
|---|---|---|---|---|---|
| **Contract No.** | | **Amendment No.:** | | **Amendment Date:** | |

| VARIABLE INFORMATION TABLE |
|---|

| Term of This Contract (Complete Dates in Just One of the Following Three Rows) | | | | | |
|---|---|---|---|---|---|
| **√ Below** | **Term Begins** | | | **Term Completion Date** | |
| | On Following Date | | | On Following Date | |
| | Upon Receipt of Notice to Proceed | | | Calendar Days Following Notice to Proceed | |
| | Upon Execution by Agency | | | Calendar Days Following Agency Contract Execution | |
| | Agency Department | | | FOB Point | |

| Terms | | Basis of Price (**Do Not √ More Than One of the Following Four Blocks**) | | | | | |
|---|---|---|---|---|---|---|---|
| Price | | | Fixed Price | Annual Price | Monthly Price | Hourly Rate | |
| Not-to-Exceed Price | | | √ if Reasonable Expenses authorized in addition to Hourly Rate | | | | |

| Contractor Contact Information | | Agency Contact Information | |
|---|---|---|---|
| Contractor | | Project Manager | |
| Address | | Address | |
| City, State & ZIP | | City, State & ZIP | |
| Telephone | | Telephone | |
| Facsimile | | Facsimile | |

**Figure P.1   Short-form contract amendment.**

| MEETINGS/MILESTONES/DELIVERABLES | | |
|---|---|---|
| Item No. | Meeting/Milestone/Deliverable Title | Due Date |
| | | |
| | | |
| | | |

| ACCOUNT INFORMATION | | |
|---|---|---|
| Account Number | Project Name | Funding |
| | | $_____ |
| | | $_____ |

| NARRATIVE |
|---|
| |

**AGENCY**

By_____

Name_____

Title_____

**CONTRACTOR**

By_____

Name_____

Title_____

**Figure P.1 (continued)    Short-form contract amendment.**

# Index

## O

# Date Due

|  |  |  |  |
|---|---|---|---|
|  |  |  |  |
|  |  |  |  |
|  |  |  |  |
|  |  |  |  |
|  |  |  |  |
|  |  |  |  |
|  |  |  |  |
|  |  |  |  |
|  |  |  |  |
|  |  |  |  |
|  |  |  |  |
|  |  |  |  |
|  |  |  |  |
|  |  |  |  |
|  |  |  |  |
|  |  |  |  |